Suffolk County

New York

W9-CBL-283

EIGHTH EDITION

GREENE

COLUMBIA

ULSTER

DUTCHESS

SULLIVAN

ORANGE

PUTNAM

WESTCHESTER

ROCKLAND

THE BRONX

MANHATTAN

QUEENS NASSAU

SUFFOLK

BROOKLYN

STATEN ISLAND

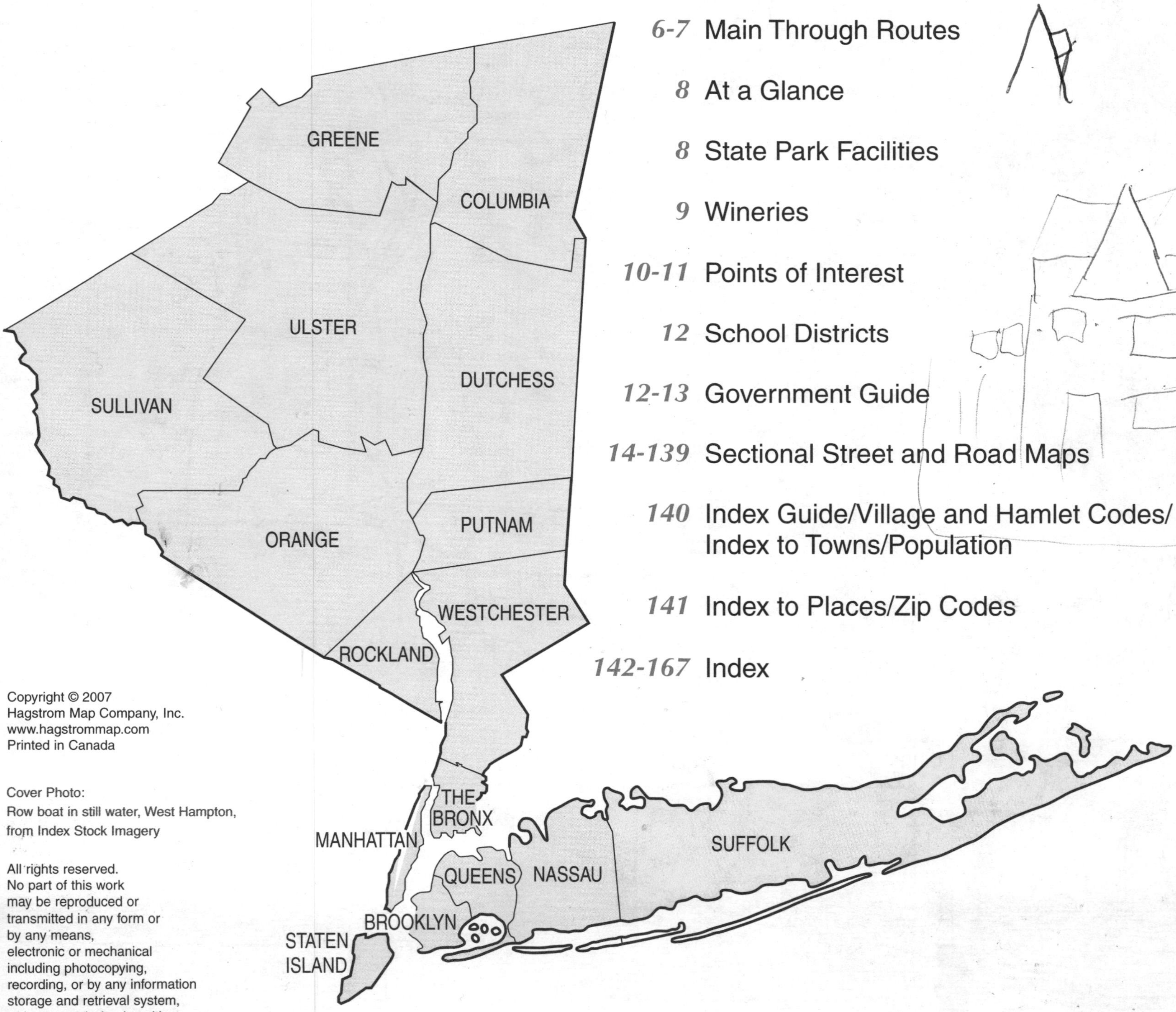

Copyright © 2007
Hagstrom Map Company, Inc.
www.hagstrommap.com
Printed in Canada

Cover Photo:
Row boat in still water, West Hampton,
from Index Stock Imagery

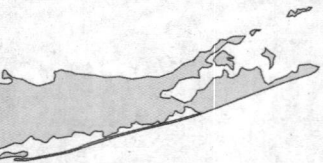

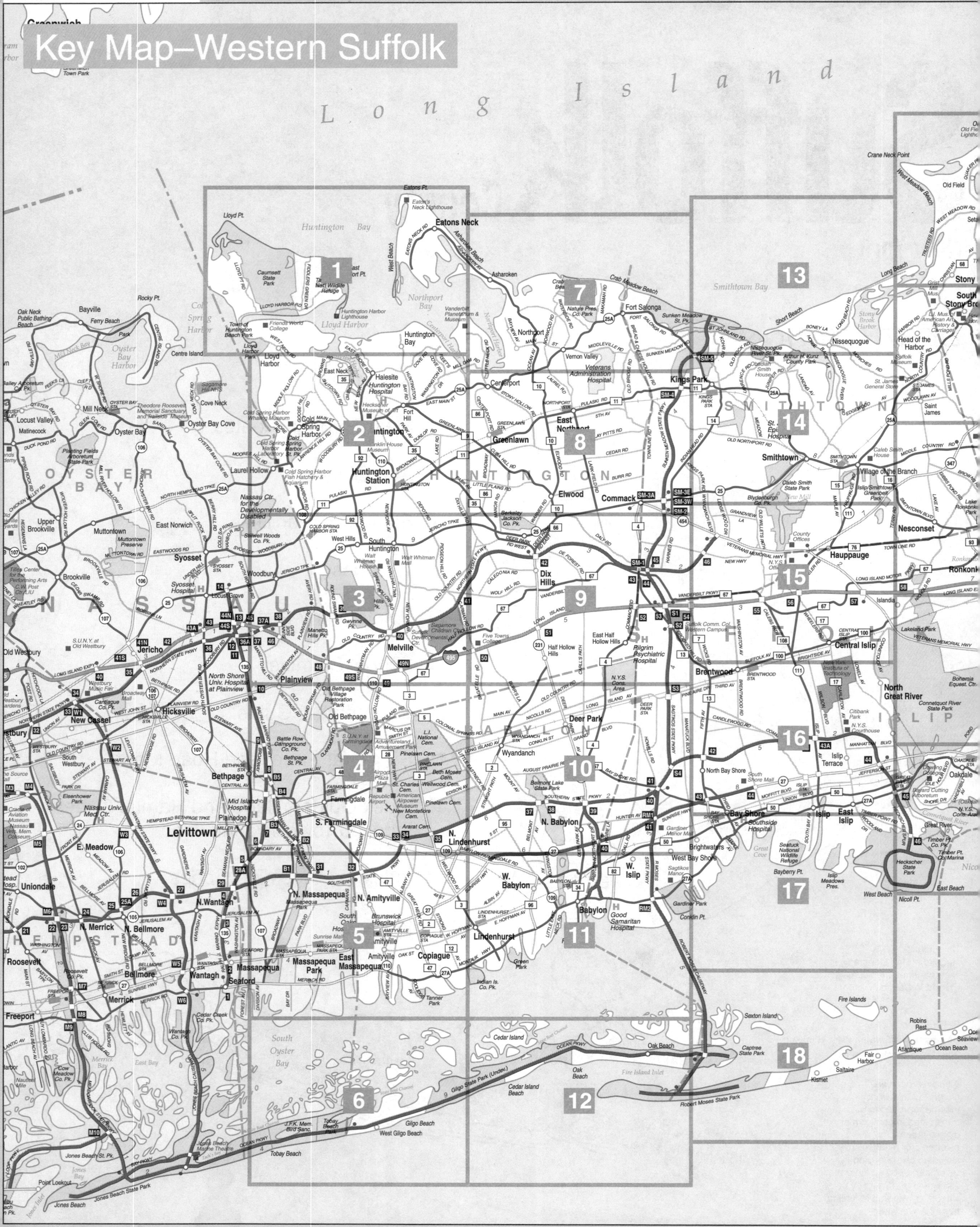

Suffolk Co.

Key Map–Western Suffolk

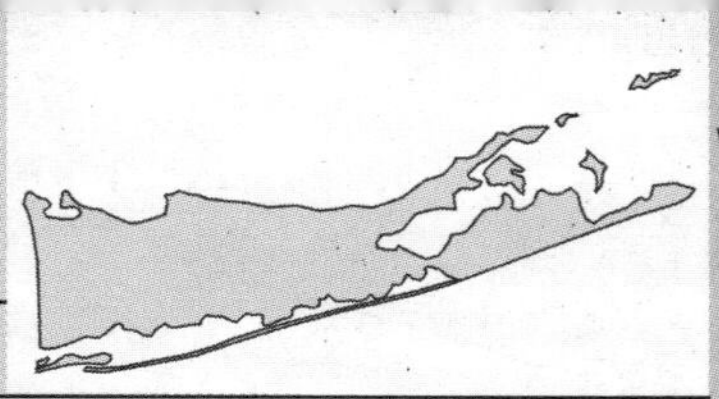

Suffolk Co.

N

S o u n d

19 **20** **21** **22** **23** **24**

25 **26** **27** **28** **29** **30**

31 **32** **33** **34** **35**

36 **37** **38** **39**

RIVERHEAD

BROOKHAVEN

SUFFOLK

SOUTHAMPTON

Port Jefferson Harbor
Mt. Misery Point
McAllister Co. Park (Water Access Only Permit Required)
Sayville Beach
West Beach
Belle Terre
St. Charles Hosp.
Cedar Beach
County Nature Preserve
Miller Place
Sound Beach
Lower Rocky Point Rd
North Shore Beach
Shoreham
Baiting Hollow State Tidal Wetlands
Wildwood St. Pk.
H.M. Reeve Park
Roanoke
Schneider Vineyards
Riverhead Field

Poquott
Mount Sinai
Rocky Point
Wading River
Calverton National Cem.
Splish Splash Water Park
Tanger Factory Outlet Center
Central Suffolk Hosp.
Port Jefferson
East Setauket
John T. Mather Mem'l Hosp.
Port Jefferson Station
Grumman Peconic River Airport
Calverton Enterprise Park
Canoe Lake
Peconic River County Park
Riverhead

Terryville
Whiskey Rd
Brookhaven St. Pk.
Lake Panamoka
Calverton
Cranberry Bog Pres.
Riverside

University Hosp.
Middle Island
Ridge
Peconic River Park
Brookhaven National Laboratory
Manorville
Suffolk Hills Pk.
Hampton Country Club

Selden
Coram
Cathedral Pines Co. Park
Yaphank
L.I. Game Farm
Our Lady of the Isl. Shrine
Suffolk County C.C. (Eastern Campus)

Centereach
Lake Grove
Farmingville
Suffolk Community College
Blue Hill Cultural Center
Yaphank Sta
National Aviation and Transportation Center (Dowling College)
Animal Farm
Eastport
Westhampton

Lake Ronkonkoma
Holtsville
Medford
Suffolk County Offices
Brookhaven Airport
Mastic
Moriches
Speonk
Remsenburg

Holbrook
South Holbrook
Holtsville Park Ecology Site and Zoo
North Patchogue
Brookhaven Memorial Medical Center
South Haven
Shirley
Center Moriches
East Moriches
County Nature Preserve
N.Y.S. Cons Area

Bohemia
L.I. MacArthur Airport
North Bellport
Brookhaven
Mastic Beach
Poospatuck Indian Res.
Swan Island
Cupsogue Beach County Pk.

Sans Souci Lakes Co. Nature Pres.
Patchogue
East Patchogue
Bellport
N.Y.S. Cons. Area
Wertheim Natl. Wildlife Refuge
Manor of St. George
William Floyd Estate

Sayville
West Sayville
Bayport
Blue Point
Patchogue Bay
Bellport Bay
Smith Pt. Co. Marina
Ridge Island
Smith Pt. County Pk.
Fire Island Natl. Seashore

Great South Bay
Great South Beach
Long Cove

Bayberry Dunes
Davis Park
Water Island
Fire Island Pines
Cherry Grove
Fire Island
Fire Island National Seashore

A t l a n t i c   O c e a n

0 ——— 5 Miles
0 ——— 5 Kilometers

Suffolk Co.

N

Key Map–Eastern Suffolk

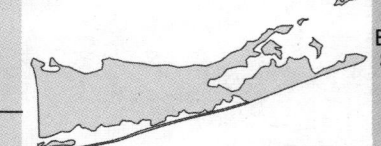

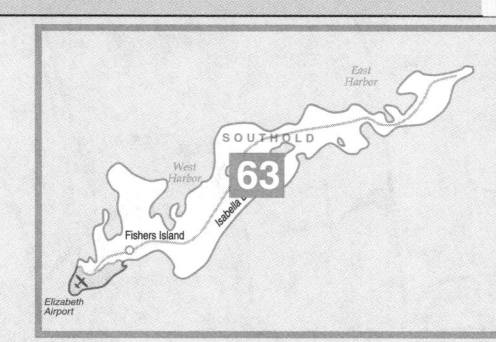

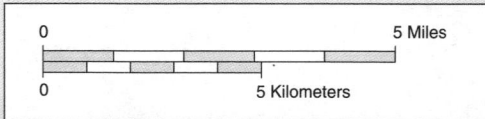

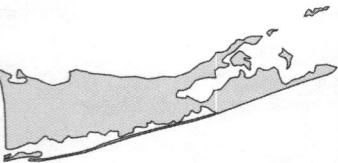

Main Through Routes

N

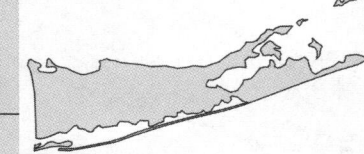

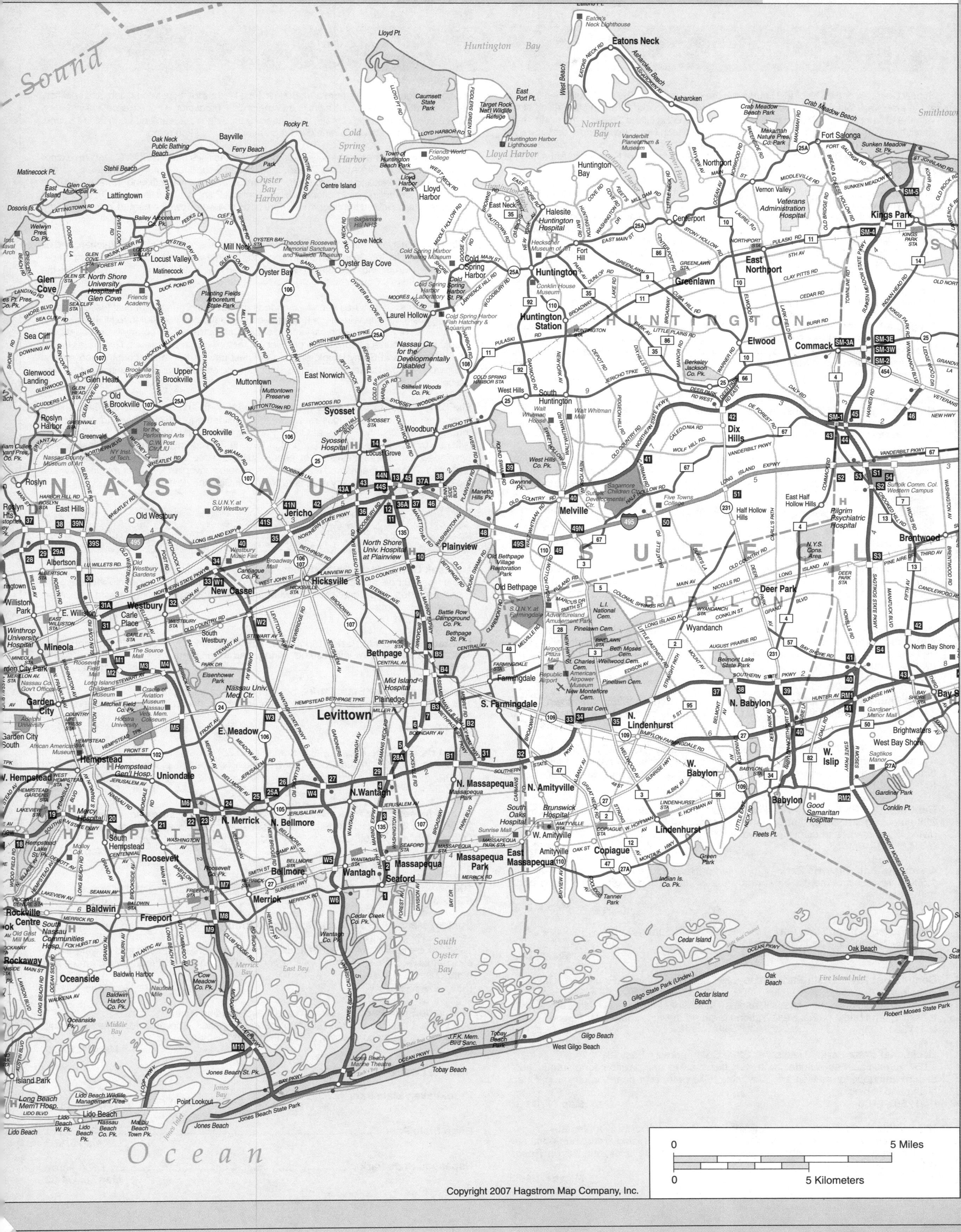

N

0 _____ 5 Miles

0 _____ 5 Kilometers

Suffolk Co.

The County at a Glance

Suffolk County is one of the oldest counties in the United States. The first English settlements in the area were founded in 1640 at what are now Southold and Southampton. Allied at first with the Connecticut and New Haven colonies across Long Island Sound to the north, these English settlements were encroachments upon the Dutch New Netherlands, settled earlier on the western part of Long Island. In 1650, the Treaty of Hartford formally divided Long Island between the Dutch and the English, but in 1664, the City of New Amsterdam and the New Netherlands were surrendered to the English.

At that time, all of Long Island along with Staten Island became the English "shire" of Yorkshire. What was later to become Suffolk County was known as East Riding, one of three administrative divisions of Yorkshire in the New World. The ridings were abolished as divisions at the first General Assembly of The Royal Colony Meeting at Hempstead in 1685. The General Assembly then established Suffolk County as one of the three counties on Long Island. Following the Revolutionary War, Suffolk became one of the counties of New York State, and Riverhead was chosen as the county seat.

Throughout most of the 19th century, farming and fishing remained the chief occupations in Suffolk. Towns in the eastern portion of the county were more populous than those in the west. In 1872, the Town of Babylon was formed out of the southern part of Huntington, bringing the number of towns in Suffolk County to 10. After World War II, these western towns grew dramatically as the county experienced rapid suburbanization and the post-war baby boom. Many people moving out of the inner city chose to settle in western Suffolk because of its proximity to New York City. Today, Suffolk County has 31 incorporated villages located within 10 towns, and a total population of more than 1.4 million.

In 1959, Suffolk County modernized its government by adopting a charter. Paralleling the structure of government in Westchester and Nassau Counties, this charter called for a chief administrative officer, the County Executive. In 1970, a county legislature was established with 18 districts based on population.

Occupying the eastern two thirds of Long Island, Suffolk County comprises 912 square miles of land. The county is 86 miles in length and 20 miles at its widest point. Its lovely and diverse landscape includes rolling hills, lush meadows, sandy beaches, sparkling lakes,

marshes, bogs, and fertile farmland. Suffolk, long famous for its potatoes, fish, and shellfish, has in recent years become a significant wine region, producing a host of excellent vintages. The county enjoys a mild climate, moderated by the Atlantic Ocean and Long Island Sound. The East End boasts world-renowned recreation and vacation areas.

The combination of natural beauty and recreational facilities make Suffolk County an exceptional place to live. The Atlantic Ocean, Long Island Sound, and many sheltered bays and inlets are ideal for sailing, motorboating, swimming, and salt-water fishing. Tuna, marlin, and swordfish offer thrilling sport offshore from Montauk Point to Fire Island Inlet. Private game reserves provide inland hunting, while shore birds and waterfowl are hunted in season along the shoreline.

Suffolk also enjoys historical importance as the birthplace of the poet Walt Whitman, and as the inspiration for the John Howard Payne song "Home Sweet Home." The whaling museums at Sag Harbor and Cold Spring Harbor recall an era, industry, and lifestyle that were the essence of Suffolk County culture prior to the Second World War.

In recent years, Suffolk has seen tremendous growth in the number of businesses located on Long Island and has drawn on its large and well-educated population to fill those jobs in the service, health, biotechnical, and technical industries. The county also boasts the Brookhaven National Laboratory, a premier center for scientific research. The State University of New York at Stony Brook, one of the finest universities in the country, and several other world-renown colleges and universities provide educational opportunities of the highest caliber.

The Long Island Railroad offers public transportation to and from New York City, while a comprehensive network of bus routes enables residents to travel safely and comfortably throughout the county. Ferries at Orient Point and Port Jefferson connect Suffolk County with nearby Connecticut, across Long Island Sound. The county also has an extensive, well-developed, and integrated system of federal, state, and county highways, expressways, and parkways. This well-maintained transportation system conveniently links communities within the county and provides easy access to New York City and destinations beyond.

Parks & Recreation

Bayard Cutting Arboretum – 440 Montauk Highway (Route 27A), Great River
690 acres. Horticulture center containing plant, tree, and shrub collections. Nature trails, guided tours, and small natural history museum. Meeting rooms and cafe.
(631) 581-1002
Map 16, B1-13

Belmont Lake State Park – Exit 38 Southern State Parkway, North Babylon
459 acres. Facilities include bridle path, basketball courts, athletic fields, bike paths, and exercise trail. Offers hiking, fishing, row boating, and ice-skating. Food stand, picnic areas, and pavilion.
(631) 667-5055
Map 10, N-12

Caleb Smith State Park/Preserve – Jericho Turnpike (Route 25), Smithtown
543 acres. Environmental park, nature trails, hiking, and fishing. Reservations required.
(631) 265-1054
Map 14, W-20

Camp Hero State Park – Montauk Point State Parkway (Route 27), Montauk
415 acres. Former military base provides surfcasting, picnic areas, horseback riding, birding, guided nature walks, environmental educational programs, and hiking.
(631) 668-3781
Map 62, E5-38

Captree State Park – Ocean Parkway at southeast end of Robert Moses Causeway
298 acres. Boat basin and boat launching ramp, fishing boats, excursion boats, and diving. Food stand and picnic area available.
(631) 669-0449
Map 12, U-4

Caumsett State Historic Park – Lloyd Harbor Road, Lloyd Neck
1,500 acres. Environmental park, nature trails, and hiking. Riding stable and bridle paths. Fishing by permit.
(631) 423-1770
Map 1, B-27

Cold Spring Harbor State Park – Route 25A, Cold Spring Harbor
40 acres. Hiking trails and bird watching.
(631) 423-1770
Map 2, D-21

Connetquot River State Park Preserve – Sunrise Highway (Route 27), Oakdale / Bohemia
3,473 acres. Guided tours, gristmill, and fish hatchery. Nature trails, hiking, cross country skiing, and bridle paths. Reservations required, permit required for fishing.
(631) 581-1005
Map 15, C1-15

Heckscher State Park – Heckscher State Spur Parkway, East Islip
1,657 acres. Facilities include campsites, picnic areas and pavilion, food stands, pool, beach, bathhouses, athletic and playfields, bike path, and boat launch ramp. Offers hiking and fishing.
(631) 581-2100
Map 17, B1-10

Hither Hills State Park – Montauk Point State Parkway (Route 27), Montauk
1,755 acres. Facilities include tent and trailer campsites, picnic areas, pump-out station, showers, food stand, store, beach, athletic and playing fields, and fishing. Reservations required.
(631) 668-2554
Map 61, S4-33

Montauk Downs State Park – South Fairview Avenue, Montauk
160 acres. 18 hole golf course, driving range, 6 fast-dry tennis courts, clubhouse, golf / tennis pro shop, and locker rooms. Swimming and wading pools. Restaurant and catering service available.
(631) 668-3781
Map 62, Z4-36

Montauk Point State Park – Montauk Point State Parkway (Route 27), Montauk
724 acres. Scenic view with fishing, hiking, and food stand.
(631) 668-3781
Map 62, E5-38

Nissequogue River State Park – St. Johnland Road, Kings Park
153 acres. Environmental park, visitor center, fishing, hiking, birding, canoe and kayak launching site.
(631) 269-4927
Map 13, W-24

Orient Beach State Park – Main Road (Route 25), Orient
357 acres. Facilities include food stand, picnic areas, beach, playfield, playground, and fishing.
(631) 323-2440
Map 49, X3-47

Robert Moses State Park – Robert Moses Causeway, western end of Fire Island
1,000 acres. Facilities include food stands, picnic areas, boat basin, and bathhouses. Offers pitch 'n' putt golf, beaches, playfields, and fishing.
(631) 669-0449
Map 12, R-2

Shadmoor State Park – Route 27, Montauk
100 acres. Facilities include hiking trails, biking, saltwater fishing and beaches.
(631)668-3781
Map 62,A5-35

Sunken Meadow State Park/Governor Alfred E. Smith – Sunken Meadow State Parkway, Kings Park
1,266 acres. Facilities include 9- and 18-hole golf courses, athletic and playing fields, bike path, beach, ¾-mile boardwalk, hiking, and fishing. Food stands, picnic areas, and bathhouses available.
(631) 269-5351
Map 7, U-25

Wildwood State Park – Hulse Landing Road, Wading River
600 acres. Facilities include tent and trailer campsites, showers, food stands, picnic areas, beach, athletic and playfields, hiking, and fishing.
(631) 929-4314
Map 31, F2-29

UNDEVELOPED STATE PARKS

Brookhaven State Park .... 1,590 acres.
Map 31, A2-27

Gilgo State Park .... 1,223 acres.
Map 6, M-3

Napeague State Park .... 1,300 acres.
Map 60, O4-32

Vineyards, Wineries, and Cellars

Long famous for its ducklings, potatoes, corn, and pumpkins, Long Island and Suffolk County now rank second only to California, in the production of wine, or "viniferous," grapes in the United States. Since the early 1970s, a burgeoning wine producing region has developed here, chiefly on the Island's North and South Forks. Blessed with rich, well-drained soil, a long growing season, mild winters, and more sunshine than any other part of New York State, Suffolk County boasts some of the finest vintages which are touted by connoisseurs and restaurateurs alike. A cadre of knowledgeable growers and vintners has transformed the area into a region known for its high-quality Merlots, Cabernets, Chardonnays, Rieslings, and Gewürztraminers.

One interesting note is that because of a damp climate, Long Island grapes are reputed to produce an extraordinarily high level of resveratrol, a phenolic compound and anti-fungal agent that occurs naturally in grape skins. As an antioxidant, resveratrol is thought to have beneficial effects.

Enjoy a vineyard tour, stop and sample some of the country's finest wines at one of the many tastings that are available to the public, or attend any of a number of happenings that include live performances, auctions, book and poetry readings, fundraising events, educational programs, and culinary demonstrations. The month of August features the annual Long Island Wine Country Weekend, when most vineyards and wineries participate in a busy series of public events. Whether you are a first-class oenophile or just enjoy an occasional glass with dinner, Suffolk County will offer a variety of pleasant opportunities to explore the many facets of viticulture, one of the oldest crafts known to man.

If you visit the Long Island wine country, please remember that hours and events are always subject to change. Check in advance either with the Long Island Wine Council, P.O. Box 74, Peconic NY 11958, (631) 477-8493, <www.liwines.com>, or with the New York Wine and Grape Foundation, 350 Elm Street, Penn Yan NY 14527, (315) 536-7442, <www.nywine.com>.

Look on Maps 36, 40, 41, 44, 45, 50, 54, 56, and 57 for the bunches of grapes that indicate the locations of individual vineyards, wineries, and cellars and please drive responsibly.

Vineyard Locations

Vineyard, Winery, Cellar	Address	Telephone	Internet	Map Location
Bedell Cellars	36225 Main Road, Route 25 Cutchogue, NY 11935	(631) 734-7537	www.bedellcellars.com	Map 44, H3-35
Bidwell Vineyards	Middle Road, Route 48 Cutchogue, NY 11935	(800) 698-9463	www.northfork.net/bidwell	Map 45, E3-34
Castello di Borghese Winery & Vineyard	17150 County Road, Route 48 - P.O. Box 957 Cutchogue, NY 11935	(631) 734-5111	www.castellodiborghese.com	Map 45, E3-34
Channing Daughters Winery	1927 Scuttlehole Road - P.O. Box 2202 Bridgehampton, NY 11932	(631) 537-7224	www.channingdaughters.com	Map 56, U3-29
Le Clos Therese	Union Avenue, Route 105 Aquebogue, NY 11931 Mailing Address - P.O. Box 1185 Mattituck, NY 11952	(631) 871-9194	www.lctwinery.com	Map 40, T2-29
Duckwalk Vineyards	231 Montauk Highway, Route 27 Water Mill, NY 11976	(631) 726-7555	www.duckwalk.com	Map 54, Q3-25
Gallucio Family Wineries	24385 Main Road, Route 25 - P.O. Box 1269 Cutchogue, NY 11935	(631) 734-7089	www.gristinawines.com	Map 45, F3-33
Jamesport Vineyards	1216 Main Road, Route 25 - P.O. Box 842 Jamesport, NY 11947	(631) 722-5256	www.jamesport-vineyards.com	Map 41, X2-28
Laurel Lake Vineyards	3165 Main Road, Route 25 Laurel, NY 11948	(631) 298-1420	www.llwines.com	Map 40, A3-30
The Lenz Winery	Route 25, Main Road - P.O. Box 28 Peconic, NY 11958	(800) 974-9899	www.lenzwine.com	Map 44, J3-36
Lieb Family Cellars	35 Cox Neck Road, at Route 48 Mattituck NY 11952 Mailing Address - P.O. Box 907 Cutchogue, NY 11935	(631) 298-1942	www.liebcellars.com	Map 45, A3-31
Macari Vineyards & Winery	150 Bergen Avenue - P.O. Box 2 Mattituck, NY 11952	(631) 298-0100	www.macariwines.com	Map 40, Z2-31
Martha Clara Vineyards	6025 Sound Avenue, Route 48 Riverhead, NY 11901	(631) 298-0075	www.marthaclaravineyards.com	Map 40, Y2-31
Old Field Vineyards	59600 Main Road, Route 25 - P.O. Box 726 Southold, NY 11971	(631) 765-0004	www.theoldfield.com	Map 44, N3-38
Osprey's Dominion Vineyard	44075 Main Road, Route 25 - P.O. Box 275 Peconic, NY 11958	(631) 765-6188	www.ospreysdominion.com	Map 44, J3-36
Peconic Bay Winery	31320 Main Road, Route 25 - P.O. Box 818 Cutchogue, NY 11935	(631) 734-7361	www.peconicbaywinery.com	Map 45, G3-34
Palmer Vineyards	108 Sound Avenue, Route 48 Riverhead, NY 11901 Mailing Address - P.O. Box Box 2125 Aquebogue, NY 11931	(631) 722-9463	www.palmervineyards.com	Map 40, U2-30
Paumanok Vineyards	1074 Main Road, Route 25 - P.O. Box 741 Aquebogue, NY 11931	(631) 722-8800	www.paumanok.com	Map 41, W2-28
Pellegrini Vineyards	23005 Main Road, Route 25 Cutchogue, NY 11935	(631) 734-4111	www.pellegrinivineyards.com	Map 45, E3-33
Pindar Vineyards	Main Road, Route 25 - P.O. Box 332 Peconic Bay, NY 11958	(631) 734-6205	www.pindar.net	Map 44, H3-35
Pugliese Vineyards	Main Road, Route 25 - P.O. Box 4067 Cutchogue, NY 11935	(631) 734-4057	www.pugliesevineyards.com	Map 45, G3-35
Raphael	39390 Main Road, Route 25 - P.O. Box 17 Peconic, NY 11958	(631) 765-1100	www.raphaelwine.com	Map 44, J3-35
Schneider Vineyards	2248 Roanoke Avenue Riverhead, NY 11901	(631) 727-3334	www.schneidervineyards.com	Map 36, P2-30
Sherwood House Vineyards	2600 Oregon Road Mattituck, NY 11952	(631) 298-1396	www.sherwoodhousevineyards.com	Map 45, C3-34
Ternhaven Cellars	331 Front Street - P.O. Box 758 Greenport, NY 11944	(631) 477-8737	www.ternhaven.com	Map 50, Q3-41
The Tasting Room	2885 Peconic Lane Peconic, NY 11958	(631) 765-6404	www.longislandwinecountry.com/tastingroom.html	Map 44, H3-36
Wölffer Estate	139 Sagg Road - P.O. Box 9002 Sagaponack, NY 11962	(631) 537-5106	www.wolffer.com	Map 57, X3-28

Suffolk Co.

Points of Interest

TOWN OF BABYLON

Adventureland Amusement Park–2245 Route 110, East Farmingdale
Rides include Hurricane Roller Coaster, Pirate Ship, Surf Dance, carrousel, Ferris wheel, and the Adventureland Railroad. Birthday party packages are available. Open year-round but limited to kiddie rides during fall and winter months. Call for official closing times, which are subject to change without notice. **Map 4, G-13**
(631) 694-6868 www.adventureland.us

Old Village Hall Museum–214 South Wellwood Avenue, Lindenhurst
Examples of home, industrial, and recreational pursuits of the early days. No admission charge. Open June-Sept., Mon., Wed., and Fri., 2pm-4pm; Oct.-May, Wed., Fri.-Sat., 2pm-4pm; first Sun. of every month, 2 pm-4 pm. **Map 5, L-7**
(631) 957-4385 www.villageoflindenhurst.com/old_village_hall_museum.htm

Village of Babylon Historical & Preservation Society
117 West Main Street, Babylon
Historical artifacts, memorabilia, and photographs pertinent to Babylon history. Donation appreciated. Open year-round, Wed. and Sat., 2pm-4pm. **Map 11, O-8**
(631) 669-7086

TOWN OF BROOKHAVEN

Brookhaven National Laboratories–William Floyd Parkway, Upton
One of the country's largest scientific research facilities. The Exhibit Center Science Museum highlights the research carried out at the facility. No admission charge. Open July-Aug., Sundays, except holidays, 10am-3pm. **Map 32, A2-23**
(631) 344-2345. Groups of 15 or more must make reservations at (631) 344-4495. www.bnl.gov

Holtsville Ecology Center & Animal Preserve–Buckley Road, Holtsville
Located on a reclaimed town landfill, the preserve offers both recreational and educational facilities. Included are a triple pool complex, exercise trails and fitness courses, a zoo, petting zoo, exhibits, tours, greenhouses, picnic area, meeting facilities, and an animal preserve featuring over 100 injured or non-releasable wild and domesticated animals. No admission charge for zoo. Open Mon.- Sun. 9am – 4pm. **Map 22, M1-16**
(631) 758-9536 www.brookhaven.org

Long Island Game Farm–Chapmans Boulevard, Manorville
Many areas where one can pet and feed over 75 different species of animals, both domestic and exotic, including goats, giraffes, and alligators. Pony rides as well as "carnival-style" rides are available for children. Picnic areas, nature trails, and a safari ride. Admission charge. Mon.-Fri., 10am-5pm; Sat., 10am-6pm. **Map 38, G2-20**
(631) 878-6644 www.longislandgamefarm.com

The Long Island Museum of American Art, History and Carriages
1208 North Country Road (Route 25A), Stony Brook
Home to the nation's largest carriage collection. The Art Museum hosts exhibitions from its permanent collection as well as traveling exhibitions; the History Museum hosts dynamic social and cultural exhibitions. Several historic buildings are on the site. Admission charge. Open year-round, Call museum for hours. **Map 13, D1-25**
(631) 751-0066 www.longislandmuseum.org

Manor House of Saint George–William Floyd Parkway, Shirley
Containing colonial furniture, documents, and portraits, this manor was granted to Colonial W. E. (Tangier) Smith in 1653. Occupied by British forces in 1776, who made it Fort Saint George, and recaptured by American soldiers in 1780. The manor was rebuilt in 1844 due to damage sustained during the revolutionary war. **Map 34, Z1-13**

William Floyd Estate, Fire Island National Seashore–Neighborhood Road, Mastic
William Floyd was a signer of the Declaration of Independence and a general in the Revolutionary War. The estate was cultivated as rich farmland and the Floyd Family occupied the house for eight generations. At one point in the Revolution, the Floyds were forced to flee to Connecticut and the British occupied the house. In addition to the colonial mansion, the estate comprises 600 acres of lush marshes, woods, and fields. Activities include house and interpretive tours with special programs for fourth-grade school groups. No Admission charge. Grounds open year round on a seasonal. Call for hours. **Map 34, E2-14**
(631) 399-2030 www.nps.gov/fiis/planyourvisit/williamfloydestate.htm

TOWN OF EAST HAMPTON

Home Sweet Home Museum–14 James Lane, East Hampton
Saltbox-style farmhouse built around 1700. Boyhood home of author John Howard Payne (1791-1852), and his inspiration for the poem *Home Sweet Home*. Grounds include a windmill, gardens, and a gallery. On the National Register of Historic Places.

Admission charge. Open year-round, May–Sept., Mon.-Sat., 10am-4pm, Sun., 2pm-4pm.; Oct.–Nov., Fri.-Sat., 10am-4PM, Sun., 2pm-4pm. **Map 56, E4-29**
(631) 324-0713 www.easthampton.com/homesweethome

Montauk Point Lighthouse Museum–Montauk Point State Park, Montauk
Located at Long Island's easternmost tip. Built by order of George Washington in 1792. It towers 168 feet above the rocks and churning waves of the Atlantic Ocean. Admission charge. Call museum for hours of operation. **Map 62, G5-38**
(631) 668-2544 www.montauklighthouse.com

Sag Harbor Whaling & Historical Museum–200 Main Street, Sag Harbor
The 19th-century whaling heritage of Sag Harbor is depicted through tools, artifacts, and etchings. Admission charge. Open Mid-May-Oct. 1, Mon.-Sat., 10am-5pm, Sun., 1pm-5pm.; Weekends only in Oct.; Group tours by appointment throughout the year.
Map 56, W3-32
(631) 725-0770 www.sagharborwhalingmuseum.org

TOWN OF HUNTINGTON

Cold Spring Harbor Fish Hatchery and Aquarium
Main Street (Route 25A), Cold Spring Harbor
Founded in 1883, it hosts the largest collection of New York State freshwater reptiles, fish, and amphibians in two buildings and eight outdoor ponds. Located in both Nassau and Suffolk. Admission charge. Open daily, except for Thanksgiving, Christmas, and Easter Sunday, 10am-5pm. **Map 2, D-21**
(516) 692-6768 www.cshfha.org

Cold Spring Harbor Whaling Museum–Main Street (Route 25A), Cold Spring Harbor
Includes tools and artifacts of the whaling trade and over 400 pieces of scrimshaw. Hands-on display of marine mammal bones, films, and dioramas are also featured. Admission charge. Open Memorial Day-Labor Day, daily, 11am-5pm; Sept.-May, Tues.-Sun. 11am-5pm. **Map 2, D-22**
(631) 367-3418 www.cshwhalingmuseum.org

Heckscher Museum–2 Prime Avenue, Huntington
Permanent collection of European and American paintings and sculptures. Features 19th-century landscapes. Changing exhibits of historic and contemporary art. Donation suggested. Open year-round, Tues.-Fri., 10am-5pm, Sat.-Sun., 1pm-5pm, first Friday of every month, 10am-8: 30pm. **Map 2, G-23**
(631) 351-3250 www.heckscher.org

Vanderbilt Mansion, Marine Museum & Planetarium–180 Little Neck Road, Centerport
Estate with mansion, gardens, decorative art objects, natural history collection, marine museum, and planetarium. Admission charge. Museum open year round, Tues.-Sat., 10am-4pm, Sun. & holidays, 12pm-5pm; Planetarium open Labor Day-June, Fri.-Sun.; Call for museum for summer hours. **Map 7, L-25**
(631) 854-5555 www.vanderbiltmuseum.org

Walt Whitman Birthplace Museum–246 Old Walt Whitman Road, Huntington Station
The boyhood home of the renowned poet. Museum includes manuscripts, pictures, and memorabilia of this great American. On the National Register of Historic Places. Admission charge. Open year-round, Memorial Day-Labor Day, Mon., Wed.-Fri, 11am-4pm, Sat.-Sun., 12pm-5pm; Winter Hours, Wed.-Fri., 1pm-4pm., Sat.-Sun., 12pm-5pm. Closed on holidays. Groups totaling seven or more must call in advance.
Map 3, H-18
(631) 427-5240 www.waltwhitman.org

TOWN OF ISLIP

Citibank Park–Court House Drive, Central Islip
Home to the Triple A Atlantic League's Long Island Ducks. Seats 6,013 and completed in 2000 the stadium features a recessed playing field, 20 luxury suites, a batting tunnel and a landscaped plaza. **Map 16, Z-13**
(631) 940-3825 www.liducks.com

Long Island Maritime Museum–Route 27A, West Sayville
Located on the Great South Bay, the museum offers permanent maritime exhibits, a library, and the largest small-craft collection on Long Island. Donation suggested. Open year-round, Mon.-Sat., 10am-3pm., Sun., 12pm-4pm. **Map 23, H1-10**
(631) 854-4974 www.limaritime.org

Sagtikos Manor–Route 27A, West Bay Shore
Historic 42 room colonial mansion built in 1692 by Stephan Van Cortland who was of Dutch descent, one of the first of five Patentees on Long Island and the first native-born Mayor of New York City. George Washington spent a night here on his Long Island tour in 1790. "Sagtikos" is derived from an American Indian word that means: "snake that

Points of Interest

hisses." Some stories claim a revolutionary-era young girl haunts the house. Admission charge. Call for hours. **Map 11, S-9**
(631) 854-0939   www.sagtikosmanor.org

TOWN OF RIVERHEAD

Atlantis Marine World Aquarium–431 East Main Street, Riverhead
More than 80 exhibits and a wide variety of programs include a 120,000-gallon "Lost City of Atlantis" shark tank, touch tanks for children and adults, environmental tour boat, ecological exhibits, and submarine simulator. Some exhibits are seasonal. Admission charge. Open, Labor Day-Memorial Day 9am-5pm; Memorial Day-Labor Day, 9am-6pm. Closed Christmas Day. Call in advance for group rates and reservations. **Map 41, S2-26**
(631) 208-9200   www.atlantismarineworld.com

Riverhead Raceway–Route 58, Riverhead
The only NASCAR stock car track in the New York metropolitan area, it includes a Figure-8 course. Events feature Super Pro trucks, demolition derbies, Enduros, train races, car roll over contests, and spectator drag racing. Admission charge. Open, April – Sept. Call or check Internet site for events and schedules. **Map 36, O2-26**
(631) 727-0010   www.riverheadraceway.com

Splish Splash Water Park–2549 Splish Splash Drive, Riverhead
A 96-acre water park with rides including the Surf City wave pool, Lazy River, and the Hollywood Stunt Rider. There are also shows, restaurants, and gift shops. Bathing suits are required on all attractions. Admission and parking charge. Open, May – Sept. Hours vary and may depend on weather. Groups and Handicap rates. **Map 36, M2-26**
(631) 727-3600   www.splishsplashlongisland.com

Suffolk County Historical Society–300 West Main Street, Riverhead
Museum contains a large collection of Native American artifacts, material on early history of eastern Long Island, and other exhibits ranging from whaling to decorative arts. The Library specializes in genealogy and Suffolk County history. Call for information on tours and educational programs. No admission charge. Open year-round, Tues.-Sat., 12:30pm-4: 30pm; Library: Wed., Thurs., Sat., 12:30pm-4: 30pm. Closed holidays. **Map 41, R2-26**
(631) 727-2881   www.riverheadli.com/rmuseum.html

Wine Country–Riverhead & Southold
Visit the wineries that produce award-winning wines. Tours and tasting available at more than a dozen wineries. Contact the Long Island Wine Council for more information. **Maps 36, 40, 41, 44, 45, 50, 54, 56, and 57**
Long Island Wine Council: (631) 369-5887   www.liwines.com

TOWN OF SHELTER ISLAND

Havens House–16 South Ferry Road, Shelter Island
Built in 1743, this house served as a general store, post office, and residence. Features include: 19th-century furnishings, children's museum room, barn, farming/fishing artifacts, and Manhanset chapel museum. Admission charge. Open summer, Fri.-Sun., 11am-3 pm. **Map 51, T3-38**
(631) 749-0025   www.shelterislandhistsoc.org

TOWN OF SMITHTOWN

St. James General Store–516 Moriches Road, St. James
In continuous operation since 1857. Fascinating and educational curios on display. Spices, old-fashioned candies, preserves, soaps, gift items, books, and handcrafts. Open year-round, daily, 10am-5pm; Jan.-Feb.; Jan.-Feb, closed Mon. **Map 13, C1-24**
(631) 854-3740

TOWN OF SOUTHAMPTON

The Big Duck–Route 24, Flanders, in Sears-Bellows County Park
Built in 1931 by farmer Martin Mauerer and now listed on The National Register of Historic Places, The Big Duck was once a stand that sold Maurer's Peking ducks. Now a famous example of roadside architecture and a symbol of Long Island, The Big Duck serves as a museum, gift shop, and tourist information center. Operated by Friends for Long Island's Heritage. Open May 1-Labor Day, daily, 10 am – 5 pm.
(631) 852-8292   **Map 42, A3-23**

Bridge Hampton Historical Society–2368 Montauk Highway, Bridgehampton
Founded in 1956 after the celebration of the hamlet's 300th anniversary. Besides maintaining the historical Strong Wheelwright Shop and the Old Bridgehampton Jail,

the Society offers lectures, tours, educational programs, and events, including the Vintage Sports Car Road Rallye & Classic Car Tour. Open: Mar.– May, Mon.–Fri., 11am–4pm; June-Sept.15th, Tues.-Sat., 11am-4pm; Sept.15th – December, Mon.-Fri., 11am-4pm; closed January, February; appointments may be scheduled. **Map 57, V3-27**
(631) 537-1088   www.hamptons.com/historicalsociety

The Halsey Homestead–South Main Street, Southampton
Built by English settlers in 1648. Named after Thomas Halsey, first English settler in Southampton. Purchased and restored from 1958-1962 by the Colonial Society. Authentic 17th and 18th-century furnishings. Period gardens with herbs. Admission charge. Open Memorial Day – Mid-Oct., Sat.- 11-5, Sun., 11am-5pm, Sun., 1pm-5pm.
(631) 283-3527   **Map 54, O3-22**

Parrish Art Museum–25 Jobs Lane, Southampton
Changing exhibits focus on 19th and 20th-century American art. Concerts, lectures, and workshops year round. Admission charge. Open year-round, Mon.-Sat., 11am-5pm, Sun., 1pm-5pm; Mid Sept.-June, Closed Tues.-Wed. **Map 54, O3-23**
(631) 283-2118   www.parrishart.org

Shinnecock Nation Cultural Center and Museum
Montauk Highway at West Gate Road, Southampton
Housed in a recreation of a pine long house, the Museum and Center feature a series of exhibits that trace the history of the Shinnecocks and their culture from the Paleolithic to the present. Included are a wigwam, canoes, other cultural artifacts, and animals. Admission charge. Open Sat., 11am-4pm, Sun., Noon-4pm. **Map 47, L3-23**
(631) 287-4923   www.shinnecock-museum.org

Southampton Historical Museum–17 Meeting House Lane, Southampton
A museum featuring regional history exhibits, military reenactments and walking tours. Located in several 17th and 18th Century buildings, headquarters are located in the 1843 Albert Rogers Mansion. Admission charge. Open year round with seasonal hours, some facilities require appointments. Call or check Internet site for details. **Map 54, O3-23**
(631) 283-2494   www.southamptonhistoricalmuseum.org

TOWN OF SOUTHOLD

Custer Institute–Bayview Road, Southold
Once frequented by Albert Einstein, the Custer Institute is a non-profit amateur astronomy education center and observatory. Facilities include a 25-foot dome observatory, museum, library and lecture facility for members. The observatories are open to the public every Saturday after sunset, weather permitting. **Map 44, L3-37**
(631) 765-2626   www.custerobservatory.org

East End Seaport Museum & Marine Foundation –Third Street, Greenport
Founded to "recognize, restore and preserve the maritime heritage of the East End of Long Island," the museum offers maritime exhibits, tours, a Maritime Festival, a blacksmith's shop, cruises, and summer programs for children. Museum admission is free. Open June 1 – Labor Day, Wed. – Mon.; Oct.-May by appointment or special event. Call or check Web site for hours. **Map 50, R3-41**
(631) 477-2100   www.eastendseaport.org

Oysterponds Historical Society Museum–Village Lane, Orient
Real working buildings that are "museums" contain memorabilia and exhibits. Hallock Building contains numerous maritime artifacts, paintings, and agricultural tools. Changing exhibits can be seen at the Old Point Schoolhouse. Webb House contains period art and furniture. Other features include dormitory/cookhouse of Hallock Farm, schoolhouse, and barn. Admission charge. Open May 31- Sept. 31, Thurs., Sat., Sun., 1pm-5pm. Exhibit times are subject to change. **Map 49, V3-44**
(631) 323-2480

Southold Indian Museum–Bayview Road, Southold
Contains large collection of artifacts and relics detailing the lives of eastern Long Island Indians before the first settlers arrived. The museum possesses a thorough Indian arrowhead and tools exhibit. Donation suggested. Open year round, Sun., 1pm-4: 30pm; July-Aug., Sat.-Sun., 1pm-4: 30 pm or call for appointment. **Map 44, L3-37**
(631) 765-5577   www.southoldindianmuseum.org

Village Green Complex–Route 25, Cutchogue
Dating back almost 350 years, this restoration features The Old House. Built in 1649 by John Budd in Southold, and later moved to its present site. The architecture of this two-story frame house is considered the finest example in the country. Furnished with 18th and 19th century items. A National Historic Landmark. The complex also features The Wickham Farm House (1704), the Old School Museum (1840), a renovated barn containing 19th-century farm tools and equipment, and the Village Library (1862). Open last weekend in June-Labor Day, Sat.-Mon., 1pm-4pm; Special group tours available, Sept.-Oct. **Map 45, G3-33**
(631) 734-7122

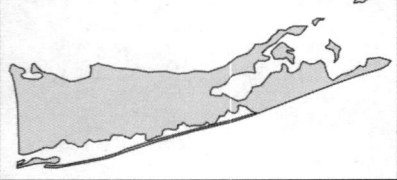

Suffolk Co.

School Districts

Reference Number	Administrative Office Number	Map No.
BABYLON		
1 Babylon UFSD	(631) 893-7900	11
2 West Babylon UFSD	(631) 321-3142	4, 5, 10, 11
3 North Babylon UFSD	(631) 321-3209	10, 11
4 Lindenhurst UFSD	(631) 226-6441	5, 11
5 Copiague UFSD	(631) 842-4015	5
6 Amityville UFSD	(631) 598-6500	5
7 Deer Park UFSD	(631) 242-6524	10
9 Wyandanch UFSD	(631) 491-1013	4, 10
BROOKHAVEN		
1 Three Village CSD (Smithtown)	(631) 474-7500	13, 19, 20, 31
3 Comsewogue UFSD	(631) 474-8100	19, 20, 26
4 South Country CSD	(631) 286-4300	27, 28, 29, 33, 34,35
5 Sachem CSD at Holbrook (Smithtown & Islip)	(631) 467-8202	27, 28, 29
6 Port Jefferson UFSD	(631) 476-4404	19
7 Mount Sinai UFSD	(631) 473-1991	19, 25, 26
8 Miller Place UFSD	(631) 474-2700	25, 26
9 Rocky Point UFSD	(631) 744-1600	25, 26, 31, 32
11 Middle Country CSD	(631) 738-2700	20, 21, 37, 38
12 Longwood CSD	(631) 345-2788	26, 31, 32, 33
24 Patchogue - Medford UFSD	(631) 758-1000	27, 28, 29, 33
32 William Floyd UFSD of the Mastics, Moriches, Shirley	(631) 874-1103	33, 34, 35
33 Center Moriches UFSD	(631) 878-0052	33, 34, 38, 39
34 East Moriches UFSD	(631) 878-0162	38, 39
36 Eastport/South Manor CSD (*)	(631) 325-3200	32, 33, 37, 38
EAST HAMPTON		
1 East Hampton UFSD	(631) 329-4100	55, 56, 57, 59, 60
2 Wainscott CSD	(631) 537-1081	55, 56, 57
3 Amagansett UFSD	(631) 267-3572	60, 61
4 Springs UFSD of East Hampton	(631) 324-0144	55, 58, 59, 62
5 Sag Harbor UFSD (Southampton)	(631) 725-5300	55, 56
6 Montauk UFSD	(631) 668-2474	61, 62

Reference Number	Administrative Office Number	Map No.
HUNTINGTON		
1 Elwood UFSD	(631) 266-5400	2, 8
2 Cold Spring Harbor CSD	(631) 692-8036	1, 2
3 Huntington UFSD	(631) 673-2054	1, 2
4 Northport - East Northport UFSD	(631) 262-6600	7, 8
5 Half Hollow Hills CSD (Babylon)	(631) 592-3000	3, 4, 9, 10
6 Harborfields CSD	(631) 754-5357	1, 2, 7, 8, 14
10 Commack (Smithtown) UFSD	(631) 912-2000	8, 14
13 South Huntington UFSD	(631) 425-5300	2, 3, 9
ISLIP		
1 Bay Shore UFSD	(631) 968-1100	10, 11, 16, 17
2 Islip UFSD	(631) 859-2200	16, 17
3 East Islip UFSD	(631) 581-1600	16, 17, 23
4 Sayville UFSD	(631) 244-6510	22, 23
5 Bayport - Blue Point UFSD (Brook.)	(631) 472-7860	22, 23
6 Hauppauge UFSD (Smithtown)	(631) 265-3630	15, 21
7 Connetquot CSD of Islip	(631) 244-2215	16, 21, 22, 23
9 West Islip UFSD	(631) 893-3200	10, 11
12 Brentwood UFSD	(631) 434-2123	9, 10, 15, 16
13 Central Islip UFSD	(631) 348-5000	15, 16
14 Fire Island UFSD (Brookhaven)	(631) 583-5626	24, 30
RIVERHEAD		
1 Shoreham - Wading River CSD (Brookhaven)	(631) 821-8100	31
2 Riverhead CSD (Southampton & Brookhaven)	(631) 369-6714	31, 32, 36, 37, 40, 41
3 Little Flower UFSD	(631) 929-4300	31
SHELTER ISLAND		
1 Shelter Island UFSD	(631) 749-0302	50, 51
SMITHTOWN		
1 Smithtown CSD	(631) 361-2200	14, 15, 20
5 Kings Park CSD	(631) 269-3200	21

Reference Number	Administrative Office Number	Map No.
SOUTHAMPTON		
1 Remsenburg - Speonk UFSD	(631) 325-0203	37, 38, 39
2 Westhampton Beach UFSD	(631) 288-3800	37, 38, 39, 42, 43,47
3 Quogue UFSD	(631) 653-4285	42, 43
5 Hampton Bays UFSD	(631) 723-2100	42, 47, 52, 56, 57
6 Southampton UFSD	(631) 591-4500	47, 48, 53, 54, 57
9 Bridgehampton UFSD	(631) 537-0271	52, 53, 54, 56, 57
10 Sagaponack CSD	(631) 537-0651	56, 57
13 Tuckahoe CSD at Southampton	(631) 283-3550	47, 54
17 East Quogue UFSD	(631) 653-5210	42, 48
36 Eastport/South Manor CSD (Brookhaven) (*)	(631) 325-3200	40, 45, 46
SOUTHOLD		
2 Oysterponds UFSD in Orient	(631) 323-2410	50
4 Fishers Island UFSD	(631) 788-7444	63
5 Southold UFSD	(631) 765-5400	44, 45, 50
9 Mattituck - Cutchogue UFSD	(631) 298-4242	40, 44, 45, 46
10 Greenport UFSD	(631) 477-1950	44, 50, 51
15 New Suffolk CSD	(631) 734-6940	45, 46

Note: The numbers used on this list and on the map pages to identify school districts are Hagstrom reference numbers only. Agreement with official school district numbers used by the Board of Cooperative Educational Services is coincidental.

The above table reflects 2001/2002 Union Free School Districts (UFSD) and Common School Districts (CSD). The district boundaries shown on the map are subject to periodic change due to development and/or district consolidation. School districts that cover portions of more than one town show the adjoining town(s) in parentheses.

(*) The South Manor UFSD of Brookhaven and the Eastport UFSD combined to become the Eastport/South Manor CSD in 2004.

Government Guide

Department	Location	Telephone
HAUPPAUGE		
County Attorney	H. Lee Dennison Building, 100 Veterans Memorial Hwy, 5th, 6th, and 7th Floors, P.O. Box 6100, Hauppauge, 11788	(631) 853-4049
Civil Service	North County Complex, Bldg. 158 Veterans Memorial Highway, P.O. Box 6100, Hauppauge, 11788-0099	(631) 853-5500
Community Development	H. Lee Dennison Building, 100 Veterans Memorial Highway, 11th Floor, P.O. Box 6100, Hauppauge, 11788-0099	(631) 853-5705
Suffolk County Comptroller's Office	H. Lee Dennison Bldg., 9th Floor, 100 Veteran's Memorial Highway, Hauppauge, 11788-0099	(631) 853-5040
Consumer Affairs	North County Complex, Bldg. 340 Veterans Memorial Highway, Hauppauge, 11788-0099	(631) 853-4600
Economic Development	H. Lee Dennison Building, 100 Veterans Highway, P.O. Box 6100, Hauppauge, 11788	(631) 853-4800
Department of Health Services	225 Rabro Drive East, Hauppauge, 11788	(631) 853-3000
	Emergencies after 5:00 PM and Weekends:	(631) 852-4820
Human Rights Commission	H. Lee Dennison Bldg., 1st Floor, 100 Veterans Memorial Highway, P.O. Box 6100, Hauppauge, 11788	(631) 853-5480
Human Services	H. Lee Dennison Building - 3rd Floor, 100 Veterans Memorial Highway, P.O. Box 6100, Hauppauge, 11788-0099	(631) 853-8282
Suffolk County Department of Labor	North County Complex, Bldg. 17, Veterans Memorial Highway, Hauppauge, 11788	(631) 853-6500
Suffolk County Legislature	William H. Rogers Building, 725 Veterans Memorial Highway, Smithtown, 11787-4311	(631) 853-4070
New York State Employment Office	State Office Building, Veterans Memorial Highway, Hauppauge, 11788	(631) 952-6500
Planning Department	H. Lee Dennison Building, 100 Veterans Memorial Highway, Hauppauge, 11788	(631) 853-5191

Department	Location	Telephone
Treasurer	H. Lee Dennison Building, 2nd Floor, 100 Veterans Memorial Highway, Hauppauge, 11788-0099	(631) 853-4641
RIVERHEAD		
County Clerk's Office	Evan K. Griffing Center, 310 Center Drive, Riverhead, 11901-3392	(631) 852-2001
County Court	Arthur M. Cromarty Court Complex, 210 Center Drive, Riverhead, 11901	
District Attorney	Evan K. Griffing Center, Riverhead Criminal Courts Complex, 200 Center Drive, Riverhead, 11901	(631) 853-2500
County Executive	Evan K. Griffing Center, County Road 51, Riverhead, 11901-3397	(631) 853-4000
Real Property Tax Service Agency	Evan K. Griffing Center, 300 Center Drive, Riverhead, 11901-3398	(631) 852-1550
Sheriff	Evan K. Griffing Center, Riverhead Correctional Facility, 100 Center Drive, Riverhead, 11901	(631) 852-2200
Department of Social Services	877 East Main Street, Riverhead, 11901	(631) 852-3500
Supreme Court Building	235 Griffing Avenue, Riverhead, 11901	
Treasurer	Evan K. Griffing Center, 330 Center Drive, Riverhead, 11901	(631) 852-1500
YAPHANK		
Board of Elections (*)	P.O. Box 700, Yaphank Ave, Yaphank, 11980-0700	(631) 852-4500
County Jail (**)	Yaphank Avenue, Yaphank, 11980	(631) 852-4704
John L. Barry Police Headquarters	30 Yaphank Avenue, Yaphank, 11980	(631) 852-6000
Department of Public Works	335 Yaphank Avenue, Yaphank, 11980	(631) 852-4010
Vector Control	335 Yaphank Avenue, Yaphank, 11980-9744	(631) 852-4270

(*) The Board of Elections is not identified on the map.
(**) The County Jail in Yaphank also receives mail for the County Jail in Riverhead.

Suffolk Co.

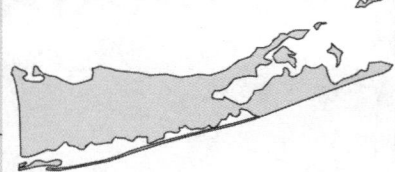

Riverhead

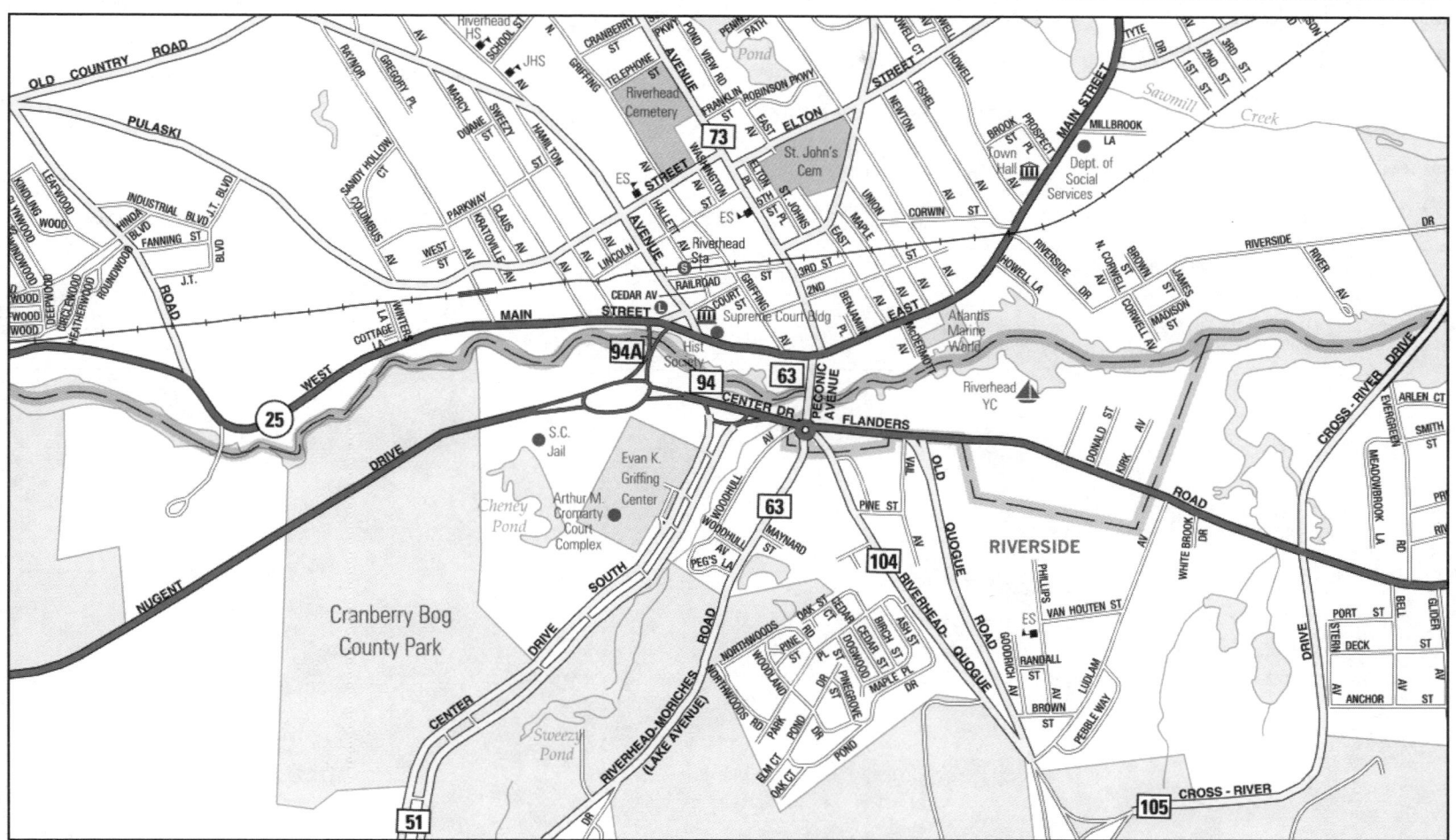

Hauppauge

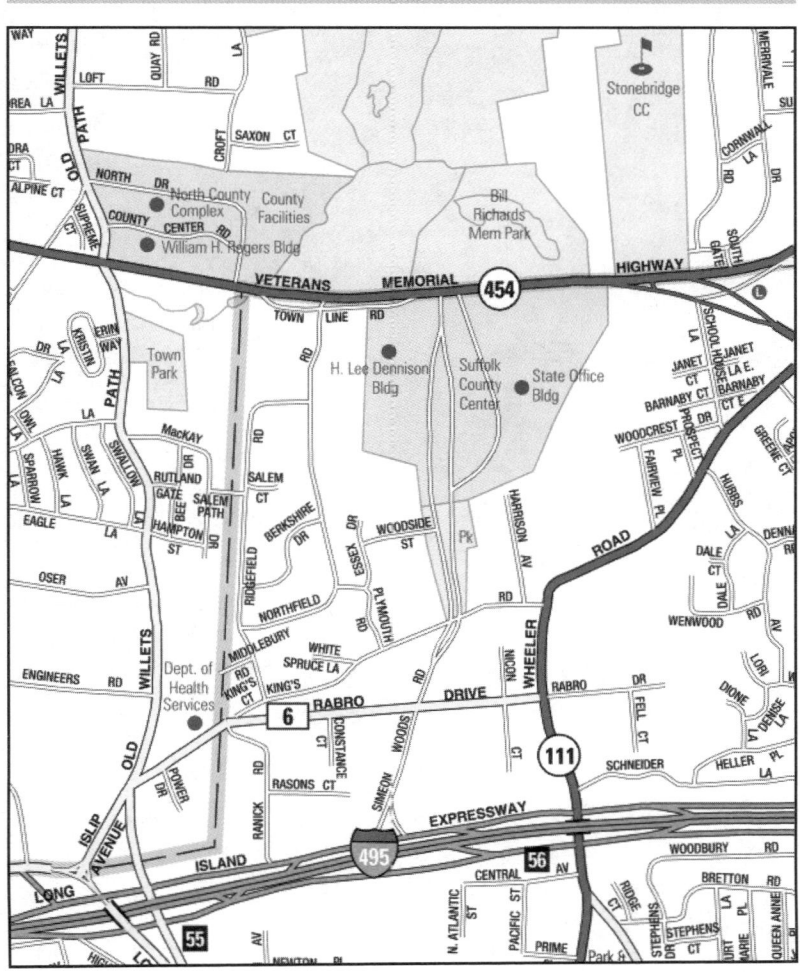

Yaphank

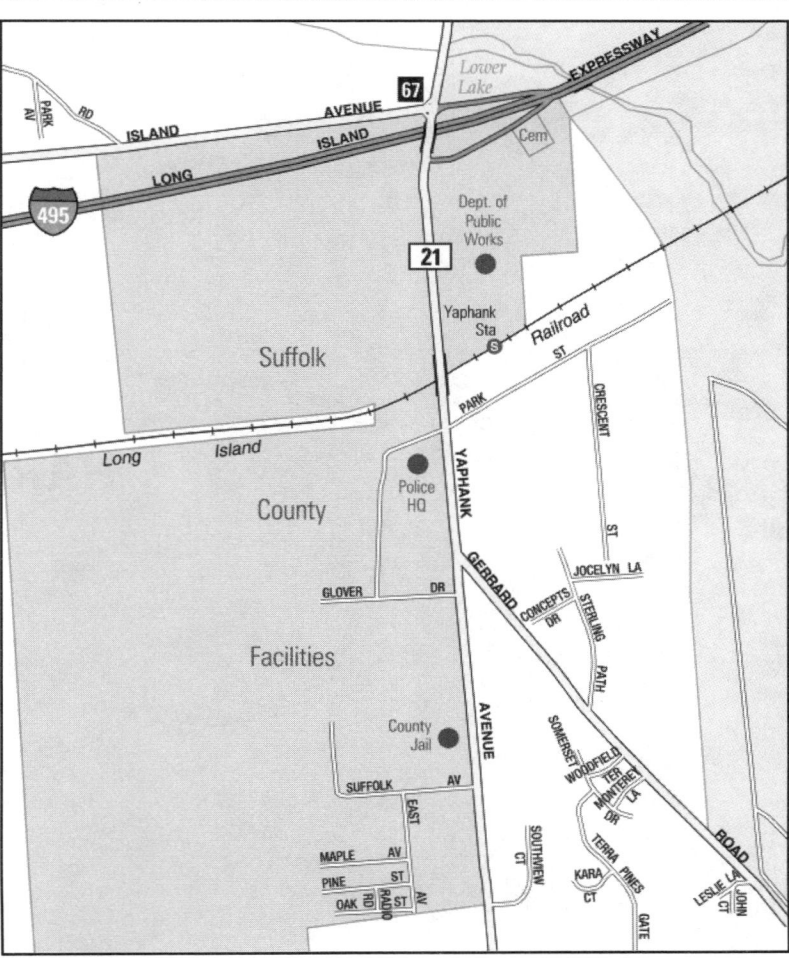

Map 1
Legend

Suffolk Co.

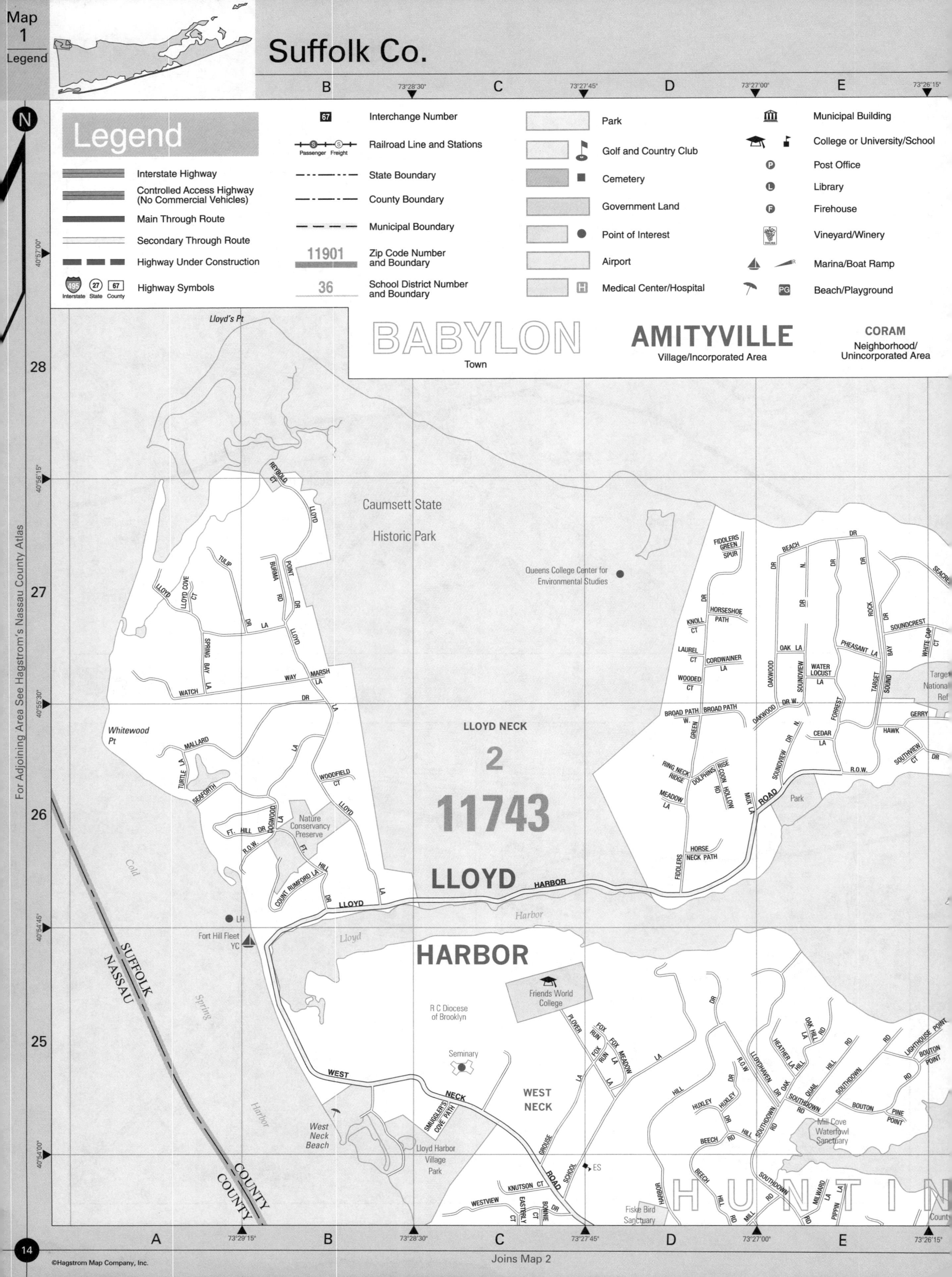

Legend

Interstate Highway	
Controlled Access Highway (No Commercial Vehicles)	
Main Through Route	
Secondary Through Route	
Highway Under Construction	
Highway Symbols	

495 Interstate **27** State **67** County

67 Interchange Number

⊕S—⊕S Railroad Line and Stations
Passenger Freight

State Boundary

County Boundary

Municipal Boundary

11901 Zip Code Number and Boundary

36 School District Number and Boundary

Park

Golf and Country Club

Cemetery

Government Land

● Point of Interest

Airport

H Medical Center/Hospital

🏛 Municipal Building

College or University/School

P Post Office

L Library

F Firehouse

Vineyard/Winery

Marina/Boat Ramp

PG Beach/Playground

BABYLON
Town

AMITYVILLE
Village/Incorporated Area

CORAM
Neighborhood/
Unincorporated Area

B 73°28'30" C 73°27'45" D 73°27'00" E 73°26'15"

40°57'00"
28
40°56'15"
27
40°55'30"
26
40°54'45"
25
40°54'00"

Lloyd's Pt

Caumsett State
Historic Park

Queens College Center for
Environmental Studies

REYBOLD CT

LLOYD
TULIP
BURMA RD
POINT DR
LLOYD COVE CT
LLOYD
SPRING BAY LA
WATCH
MARSH LA
WAY
DR

Whitewood Pt

MALLARD
TURTLE LA
SEAFORTH
WOODFIELD CT
LLOYD
Nature Conservancy Preserve
FT. HILL DR
DOGWOOD
R.O.W.
FT. HILL
COURT RUMFORD LA
LLOYD
DR

Cold

Spring

SUFFOLK
NASSAU

Harbor

● LH
Fort Hill Fleet YC

Lloyd

West
Neck
Beach

WEST
NECK
SMUGGLERS COVE PATH

Lloyd Harbor
Village Park

R C Diocese
of Brooklyn

Seminary

Friends World
College

WEST
NECK

LLOYD NECK

2

11743

LLOYD HARBOR

Harbor

HARBOR

FIDDLERS GREEN SPUR
BEACH
DR
DR
DR
N.
DR
DR
SEACREST
ROCK
SOUNDCREST
WHITE CAP
BAY
HORSESHOE PATH
KNOLL CT
LAUREL CT
CORDWAINER LA
WOODED CT
OAK LA
OAKWOOD
SOUNDVIEW
WATER LOCUST LA
PHEASANT LA
TARGET
SOUND
Target National Ref
BROAD PATH W.
BROAD PATH
OAKWOOD DR W.
GREEN
SOUNDVIEW DR N.
FORREST
CEDAR LA
GERRY
HAWK
SOUTHVIEW CT
DR
RING NECK RIDGE
DOLPHINS
RISE
COON HOLLOW RD
MUX LA.
SOUNDVIEW DR N.
ROAD
R.O.W.
Park
MEADOW LA
HORSE NECK PATH
FIDDLERS

FOX RUN
FOX MEADOW LA
FOX RUN LA
PLOVER LA
DR
OAK HILL LA
HILL
LIGHTHOUSE POINT
BOUTON POINT
LLOYDHAVEN
R.O.W.
HEATHER LA
OAK
HUXLEY
HUXLEY DR
HILL
SNAIL HILL RD
SOUTHDOWN
SOUTHDOWN
SOUTHDOWN
BOUTON
PINE POINT
Mill Cove Waterfowl Sanctuary
BEECH
BEECH RD
HILL
GROUSE
WEST
NECK
ROAD
SCHOOL
● ES
KNUTSON CT
WESTVIEW
EASTRLY CT
BONNIE DR
HABRAH
MILL
SOUTHDOWN RD
BEECH HILL RD
MILL RD
PIPPIN LA
MILWARD LA
SOUTHDOWN
HUNTIN
Fiske Bird
Sanctuary

A 73°29'15" B 73°28'30" C 73°27'45" D 73°27'00" E 73°26'15"

Map 1

Tip! Quickly estimate distance:
Each grid box represents approximately 0.65 mi. horizontally by 0.86 mi. vertically.

Scale 1:24,000

| 0 | 1,000 | 2,000 | 3,000 | 4,000 | 5,000 Feet |

| 0 | 200 | 400 | 600 | 800 | 1,000 | 1,200 | 1,400 Meters |

N

11768

Eatons Neck Pt
U.S. Coast Guard
LH

4

EATONS NECK

ASHAROKEN

Duck Island Harbor

Target Rock

East Fort Pt

Huntington Bay

Duck Island

Park

Prices Bend

Winkle Pt

Hobart Beach

West Beach

Sand City

East Beach

Northport Bay

Old Tower U.S. Govt Prop.

Little Neck Pt

Huntington Harbor Light

Sandy Pt

Crescent Beach

Huntington Crescent YC

Knollwood Beach

Sr. Citizens Beach

Little Neck

LITTLE NECK

Centerport Park

11721

6

HUNTINGTON BAY

3

WEST SHORE Park

Centerport Beach

Centerport Harbor

Joins Map 7

©Hagstrom Map Company, Inc.

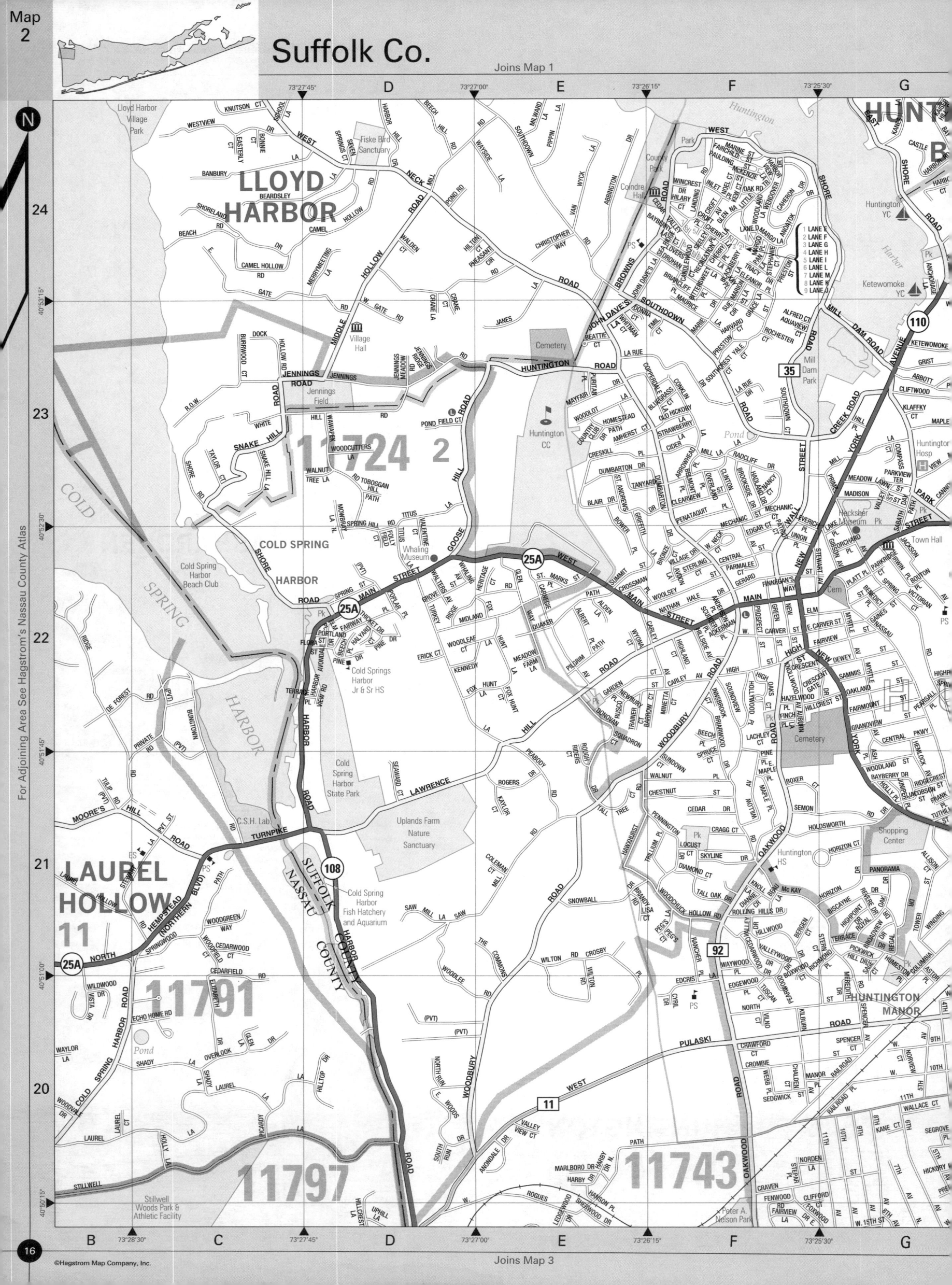

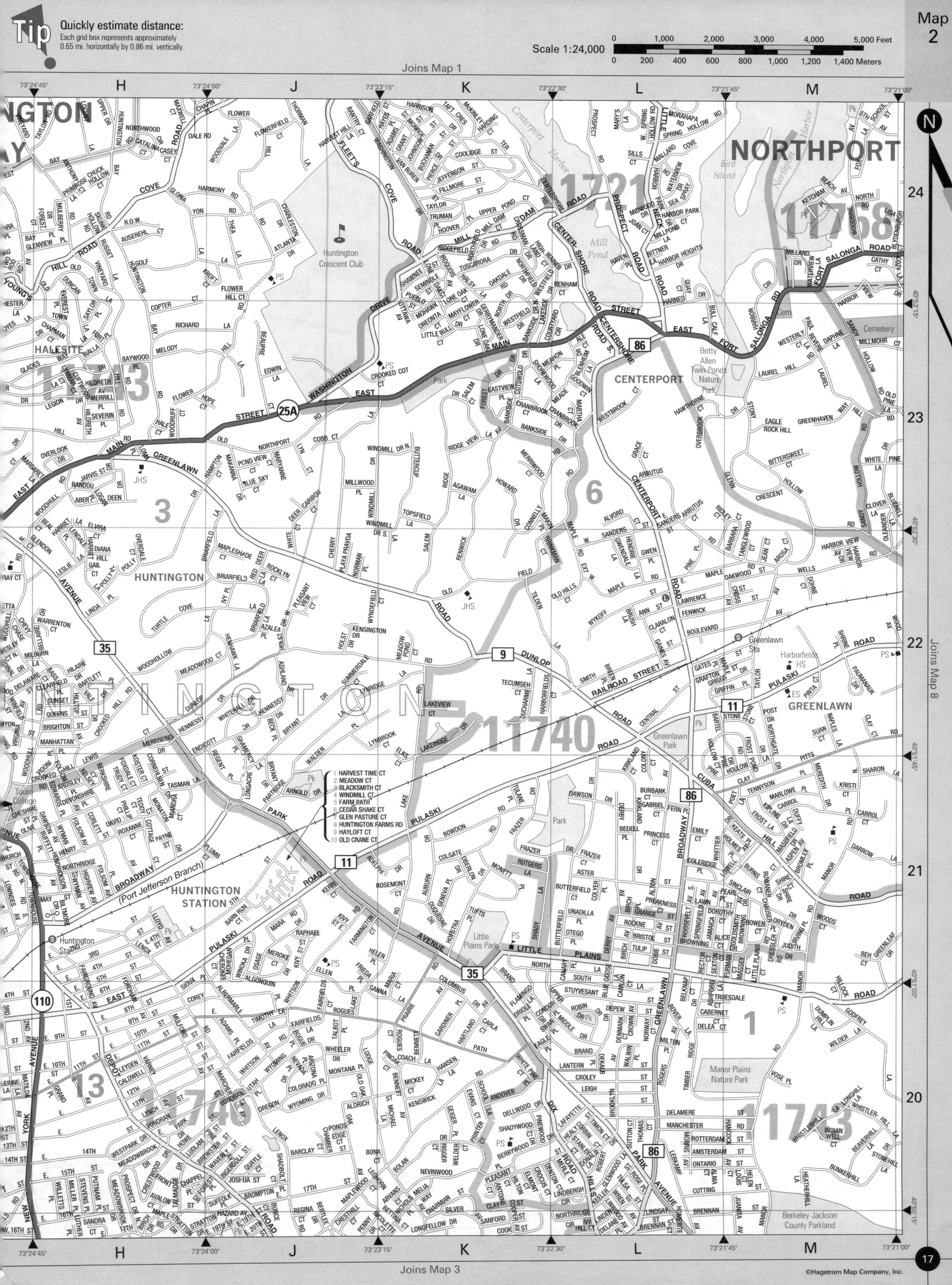

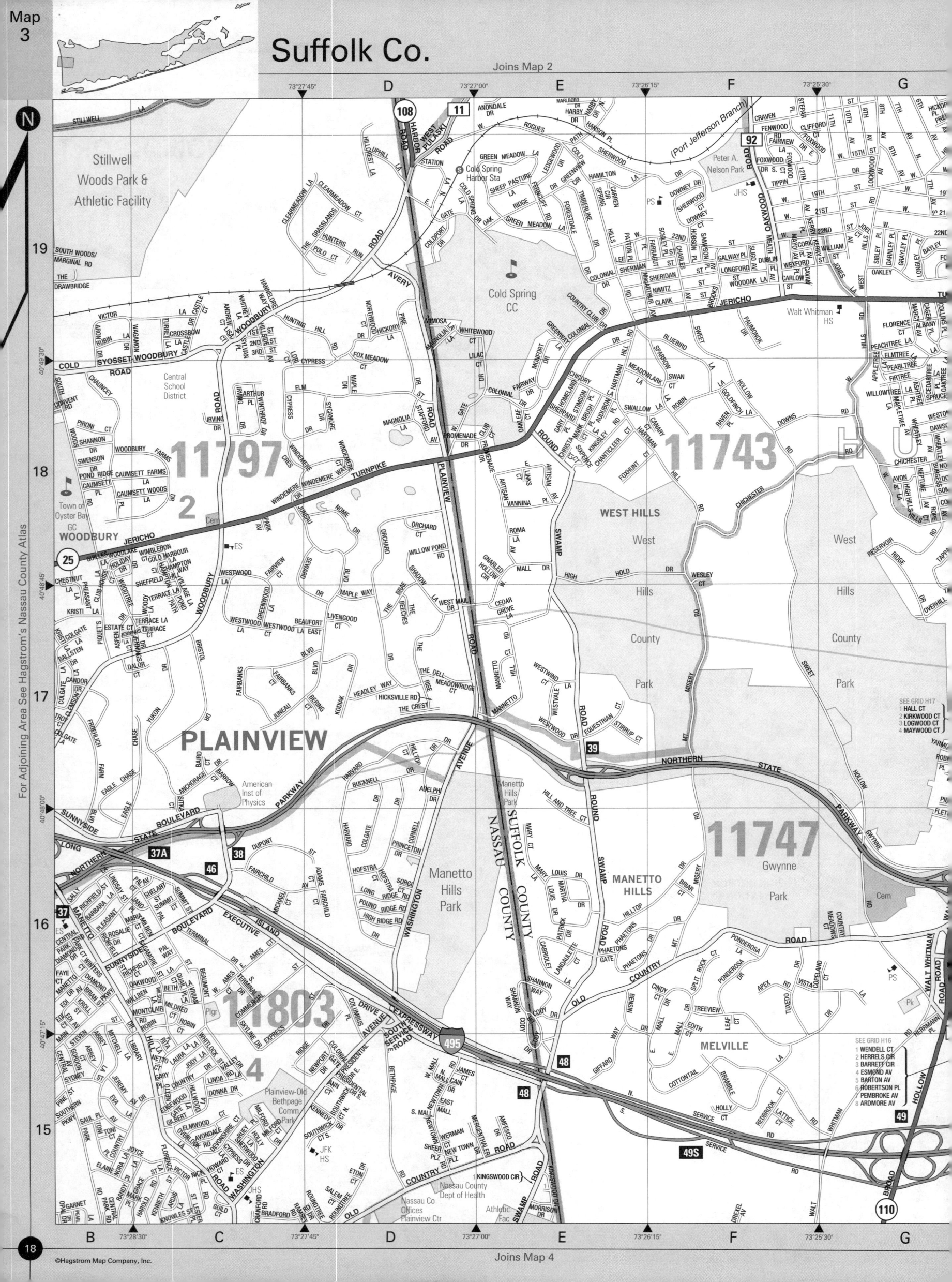

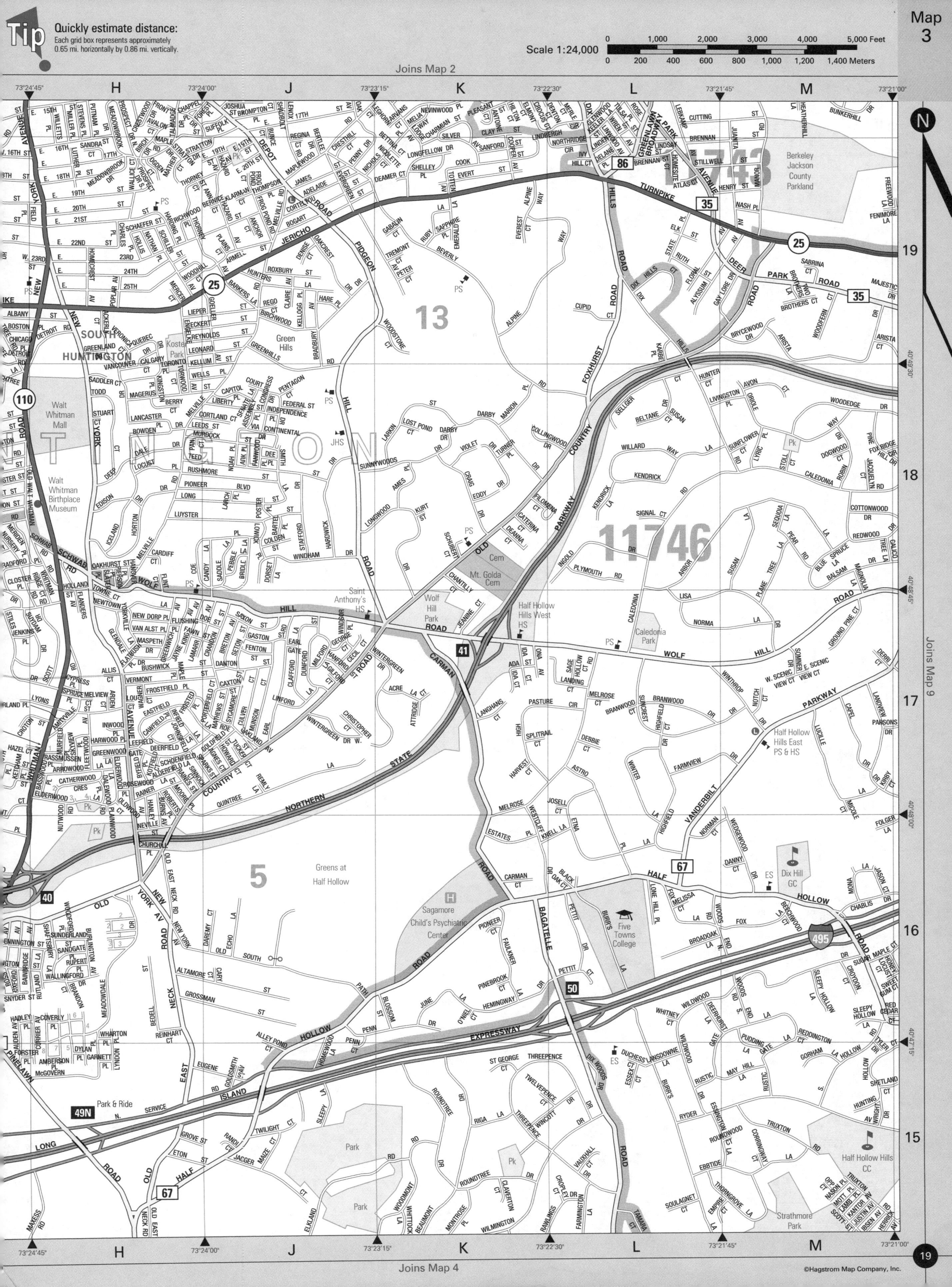

Map
3

Map
4

Tip! Quickly estimate distance:
Each grid box represents approximately
0.65 mi. horizontally by 0.86 mi. vertically.

Scale 1:24,000

Joins Map 3

©Hagstrom Map Company, Inc.

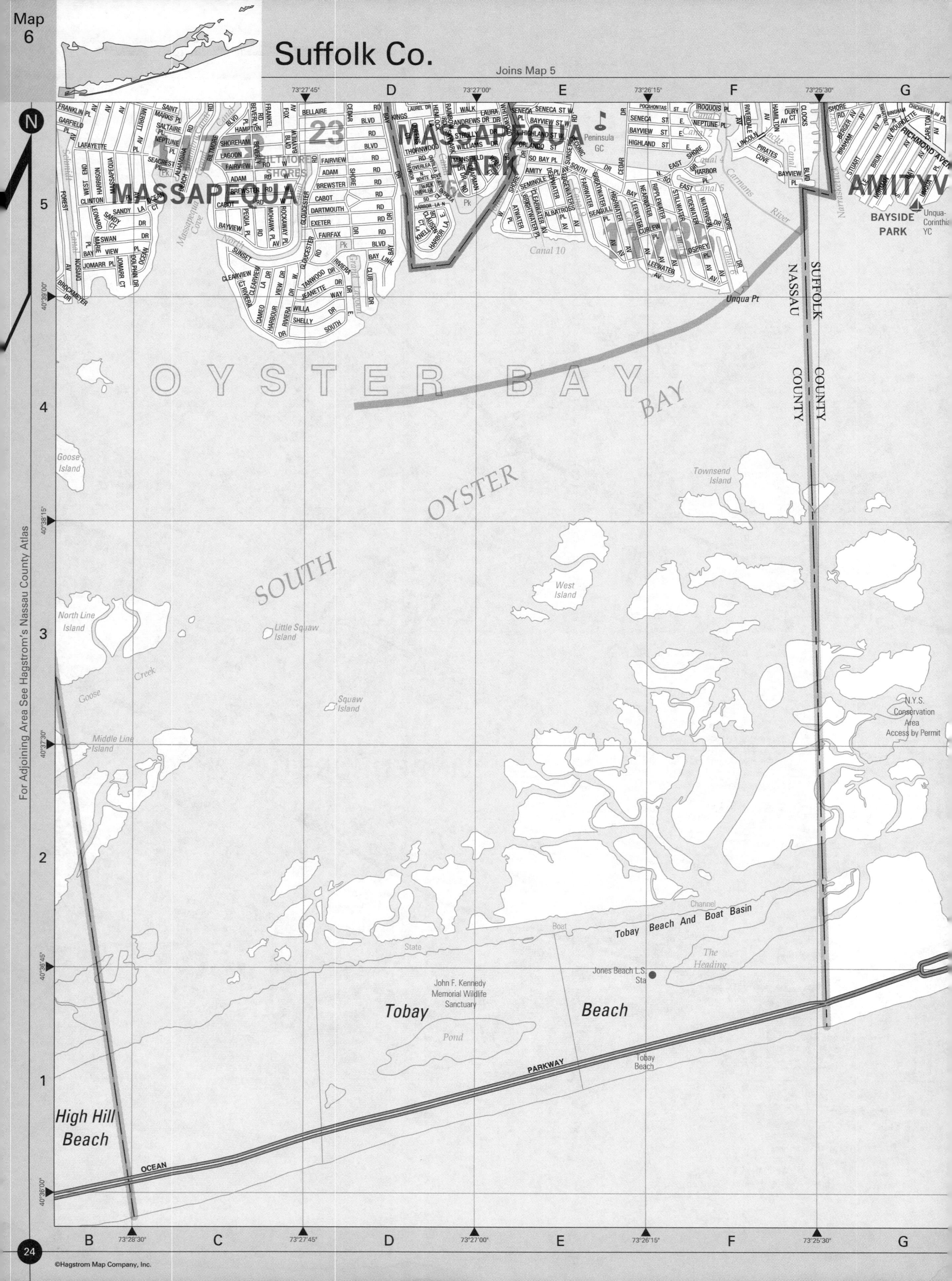

Map
6

Tip!

Quickly estimate distance:
Each grid box represents approximately
0.65 mi. horizontally by 0.86 mi. vertically.

Scale 1:24,000

0   1,000   2,000   3,000   4,000   5,000 Feet

0   200 400 600 800 1,000 1,200 1,400 Meters

Joins Map 5

73°24'45"   H   73°24'00"   J   73°23'15"   K   73°22'30"   L   73°21'45"   M   73°21'00"

ILLE

11701

AMITYVILLE

AMITY HARBOR

11726

Tanner Park

Copiague Beach

Howell Pt

Amityville Beach

GREAT   SOUTH   BAY

40°39'00"

N.Y.S. Conservation Area
Access by Permit

Little Isl

Elder Isl

Hole

CEDAR ISLAND

Brant Cove

Great Isl

West Fox Creek

40°38'15"

THATCH ISL

Creek

B A B Y L O N

State

Gilgo State Park   PARKWAY

Gilgo ISL

Joins Map 12

40°37'30"

York

OCEAN

New

OCEAN

PARKWAY

Gilgo Beach

OCEAN

O C E A N

40°36'45"

ATLANTIC

40°36'00"

73°24'45"   H   73°24'00"   J   73°23'15"   K   73°22'30"   L   73°21'45"   M   73°21'00"

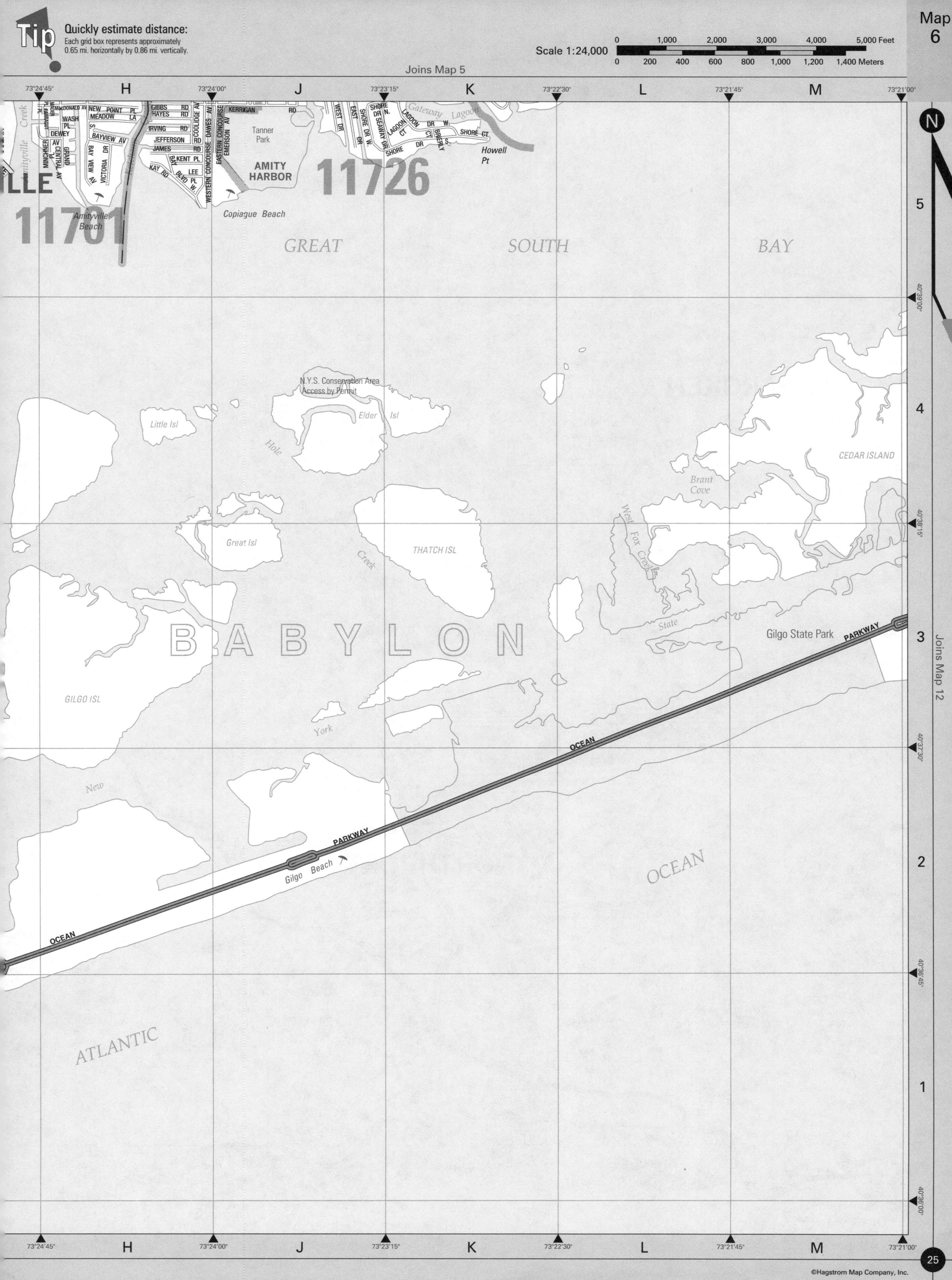

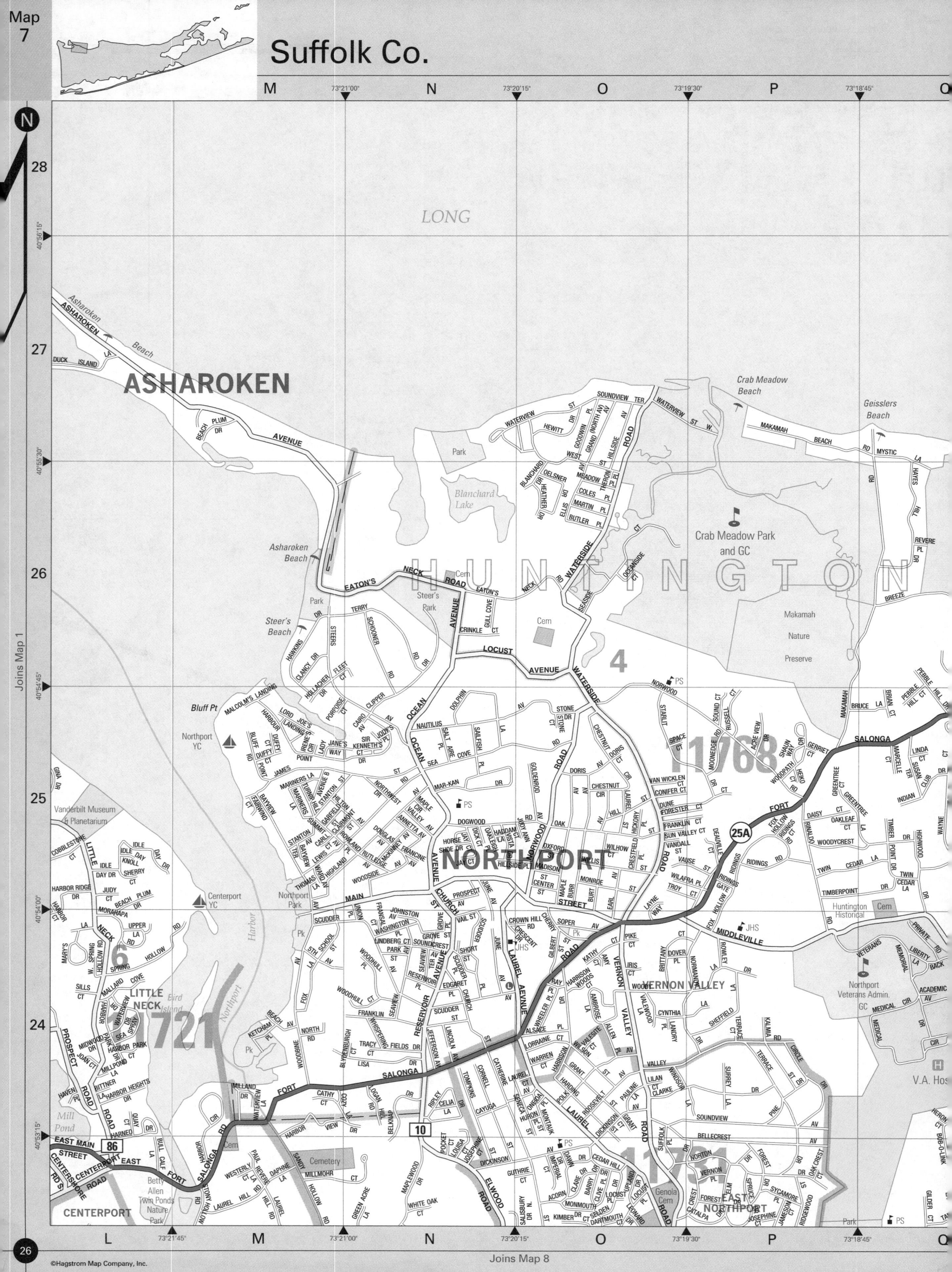

Map
7

Suffolk Co.

Map 7

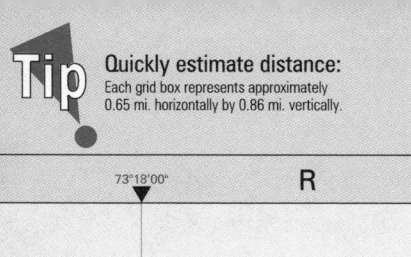

Tip Quickly estimate distance: Each grid box represents approximately 0.65 mi. horizontally by 0.86 mi. vertically.

Scale 1:24,000

0 1,000 2,000 3,000 4,000 5,000 Feet

0 200 400 600 800 1,000 1,200 1,400 Meters

73°18'00" 73°17'15" 73°16'30" 73°15'45" 73°15'00"

R S T U V

N

28

40°56'15"

ISLAND *SOUND*

27

40°55'30"

SMITHTOWN *BAY*

Indian Hills CC

Fresh Pond

Callahan's Beach Park

Sunken Meadow State Park 3 Golf Courses

Board Walk

Bathhouse

Parking-Field 2 Parking-Field 1 Parking-Field 3

Sunken Meadow Creek

26

40°54'45"

FORT SALONGA

Sunken Meadow State Park

Picnic Area Parking-Field 4

Society of St. Johnland

25

40°54'00"

S M I T H T O W N

MIDDLEVILLE

Sunken Meadow State Park

Parking Field 5

11754

25A SM5 SM4

24

40°53'15"

KINGS PARK

Kings Park HS

Port Jefferson Branch

Long Island Railroad

4 11 14

73°18'00" 73°17'15" 73°16'30" 73°15'45" 73°15'00"

R S T U V

Joins Map 13

Joins Map 8

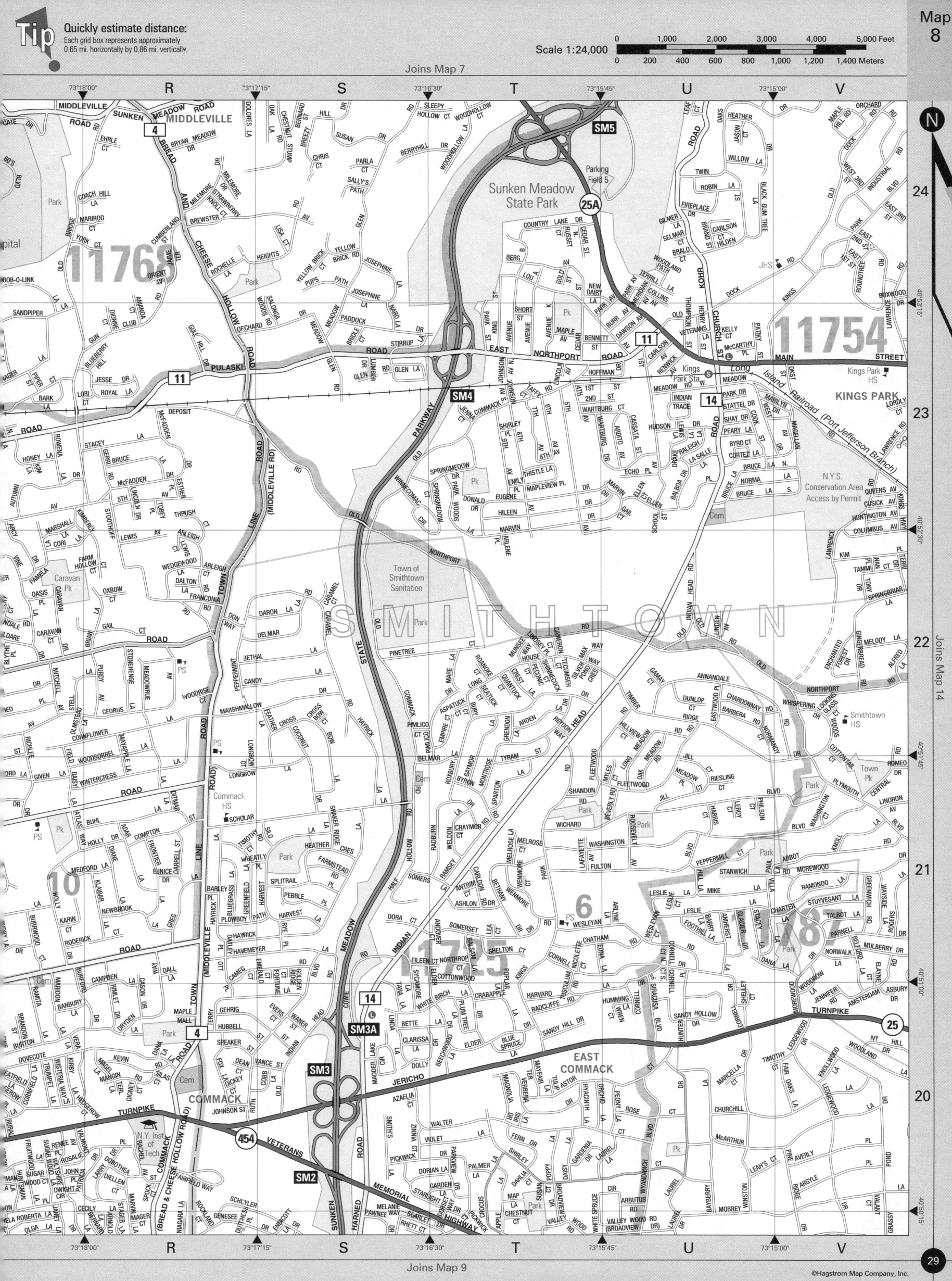

Map
11

Suffolk Co.

Joins Map 10

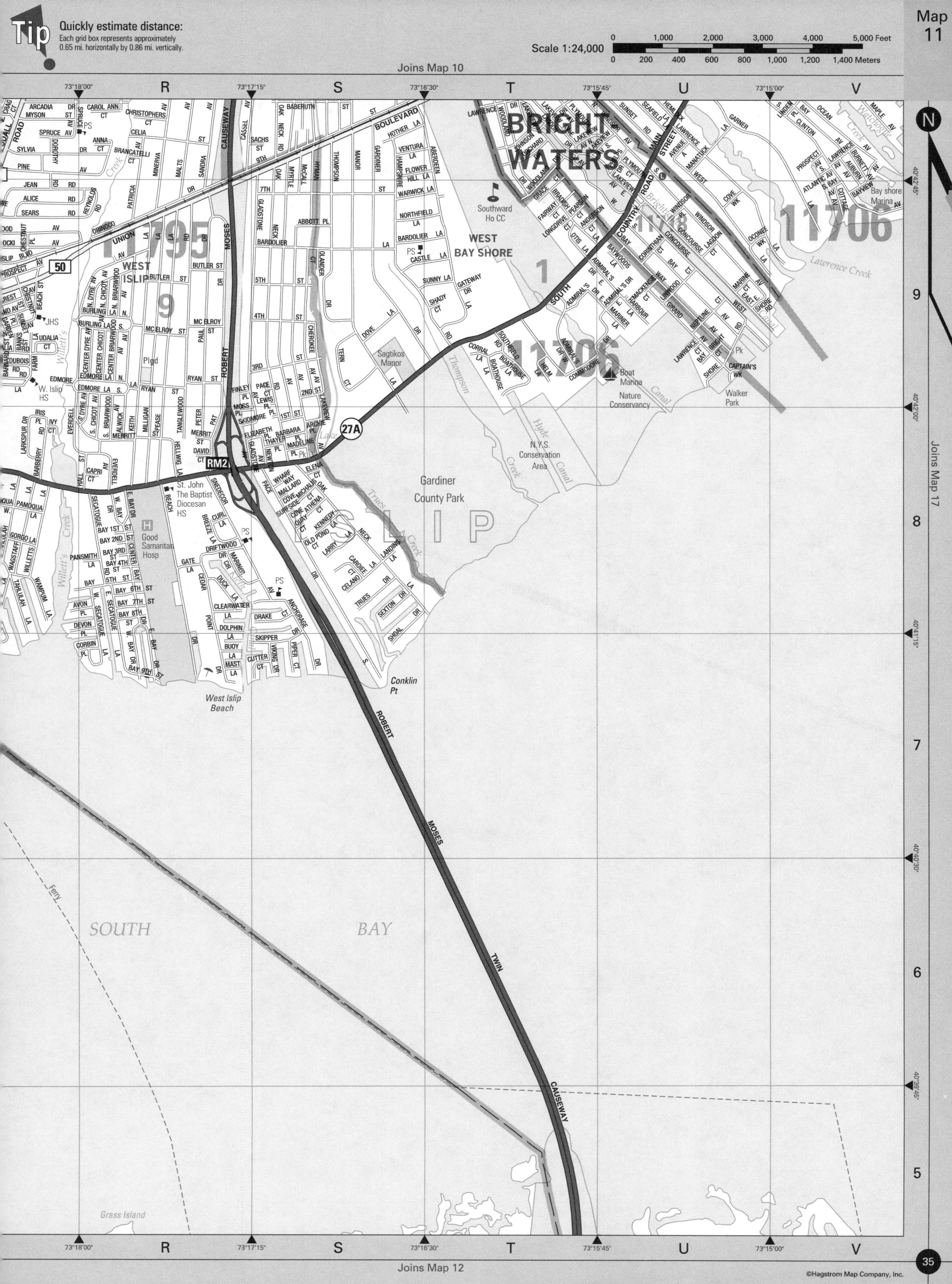

Map
11

Tip! Quickly estimate distance:
Each grid box represents approximately
0.65 mi. horizontally by 0.86 mi. vertically.

Scale 1:24,000

5,000 Feet
1,400 Meters

BRIGHT WATERS

WEST BAY SHORE

WEST ISLIP

Southward Ho CC

Sagtikos Manor

St. John The Baptist Diocesan HS

Good Samaritan Hosp

West Islip Beach

Gardiner County Park

Conklin Pt

N.Y.S. Conservation Area

Nature Conservancy

Boat Marina

Walker Park

Captain's WK

Bay shore Marina

Lawrence Creek

SOUTH BAY

Grass Island

©Hagstrom Map Company, Inc.

Joins Map 17

Map
12

Suffolk Co.

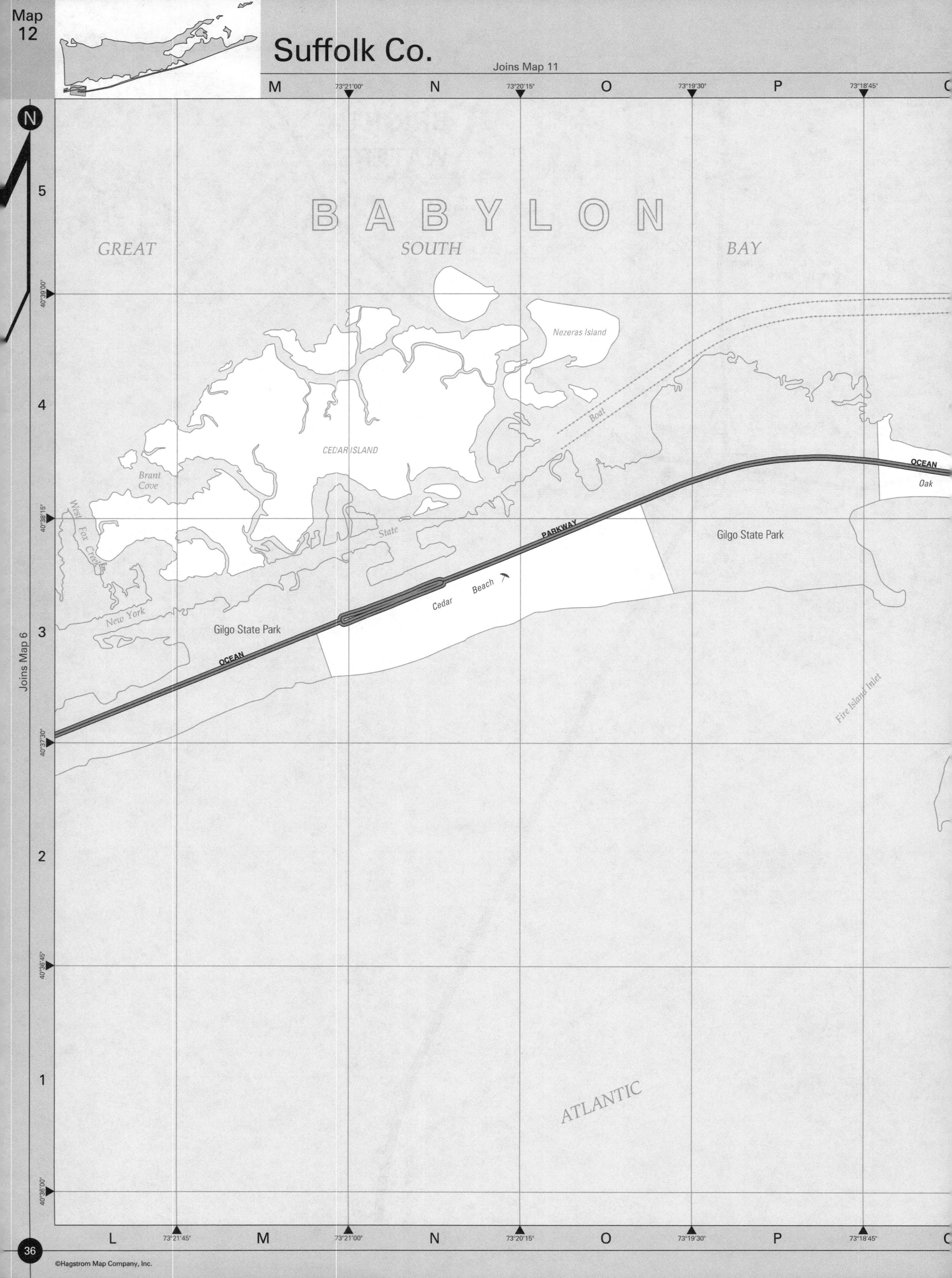

M   73°21'00"   N   73°20'15"   O   73°19'30"   P   73°18'45"   C

N

5

B A B Y L O N

GREAT   SOUTH   BAY

40°39'00"

Nezeras Island

4

Boat

CEDAR ISLAND

Brant
Cove   OCEAN

Oak

40°38'15"

West Fox Creek   State   PARKWAY   Gilgo State Park

Cedar   Beach

New York   Gilgo State Park

Gilgo State Park

3   OCEAN   Fire Island Inlet

40°37'30"

2

1

ATLANTIC

40°36'45"

40°36'00"

L   73°21'45"   M   73°21'00"   N   73°20'15"   O   73°19'30"   P   73°18'45"

Joins Map 6

Map
12

Tip
Quickly estimate distance:
Each grid box represents approximately
0.65 mi. horizontally by 0.86 mi. vertically.

Scale 1:24,000

0   1,000   2,000   3,000   4,000   5,000 Feet
0   200 400 600 800 1,000 1,200 1,400 Meters

Joins Map 11

N

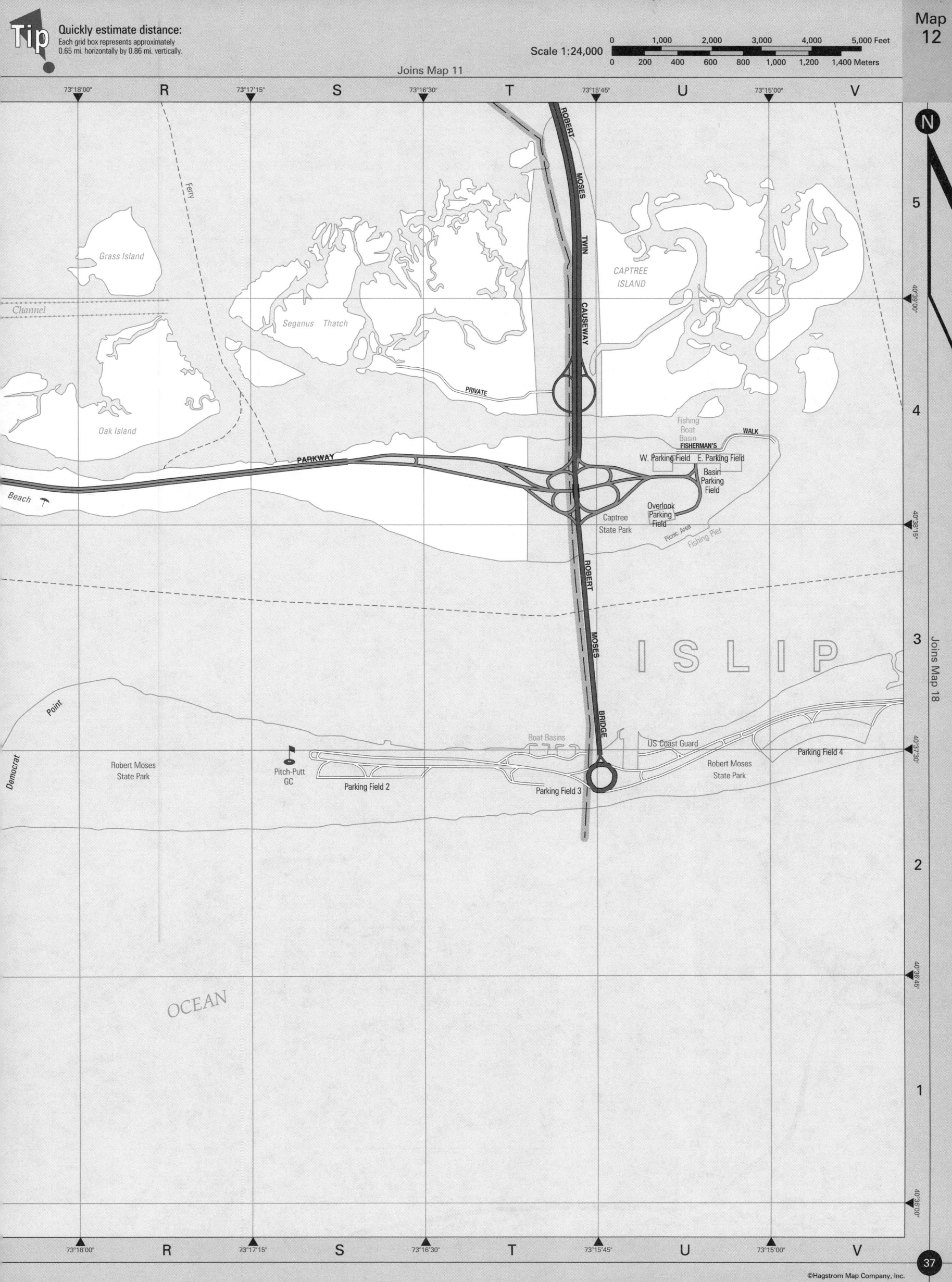

73°18'00"   R   73°17'15"   S   73°16'30"   T   73°15'45"   U   73°15'00"   V

Ferry

Grass Island

Channel

Seganus   Thatch

CAPTREE
ISLAND

40°39'00"   5

Oak Island

PRIVATE

PARKWAY

Beach

ROBERT

MOSES

TWIN

CAUSEWAY

Fishing
Boat
Basin   WALK
FISHERMAN'S
W. Parking Field   E. Parking Field
Basin
Parking
Field
Overlook
Parking
Field
Captree
State Park
Picnic Area
Fishing Pier

40°38'15"   4

ROBERT

MOSES

I S L I P

40°38'15"

Point

Democrat

Robert Moses
State Park

Pitch-Putt
GC

Parking Field 2

BRIDGE

Boat Basins

US Coast Guard
Parking Field 4
Robert Moses
State Park

Parking Field 3

40°37'30"   3

Joins Map 18

OCEAN

40°36'45"

40°36'00"

73°18'00"   R   73°17'15"   S   73°16'30"   T   73°15'45"   U   73°15'00"   V

Map
13
Suffolk Co.

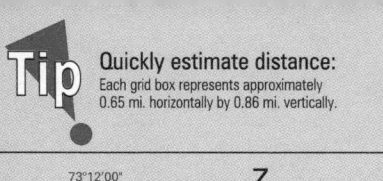

Tip Quickly estimate distance:
Each grid box represents approximately 0.65 mi. horizontally by 0.86 mi. vertically.

Scale 1:24,000

Map 13

NISSEQUOGUE

HEAD OF THE HARBOR

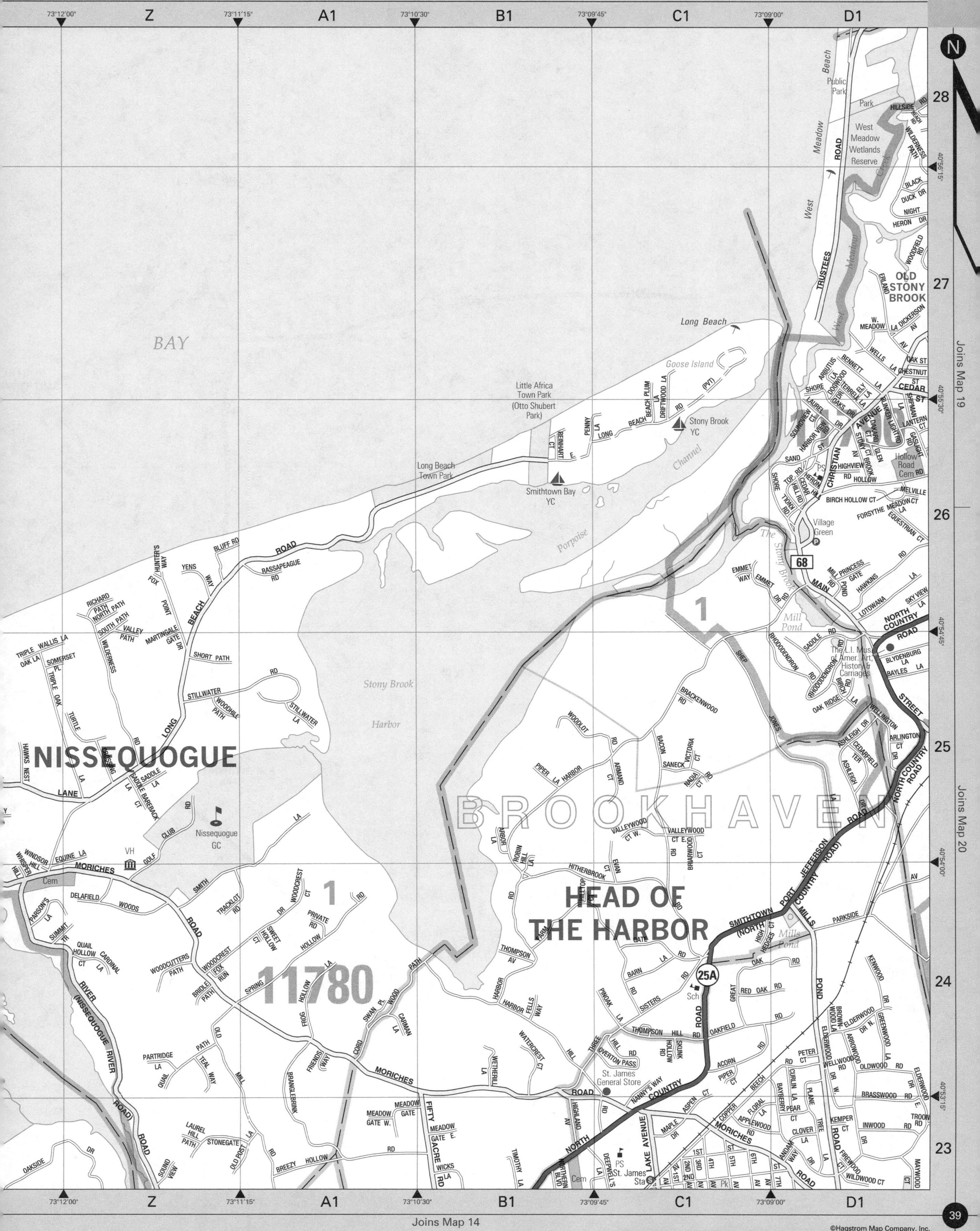

11780

BROOKHAVEN

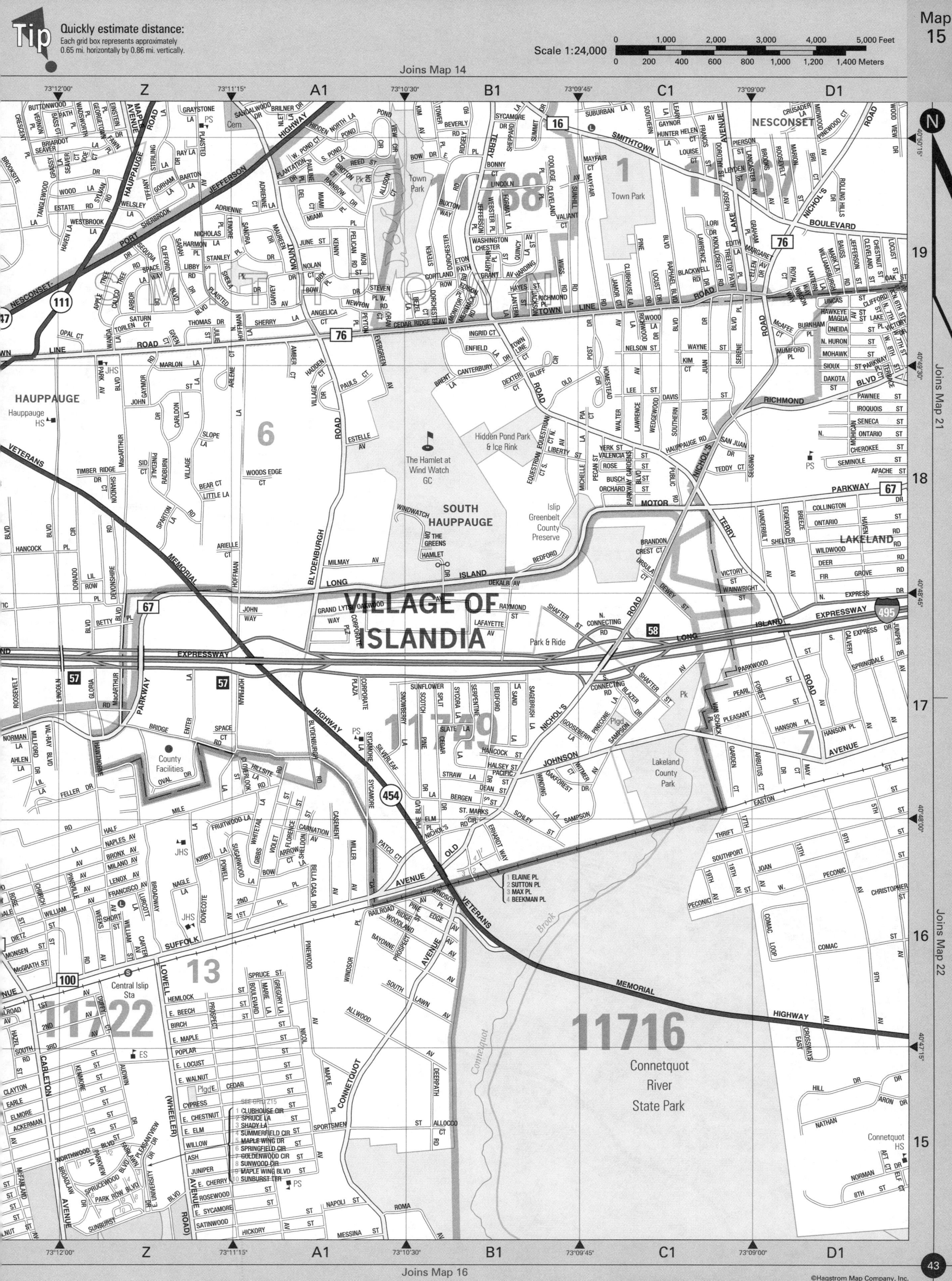

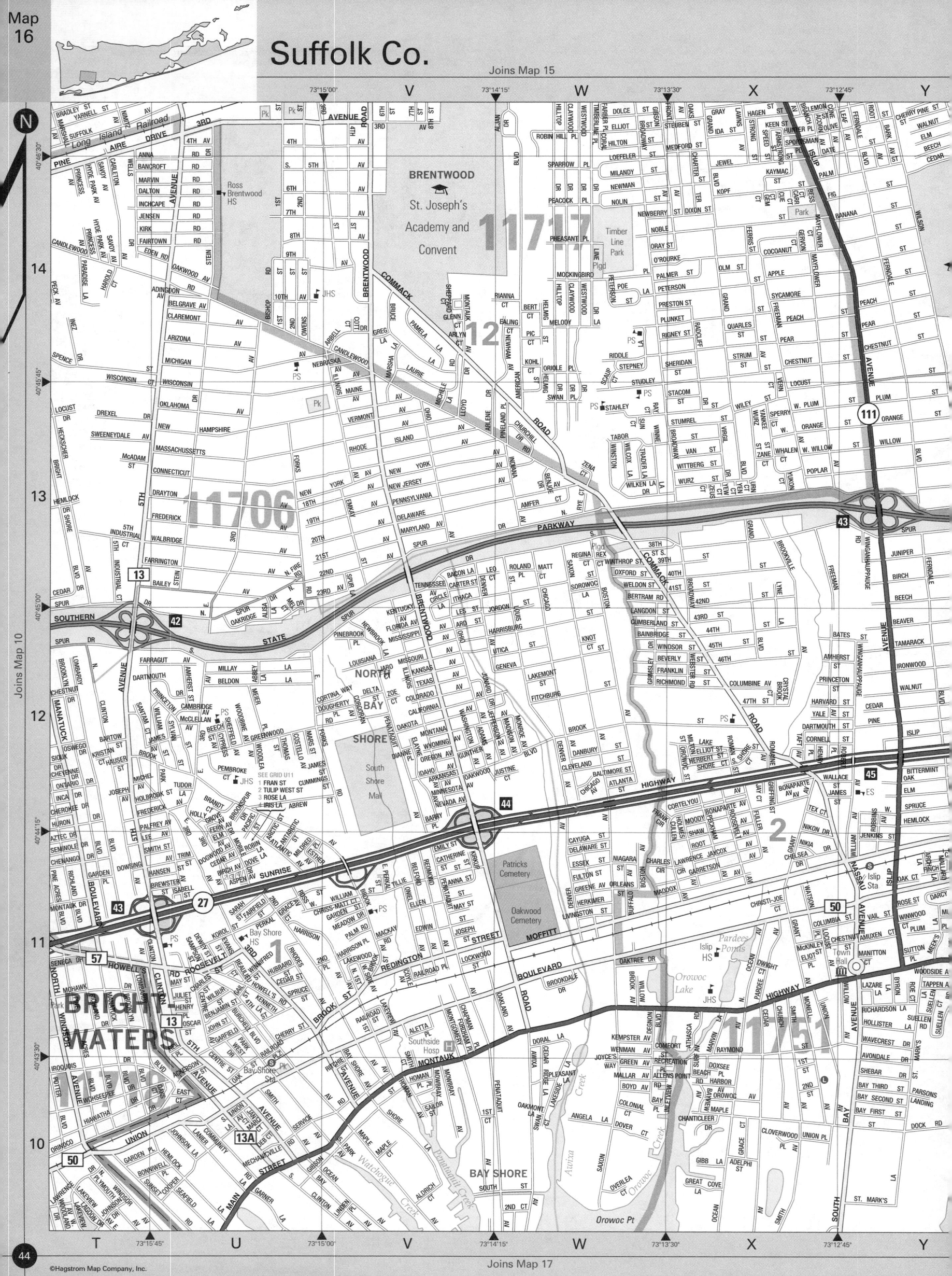

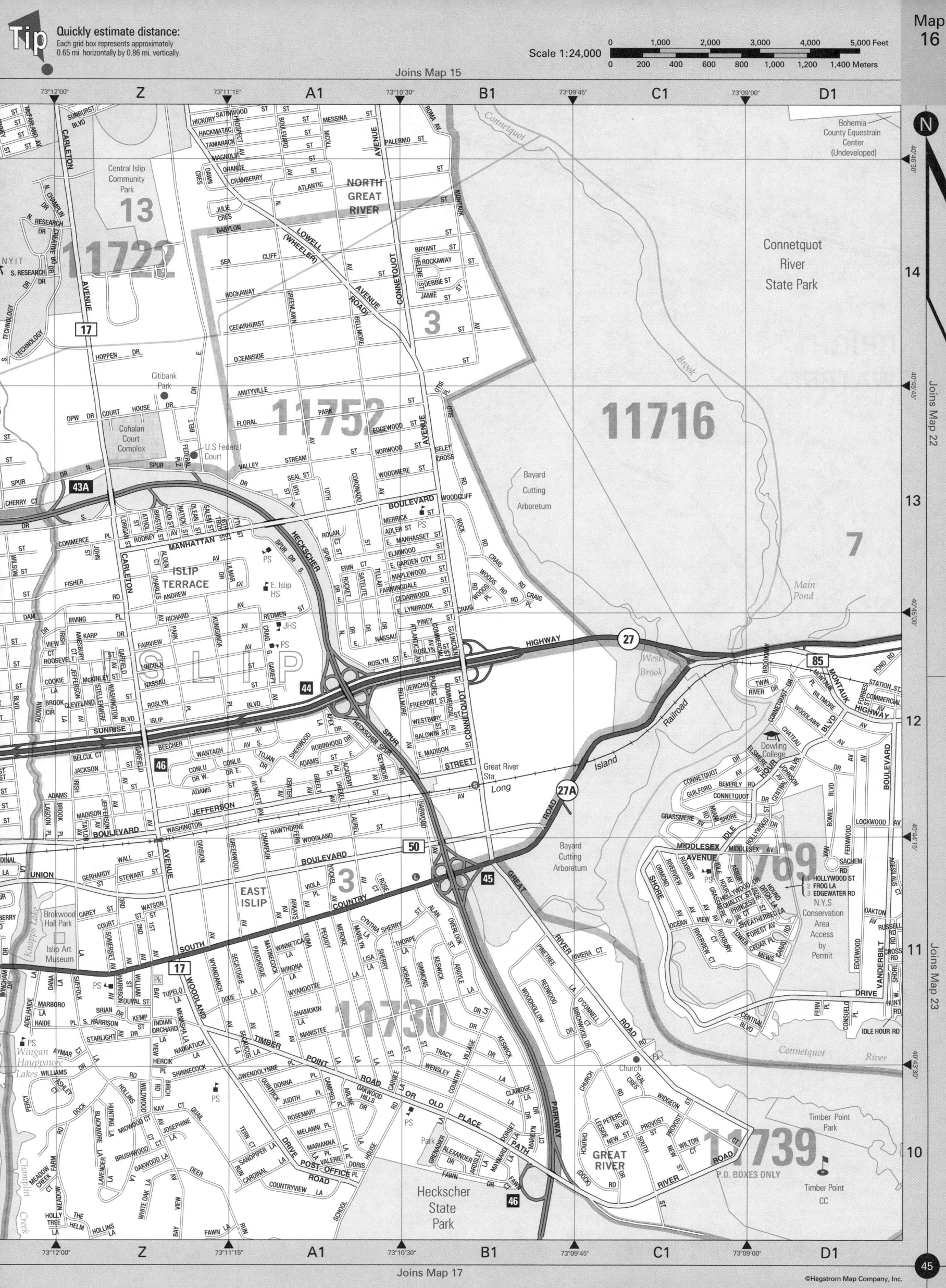

Map
16

Joins Map 15

Joins Map 17

Tip! Quickly estimate distance:
Each grid box represents approximately 0.65 mi. horizontally by 0.86 mi. vertically.

Scale 1:24,000

©Hagstrom Map Company, Inc.

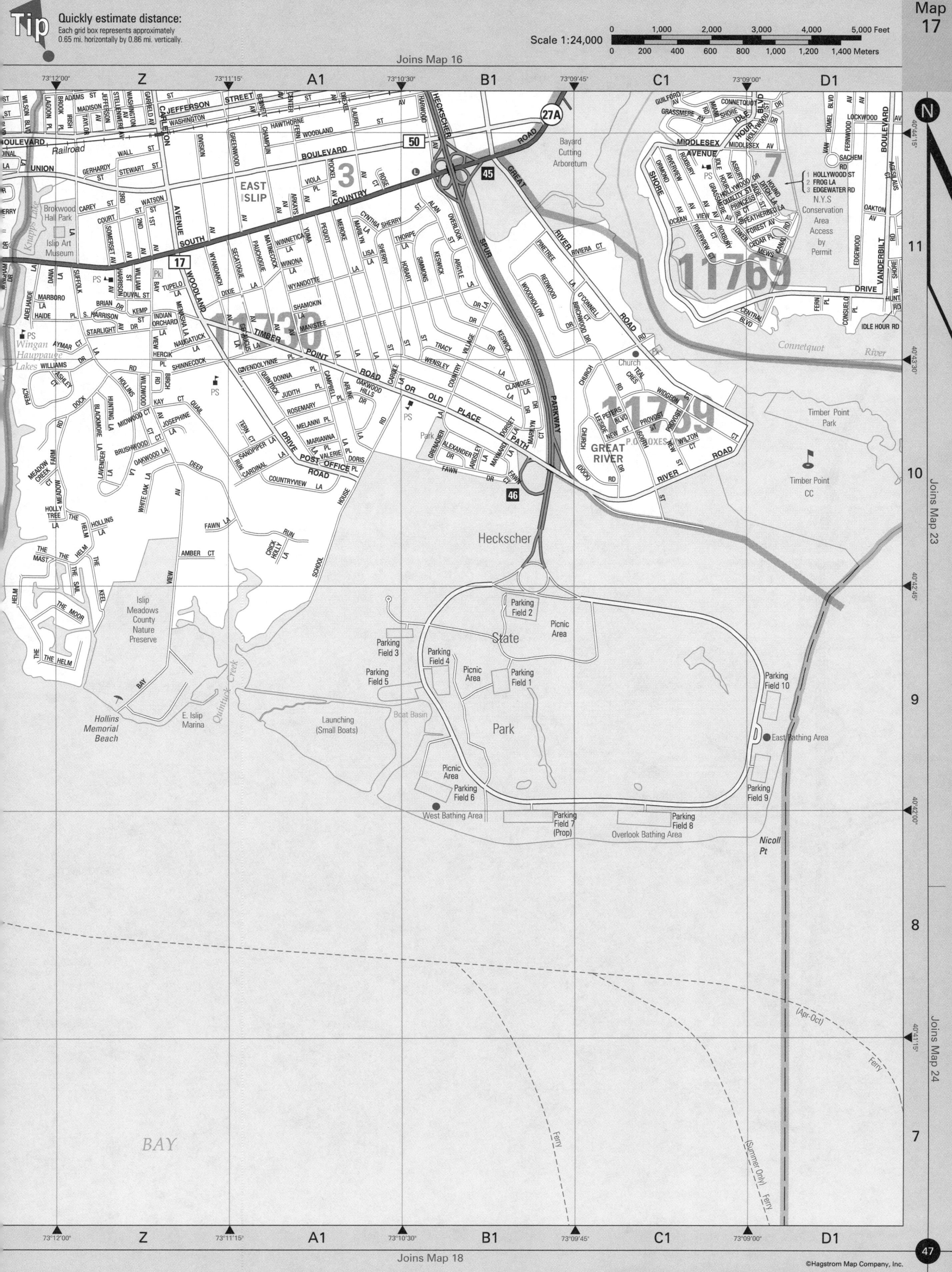

Map
18

Suffolk Co.

GREAT

ISLIP

Sexton Island

CAPTREE
ISLAND

ROBERT

MOSES

TWIN

CAUSEWAY

PRIVATE

Fishing
Boat
Basin
FISHERMAN'S   WALK

W. Parking Field   E. Parking Field

Basin
Parking
Field

Overlook
Parking
Field

Captree
State Park   Picnic Area   Fishing Pier

ROBERT

MOSES

BRIDGE

KISMET

BAY

W.
LIGHTHOUSE

E.
LIGHTHOUSE

CEDAR

LH

Fire Island Lighthouse
Visitors Center

Parking
Fields

Robert Moses
State Park

Boat Basins   US Coast Guard

Parking Field 4

Parking Field 3

ATLANTIC

Joins Map 11

Joins Map 12

Map
18

Tip
Quickly estimate distance:
Each grid box represents approximately
0.65 mi. horizontally by 0.86 mi. vertically.

Scale 1:24,000

Joins Map 17

73°12'00"   Z   73°11'15"   A1   73°10'30"   B1   73°09'45"   C1   73°09'00"   D1

N

40°40'30"

6

SOUTH   *BAY*

Ferry

(Summer Only)
Ferry

40°39'45"

5

Fire Islands

West Fire Island

East Fire Island

OCEAN BAY PARK

40°39'00"

CORNEILLE ESTATES
SUMMER CLUB

OCEAN BEACH

SEAVIEW

PS

4

ROBINS REST
DUNEWOOD
OLD LONELYVILLE

Town Park

ATLANTIQUE

SHELL WK
EAST WK
WEST WK

Seashore

National

Fire   *Island*

BAY PROMENADE

Saltaire Harbor

40°38'15"

FAIR HARBOR

Fire Horn

SALTAIRE

OCEAN

3

40°37'30"

2

Joins Map 24

©Hagstrom Map Company, Inc.

Map
19

Suffolk Co.

LONG   ISLAND

Old Field Pt

OLD FIELD

STRONG'S
NECK

CRANE
NECK

Crane Neck Pt

Flax Pond
Marine Lab

Flax Pond

Conscience
Bay

N.Y.S
Conservation
Area

Little
Bay

Setauket
Harbor

SETAUKET

Setauket
Millpond

Three
Village
Arboretum

1733

1

MEADOW   ROAD

WEST

Public
Park

West Meadow
Wetlands
Reserve

OLD
STONY
BROOK

Bethel
Cem

1756

NISSEQUOGUE

Long Beach
YC

Goose Island (PVT)

Stony Brook
YC

State University
of New York
at Stony Brook

Stony Brook
Sta

11734

St George's
GC & CC

POND PATH
DRIVE

BRO

Porpoise

Channel

Joins Map 13

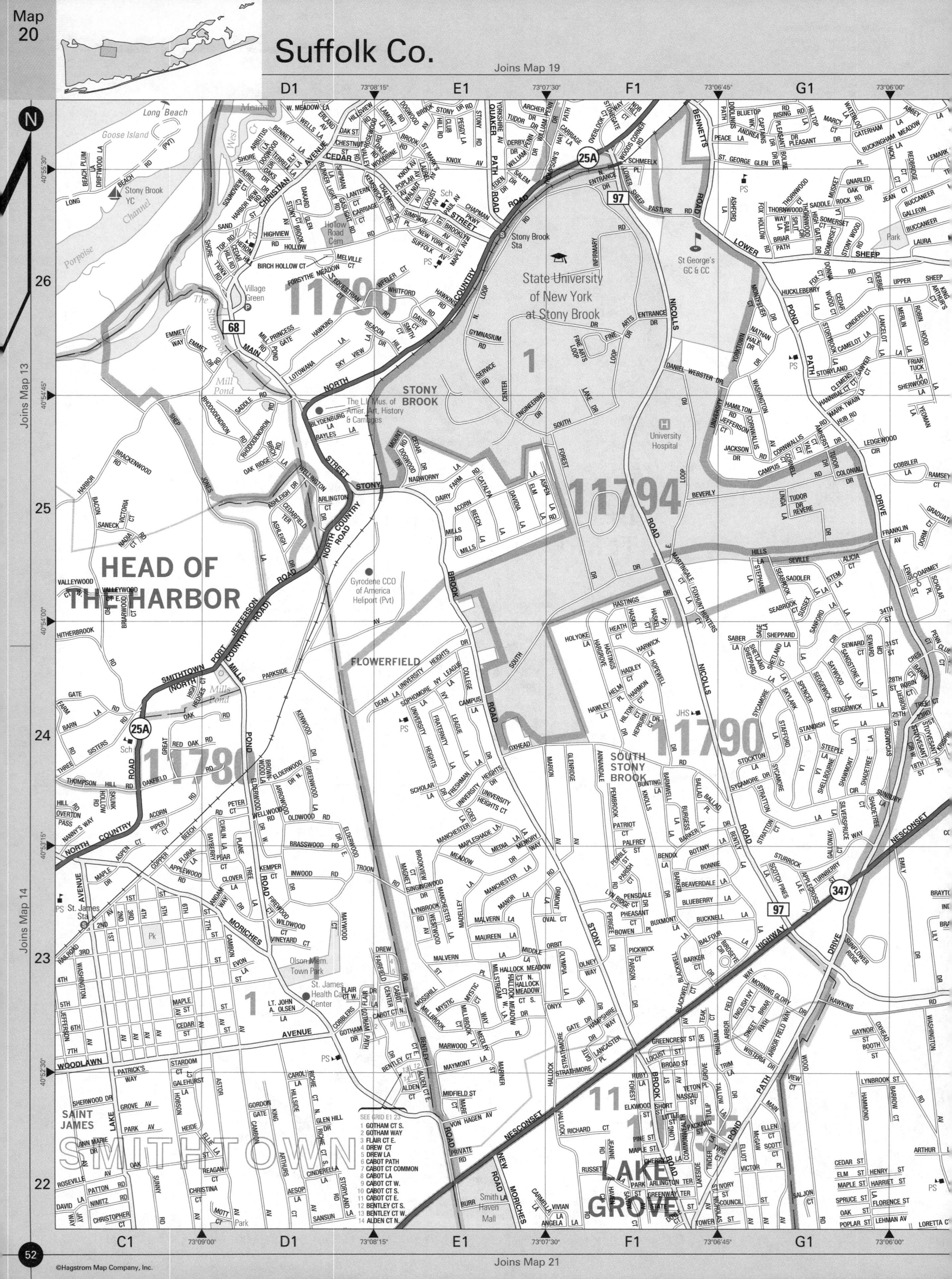

Map
21

Map
22

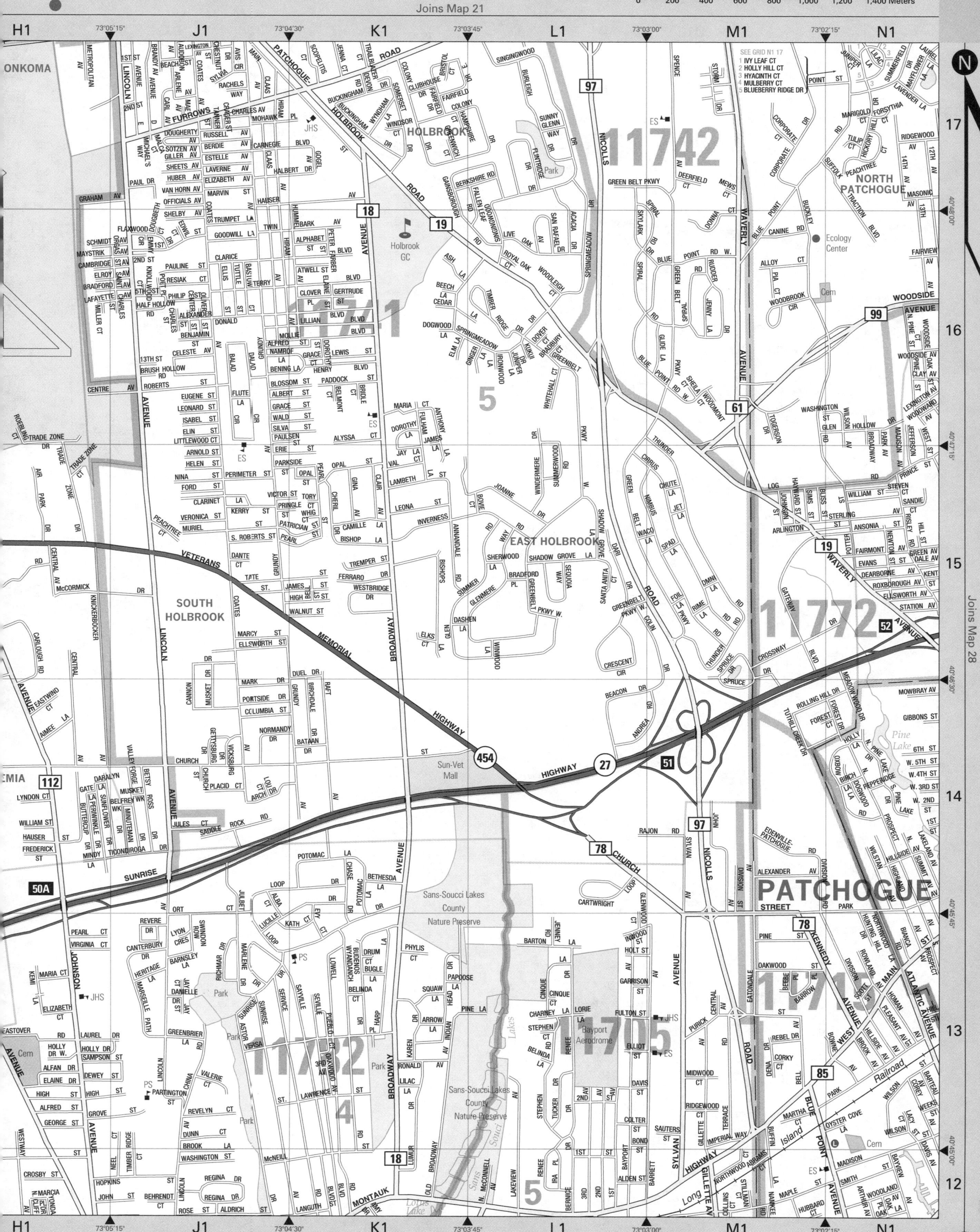

Tip Quickly estimate distance: Each grid box represents approximately 0.65 mi. horizontally by 0.86 mi. vertically.

Scale 1:24,000

©Hagstrom Map Company, Inc.

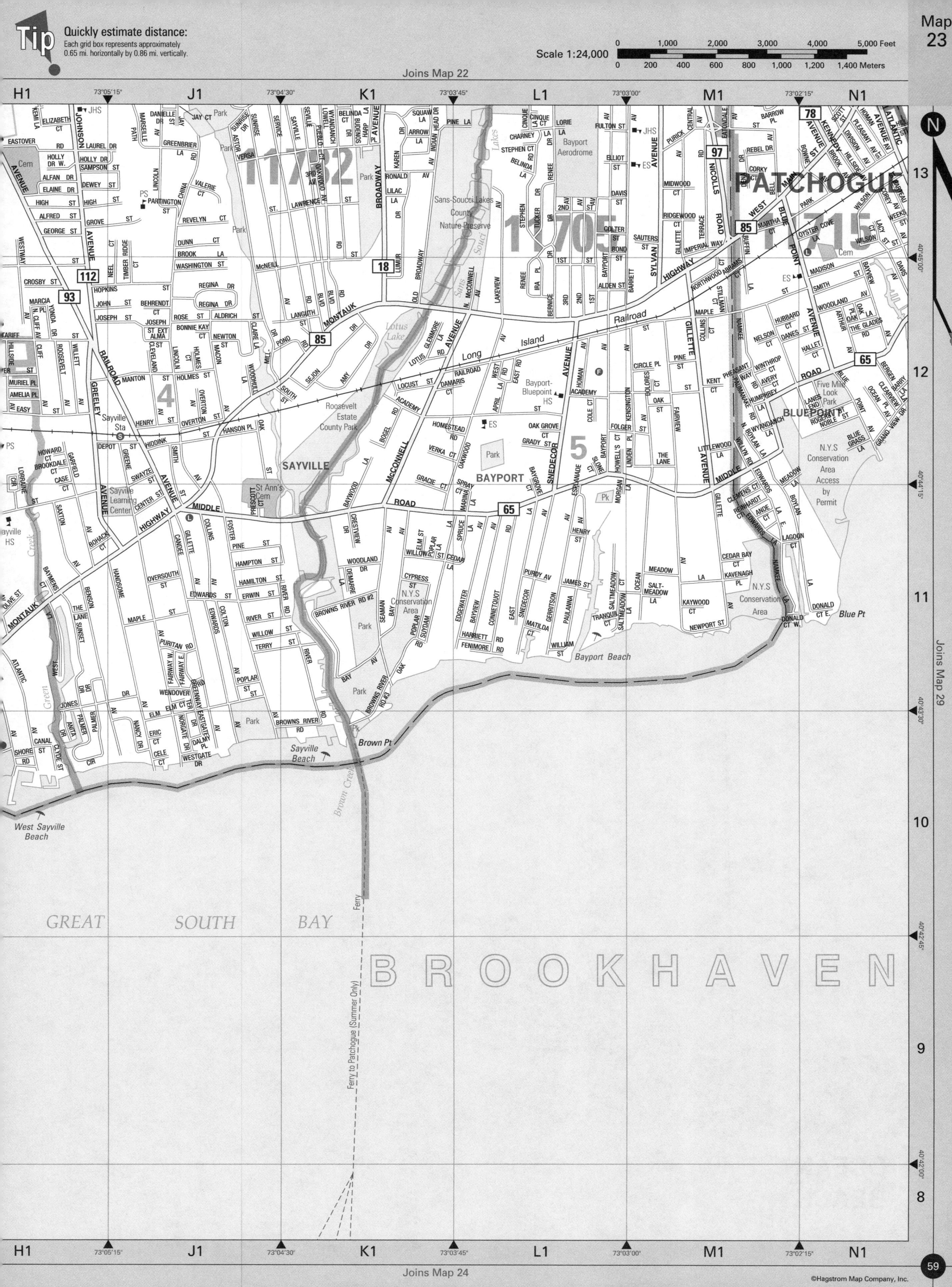

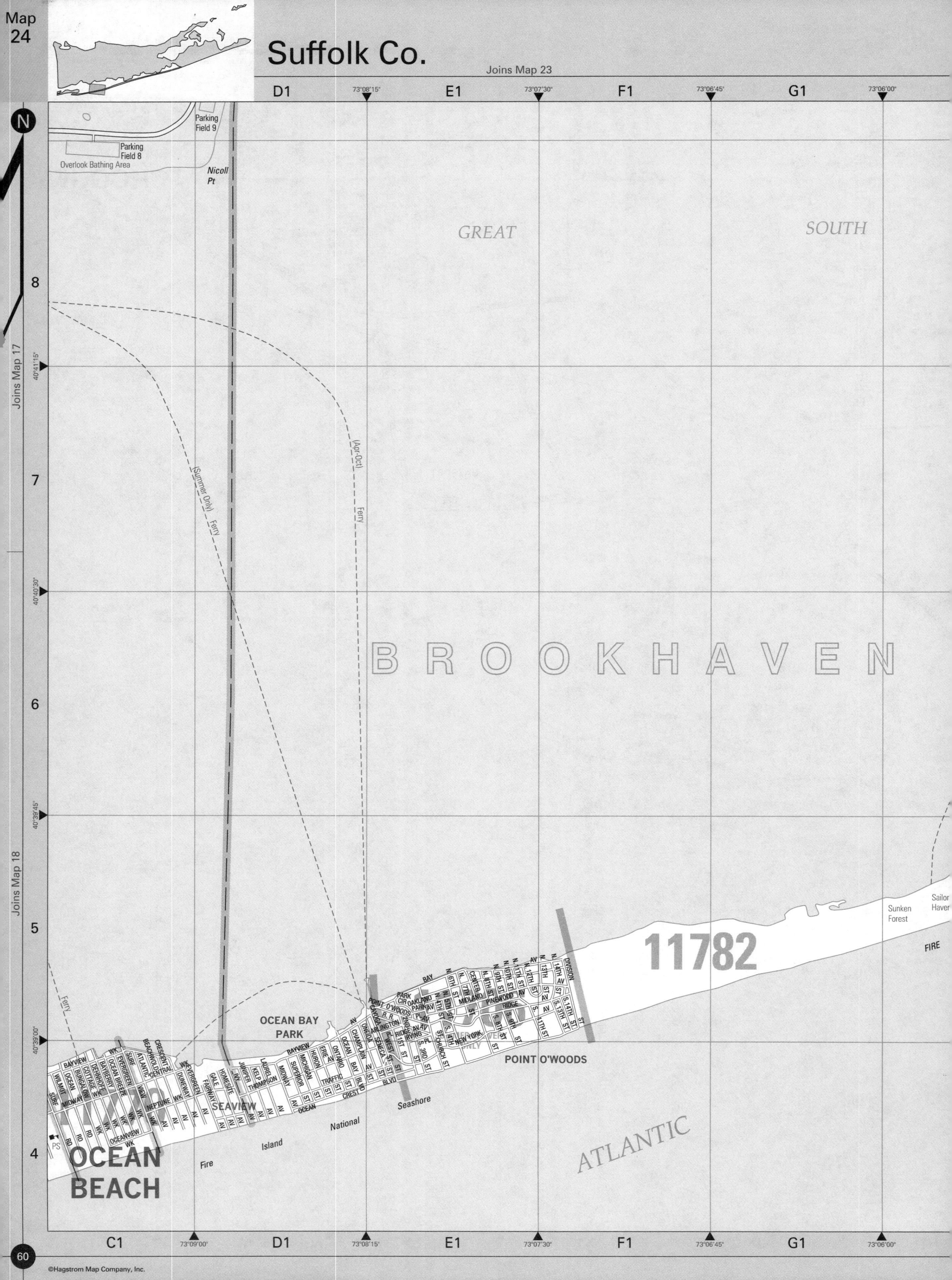

Map
24

Suffolk Co.

Joins Map 23

GREAT   SOUTH

Parking
Field 9

Parking
Field 8
Overlook Bathing Area

Nicoll
Pt

Joins Map 17

(Summer Only) Ferry

(Apr-Oct) Ferry

B R O O K H A V E N

Sunken
Forest

Sailor
Haven

FIRE

11782

Joins Map 18

Ferry

Point O'Woods
R.R.

OCEAN BAY
PARK

POINT O'WOODS

Seashore

National

Island

ATLANTIC

OCEAN
BEACH

Fire

PS

Map
24

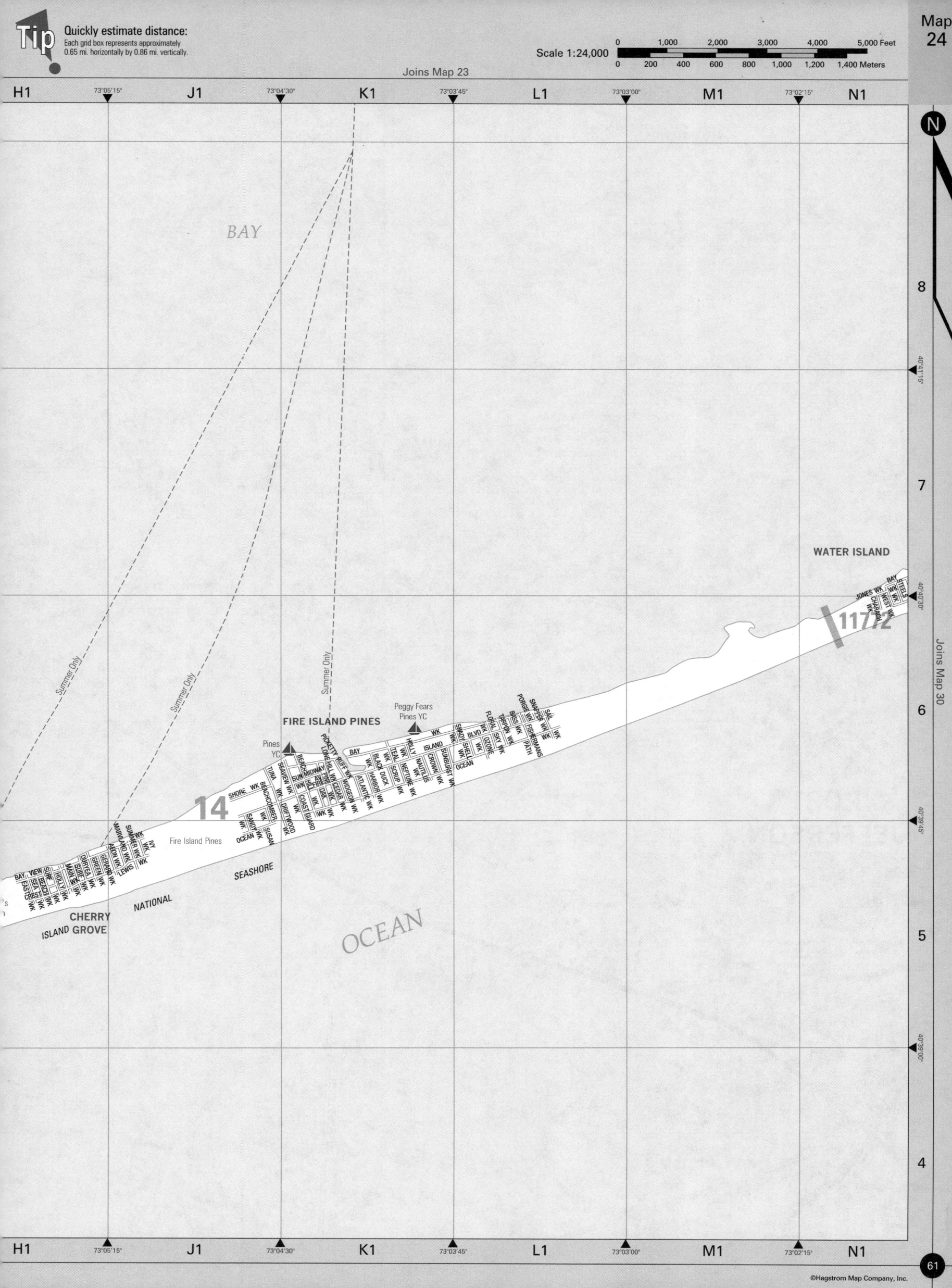

Tip **Quickly estimate distance:**
Each grid box represents approximately
0.65 mi. horizontally by 0.86 mi. vertically.

Scale 1:24,000

0   1,000   2,000   3,000   4,000   5,000 Feet

0   200   400   600   800   1,000   1,200   1,400 Meters

Joins Map 23

H1   73°05'15"   J1   73°04'30"   K1   73°03'45"   L1   73°03'00"   M1   73°02'15"   N1

N

8

40°41'15"

7

WATER ISLAND

40°40'30"

Joins Map 30

6

Peggy Fears
Pines YC

FIRE ISLAND PINES

Pines
YC

BAY

Fire Island Pines

14

Summer Only

Summer Only

Summer Only

SEASHORE

NATIONAL

**CHERRY
ISLAND GROVE**

OCEAN

40°39'45"

40°39'00"

5

4

H1   73°05'15"   J1   73°04'30"   K1   73°03'45"   L1   73°03'00"   M1   73°02'15"   N1

Map
26

Suffolk Co.

Joins Map 25

Map 26

Tip Quickly estimate distance:
Each grid box represents approximately
0.65 mi. horizontally by 0.86 mi. vertically.

Scale 1:24,000

0 1,000 2,000 3,000 4,000 5,000 Feet
0 200 400 600 800 1,000 1,200 1,400 Meters

R1 72°58'30" S1 72°57'45" T1 72°57'00" U1 72°56'15" V1 72°55'30" W1

N

8
11764

9
N.Y.S. 11778
Conservation Area
(Access by Permit)

27
40°55'30"
26
40°54'45"
25
40°54'00"
24
40°53'15"
23
40°52'30"
22

SEE GRID Q1 24
1 PARTRIDGE TR   10 RACCOON PATH
2 DEER PATH   11 WOODCHUCK TR
3 WREN PATH   12 DOE PATH
4 POSSUM PATH   13 BADGER TR
5 BEAVER TR   14 FOX PATH
6 MALLARD PATH   15 DOVE PATH
7 EGRET PATH   16 THRUSH PATH
8 GROUSE PATH   17 PEACOCK PATH
9 HERON PATH   18 CHIPMUNK TR

Washington
Memorial
Park &
Crematorium

Twin Ponds
Nat Pres
Twin Ponds

WHISKEY   ROAD

1 ROBERT LA   8 RICHARD LA
2 LORI LA   9 CHARLEY LA
3 LAVERN DR   10 JILLIAN LA
4 CAIN LA   11 CASEY LA
5 TRACIE LA   12 JENNIFER LA
6 SARA LA   13 ALEXANDRA LA
7 MARTIN DR

B R O O K H A V E N

11953

12

Pine
Lake

MIDDLE
ISLAND

Artist
Lake

Spring Lake
GC

Bartlett
Pond Park

Cathedral
Pines
County
Park

Prosser Pines
County Park

GORDON HEIGHTS

11961

R1 72°58'30" S1 72°57'45" T1 72°57'00" U1 72°56'15" V1 72°55'30" W1

©Hagstrom Map Company, Inc.

Map 27
Suffolk Co.
Joins Map 26

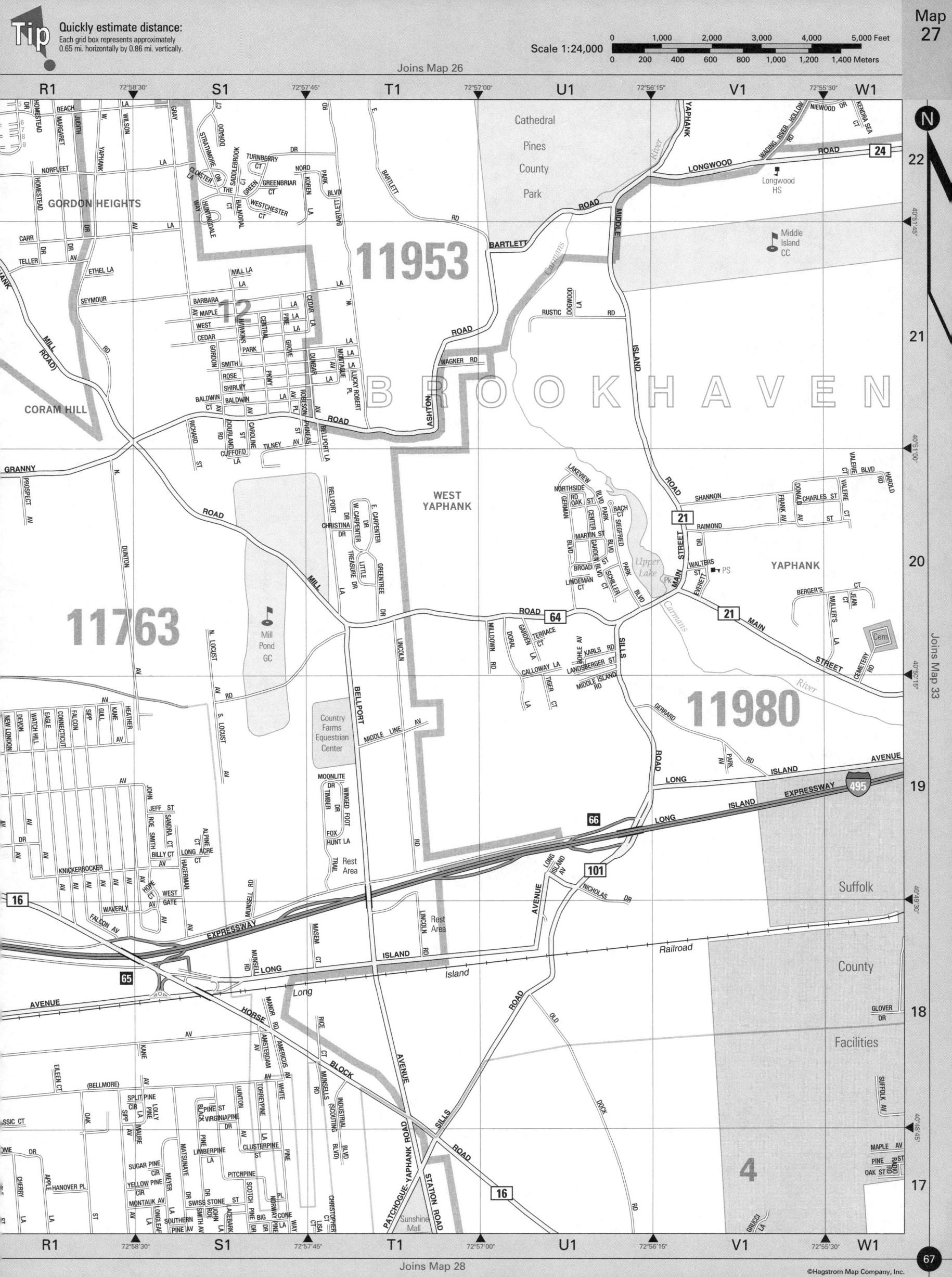

Map 27

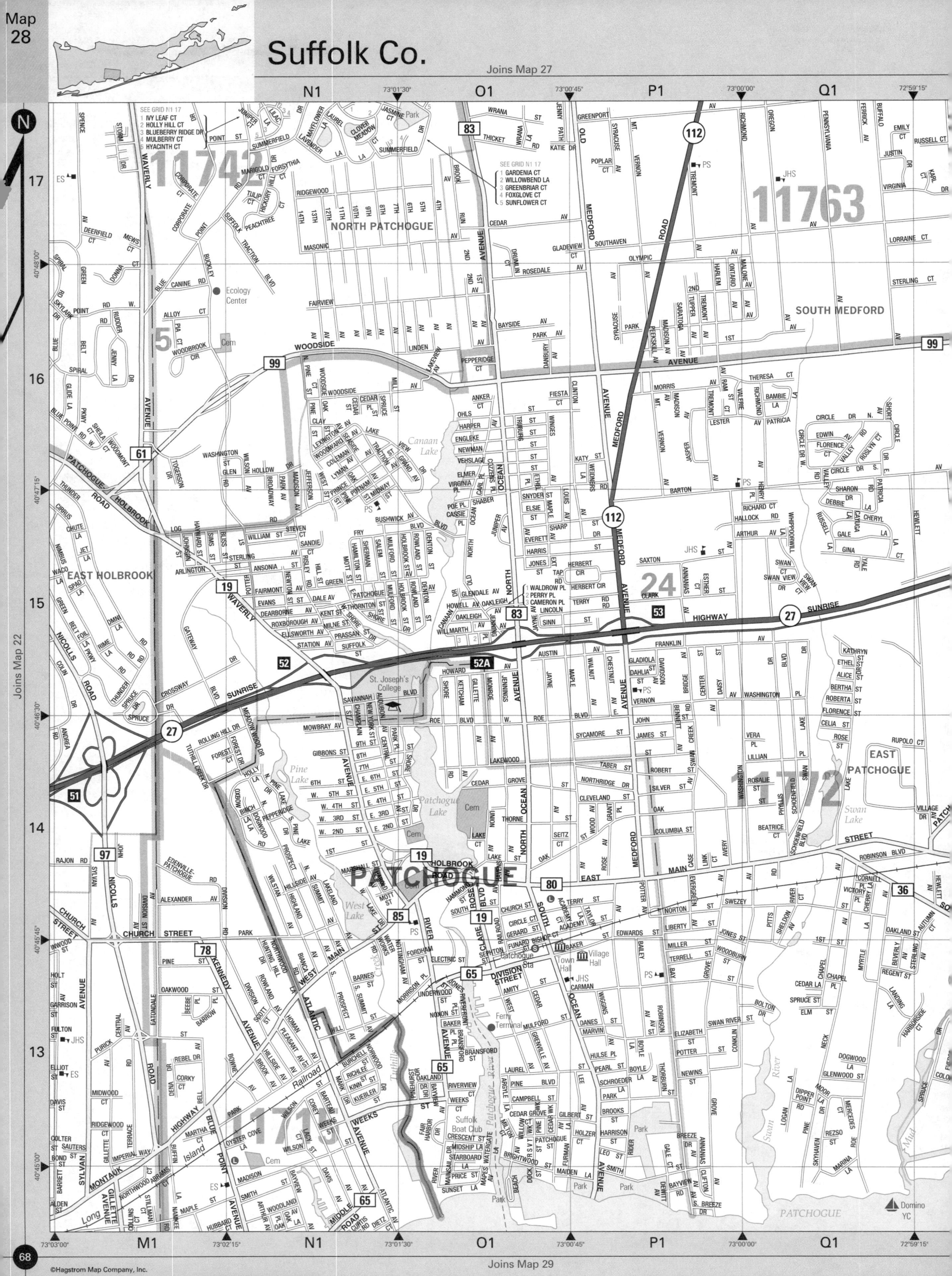

Map
28

Suffolk Co.

Joins Map 27

Map
28

Map
29

Suffolk Co.

Joins Map 28

PATCHOGUE

11715

11705

11772

24

PATCHOGUE
BAY

BROOKHAVEN

GREAT   SOUTH   BAY

Joins Map 23

©Hagstrom Map Company, Inc.

Joins Map 30

Map 29

Map
30

Suffolk Co.

N1   73°01'30"   O1   73°00'45"   P1   73°00'00"   Q1   72°59'15"

N

10

GREAT   SOUTH

40°42'45"

B R O O K H A V E N

40°42'00"

Joins Map 24

9

Ferry to Patchogue (Summer Only)

8

Watch
Hill

40°41'15"

WHALEBONE WK
LEEWARD WK
SANDPIPER WK

BAYBERRY DUNES

WINDWARD WK
DRIFTWOOD WK
SEAFOAM WK

DAVIS PARK

SPINDRIFT WK
DUNE WK

74

EAST WK
WEST WK
TRUSTEES Pk

DONELLA WK
SEAWAY WK

BEACH PLUM WK
PEPPERIDGE WK
FIRST WK

SECOND WK
THIRD WK

FOURTH WK
ELDER DRIVE WK

CENTER WK

11772

7

WATER ISLAND

EAST WK
BAY WK
OCEAN WK

JONES WK
CALDWELLS WK
STEELS WK

CHARACH WK
WEST WK

40°40'30"

ATLANTIC

11782

6

14

M1   73°02'15"   N1   73°01'30"   O1   73°00'45"   P1   73°00'00"   Q1   72°59'15"

Map
30

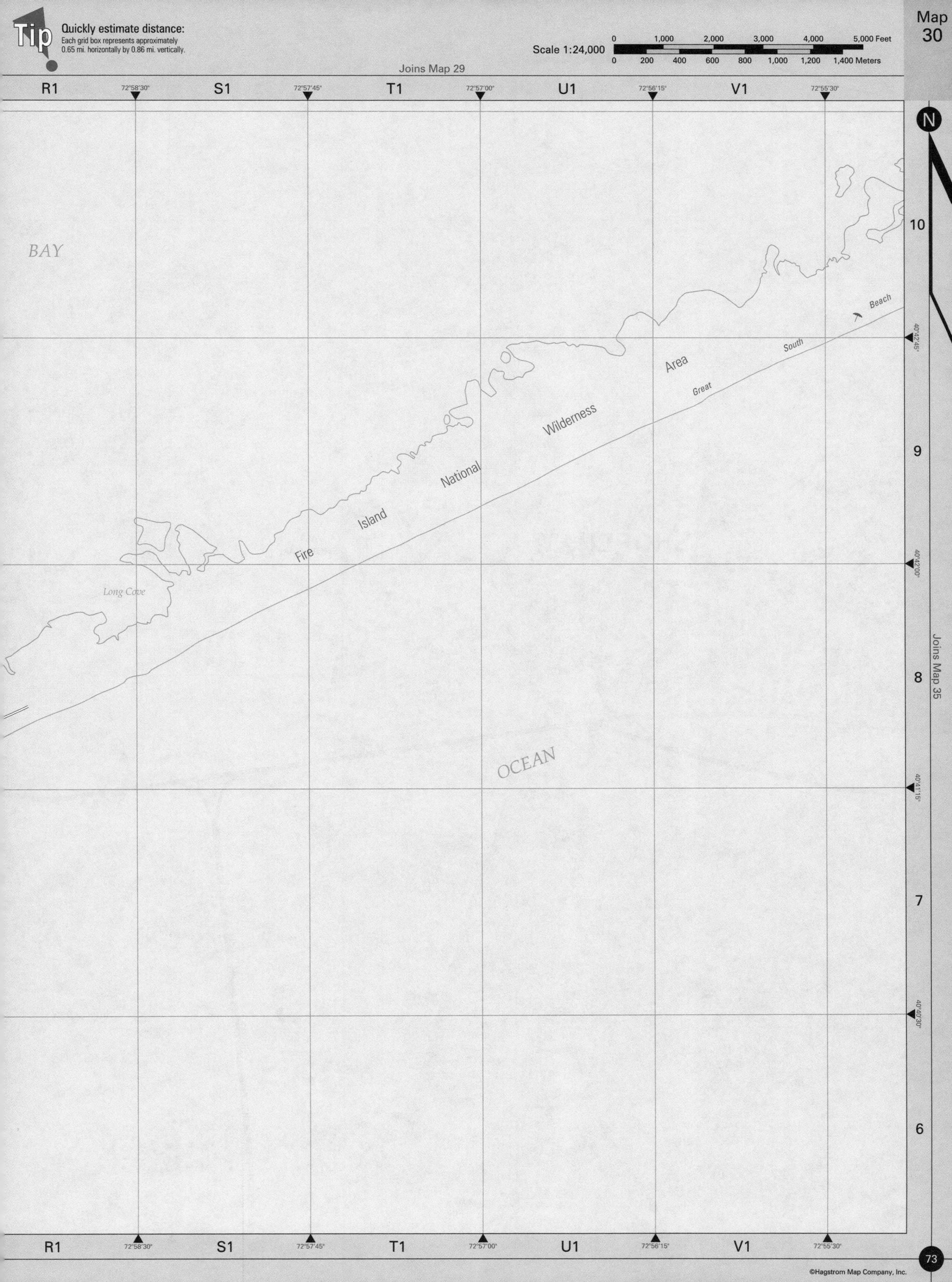

Tip! Quickly estimate distance:
Each grid box represents approximately
0.65 mi. horizontally by 0.86 mi. vertically.

Scale 1:24,000

| 0 | 1,000 | 2,000 | 3,000 | 4,000 | 5,000 Feet |

| 0 | 200 | 400 | 600 | 800 | 1,000 | 1,200 | 1,400 Meters |

Joins Map 29

R1   72°58'30"   S1   72°57'45"   T1   72°57'00"   U1   72°56'15"   V1   72°55'30"

N

BAY

10

40°12'45"

South

Beach

Area

Great

Wilderness

National

Island

Fire

9

40°12'00"

Long Cove

Joins Map 35

8

OCEAN

40°11'15"

7

40°10'30"

6

R1   72°58'30"   S1   72°57'45"   T1   72°57'00"   U1   72°56'15"   V1   72°55'30"

73

Map
31

Suffolk Co.

SHOREHAM

EAST
SHOREHAM

ISLAND

LONG

11786

1

11778

N.Y.S.

Conservation Area

(Access by Permit)

BROOKHAVEN

Tall Grass
Golf Club

Shoreham
Wading River
HS

Brookhaven

State Park

(Undeveloped)

11961

12

9

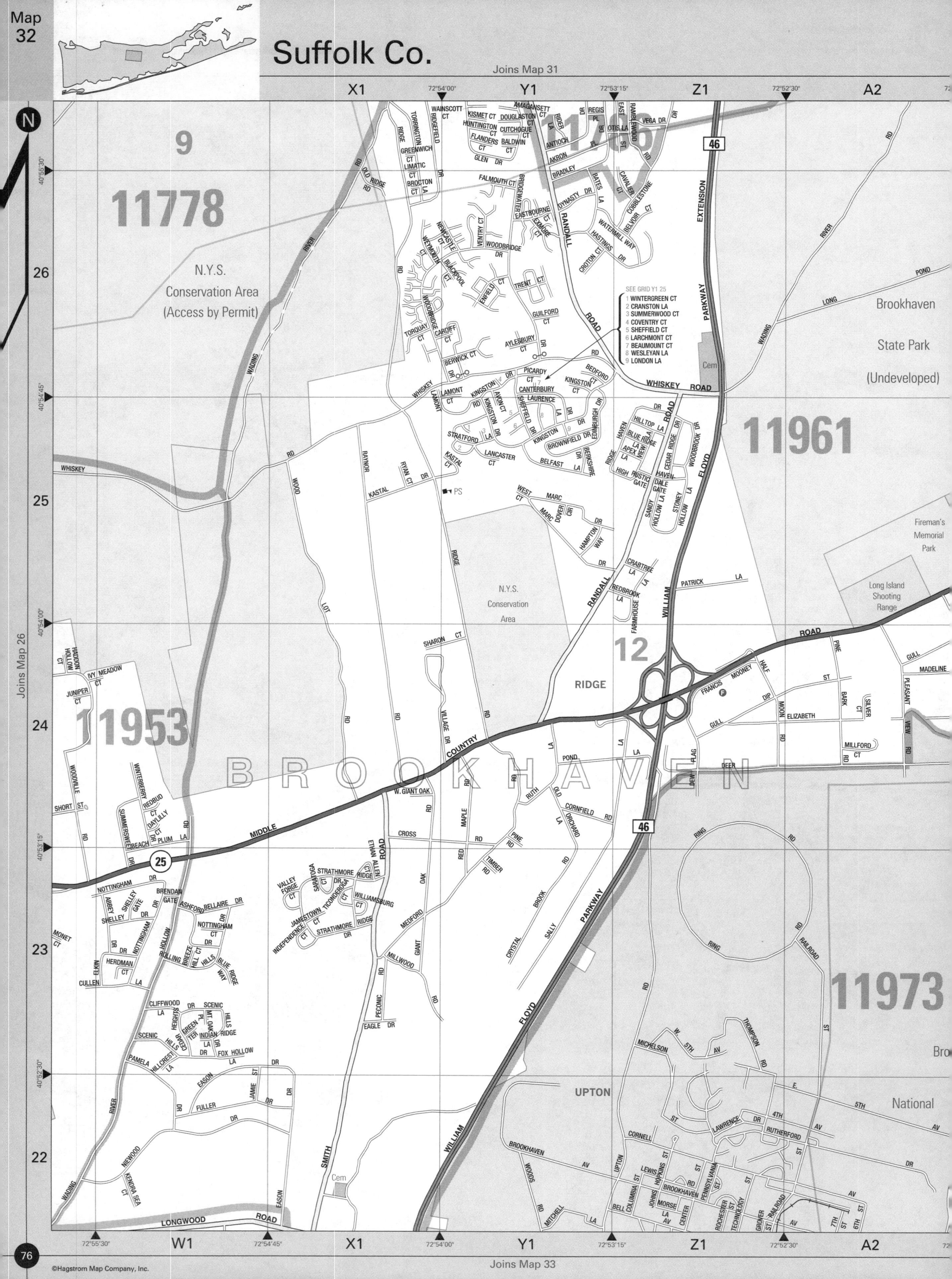

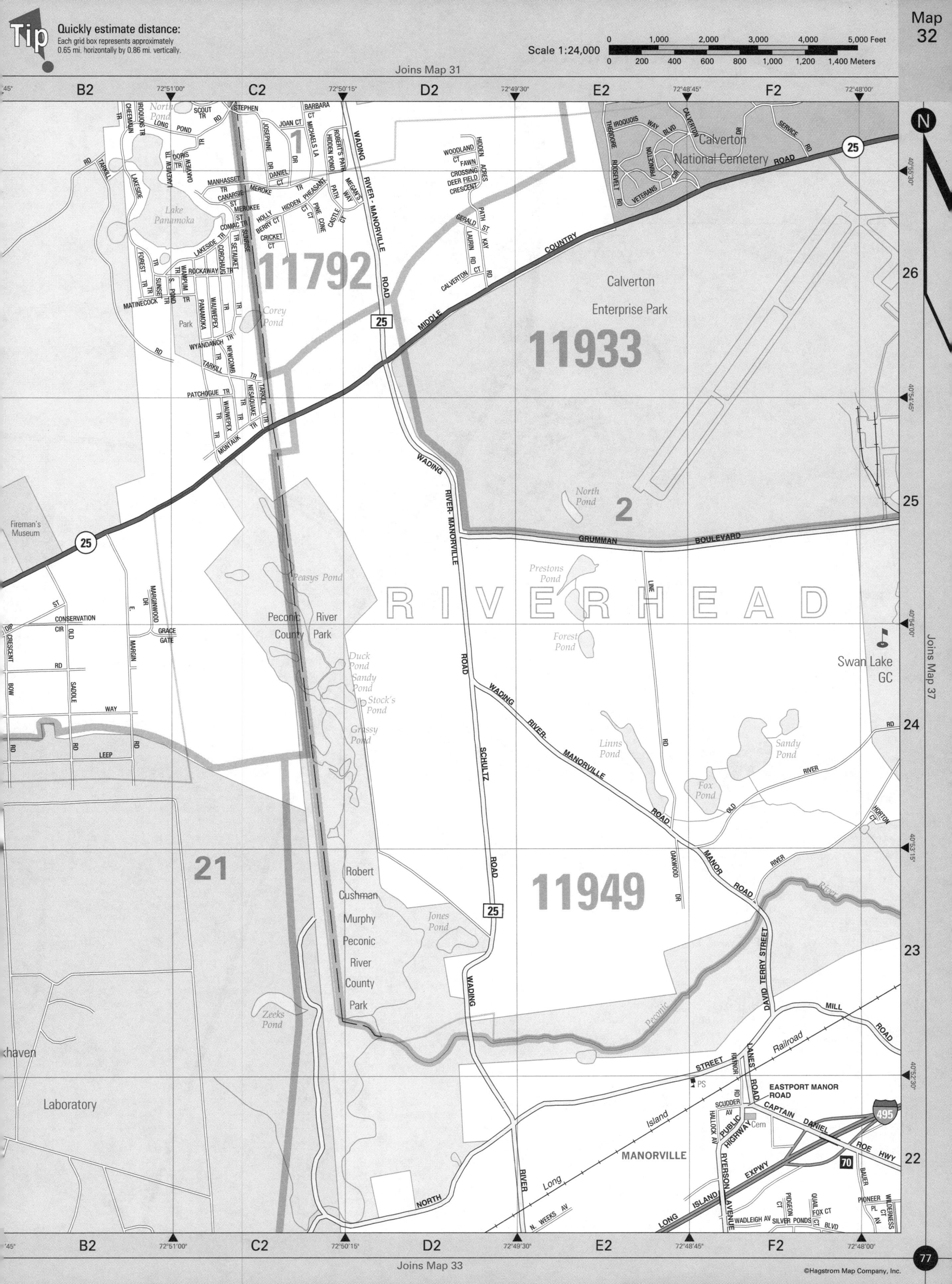

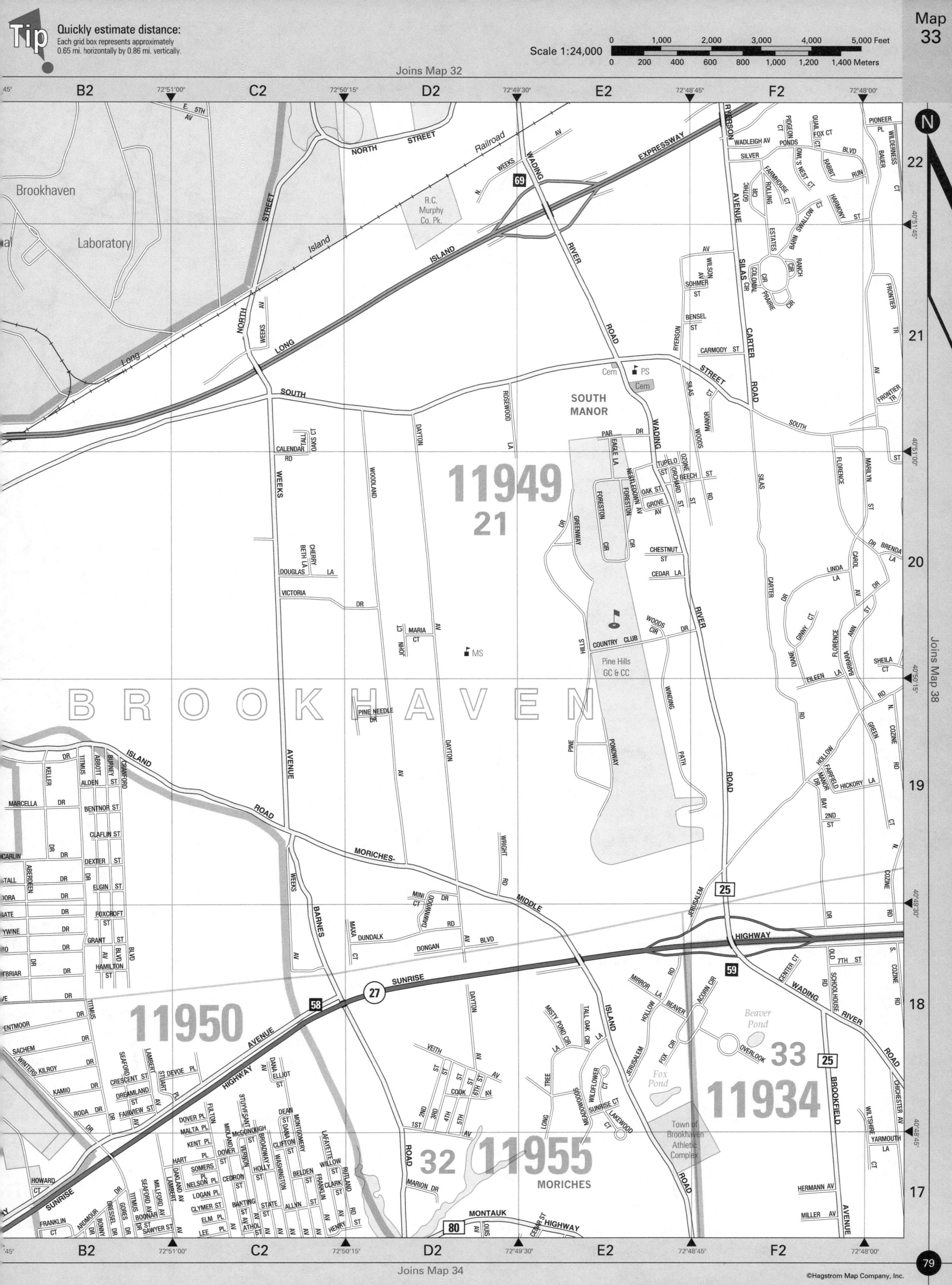

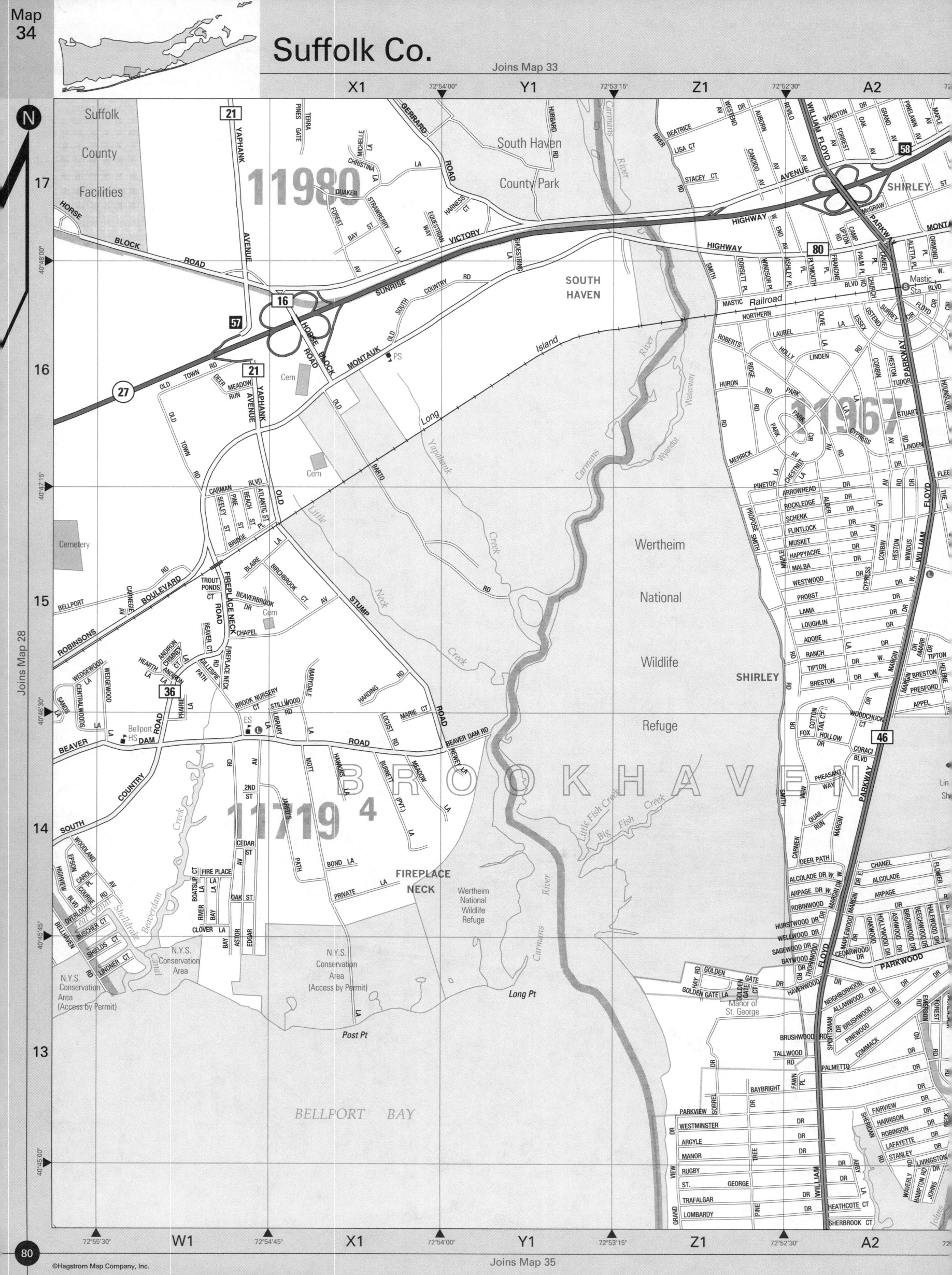

Map
34

Suffolk Co.

Joins Map 33

©Hagstrom Map Company, Inc.

Map
35

Suffolk Co.

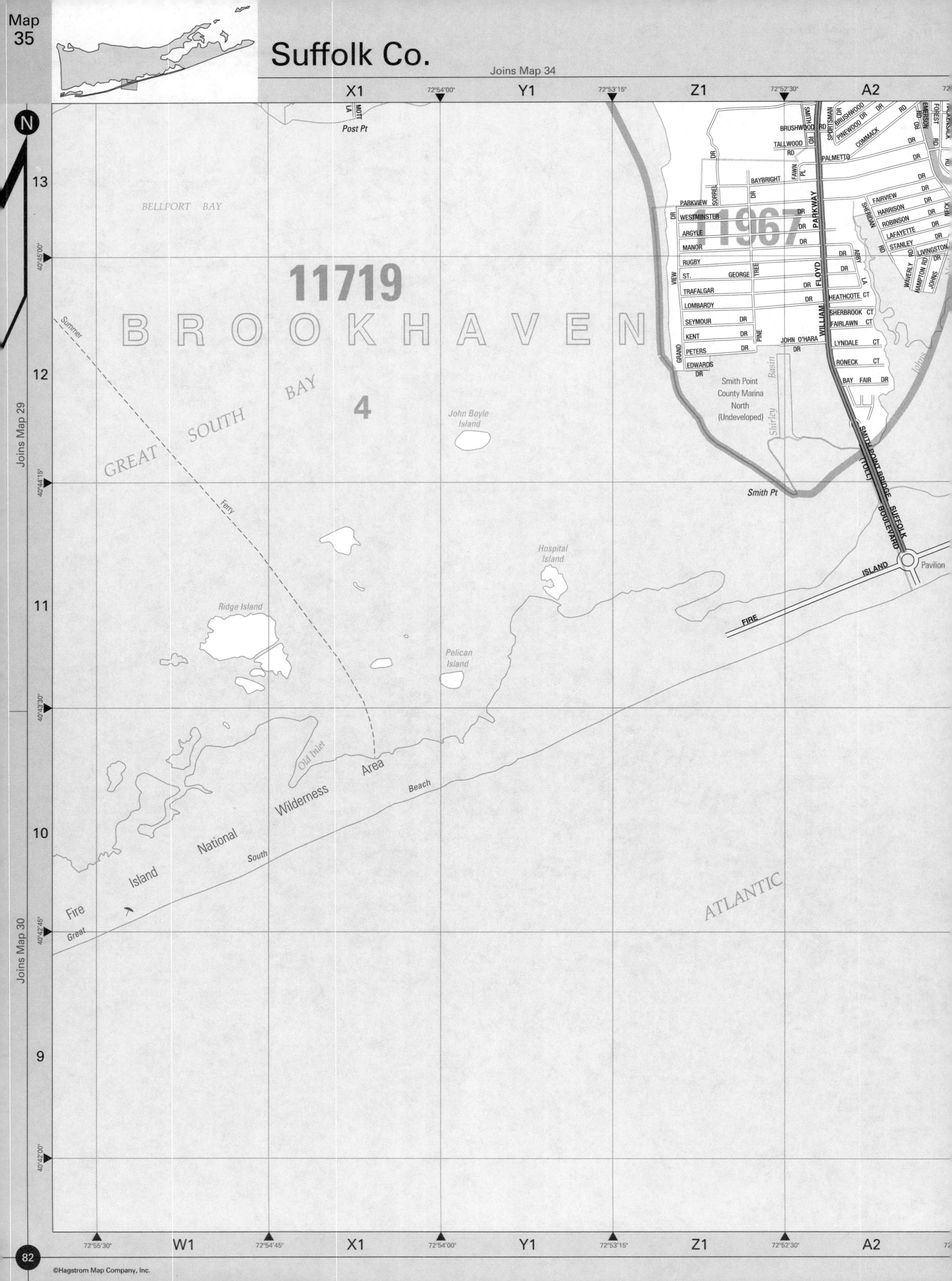

N

X1   72°54'00"   Y1   72°53'15"   Z1   72°52'30"   A2

LA   MOTT
Post Pt

13

BELLPORT BAY

40°45'00"

SPORTSMAN RD
SMITH RD
BRUSHWOOD DR
PINEWOOD DR
COMMACK DR
FOREST DR
EMERSON RD DR
BRUSHWOOD
TALLWOOD RD
PALMETTO DR
BAYBRIGHT
FAWN PL
PARKVIEW DR
SORREL DR
FAIRVIEW DR
WESTMINSTER DR
SHERIDAN RD
HARRISON DR
ARGYLE DR
ROBINSON DR
MANOR DR
LAFAYETTE DR
STANLEY DR
RUGBY DR
VIEW
ST. GEORGE TREE DR
ABBY LA
WAVERLY RD
LIVINGSTON
HAMPTON RD
JOHNS
TRAFALGAR DR
HEATHCOTE CT
LOMBARDY DR
WILLIAM FLOYD PARKWAY
SHERBROOK CT
SEYMOUR DR
FAIRLAWN CT
KENT DR
PINE
JOHN O'HARA
GRAND
PETERS DR
LYNDALE CT
EDWARDS DR
RONECK CT
BAY FAIR DR

11719

BROOKHAVEN

1967

4

GREAT SOUTH BAY

Summer

John Boyle
Island

Smith Point
County Marina
North
(Undeveloped)

Shirley Basin

40°44'15"

Ferry

Smith Pt

SMITH POINT BRIDGE

SUFFOLK BOULEVARD

12

Hospital
Island

ISLAND

Pavilion

11

Ridge Island

FIRE

40°43'30"

Pelican
Island

Old Inlet
Area

Wilderness
Beach

National
South

Island

10

Fire
Great

ATLANTIC

40°42'45"

9

40°42'00"

72°55'30"   W1   72°54'45"   X1   72°54'00"   Y1   72°53'15"   Z1   72°52'30"   A2

Map
35

Tip

Quickly estimate distance:
Each grid box represents approximately
0.65 mi. horizontally by 0.86 mi. vertically.

Scale 1:24,000

| 0 | 1,000 | 2,000 | 3,000 | 4,000 | 5,000 Feet |

| 0 | 200 | 400 | 600 | 800 | 1,000 | 1,200 | 1,400 Meters |

Joins Map 34

B2   72°51'00"   C2   72°50'15"   D2   72°49'30"   E2   72°48'45"   F2   72°48'00"

N

33

Smith   Point   Great   South   Beach   County   Park

32
11951

Smith   Point   County   Park

75   ROAD   BEACH

OCEAN

N.Y.S.
Conservation
Area
(Access by Permit)

Pattersquash
Reservation

Mastic
Beach
YC

Pattersquash   Creek

13

40°45'00"

12

40°44'15"

11

40°43'30"

10

40°42'45"

9

40°42'00"

B2   72°51'00"   C2   72°50'15"   D2   72°49'30"   E2   72°48'45"   F2   72°48'00"

Map
36

Suffolk Co.

LONG   ISLAND

1 9TH ST
2 8TH ST
3 7TH ST
4 5TH ST
5 12TH ST
6 11TH ST

Jericho Landing

WARNER CT

Fresh Pond
Landing

BEACH WAY EDWARDS

Fox Hill
GC & CC

N.Y.S.
Conservation Area
Access by Permit

FOUNDERS
PATH

OAKLEIGH
AV

Bath
House

Parking
Field

N.
RIVER

WADING
RD

Overnight
Camping Area

Trailer
Camping

Camping
Area

Boy Scouts of
America
Camp Baiting
Hollow

PARK
PL

DOGWOOD LA

CEDAR
RD
LAUREL
LA

MAPLE RD

FERN
KINGS
HWY
GLEN

HICKORY
LA

HARPER RD

RD

RD

GEORGE BENSON WAY

OSPREY
OVERLOOK

SILVER

SUMMIT
DR

MEADOW
DR

BEECH
LA

BATTI
HOLL
CE

Wildwood State Park

11792

AVENUE

BAITING HOLLOW

2

FIRE
CT

KAREN
LA

GREGORY
WAY

KRISTEN
PL

54

HULSE

SOUND

AVENUE

MARGE
LA

TWOMEY

WILLIAMS

CAROL
CT

KIMBERLY
CT

WILLIAMS
WAY N.

DONNA

GORDON
CT

1ST
7TH AV
6TH
5TH
4TH

2ND ST
3RD
ST

AV
3RD

E. 3RD AV

E. 4TH
AV

E. 5TH
AV

6TH ST
7TH ST
6TH

AV
2ND AV E.

E. 2ND
AV

E.
1ST
ST

VILLAGE
GREEN N.

VILLAGE
GREEN S.

SUNWOOD DR

FRESH

11933

2

LANDING

ROAD

POND

PARKER

PATH

TRIANGLE
LA

GNOSE
LA

KAR

PHEASANT
LA

LA

EDWARDS

RILEY

John Jay
RD

Michigan
WAY

ALEXANDER
HAMILTON
RD

Calverton
National Cemetery

SOUTH

PENNY

TIMBER

WILDWOOD
DR

DR

AV

CALVERTON
DR

SUNNY LINE DR

OLD STONE RD

CALVERTON

SERVICE
RD

MIDDLE

COUNTRY

25A

ROAD

COUNTRY

ROAD

25

Grumman
Memorial
Park

Calverton
Enterprise Park

AVENUE

Joins Map 31

Map
36

Map
37

Suffolk Co.

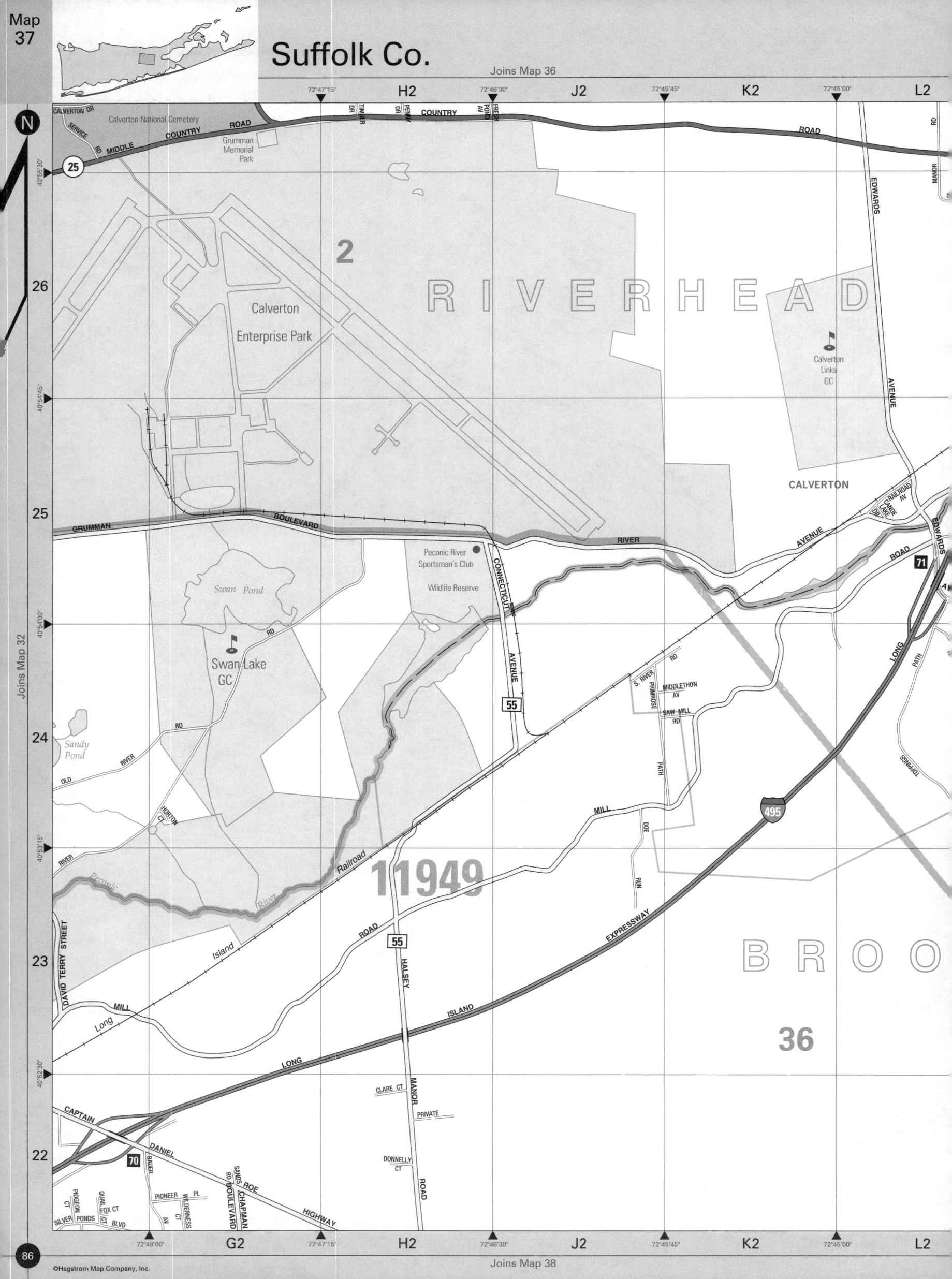

72°47'15"   H2   72°46'30"   J2   72°45'45"   K2   72°45'00"   L2

N

CALVERTON DR
SERVICE
Calverton National Cemetery
ROAD
COUNTRY
RD MIDDLE
Grumman Memorial Park
25
COUNTRY
FRET
PENNY DR
TIMBER DR
POND AV
ROAD
EDWARDS
RD
MOWN
40°55'30"

2

RIVERHEAD

26

Calverton
Enterprise Park

Calverton Links GC

40°54'45"

CALVERTON

25

GRUMMAN
BOULEVARD
RIVER
AVENUE
C RAILROAD AV
CANOE LANE
EDWARDS
71

Peconic River Sportsman's Club
Wildlife Reserve

Joins Map 32

Swan Pond

40°54'00"

RD
CONNECTICUT
AVENUE
55
S. RIVER RD
PRIMROSE
MIDDLETHON AV
SAW MILL RD

Swan Lake GC

LONG
PATH
TOPHICS

Sandy Pond

24

RD
RIVER
OLD
HORTON CT
PATH
DOE
MILL
RUN
495
40°53'15"

RIVER
River
Peconic

Railroad
11949
Expressway
BROO
40°52'30"

David Terry Street
Island
ROAD
55
HALSEY
ISLAND

36

23

MILL
Long
LONG
ISLAND

22

CAPTAIN
DANIEL
70
BAUER
CLARE CT
MANOR
PRIVATE
DONNELLY CT
ROAD

PIGEON CT
QUAIL CT
SILVER PONDS CT
FOX CT
PIONEER PL
WILDERNESS AV
SANDS ROE PL
CHAPMAN BOULEVARD
HIGHWAY

72°48'00"   G2   72°47'15"   H2   72°46'30"   J2   72°45'45"   K2   72°45'00"   L2

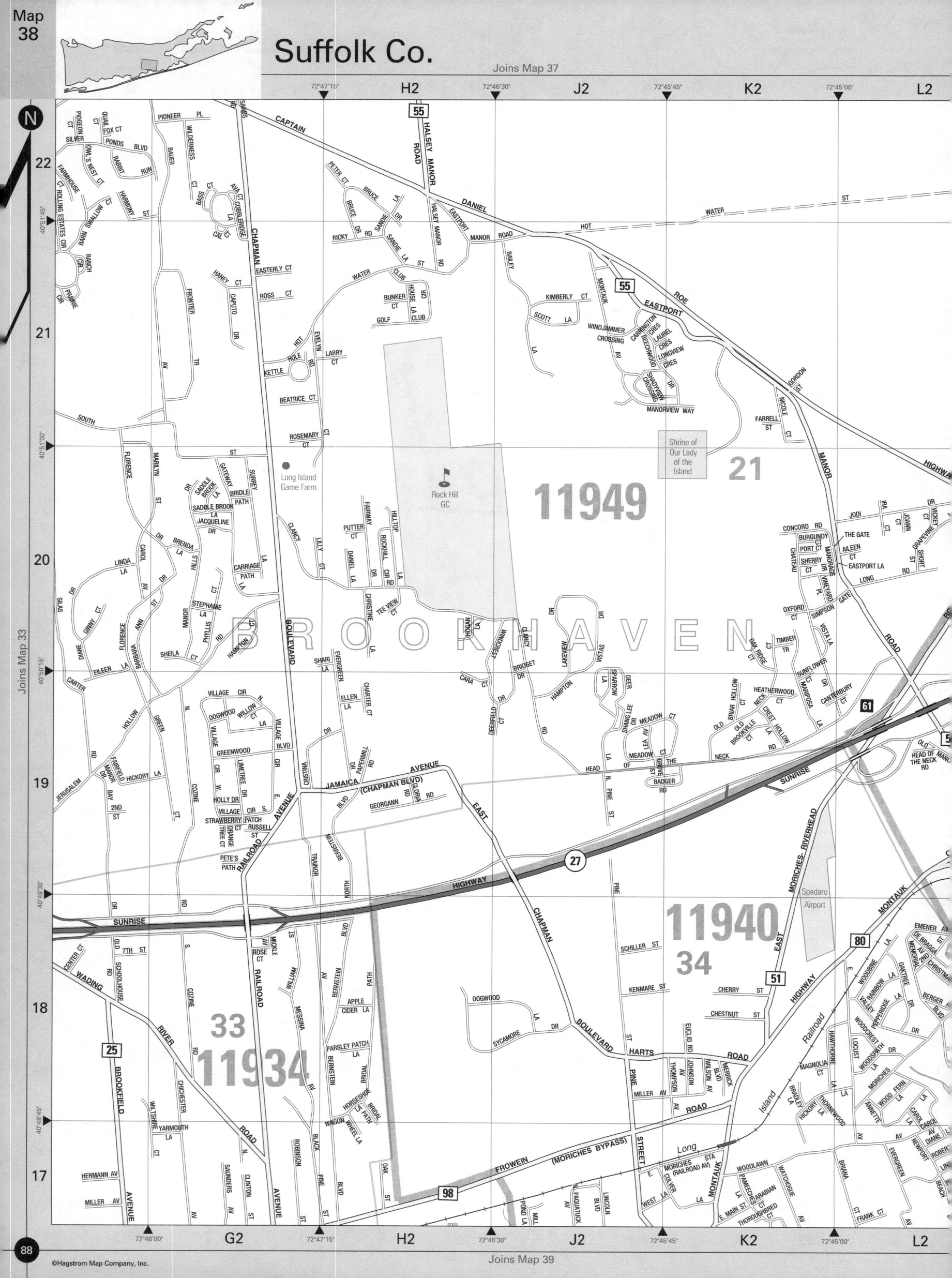

Map
38

Suffolk Co.

Joins Map 37

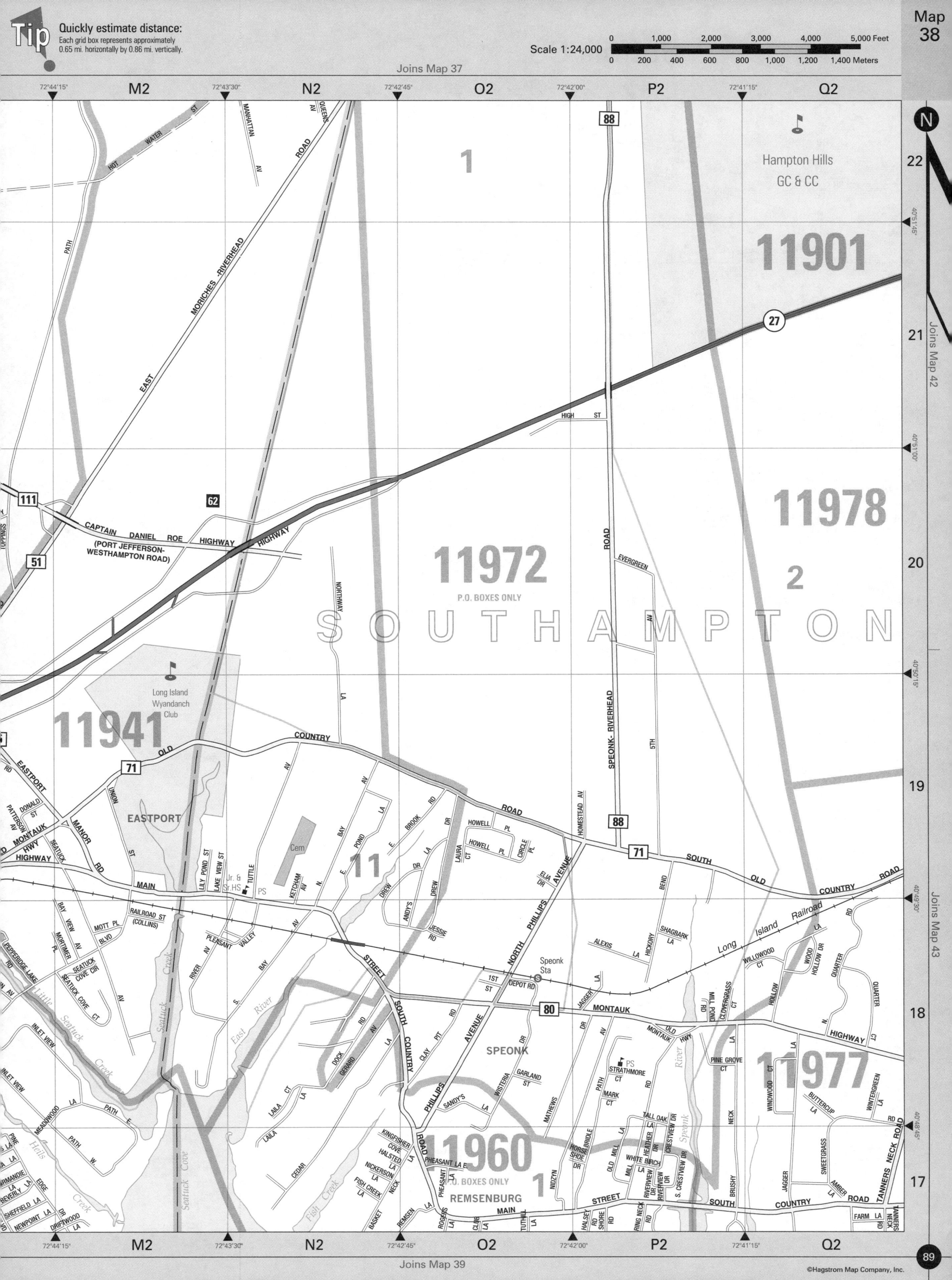

Map
38

Joins Map 37

Tip!
Quickly estimate distance:
Each grid box represents approximately
0.65 mi. horizontally by 0.86 mi. vertically.

Scale 1:24,000

| 0 | 1,000 | 2,000 | 3,000 | 4,000 | 5,000 Feet |

| 0 | 200 | 400 | 600 | 800 | 1,000 | 1,200 | 1,400 Meters |

N

Hampton Hills
GC & CC

11901

11978

2

27

11972

P.O. BOXES ONLY

S O U T H A M P T O N

11941

Long Island
Wyandanch
Club

CAPTAIN DANIEL ROE HIGHWAY
(PORT JEFFERSON-
WESTHAMPTON ROAD)

MORICHES - RIVERHEAD

EASTPORT

11

EASTPORT

SPEONK

11977

11960

P.O. BOXES ONLY

REMSENBURG

Speonk
Sta

Joins Map 42

Joins Map 43

©Hagstrom Map Company, Inc.

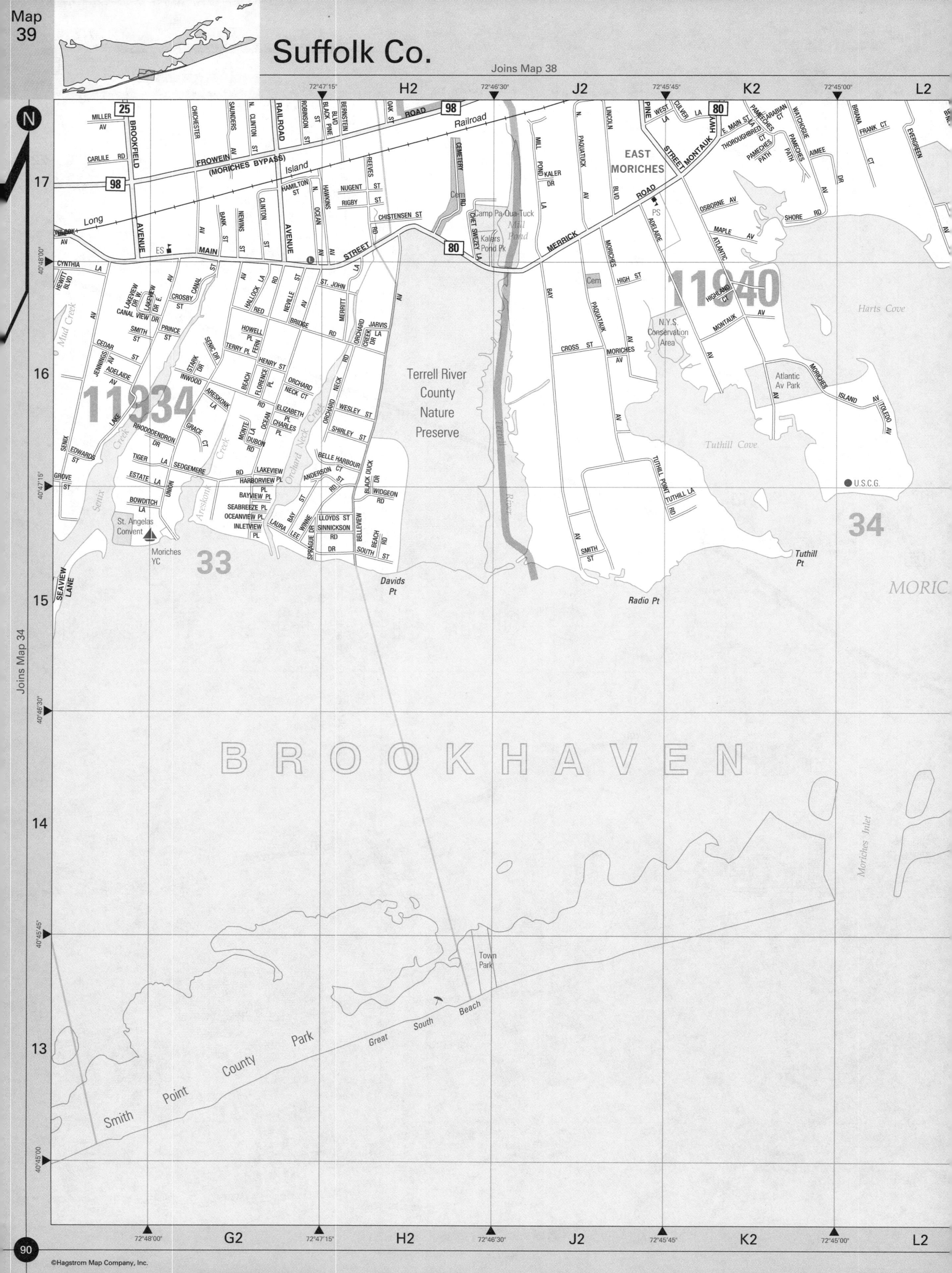

Map
39

Suffolk Co.

N

BROOKHAVEN

Terrell River
County
Nature
Preserve

EAST
MORICHES

11940

11934

11934

33

34

34

Harts Cove

Tuthill Cove

Davids
Pt

Radio Pt

Tuthill
Pt

Great   South   Beach

Smith   Point   County   Park

Moriches Inlet

Map
39

Tip Quickly estimate distance:
Each grid box represents approximately
0.65 mi. horizontally by 0.86 mi. vertically.

Scale 1:24,000

| 0 | 1,000 | 2,000 | 3,000 | 4,000 | 5,000 Feet |
| 0 | 200 | 400 | 600 | 800 | 1,000 | 1,200 | 1,400 Meters |

Joins Map 38

72°44'15"   **M2**   72°43'30"   **N2**   72°42'45"   **O2**   72°42'00"   **P2**   72°41'15"   **Q2**

N

SHEFFIELD LA   PINE EDGE LA
NEWPOINT LA
BEACH BLVD   DRIFTWOOD LA
TIMBERPOINT DR

Hells Creek

Seatuck Cove

CEDAR LA
FISH CREEK LA
HOLLY LA
BASKET NECK LA
CROSS REMSEN PATH
CRICKET PATH
ROGERS
SOUTHWIND LA
DRIFTWOOD LA
SEATUCK

MAIN   STREET
NIDZYN AV
BRIDLE PATH
MILL RD
RIVERVIEW DR
BRUSH NECK LA
SOUTH COUNTRY LA
AMBER ROAD
FARM LA
JAGGER LA
SHORE LA   TANNERS NECK
BAYVIEW DR   BAY MEADOW LA   SANDPIPER CT

11960

FELY AV
OLD POND LA
GODFREY LA
CUTLER LA
WETZEL CT
P.O. BOXES ONLY
1
TUTHILL
BAYBERRY LA
CLUB CT
NEW ST
STOKES LANE
HALSEY BAY
SHORE VIEW
DUCK
SPEONK POINT RD

1

MALLARD LA
WOODCOCK LA
BOB WHITE LA
RING NECK
PINE TREE LA

Lagoon

2
11977

N.Y.S.
Conservation Area
Access by Permit

Havens Pt

Westhampton
Yacht Squadron

Speonk Pt

17

40°48'00"

S O U T H A M P T O N

16

Gunning Pt

40°47'15"

HES BAY

**WEST HAMPTON
DUNES**

Swan
Island

Suffolk County
Water Authority

WIDGEON WAY
DUNE LA
DAISEY LA PVT
COVE LA

Pikes Beach

ROAD

89

WIDGEON WAY
DUNE LA
COVE LA

15

40°46'30"

Cupsogue Beach
County Park

O C E A N

14

40°45'45"

A T L A N T I C

13

40°45'00"

72°44'15"   **M2**   72°43'30"   **N2**   72°42'45"   **O2**   72°42'00"   **P2**   72°41'15"   **Q2**

Joins Map 43

Map
40

Suffolk Co.

Joins Map 36

S2 72°39'45" T2 72°39'00" U2 72°38'15" V2 72°37'30"

41°00'45"

33

41°00'00"

32

40°59'15"

ISLAND

Luce Landing

LONG

31

Jacobs Pt

Roanoke Pt

SOUND

2

NORTH WALK
E. FAIRVIEW AV
W. FAIRVIEW AV
BLOCK
SHORE

1 LOWE DR
2 JAMES DR
3 RALPH DR
4 OVERLOOK DR
5 SOUND DR

40°58'30"

CEDAR
PA
WILLOW
POND
DR
BAYBERRY
PATH

R I V E R H E A D

NORTHVILLE
Palmer
Vineyards

30

SOUND

AVENUE

SOUND

NATE'S WAY

AVENUE

FOX TRAIL

48

105

43

Long
Island
National
GC

CHRIS CT
WEST

PHILIPS

CLOVER
PL

40°57'45"

11901

Riverhead
Air Park

CROSS RIVER
(UNION AVENUE)

TURNPIKE

11931
P.O. BOXES ONLY

DOCTORS

LANE
CHURCH
IDA
LA

REEVES

AV

MUET
DR

PATH

NORTHVILLE

DRIVE

UNION AV

Le Clos
Thérèse

VERONICA
LA

LA

HUCKLEBERRY
HILL

29

Q2 72°40'30" R2 72°39'45" S2 72°39'00" T2 72°38'15" U2 72°37'30" V2

Map
40

©Hagstrom Map Company, Inc.

Map
41

Tip! Quickly estimate distance:
Each grid box represents approximately
0.65 mi. horizontally by 0.86 mi. vertically.

Scale 1:24,000

Joins Map 40

| 0 | 1,000 | 2,000 | 3,000 | 4,000 | 5,000 Feet |

| 0 | 200 | 400 | 600 | 800 | 1,000 | 1,200 | 1,400 Meters |

11948

11947
P.O. BOXES ONLY

JAMESPORT

SOUTH JAMESPORT

11970
P.O. BOXES ONLY

Flanders
Bay

Simmons
Pt

Miamogue
Pt

Browns Pt

State
Boat
Marina
Town
Park

Town Beach

Indian
Isl

Iron
Pt

Red
Cedar
Pt

REEVES

BAY

Goose Creek
Pt

Red
Creek
Pond

SOUTHPORT

11946

Flanders
County
Parkland

Flanders
Men's
Club
(Private)

Hubbard
County
Parkland

FLANDERS

Maple Swamp
County Park
(Pine Barrens)

2

Birch Creek Pond
County Park

Birch
Creek
Pond

Penny
Pond

Paumanok
Vineyards

Jamesport
Vineyards

Cow Yard Beach

Joins Map 46

Joins Map 47

Joins Map 42

©Hagstrom Map Company, Inc.

Map
42

Suffolk Co.

S2   T2   U2   V2

N

72°39'45"   72°39'00"   72°38'15"   72°37'30"

CONCORD ST

GOLDENLEAF TR

TREE HAVEN LA

BROOK HAVEN AV

OAK

McKINELY AV

ARTHUR ST AV

DRIVE

51

RIVERHEAD-MORICHES ROAD

(LAKE AVENUE)

TOPPING DR

ANN AV

ELY RD

LAKEVIEW

LAKEVIEW (OLD WESTHAMPTON RD)

N. Y. S.
Conservation Area
(Access by Permit)

N. Y. S.
Conservation Area
(Access by Permit)

24

51

Wildwood Lake

WILDWOOD

PINE PATH

CT

PINE

BIRCH CT

WILDWOOD PATH TR

RIVERHEAD - QUOGUE

11901

MARC PL

ALISSA CT

RISA

S O U T H A M P T O N

40°53'15"

Joins Map 37

23

NORTHAMPTON

ROAD

104

31

40°52'30"

Hampton Hills
GC & CC

22

OLD

RIVERHEAD

ROAD

HIGHWAY

63

40°51'45"

SUNRISE

27

31

21

OLD

WEST

HAMPTON

RD

40°51'00"

Joins Map 38

2

11978

RIVERHEAD

ROAD

Francis Gabreski
Airport

20

BOLLING AV

DR

AV

New York
Air Guard

STEWART

AV

ENT AV

EDWARDS

VAIL CT

HAMILTON AV

OLD

Q2   R2   S2   T2   U2   V2

72°40'30"   72°39'45"   72°39'00"   72°38'15"   72°37'30"

Map
42

Quickly estimate distance:
Each grid box represents approximately
0.65 mi. horizontally by 0.86 mi. vertically.

Scale 1:24,000

0   1,000   2,000   3,000   4,000   5,000 Feet
0   200   400   600   800   1,000   1,200   1,400 Meters

Joins Map 41

FLANDERS

W2   72°36'45"   72°36'00"   X2   72°35'15"   Y2   72°34'30"   Z2   72°33'45"   A3

24

2

Birch Creek Pond

RIVERHEAD-HAMPTON BAYS

Flanders Men's Club (Private)

Hubbard County Parkland

Birch Creek Pond County Park

Penny Pond

11946

Maple Swamp County Park (Pine Barrens)

Flanders Men's Club (Private)

Sears Pond

House Pond

The Big Duck

Maple Swamp

Division Pond

Sears-Bellows Pond County Park

Bellows Pond

HIGHWAY

64

27   SUNRISE

SOUTH FLANDERS

5

104

Henry's Hollow

Kate Ct

Corbett

Clara Dr

Maggie

Corbett

Chardonnay Dr

(Montauk Branch) HIGHWAY

11942

OAKVILLE

Candace Dr

WEST TIANA

17

Corbett

Malloy

Gleason

Railroad

MONTAUK

LEWIS

QUOGUE-RIVERHEAD

Cem

80

Long Island COUNTRY

EAST QUOGUE

PINE NECK

3

11959

Bird

P.O. Box Only

QUOGUE

64

OLD COUNTRY ROAD

W2   72°36'45"   72°36'00"   X2   72°35'15"   Y2   72°34'30"   Z2   72°33'45"   A3

Joins Map 43

N

24

23

22

21

20

Joins Map 47

Joins Map 48

©Hagstrom Map Company, Inc.

Map
43

Suffolk Co.

©Hagstrom Map Company, Inc.

Map
43

Tip

Quickly estimate distance:
Each grid box represents approximately
0.65 mi. horizontally by 0.86 mi. vertically.

Scale 1:24,000

0   1,000   2,000   3,000   4,000   5,000 Feet
0   200   400   600   800   1,000   1,200   1,400 Meters

Joins Map 42

W2   X2   Y2   Z2   A3

72°36'45"   72°36'00"   72°35'15"   72°34'30"   72°33'45"

N

20

19

18

17

16

15

Joins Map 48

Quogue Bird Sanctuary

North Pond

Old Ice Pond

QUOGUE

11959
P.O. BOXES ONLY

3

11942

PINE NECK

80

104

89

89

Village Hall

Village

Quogue Field Club

Quogue Beach Club

Surf Club of Quogue

Shinnecock YC

Village Park

Stone Creek

Penniman Cove

Penniman Creek

Phillips Pt

Hampton Pt

Sedge Island

Weesuck Creek

Phillips Creek

Daves Creek

Ogdens Pond

Bay

Hampton Beach

OCEAN

ATLANTIC

RIVERHEAD ROAD

QUOGUE STREET

MONTAUK HIGHWAY

LEWIS ROAD

BEACH ROAD

NIAMOGUE LANE

DUNE ROAD

QUAQUANANTUCK LANE

JESSUP AVE

POST

40°50'15"

40°49'30"

40°48'45"

40°48'00"

40°47'15"

©Hagstrom Map Company, Inc.

Map
44

Map
45

Tip Quickly estimate distance:
Each grid box represents approximately
0.65 mi. horizontally by 0.86 mi. vertically.

Scale 1:24,000

| 0 | 1,000 | 2,000 | 3,000 | 4,000 | 5,000 Feet |

| 0 | 200 | 400 | 600 | 800 | 1,000 | 1,200 | 1,400 Meters |

Joins Map 44

G3   H3   J3   K3   L3

72°29'15"   72°28'30"   72°27'45"   72°27'00"   72°26'15"

The Lenz
Winery

11977

N

41°02'15"

25

Pindar
Vineyards

35

11958

Raphael
Vineyards

Richmond Creek

5

9

Bedell
Cellars

11935

Pugliese
Vineyards

PS

HOG NECK

41°01'30"

EAST
CUTCHOGUE

BAY

34

Cutchogue Cem

Peconic Bay
Winery

41°00'45"

FLEET
NECK

Joins Map 52

Village
Green

Cedars
GC

33

11956
P. O. BOXES ONLY

North Fork
CC

Marsh Pt

Cutchogue
Harbor

Haywater
Cove

NASSAU
POINT

9

West Creek

Horseshoe
Cove

41°00'00"

Wunneweta
Pond

32

Old Cove
YC

Lagoon

Kimogener
Pt

40°59'15"

NEW SUFFOLK

15

Nassau Pt

LITTLE   PECONIC   BAY

31

Race

North

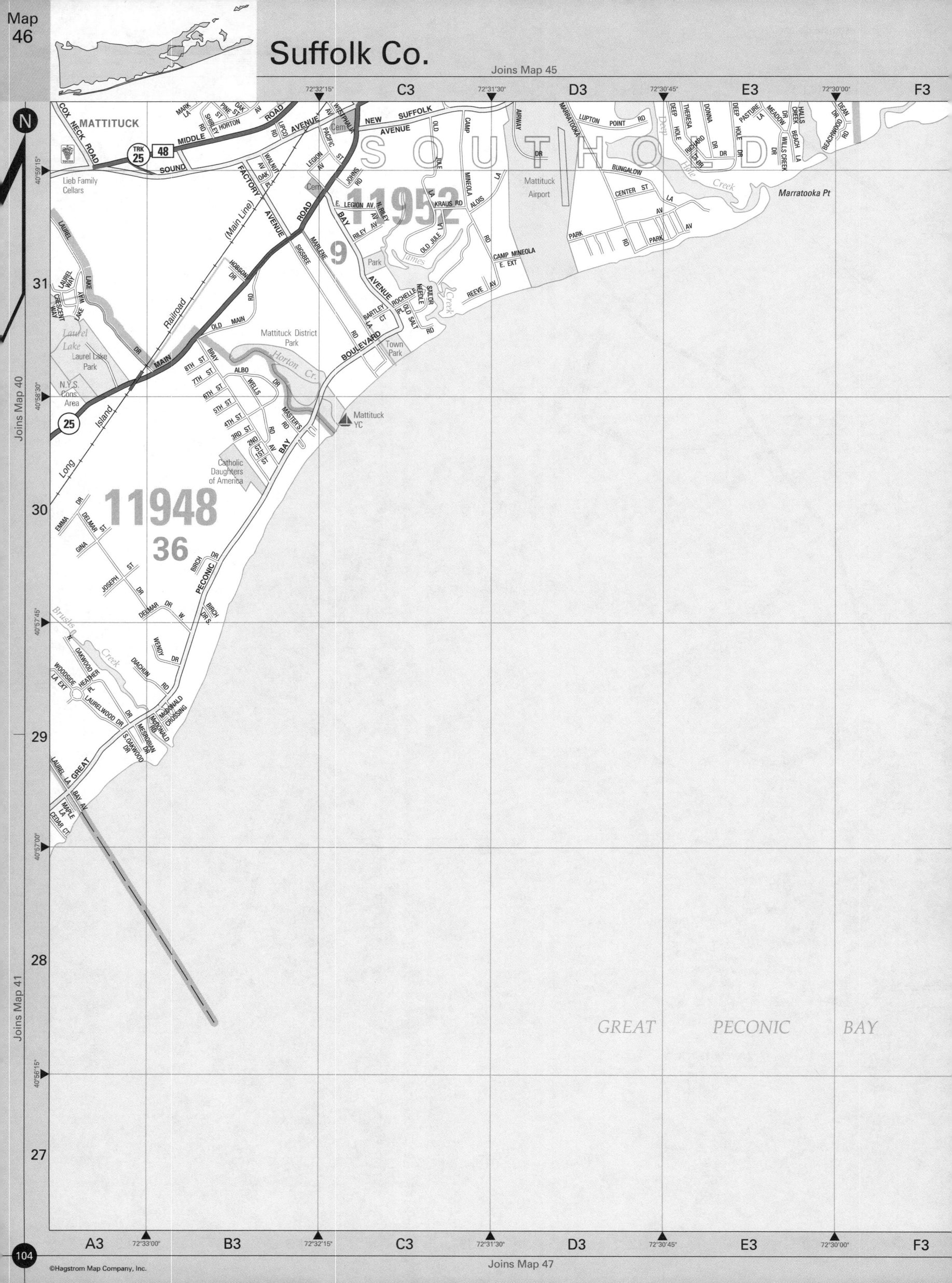

Map
46

Tip

Quickly estimate distance:
Each grid box represents approximately
0.65 mi. horizontally by 0.86 mi. vertically.

Scale 1:24,000

| 0 | 1,000 | 2,000 | 3,000 | 4,000 | 5,000 Feet |

| 0 | 200 | 400 | 600 | 800 | 1,000 | 1,200 | 1,400 Meters |

Joins Map 45

N

72°29'15" G3   72°28'30" H3   72°27'45" J3   72°27'00" K3   72°26'15" L3

40°59'15"

11956

NEW SUFFOLK

P. O. BOXES ONLY

Kimogener Pt

NEW SUFFOLK AVENUE

North Race

31

40°58'30"

ROBINS
ISLAND

LITTLE   PECONIC

BAY

30

40°57'45"

South Race

29

40°57'00"

North Sea Bathing Beach

Cow Neck
Pt

**COW
NECK**

*Scallop
Pond*

28

40°56'15"

11968
6

Scallop
Pond
Preserve

27

West Cove Creek

Nassau Pt

NASSAU POINT RD

72°29'15" G3   72°28'30" H3   72°27'45" J3   72°27'00" K3   72°26'15" L3

Joins Map 47

Joins Map 53

Map 47

©Hagstrom Map Company, Inc.

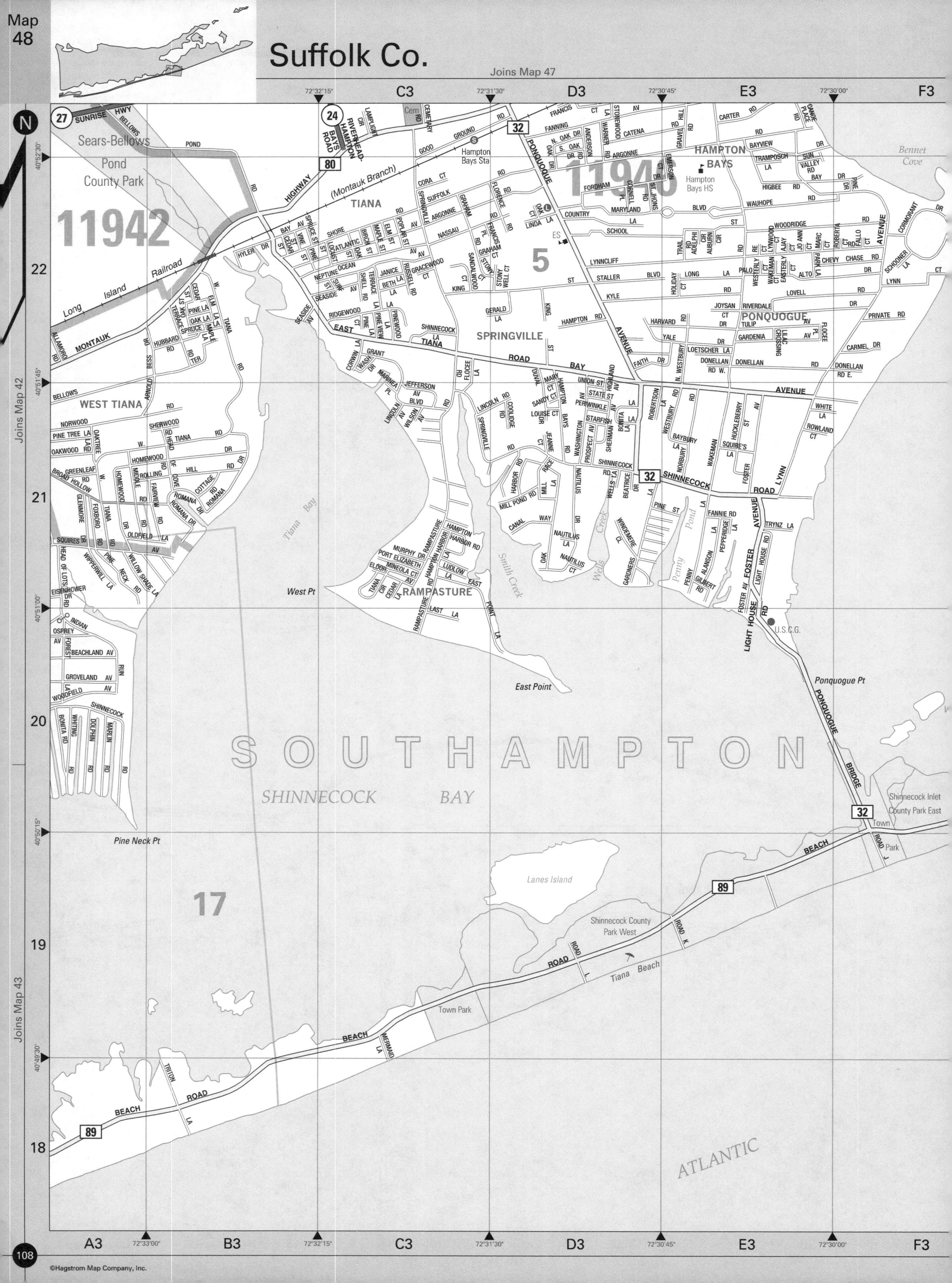

Map
48

Suffolk Co.

Joins Map 47

Map
48

Tip
Quickly estimate distance:
Each grid box represents approximately
0.65 mi. horizontally by 0.86 mi. vertically.

Scale 1:24,000

| 0 | 1,000 | 2,000 | 3,000 | 4,000 | 5,000 Feet |

| 0 | 200 | 400 | 600 | 800 | 1,000 | 1,200 | 1,400 Meters |

Joins Map 47

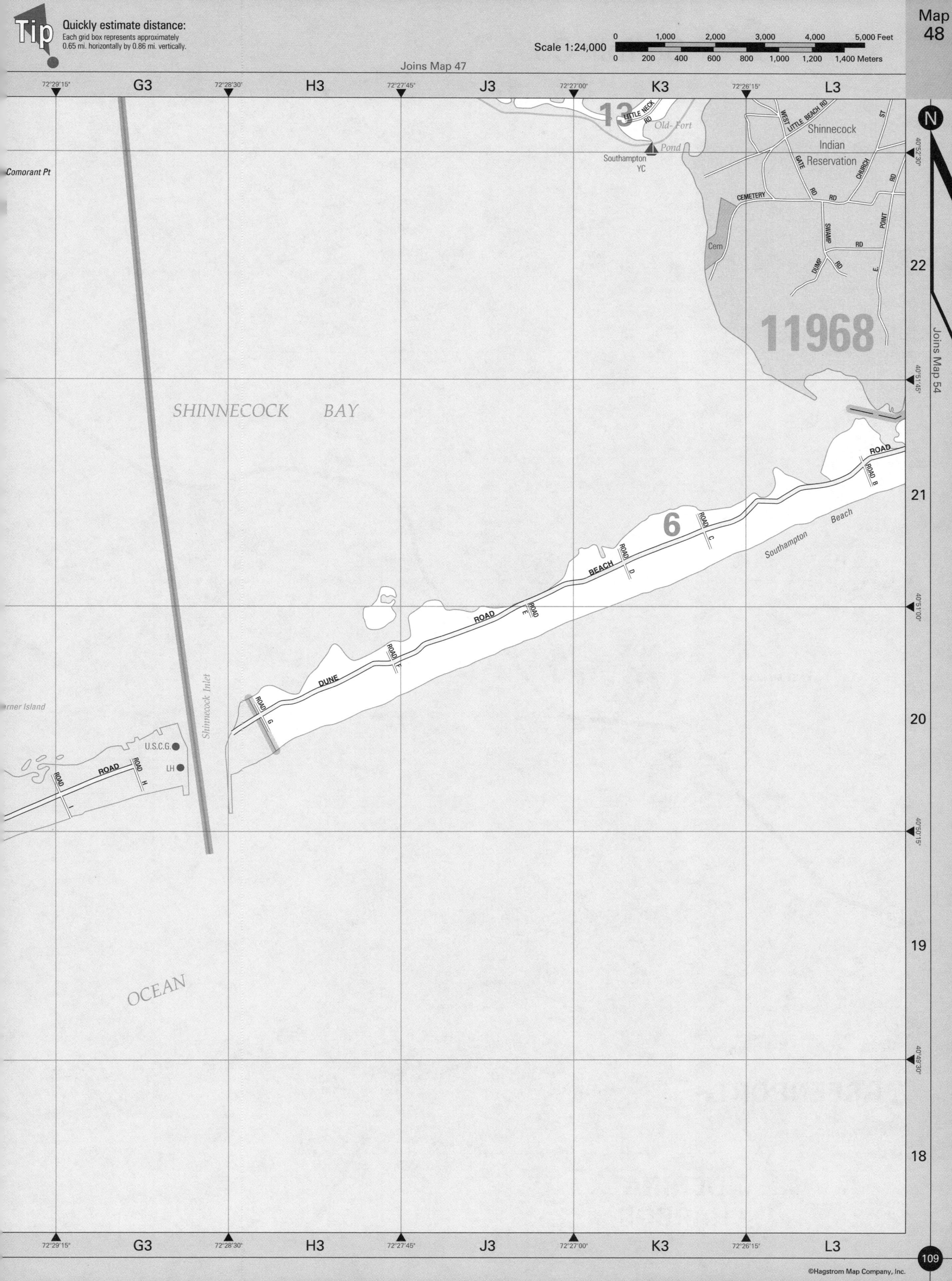

G3   H3   J3   K3   L3

72°29'15"   72°28'30"   72°27'45"   72°27'00"   72°26'15"

N

Comorant Pt

Joins Map 54

SHINNECOCK BAY

Southampton YC
Old Fort
Pond
LITTLE NECK RD

13

Shinnecock Indian Reservation

WEST LITTLE BEACH RD
CHURCH ST
GATE
CEMETERY
SWAMP RD
DUMP RD
POINT RD
E.
Cem

11968

22

Shinnecock Inlet

6
BEACH
ROAD
DUNE
ROAD C
ROAD D
ROAD E
ROAD F
ROAD G
ROAD B
ROAD
Southampton Beach

21

Turner Island

U.S.C.G.
LH
ROAD
ROAD H

20

19

OCEAN

18

40°52'30"
40°51'45"
40°51'00"
40°50'15"
40°49'30"

©Hagstrom Map Company, Inc.

Map
49

Suffolk Co.

N

45

LONG ISLAND SOUND

44

N. VIEW DR
S. VIEW DR
BROWNS

EDWARDS LA

DIEDERICKS RD

Terry Pt
Munn Lake

ORIENT

PLATT

Cem MUNN
MAPLE LA
BACK LA
PETE HILL
YOUNGS

STEVENSON RD
BIRDS PT
LA

ROAD
PS

Cem

TABOR

East Marion
Orient Park

RACKETT'S CT
OYSTER PONDS LA

Central
Cem

ORCHARD

Rocky Pt

AQUAVIEW
CIRCLE
DR
TOWN STARS
RD W. STARS
PRIVATE RD

Truman Beach

SKIPPERS LA
HARBOR RIVER
Historical
Society Mus.

HALYOKE AV

OLD FARM RD

FIRE RD 3
STRATMORS RD
RD
CEDAR
BLVD

PRIVATE RD #1

Orient
YC
VILLAGE
VINCENT ST NAVY ST

43

ROCKY
SOUTHERN

PINE TER
WILLOW

KAYLEIGH'S

MAIN

FLETCHER
ST
WILLOW
ST
NAVY ST KING

NELSON DR
MAJOR
POND RD

EAST MARION

PRIVATE

*Dam
Pond*

Orient   Harbor

WILLOW
NAVY ST
HOWE DR
TERRACE LA

STREET KING

DOUGLAS RD
HARBOR RD

PETERS

THE
CROSS WAY

MAPLE PL

CEDAR DR
OAK CT

PS

CT
11939

25

THE
SHORT LA

ROAD

CEMETERY RD
Cem

TRUMAN'S PATH

42

*Marion
Lake*

BAY
MARION MARION
LA PL
LAKEVIEW
TER

AV DABBIT LA

THE
WAY

OLD

ORCHARD

NORTH LA
EAST
WEST LA
LOCUST CT
SOUTH LA RUCKLEBERRY HILL RD

SOUTHOLD

Islands
End
GC & CC

25

MAIN

CEDAR LA

DOGWOOD LA
PARSONAGE DR
BLVD
STEPHEN DR
S. SOUTH LA
KNOLL DR

MANOR PL
E. GILLETTE
GILLETTE
MIDLAND PL
BAYVIEW

PINE PL

Bird Sanctuary

WIGGINS LA
DAWN
DR

SHIPYARD

BEACH CT

MARINE PL
SNUG HARBOR RD
RD OSPREY NEST RD
DR CLEVES
POINT
RD

Long Beach
Pt
• LH

Sull Pt
10

Dawn Lagoon
Pearhnan
Canal

Cleves Pt

ANGLER'S LA
MEADOW LA
WOOD LA
BENJAMINS LA

MANHASSET

AV

GREENPORT

SHELTER

DERING
HARBOR

Youngs Pt

Hay Beach Pt

ISLAND

41

CHANNING
BAY
BEACH RD
LA
BEACH RD

• LH

PINE POINT LA
GARDINERS LA
ORIENT LA
HAY BEACH
VIEW
RD
BAY
DR
BLACK RD
GRADE
CRESCENT
CIRCLE
WAY
EAST RD
RD

©Hagstrom Map Company, Inc.

Map
49

Tip

Quickly estimate distance:
Each grid box represents approximately
0.65 mi. horizontally by 0.86 mi. vertically.

Scale 1:24,000

0	1,000	2,000	3,000	4,000	5,000 Feet
0	200 400	600 800	1,000	1,200	1,400 Meters

N

72°17'15"   X3   72°16'30"   Y3   72°15'45"   Z3   72°15'00"   A4   72°14'15"   B4   72°13'30"

LH

Orient
Pt

45

Mulford Pt

PETTYS BIGHT

SOUND VIEW RD
SEA DR
PLUM LA
THREE WATERS LA
LANDS END
LATHAM RD

Orient Point
County Park

RD

N. SEA DR
RYDER FARM
UHL LA
ISLAND LA

GREENWAY RD W
GREENWAY RD

PARK VIEW LA

POINT

Ferry to New London, Connecticut

41°09'00"

HILLCREST DR S
SOUNDVIEW RD
DEMAREST DR
HILLCREST DR
HILL
RD
ROBIN RD

GRANDVIEW DR
PETTY'S
MULFORD CT

BEACH LA

OLD MAIN

BIGHT RD
WINDWARD RD

SOUND VIEW RD
LONG BOAT LA
WHALERS RD

Charles
Rose
Airport

OLD MAIN

PARKVIEW DR

25

ROAD

CEDAR LA
BIRCH LA

STATE PARKWAY

MAIN

RIVER ROAD

NARROW

2

ORIENT POINT

11957

Cem

44

RD

STREET

Narrow River

Eagle Pt

Little Bay

41°08'15"

Long Beach Bay

Ben's Pt

Long Beach Bay
State Tidal
Wetlands

Long

Beach   Bay

Orient Beach

Park Office

Bath
House
Parking

ORIENT

48

Browns Pt

41°11'15"

Peters Neck Pt

Long   Beach   Bay

Orient Beach
State Park

Long Beach

Fort Terry

47

Plum Island
Animal Disease Center
(Restricted)

PLUM ISLAND

41°10'30"

LH

Plum Island Rock

Plum Island

Ferry to Plum Gut

46

72°17'15"   X3   72°12'45"   D4   72°12'00"   E4   72°11'15"   F4   72°10'30"   G4   72°09'45"

Map
50

Suffolk Co.

ISLAND   SOUND

LONG

N

44

43

42

41

40

39

©Hagstrom Map Company, Inc.

Joins Map 44

STIRLING

GREENPORT

10

Silver
Lake

Koa
Trailer
Park

Greenport
HS

GREENPORT WEST

25

11971

11944

Hashamomuck
Pond
Park

Hashamomuck

Inlet Pt

Inlet
Pond

Inlet Point
County Park

SOUND VIEW AVENUE

Pipes Cove

Fanning Pt

5

48

25

48

TRK
25

25

48

Map
50

Tip Quickly estimate distance:
Each grid box represents approximately
0.65 mi. horizontally by 0.86 mi. vertically.

Scale 1:24,000

Joins Map 49

Map
51

Suffolk Co.

Joins Map 50

Map
51

Tip!
Quickly estimate distance:
Each grid box represents approximately
0.65 mi. horizontally by 0.86 mi. vertically.

Scale 1:24,000

0   1,000   2,000   3,000   4,000   5,000 Feet
0   200 400 600 800 1,000 1,200 1,400 Meters

Joins Map 50

N

72°19'30"   U3   72°18'45"   V3   72°18'00"   W3   72°17'15"   X3   72°16'30"   Y3

41°05'15"

39

41°04'30"

38

Joins Map 55

41°03'45"

37

41°03'00"

36

41°02'15"

35

SHEEP PASTURE LA
LANE
HARBOR HEAD RD
RAM
W. HAR-BAY RD
ISLAND
ROAD
LARI LA
CTWRIGHT AD
WILLOW LA
69
HUDSON AV
Little Cedar Isl
LITTLE RAM ISLAND
LITTLE RAM ISLAND DR
Lower Beach
DRIVE
MIDDLE HAR-BAY RD
N.
RAM
SOUTH
BIG RAM ISLAND
ISLAND
DRIVE
Ram Head
ROAD
Passionist Monastery
Neck Pt
RAM
TUTHILL
ISLAND
OAK RD
DRIVE
DR
CLUB DRIVE
Shanty Bay
Ram Island YC
N.Y.S. Conservation Area Access by Permit
LOCUST LA
CHERRY LA
EMERSON LA
MEADOW LA
69
NORTH CARTWRIGHT
Coecles Harbor Marina
Coecles
Harbor
Pomps Pt
Reel Pt
CONGDON RD
Town Dock
JUPITER'S
Congdons Pt
Coecles Inlet
Sungic Pt
PRICE LA
SHELTER
Congdons Creek
Foxen Creek
Cedar Island Cove
SOUTH CARTWRIGHT
ROAD
ISLAND
TOWN
FOXEN
Sungic Creek
Medical Center
CREEK
RD
PRIVATE
H
DR
Preserve Parking
Mashomack Preserve
The Nature Conservancy
PARK LA
FERRY
VALLEY RD
LINDA RD
MEIKEL
IRENE LA
ROBIN
THOMPSON LA
Nicoll's Creek
RD
Nichols Pt
CLARK PL
SUNSET LA
ROAD
Smith   Cove
114
Cedar Island
LH
OSPREY LA
Bass Creek
PPLE ORCHARD
PHEASANT RD
SEA GULL
Gibson's
Sachems Beach
PHEASANT CIR
Ferry
Tyndal Pt
Majors Pt
Majors Harbor
HAMPTON
SOUTH
FERRY
Genet Creek
NORTH DR
WEST DR
EAST DR
DEERFIELD RD
ROAD
HAVEN WAY
EZEKELLS HOLLOW
WIDOW CLIPPERS PATH
SOUTH DR
CORWIN LA
COLONY RD
GARDINERS PATH
STOCK FARM LA
ACTORS
CEDAR
ESPLANADE
THE
HAWTHORNE AV
MASHOMACK DR
BAY VIEW
11963 5
GLEASON PATH
FAIRLEA CT
SALTMEADOW LA
Mashomack Pt Preserve

72°19'30"   U3   72°18'45"   V3   72°18'00"   W3   72°17'15"   X3   72°16'30"   Y3

©Hagstrom Map Company, Inc.

Map
52

Suffolk Co.

Joins Map 44

11971

SOUTHOLD

Corey Creek

BAYVIEW

CEDAR BEACH

Cedar Beach County Park

Cedar Beach Point

JESSUP NECK

Morton

National

Wildlife

Refuge

HOG NECK

BAY

SOUTHAMP

Clam Island

Noyac Creek

NORTH SIDE HILLS

Noyac GC & CC

38

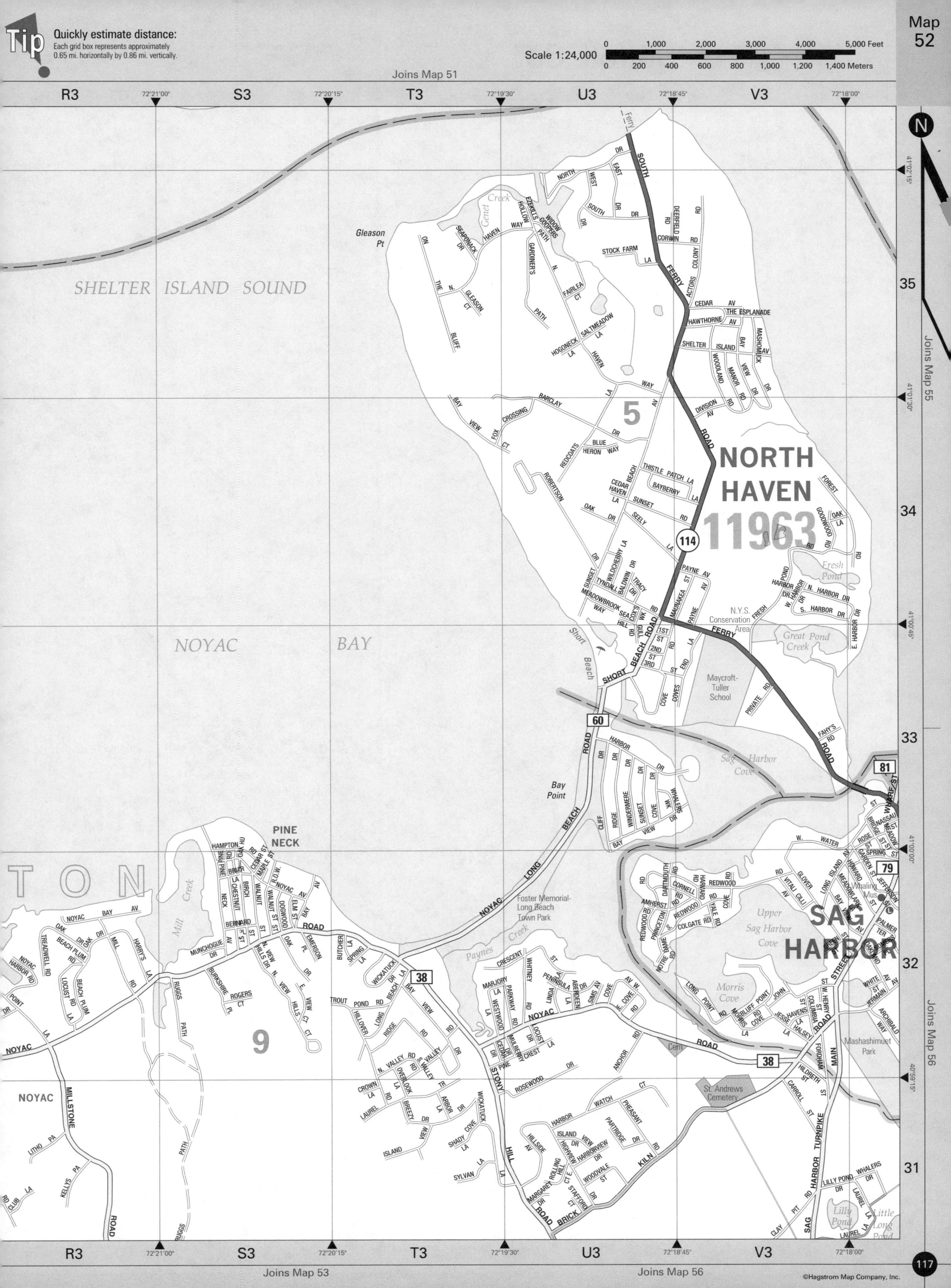

Map
53

Suffolk Co.

N

Joins Map 46

40°58'30"
30
40°57'45"
29
40°57'00"
28
40°56'15"
27
40°55'30"
26

Joins Map 47

LITTLE PECONIC

BAY

Whalebone
Landing

Fresh
Pond

Little Peconic
YC

Wooley
Pond

South Race

Turtle
Cove

North Sea Bathing Beach   Towd Pt

Davis Creek

Cow Neck
Pt

SOUTHAMPTON

11968

COW
NECK

Scallop
Pond

Conscience
Point
National
Wildlife
Refuge

North
Sea Harbor

NORTH SEA

Scallop
Pond
Preserve

6

Fish
Cove

Cow Cove Creek

West Sebonac Creek

Scallop
Pond
Preserve

Millstone

Wolf Swamp
Sanctuary

Big
Fresh Pond

Little
Fresh Pond

MacKay
Radio

Little Sebonac Creek

Island Creek

Sebonac Creek

Bullhead
YC

38

38

38

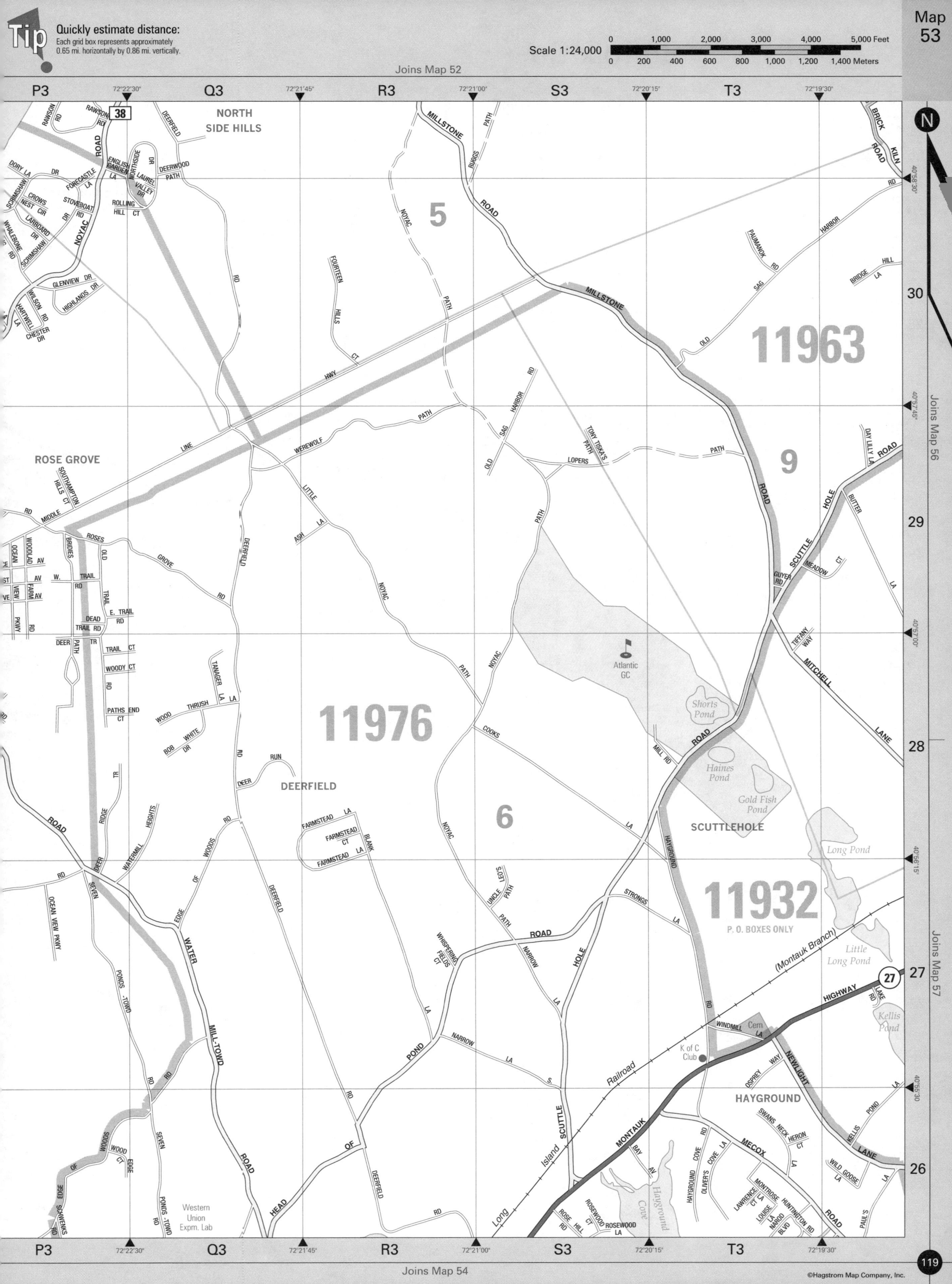

Map
53

Quickly estimate distance:
Each grid box represents approximately
0.65 mi. horizontally by 0.86 mi. vertically.

Scale 1:24,000

| 0 | 1,000 | 2,000 | 3,000 | 4,000 | 5,000 Feet |

| 0 | 200 | 400 | 600 | 800 | 1,000 | 1,200 | 1,400 Meters |

P3   72°22'30"   Q3   72°21'45"   R3   72°21'00"   S3   72°20'15"   T3   72°19'30"

N

NORTH
SIDE HILLS

ROSE GROVE

5

11963

9

11976

DEERFIELD

6

Atlantic
GC

Shorts
Pond

Haines
Pond

Gold Fish
Pond

SCUTTLEHOLE

Long Pond

11932
P. O. BOXES ONLY

Little
Long Pond

Kellis
Pond

(Montauk Branch)

HAYGROUND

Western
Union
Expm. Lab

K of C
Club

Hayground
Cove

P3   72°22'30"   Q3   72°21'45"   R3   72°21'00"   S3   72°20'15"   T3   72°19'30"

©Hagstrom Map Company, Inc.

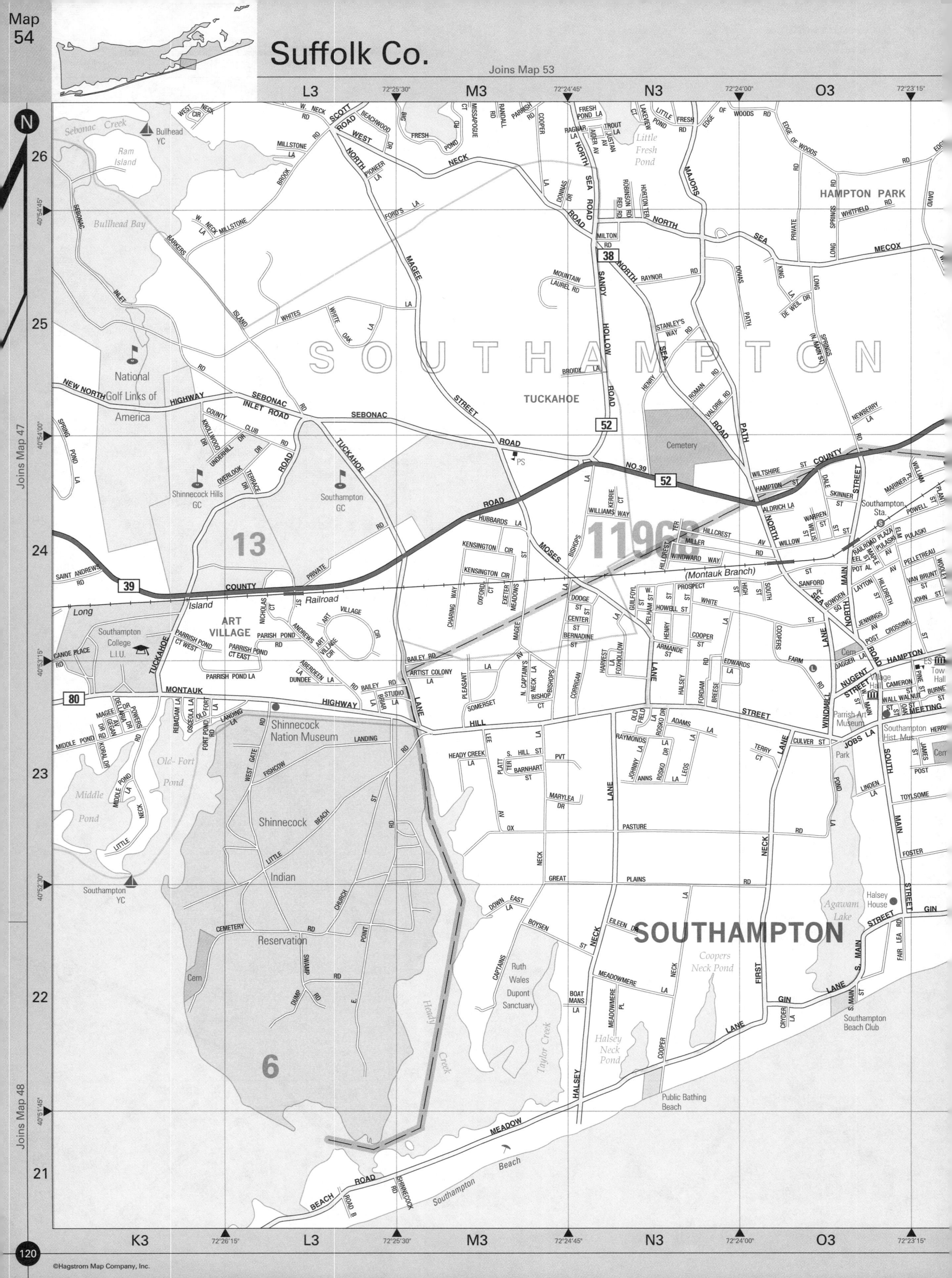

Map 54

Tip

Quickly estimate distance:
Each grid box represents approximately
0.65 mi. horizontally by 0.86 mi. vertically.

Scale 1:24,000

| 0 | 1,000 | 2,000 | 3,000 | 4,000 | 5,000 Feet |

| 0 | 200 | 400 | 600 | 800 | 1,000 | 1,200 | 1,400 Meters |

Joins Map 53

P3 72°22'30" Q3 72°21'45" R3 72°21'00" S3 72°20'15" T3 72°19'30"

N

26

40°54'45"

25

40°54'00"

24

40°53'15"

Joins Map 57

23

40°52'30"

22

40°51'45"

21

11976

WATER MILL

COBB

FLYING POINT

WICKAPOGUE

Southampton HS

Southampton Hosp.

Western Union Exprm. Lab

Villa Maria Sisters of St. Dominic

Duckwalk Vineyards

Mill Pond

Mecox Bay

Hayground Cove

Calf Creek

Mill Creek

Channel Pond

Jule Pond

Phillips Pond

Wickapogue Pond

Old Town Pond

OCEAN

ATLANTIC

Water Mill Beach Club

6

9

27

39A

NO. 39

P3 72°22'30" Q3 72°21'45" R3 72°21'00" S3 72°20'15" T3 72°19'30"

Map
55

Suffolk Co.

Joins Map 51

V3 · 72°18'00" · W3 · 72°17'15" · X3 · 72°16'30" · Y3 · 72°15'45" · Z3

N

114 SOUTH FERRY ROAD

Smith Cove

Cedar Island
LH

Cedar

36

Tyndal Pt

PRIVATE RD

Bass Creek

Mashomack Preserve

The Nature Conservancy

Gibson's Beach

Sachems Neck

S H E L T E R

Majors Pt

Majors Harbor

I S L A N D

Mashomack
Pt Preserve

35

FERRY ROAD

CEDAR AV
THE ESPLANADE
HAWTHORNE
SHELTER ISLAND
WOODLAND
BAY VIEW DR
MANOR RD
MASHOMUCK

34

DIVISION AV

NORTH
HAVEN

5

11963

FOREST RD

OAK LA
GOODWOOD RD

Fresh Pond

114

PAYNE AV
MADNALEA
PAYNE LA

HARBOR DR
N. HARBOR DR
W. HARBOR
S. HARBOR DR
E. HARBOR DR

N.Y.S.
Conservation
Area

Fresh Pond

Barcelona Pt

33

FERRY ROAD

Great Pond Creek

FAHY'S ROAD
PRIVATE RD

Maycroft-
Tuller School

60

SHORT BEACH ROAD

Sag Harbor Cove

81

Sag Harbor

BARCELONA
NECK

Bay Point

WHARF ST

Sag Harbor
YC

Northwest Creek

Sag Harbor
State GC

N.Y.S.
Conservation
Area Access
by Permit

32

Paynes Creek

NOYAC ROAD

Upper Sag
Harbor Cove

SAG
HARBOR

79

Morris Cove

Long Point

Oakland
Cemetery

HAMPTON

Havens Beach

MADISON STREET

STREET

2

Cem

114

U3 · 72°18'45" · V3 · 72°18'00" · W3 · 72°17'15" · X3 · 72°16'30" · Y3 · 72°15'45" · Z3

38

BRICK KILN ROAD

Mashashimuet
Park

St. Andrews
Cemetery

Round
Pond

SWAMP

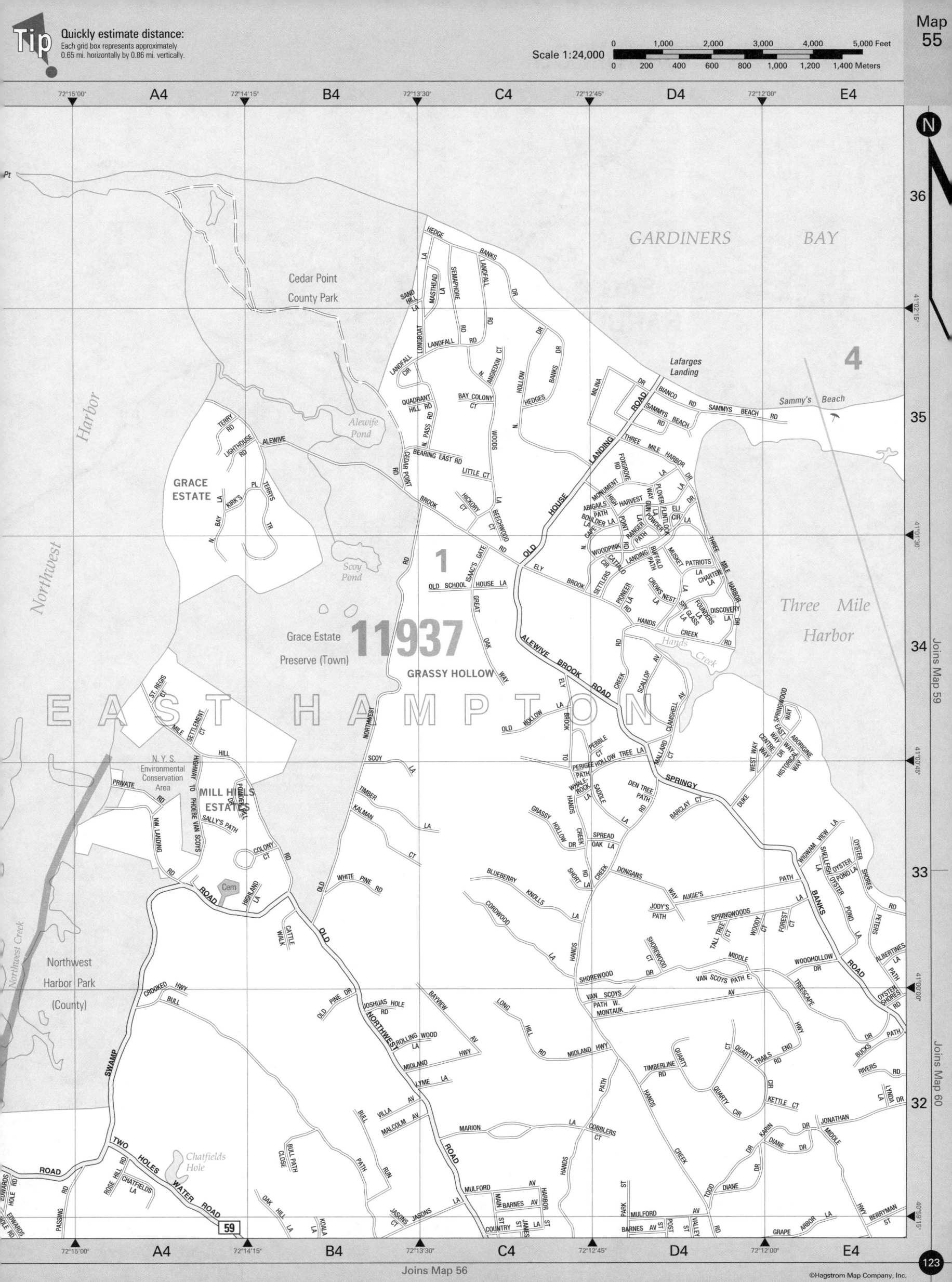

Map 55

©Hagstrom Map Company, Inc.

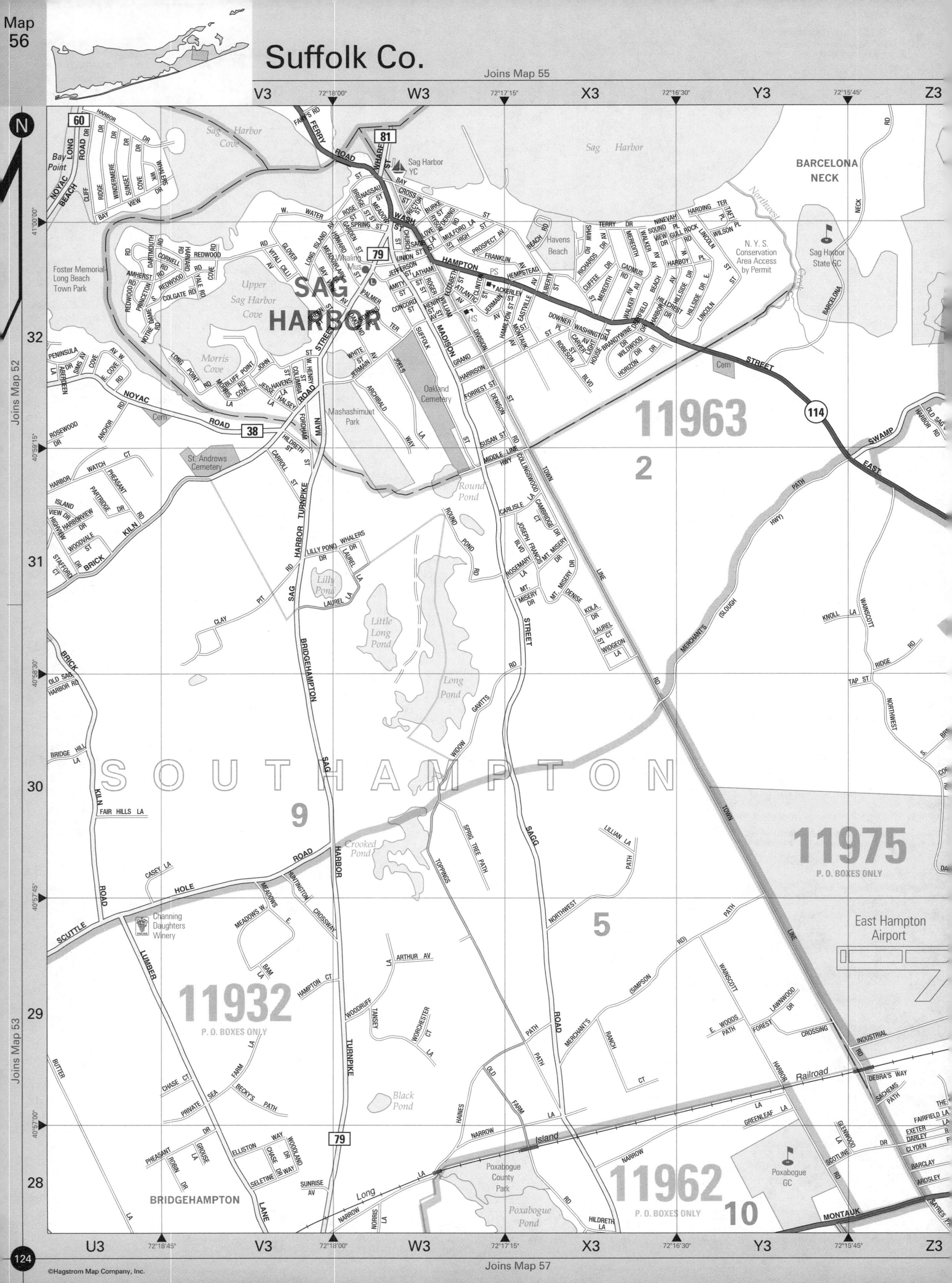

Map 56

Map
57

Suffolk Co.

Map
58

Suffolk Co.

N

42

41°06'45"

41

41°06'00"

Cherry H
Pond

40

41°05'15"

39

E A S T

41°04'30"

38

GARDINERS   BAY

Joins Map 59

Map
58

Tip Quickly estimate distance:
Each grid box represents approximately
0.65 mi. horizontally by 0.86 mi. vertically.

Scale 1:24,000

| 0 | 1,000 | 2,000 | 3,000 | 4,000 | 5,000 Feet |

| 0 | 200 | 400 | 600 | 800 | 1,000 | 1,200 | 1,400 Meters |

N

K4 72°07'30" L4 72°06'45" M4 72°06'00" N4 72°05'15" O4

72°08'15"

42

41°06'45"

41

Bostwick Bay

Bostwick Creek

Upper Willow Br

41°06'00"

41

Willow Br

GARDINERS ISLAND

Home Pond

40

Gaylor Hole

11937

Tobaccolot Pond

41°05'15"

Tobaccolot Bay

H A M P T O N

39

41°04'30"

Little Pond

GARDINERS ISLAND

38

Gales Pond

Airport Pond

K4 72°07'30" L4 72°06'45" M4 72°06'00" N4 72°05'15" O4

72°08'15" 72°04'30"

Map
59

Suffolk Co.

Joins Map 58

N

GARDINERS BAY

Lionhead Rock

Hog Creek Pt

Joins Map 55

Lafarges
Landing

Sammy's Beach

SAMMYS BEACH RD

11937

Three   Mile

Harbor

E A S T   H A M P T O N

1

MAIDSTONE
PARK

Town Park

THREE
MILE HARBOR

FIREPLACE

GERARD
PARK

Kaplan
Meadows
Sanctuary

Merrill Lake
Sanctuary

Woo
Tick
Isl

4

SPRINGS

OLD STONE HWY

KINGSTOWN

4

Accabonac

D4   E4   F4   G4   H4   J4

Map
59

Tip

Quickly estimate distance:
Each grid box represents approximately
0.65 mi. horizontally by 0.86 mi. vertically.

Scale 1:24,000

0   1,000   2,000   3,000   4,000   5,000 Feet
0   200   400   600   800   1,000   1,200   1,400 Meters

Joins Map 58

K4   72°07'30"   L4   72°06'45"   M4   72°06'00"   N4   72°05'15"   O4   72°04'30"

72°08'15"

N

41°03'45"

Airport
Pond

Great Pond

37

41°03'00"

36

Cartwright
Island

41°02'15"

Joins Map 61

35

41°01'30"

C Gerard
Park

Edwards
Island
Sanctuary

11930

P. O. BOXES ONLY

34

East
Harbor

Accabonac
Cliff

41°00'45"

Y.S
ons
rea

45

WINDING
HARBOR HILL
CARRIAGE LA
WAY
CAPTAINS
WK
WINDWARD ST
EDGE

SPRINGS
AMAGANSETT ROAD
SHORE LA
SHADOW
RIDGE
GLENWAY
ROBINS
BEACHWAY

NORTHWAY
HIGHWOOD
LANTERN
RD LA

33

Cherry
Pt

3

QUALITY
ROW
WAY

BARNES HOLE
ROAD

Barnes Landing

GERARD

DR

RD

LOOKOUT
POINT LA

LOUISE

WATERS

HWAY

K4   72°07'30"   L4   72°06'45"   M4   72°06'00"   N4   72°05'15"   O4   72°04'30"

72°08'15"

Map
60

Quickly estimate distance:
Each grid box represents approximately 0.65 mi. horizontally by 0.86 mi. vertically.

Scale 1:24,000

Joins Map 59

| K4 | L4 | M4 | N4 | O4 | P4 |

DEVON

11930
P. O. BOXES ONLY

HAMPTON

Dennistown Bell Park

Fresh Pond

Alberts Landing

Devon YC

NAPEAGUE MEADOW ROAD

Cherry Pt

Napeague State Park

PROMISED LAND

Montauk Branch

MONTAUK HIGHWAY

Napeague

Beach

BEACH HAMPTON

South Fork CC

Marine Museum

OCEAN

©Hagstrom Map Company, Inc.

Joins Map 61

Map
61

Suffolk Co.

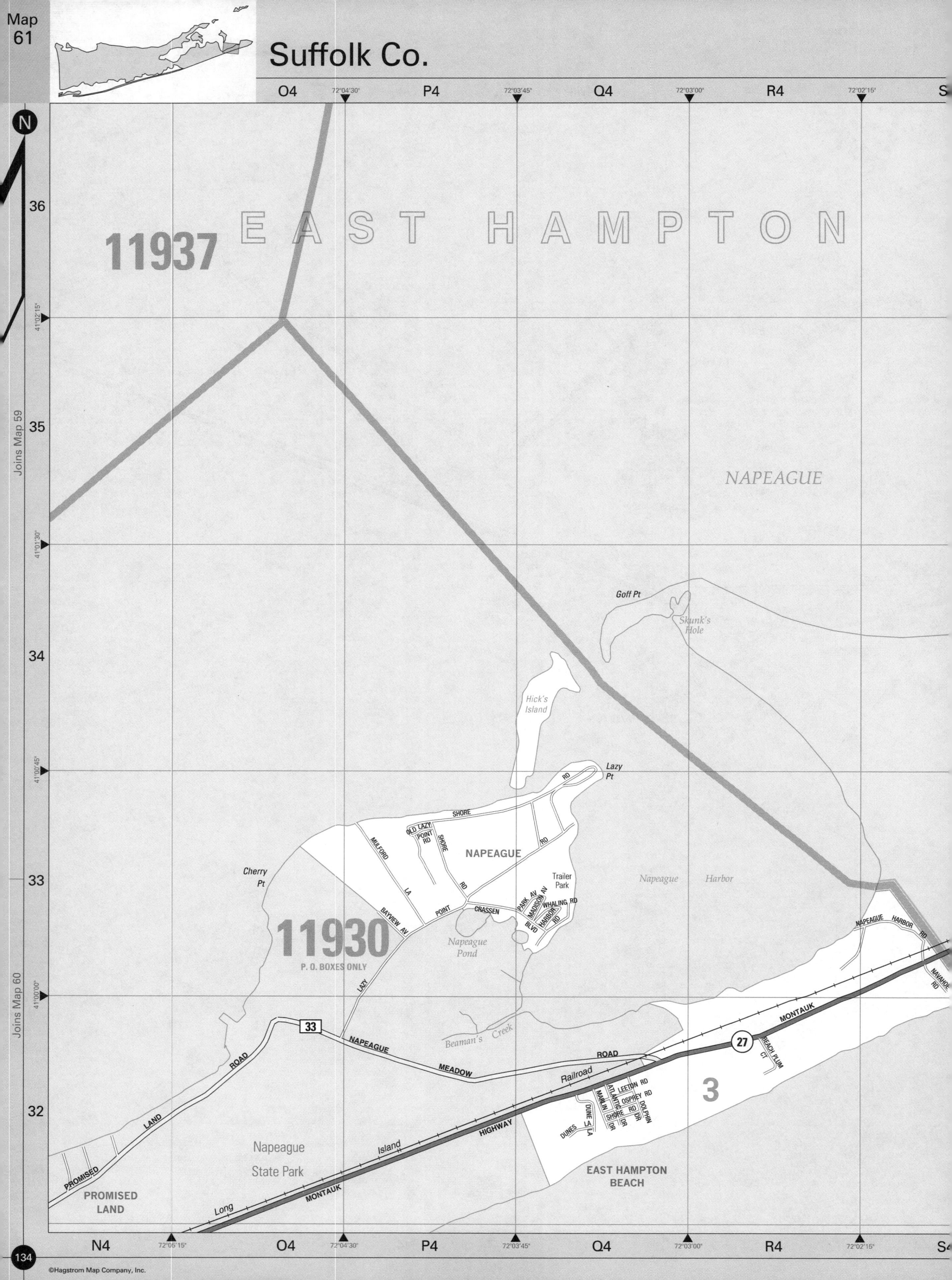

O4   72°04'30"   P4   72°03'45"   Q4   72°03'00"   R4   72°02'15"   S

N

36

11937

E A S T   H A M P T O N

NAPEAGUE

35

Joins Map 59

41°02'15"

41°01'30"

Goff Pt

Skunk's Hole

34

Hick's Island

41°00'45"

Lazy Pt

RD

SHORE

OLD LAZY POINT RD

SHORE RD

NAPEAGUE

RD

MILFORD

Cherry Pt

LA

POINT RD

Trailer Park

Napeague   Harbor

33

BAYVIEW AV

POINT RD

CRASSEN

PARK AV

MADISON AV

HARBOR RD

WHALING RD

BLVD

11930

P. O. BOXES ONLY

Napeague Pond

NAPEAGUE   HARBOR   RD

NAVAHOE RD

LAZY

Beaman's   Creek

33

NAPEAGUE

MEADOW

ROAD

Railroad

27

MONTAUK

BEACH PLUM CT

41°00'00"

Joins Map 60

ROAD

LAND

3

LEETON RD

OSPREY RD

32

PROMISED

Napeague

State Park

Island

HIGHWAY

MARLIN

ATLANTIC

SHORE RD

DOLPHIN DR

DUNES DR

DUNES S LA

EAST HAMPTON BEACH

PROMISED LAND

Long

MONTAUK

Map
61

Tip Quickly estimate distance:
Each grid box represents approximately
0.65 mi. horizontally by 0.86 mi. vertically.

Scale 1:24,000

0   1,000   2,000   3,000   4,000   5,000 Feet

0   200   400   600   800   1,000   1,200   1,400 Meters

72°01'30"   T4   72°00'45"   U4   72°00'00"   V4   71°59'15"   W4   71°58'30"   X4

N

Rocky
Pt

Fort Pond
Bay

36

Railroad

41°02'15"

Island

Hither Woods Preserve

(State-County-Town)

MONTAUK

Quincetree
Landing

Long

11954

35

27   WASHINGTON

BAY

Lee Koppelman

Nature Preserve

(County)

41°01'30"

PARKWAY

Water   Fence   Beach

6

STATE

34

Joins Map 62

Fresh
Pond

MONTAUK

BEACH

MONTAUK

Hither Hills

State Park

Parking
Field

POINT

OCEAN

41°00'45"

MONTAUK

Parking
Field

Park-
Supt

(Montauk Branch)

Parking   MONTAUK
Field

Picnic
Area

33

CEMETERY
ROAD

OLD

Bath
House

HIGHWAY

Napeague   Beach

41°00'00"

ATLANTIC

32

72°01'30"   T4   72°00'45"   U4   72°00'00"   V4   71°59'15"   W4   71°58'30"   X4

Map
62

Suffolk Co.

BLOCK ISLAND SOUND

Culloden Pt

EAST

LAKE MONTAUK

Montauk Airport

U.S. Coast Guard

Montauk YC

Star Island

Montauk Downs State Park

Fort Hill Cemetery

Stepping Stones Pond

Tuthill Pond

Rocky Pt

Fort Pond Bay

Montauk Sta

Fort Pond

Hither Woods Preserve
(State-County-Town)

Long

Lee Koppelman
Nature Preserve
(County)

1 HOUSTON DR
2 McKINLEY RD
3 CLEVELAND DR
4 TAFT DR
5 WOOD DR
6 WEBSTER RD

MONTAUK

Shadmoor
State
Park

DITCH
PLAINS

ATLANTIC

Map
62

Tip! Quickly estimate distance:
Each grid box represents approximately
0.65 mi. horizontally by 0.86 mi. vertically.

Scale 1:24,000

| 0 | 1,000 | 2,000 | 3,000 | 4,000 | 5,000 Feet |

| 0 | 200 | 400 | 600 | 800 | 1,000 | 1,200 | 1,400 Meters |

B5   71°54'45"   C5   71°54'00"   D5   71°53'15"   E5   71°52'30"   F5   71°51'45"   G5

N

39

38

37

36

35

Shagwong Point

Big Reed
Pond

Little
Reed
Pond

Montauk
County Park

Lake Munchogue
(Oyster Pond)

Montauk Point
State Park

False Pt

Refreshment
Bldg

Parking

LH

U.S.C.G.

Montauk
Pt

HAMPTON

BIG REED PATH WAY
DEER LA
LAKE
THI LA
PROSPECT
POCAHONTAS LA
HOMEWARD RD
MELCHIONNA LA
LEON CT
STARTOP DR
RANCH CT

11954

DRIVE

27

30

PARKWAY

RANCH
RD

OLD   MONTAUK   HWY

New York State
Preserve
"The Sanctuary"

MONTAUK
(MONTAUK

STATE
POINT
POINT

STATE
BLVD)

PARKWAY

CAMP
MADISON
WASHINGTON AV
HILL
JEFFERSON DR
EDISON DR

HERO   RD

Camp Hero State Park
(Undeveloped-
Access by Permit only)

STATE

S. LAKE DR

WEST
LAKE DR
S. GREENBRIAR RD
PL
GOODRIDGE PL
BENSON
HOYT
DU
VAL
CASWELL RD
RENAM AV
FLAGG PL
BRISBANE AV
REUTER PL
AGNEW AV
SANGER PL
OTIS
AV DEFOREST
CROSS
W. END AV
SWORDFISH AV
E. END AV
TUNA DR
MIDWAY
SNAPPER AV
MARLIN DR
EDGEWATER DR
PRENTICE PL
HOPPIN AV

Ditch Plains
U.S. Coast Guard

OCEAN

B5   71°54'45"   C5   71°54'00"   D5   71°53'15"   E5   71°52'30"   F5   71°51'45"   G5

©Hagstrom Map Company, Inc.

Map 63

Suffolk Co.

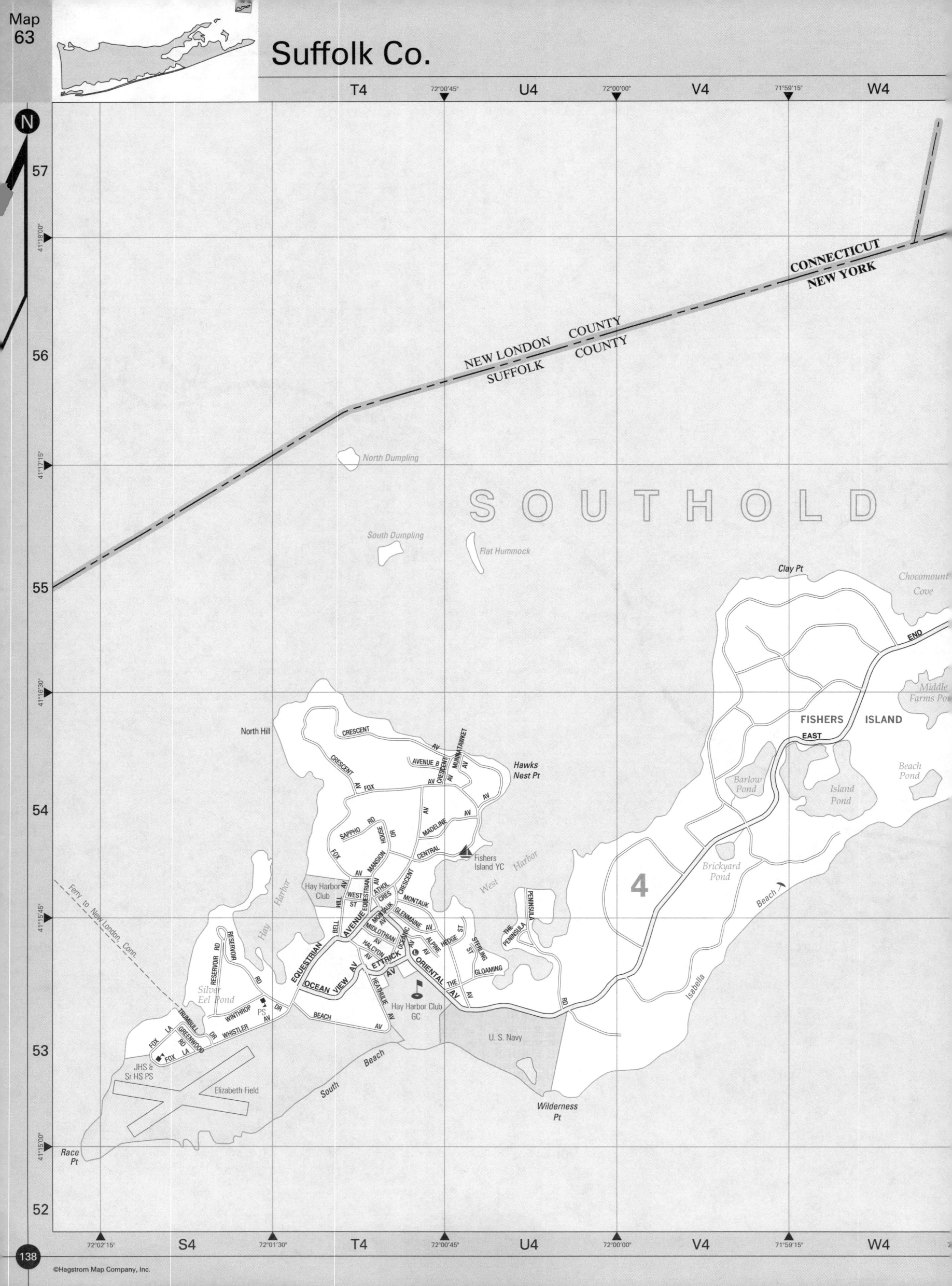

Map
63

Tip

Quickly estimate distance:
Each grid box represents approximately
0.65 mi. horizontally by 0.86 mi. vertically.

Scale 1:24,000

06390

FISHERS   ISLAND   SOUND

Brooks Pt

Hungry Pt

East Harbor

Fishers Island CC & GC

U.S.C.G.

EAST   END

ROAD

South   Beach

Barleyfield Cove

Chocomount Beach

Treasure Pond

BLOCK   ISLAND   SOUND

Wreck Island

Money Pond

East Pt

Wicopesset Passage

Wicopesset Island

LH   Latimer Reef

ROAD

Suffolk Co.

Index Guide

Using the Grid Square Location System

Blue lines are drawn horizontally and vertically on the map, forming grid squares. These squares can be identified by letters and numbers appearing in the map margins. Streets and roads are listed alphabetically in the index by political divisions within the county. The letters and numbers after the name give the map number and grid square in which the street appears.

For example, to locate Lenox Rd., in Babylon, find the heading for Babylon in the index. The 11 N9 after the street name shows that Lenox Rd. can be located on Map 11, within grid square N9 as shown to the right.

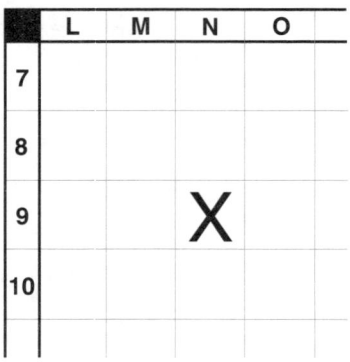

NOTE: Numbered streets are indexed after alphabetical listing.
"*" indicates that street name is not shown on map due to lack of space.

Abbreviations Used on Hagstrom Maps

Al	Alley
Av	Avenue
Blvd	Boulevard
Bk	Brook
Boro	Borough
CC	Country Club
Cem	Cemetery
Cir	Circle
CO	County
Cor	Corner
Cr	Creek
Cres	Crescent
Ct	Court
Dr	Drive
E	East
ES	Elementary School
Expwy	Expressway
GC	Golf Club
HS	High School
Hwy	Highway
JHS	Junior High School
La	Lane
MS	Middle School
Mt	Mount
Mun Bldg	Municipal Building
N	North
Pk	Park
Pkwy	Parkway
Pl	Place
Rd	Road
Riv	River
RR	Railroad
S	South
Sq	Square
St	Saint
St	Street
Sta	Station
Ter	Terrace
Term	Terminal
Tpk	Turnpike
Tr	Trail
Twp	Township
W	West
Wk	Walk

Index to Places

Village Code System

Streets located within an incorporated village are indexed under the town in which the village is located. If a street is indexed under a town more than once, a 2-letter code immediately following the street name identifies the village in which the street is located.

Village	Code	In town of	Village	Code	In town of	Village	Code	In town of
Amityville	(AM)	Babylon	Islandia	(IS)	Islip	Port Jefferson	(PJ)	Brookhaven
Asharoken	(AK)	Huntington	Lake Grove	(LG)	Brookhaven	Quogue	(QG)	Southampton
Babylon	(BV)	Babylon	Lindenhurst	(LI)	Babylon	Sag Harbor	(SH)	East Hampton & Southampton
Belle Terre	(BT)	Brookhaven	Lloyd Harbor	(LH)	Huntington			
Bellport	(BP)	Brookhaven	Nissequogue	(NQ)	Smithtown	Saltaire	(SA)	Islip
Brightwaters	(BR)	Islip	North Haven	(NH)	Southampton	Shoreham	(SR)	Brookhaven
Dering Harbor	(DH)	Shelter Island	Northport	(NP)	Huntington	Southampton	(SV)	Southampton
East Hampton	(EV)	East Hampton	Ocean Beach	(OB)	Islip	Village of the Branch	(VB)	Smithtown
Greenport	(GR)	Southold	Old Field	(OF)	Brookhaven	Westhampton Beach	(WB)	Southampton
Head of the Harbor	(HH)	Smithtown	Patchogue	(PG)	Brookhaven	West Hampton Dunes	(WD)	Southampton
Huntington Bay	(HB)	Huntington	Poquott	(PQ)	Brookhaven			

Hamlet Code System for Brookhaven and Southold

For the town of Brookhaven, some street names in hamlets have a code. If a street name appears in the index more than once, it means that a street name with that name can be found in more than one place within Brookhaven.

A 2-letter code immediately following the street name identifies the hamlet. For example, in the Brookhaven index, you will find Tyler Av. (mp) 25 S1-28, located in the general area of Miller Place, and Tyler Av. (co) 26 O1-22, located in the general area of Coram. Please see accompanying list of codes.

Place	Code	Place	Code	Place	Code	Place	Code
Brookhaven	(bk)	Fishers Island	(fi)	Manorville	(mv)	Selden	(sd)
Blue Point	(bt)	Fire Island Pines	(fp)	North Bellport	(nb)	South Medford	(sf)
Cherry Grove	(cg)	Farmingville	(fv)	North Centereach	(nc)	Strong's Neck	(sg)
Coram Hill	(ch)	Gordon Heights	(gh)	New Suffolk	(nk)	Shirley	(sh)
Center Moriches	(cm)	Greenport West	(gw)	North Patchogue	(np)	Setauket	(sk)
Coram	(co)	Holbrook	(hb)	North Shore Beach	(nr)	Stony Brook	(sn)
Centereach	(cr)	Hagerman	(hg)	North Selden	(ns)	South Stony Brook	(so)
Davis Park	(dp)	Holtsville	(hv)	Ocean Bay Park	(ob)	South Manor	(sr)
East Setauket	(ek)	Lake Ronkonkoma	(lr)	Port Jefferson Station	(ps)	South Setauket	(ss)
East Moriches	(em)	Mastic Beach	(mb)	Point O'Woods	(pw)	Old Stony Brook	(sy)
East Patchogue	(ep)	Mastic	(mc)	Ridge	(ri)	Terryville	(tv)
East Shoreham	(er)	Medford	(mf)	Ronkonkoma	(rk)	Upton	(up)
Eastport	(et)	Middle Island	(mi)	Rocky Point	(rp)	West Bellport	(wb)
East Yaphank	(ey)	Miller Place	(mp)	South Haven	(sa)	Water Island	(wi)
Five Corners	(fc)	Moriches	(mr)	Sound Beach	(sb)	West Yaphank	(wy)
Flowerfield	(ff)	Mount Sinai	(ms)	South Centereach	(sc)	Yaphank	(ya)

Index to Towns / Population

Place	Map	Population	Place	Map	Population
Babylon	4-6, 9-11	211,792	Smithtown	7-19, 13-15, 19-21	115,715
Brookhaven	3, 13-15, 18-35, 38, 39	448,248	Southampton	37-39, 41-43, 46-48, 51-57	54,712
East Hampton	55-57, 59-63	19,719	Southold	40, 41, 44-46, 49-52	20,599
Huntington	1-4, 7-10, 15	195,289			
Islip	9-12, 15-18. 21-24, 27-29	322,612	**County Total**		**1,419,369**
Riverhead	31, 32, 36, 37, 40, 41, 44, 46	27,680			
Shelter Island	44, 49-51, 55	2,228	Source: U.S. Census Bureau, Census 2000		

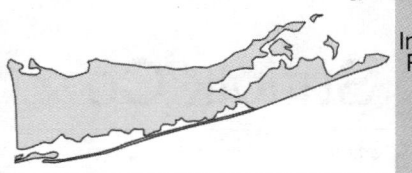

Index to Places/Zip Codes

Place	Indexed Under Town Of	Map	Zip Codes
Amagansett	East Hampton	60	11930
Amity Harbor	Babylon	5	11701
Amityville (Village)	Babylon	5	11701
Apaquogue	East Hampton	57	11937
Aquebogue	Riverhead	41	11931
Art Village	Southampton	54	11968
Asharoken (Village)	Huntington	7	11768
Atlantique	Islip	18	11706, 11770
Babylon (Village)	Babylon	11	11702
Baiting Hollow	Riverhead	36	11933
Barcelona Neck	East Hampton	55	11963
Barnes Hole	East Hampton	60	11937
Bay Shore	Islip	16	11706
Bayberry Dunes	Brookhaven	30	N/A
Bayport	Islip	23	11705
Bayside Park	Babylon	5	11701
Bayview	Southold	44	11971
Baywood	Islip	10	11706
Beach Hampton	East Hampton	60	11930
Belle Terre (Village)	Brookhaven	19	11777
Bellport (Village)	Brookhaven	29	11703
Biexedon	Southold	44	11971
Blue Point	Brookhaven	23	11715
Bohemia	Islip	22	11716
Brentwood	Islip	9	11717
Bridgehampton	Southampton	57	11932
Bright Waters (Village)	Islip	10	11718
Brookhaven (Hamlet)	Brookhaven	34	11719
Calverton	Riverhead & Brookhaven	37	11933
Canoe Place	Southampton	47	11946
Captain Kidd Estates	Southold	40	11952
Captree Island	Babylon & Islip	12	11702
Cedar Beach	Southold	44	11971
Center Moriches	Brookhaven	34	11934
Centereach	Brookhaven	21	11720
Centerport	Huntington	2	11721
Centerville	Riverhead	36	11901
Central Islip	Islip	15	11722
Cherry Grove	Brookhaven	24	11782
Cobb	Southampton	54	11976
Cold Spring Harbor	Huntington	2	11724
Commack	Smithtown & Huntington	8	11725
Copiague	Babylon	5	11726
Coram	Brookhaven	26	11727
Coram Hill	Brookhaven	27	11727
Corneille Estates	Islip	18	11770
Cutchogue	Southold	45	11935
Cow Neck	Southampton	46	11968
Crane Neck	Brookhaven	19	11733
Davis Park	Brookhaven	30	11772
Deer Park	Babylon	10	11729
Deerfield	Southampton	53	11976
Dering Harbor (Village)	Shelter Island	49	11964-5
Devon	East Hampton	60	11930
Ditch Plains	East Hampton	62	11954
Dix Hills	Huntington	9	11746
Dunewood	Islip	18	11706
East Commack	Smithtown	8	11725, 11787
East Cutchogue	Southold	45	11935
East Farmingdale	Babylon	4	11735
East Half Hollow Hills	Huntington	9	11746
East Hampton (Village)	East Hampton	60	11937
East Hampton North	East Hampton	60	11937
East Holbrook	Islip	22	11741
East Islip	Islip	16	11730
East Marion	Southold	50	11939
East Mattituck	Southold	45	11952
East Moriches	Brookhaven	39	11940
East Northport	Huntington	8	11731
East Patchogue	Brookhaven	28	11772
East Quogue	Southampton	42	11942
East Setauket	Brookhaven	19	11733
East Shoreham	Brookhaven	31	11786
East Yaphank	Brookhaven	33	11967
Eastport	Brookhaven & Southampton	38	11941
Eatons Neck	Huntington	1	11768
Edgewood	Islip	10	11717
Elwood	Huntington	8	11731
Fair Harbor	Islip	18	11706
Farmingville	Brookhaven	21	11738
Fire Island Pines	Brookhaven	24	11782
Fireplace	East Hampton	59	11937
Fireplace Neck	Brookhaven	34	11719
Fishers Island	Southold	63	06390
Five Corners	Brookhaven	21	11779
Flanders	Southampton	42	11901
Flowerfield	Brookhaven	20	11780
Flying Point	Southampton	54	11968
Fort Salonga	Huntington & Smithtown	7	11768
Freetown	East Hampton	56	11937
Gardiners Island	East Hampton	58	11937
Georgica	East Hampton	56	11963, 11962
Georgica Neck	East Hampton	57	11937
Gerard Park	East Hampton	59	11937
Gordon Heights	Brookhaven	27	11727
Grace Estate	East Hampton	55	11937
Grassy Hollow	East Hampton	55	11937
Great Hog Neck	Southold	44	11971
Great River	Islip	16	11739
Greenlawn	Huntington	2	11740
Greenport (Village)	Southold	50	11944
Greenport West	Southold	50	11944
Hagerman	Brookhaven	28	11772
Halesite	Huntington	2	11743
Half Hollow Hills	Huntington	10	11746-7
Hampton Bays	Southampton	47	11946
Hampton Park	Southampton	54	11968, 11976
Hardscrabble	East Hampton	56	11937, 11975
Hauppauge	Islip & Smithtown	15	11788
Hayground	Southampton	53	11932, 11976
Head of the Harbor (Village)	Smithtown	14	11780
Holbrook	Islip & Brookhaven	22	11741
Holtsville	Brookhaven	21	11742
Huntington (Hamlet)	Huntington	2	11743
Huntington Bay (Village)	Huntington	1	11743
Huntington Manor	Huntington	2	11743
Huntington Station	Huntington	2	11746
Islandia (Village)	Islip	15	11749
Islip (Hamlet)	Islip	16	11751
Islip Terrace	Islip	16	11752
Jamesport	Riverhead	41	11947
Jericho	East Hampton	56	11937
Jessup Neck	Southampton	52	11963
Kings Park	Smithtown	8	11754
Kingstown	East Hampton	59	11973
Kismet	Islip	18	11706
Lake Grove (Village)	Smithtown	21	11755
Lake Ronkonkoma	Brookhaven & Smithtown	21	11779
Lakeland	Islip	15	11779
Laurel	Southold	40	11948
Lindenhurst (Village)	Babylon	11	11757
Lloyd Harbor (Village)	Huntington	1	11743
Lower Melville	Huntington	4	11704, 11741
Maidstone Park	East Hampton	59	11937
Manetto Hills	Huntington	3	11747
Manorville	Riverhead	32	11949
Mastic	Brookhaven	34	11940
Mastic Beach	Brookhaven	34	11951
Mattituck	Southold	40	11952
Mecox	East Hampton	57	11932, 11976
Medford	Brookhaven	27	11763
Melville	Huntington	3	11747
Middle Island	Brookhaven	26	11953
Middleville	Smithtown & Huntington	7	11768
Mill Hills Estates	East Hampton	55	11937
Miller Place	Brookhaven	25	11764
Montauk	East Hampton	61	11954
Montauk Beach	East Hampton	61	11954
Moriches	Brookhaven	33	11955
Mt Sinai	Brookhaven	25	11766
Napeague	East Hampton	61	11930
Nassau Point	Southold	45	11935
Nesconset	Smithtown	21	11767
New Suffolk	Southold	46	11956
Nissequogue (Village)	Smithtown	19	11780
North Amityville	Babylon	5	11701
North Babylon	Babylon	10	11703
North Bay Shore	Islip	10	11706
North Bellport	Brookhaven	28	11713
North Centereach	Brookhaven	20	11720
North Great River	Islip	16	11752
North Haven (Village)	Southampton	52	11963
North Lindenhurst	Babylon	5	11757
North Patchogue	Brookhaven	28	11772
North Sea	Southampton	53	11968
North Selden	Brookhaven	20	11784
North Side Hills	Southampton	53	11963, 11976
North Smithtown	Smithtown	14	11787
Northampton	Southampton	42	11901
Northport (Village)	Huntington	7	11768
Northville	Riverhead	40	11901, 11931
Noyac	Southampton	52	11937
Oakdale	Islip	22	11769
Oakville	Southampton	42	11942
Ocean Bay Park	Brookhaven	24	11770
Ocean Beach (Village)	Islip	24	11770
Old Field (Village)	Brookhaven	19	11733
Old Lonelyville	Islip	18	11706
Old Mastic	Brookhaven	34	11951
Old Stony Brook	Brookhaven	19	11790
Oregon	Southold	45	11935, 11952
Orient	Southold	49	11957
Orient Point	Southold	49	11957
Pantigo	East Hampton	60	11937
Patchogue (Village)	Brookhaven	22	11717
Peconic	Southold	44	11958
Pine Aire	Islip	9	11717
Pine Neck	Southampton	42	11942
Point O'Woods	Brookhaven	24	11706
Ponquogue	Southampton	48	11946
Poospatuck American Indian Reservation	Brookhaven	33	11950
Poquott (Village)	Brookhaven	19	11733
Port Jefferson (Village)	Brookhaven	19	11777
Port Jefferson Station	Brookhaven	19	11776
Promised Land	East Hampton	60	11930
Quiogue	Southampton	43	11959
Quogue (Village)	Southampton	43	11959
Rampasture	Southampton	48	11946
Reeves Park	Riverhead	36	11901
Remsenburg	Southampton	38	11960
Ridge	Brookhaven	32	11961
Riverhead (Hamlet)	Riverhead	41	11901
Riverside	Southampton	41	11901
Roanoke	Riverhead	36	11901
Robin Rest	Islip	18	11956
Robins Island	Southold	46	11706
Rocky Point	Brookhaven	25	11778
Ronkonkoma	Islip & Brookhaven	21	11779
Rose Grove	Southampton	53	11968
Sag Harbor	East Hampton & Southampton	56	11963
Sagaponack	Southampton	57	11962
St James	Smithtown	14	11780
San Remo	Smithtown	13	11754, 11787
Sayville	Islip	23	11782
Scuttlehole	Southampton	53	11976
Seaview	Islip	18	11770
Sebonac Neck	Southampton	47	11968
Selden	Brookhaven	27	11784
Setauket	Brookhaven	19	11733
Shelter Isl Heights	Shelter Island	51	11964-5
Shinnecock American Indian Reservation	Southampton	54	11969
Shinnecock Hills	Southampton	47	11946, 11968
Shirley	Brookhaven	34	11967
Shoreham (Village)	Brookhaven	25	11786
Smithtown (Hamlet)	Smithtown	14	11787
Sound Beach	Brookhaven	25	11789
South Centereach	Brookhaven	21	11738, 11779
South Flanders	Southampton	42	11942
South Hauppauge	Islip	15	11788
South Haven	Brookhaven	34	11950, 11967
South Holbrook	Islip	22	11751
South Huntington	Huntington	3	11746
South Jamesport	Riverhead	41	11970
South Manor	Brookhaven	33	11949
South Medford	Brookhaven	28	11763, 11772
South Setauket	Brookhaven	20	11720
South Stony Brook	Brookhaven	20	11790
South Yaphank	Brookhaven	28	11980
Southampton (Village)	Southampton	54	11968
Southold (Hamlet)	Southold	44	11971
Southport	Southampton	47	11946
Speonk	Southampton	38	11972
Springs	East Hampton	59	11937
Springville	Southampton	48	11946
Squiretown	Southampton	47	11946
Stirling	Southold	50	11944
Stony Brook	Brookhaven	20	11790, 11794
Strong's Neck	Brookhaven	19	11733
Summer Club	Islip	18	11776
Terryville	Brookhaven	20	11937
Three Mile Harbor	East Hampton	59	11937
Tiana	Southampton	48	11946
Tuckahoe	Southampton	54	11968
Upton	Brookhaven	32	11973
Vernon Valley	Huntington	7	11731, 11768
Village of the Branch (Village)	Smithtown	14	11787
Wading River	Riverhead	31	11792
Wainscott	East Hampton	57	11975
Water Island	Brookhaven	30	11772
Water Mill	Southampton	54	11976
West Amagansett	East Hampton	60	11930
West Babylon	Babylon	10	11704
West Bay Shore	Islip	11	11706
West Brentwood	Islip	10	11717
West Hills	Huntington	3	11743
West Islip	Islip	11	11795
West Neck	Shelter Island	51	11964-5
West Sayville	Islip	23	11796
West Tiana	Southampton	42	11946
West Yaphank	Brookhaven	27	11980
Westhampton	Southampton	43	11977
Westhampton Beach (Village)	Southampton	43	11978
Westhampton Dunes (Village)	Southampton	39	11978
Wheatley Heights	Babylon	4	11798
Wickapogue	Southampton	54	11968
Wyandanch	Babylon	4	11798
Yaphank	Brookhaven	33	11980

Suffolk Co.

BABYLON

STREET	MAP	GRID
A St	4 M	10
Abbington Ct	5 J	6
Abbott St	11 N	8
Acorn St	10 M	13
Adams Av (LI)	11 L	7
Adams Av	10 M	13
Adams Blvd	5 G	10
Adams St	4 F	12
Adams St	5 G	9
Adams St	10 M	13
Adrian Ct	5 F	9
Advent Pl	10 P	11
Airport Plaza Blvd	4 G	11
Akron St	5 J	7
Albany Av	5 H	10
Albany Av (LI)	5 K	7
Albany Av (AM)	5 G	7
Albany Av	10 M	12
Albany St	9 P	15
Albermarle Av	11 N	8
Albert Rd	5 H	6
Albert St (LI)	5 L	8
Albin Av	5 M	9
Alder St	4 J	11
Alexander Av	4 F	12
Alexander St	11 O	9
Alfred St	10 N	11
Algonquin St	10 Q	12
Alicia Dr	10 O	10
Allen Blvd	4 G	10
Allen Blvd	5 G	10
Alo Ct	10 O	12
Alto St	11 M	9
Alton Rd	11 O	7
America Av	10 M	10
Americo Vespucci Av	5 H	7
Amity Pl	5 H	8
Amsterdam Av	10 M	10
Anawanda Rd	10 P	11
Anchor Ct	11 N	9
Anderson Av	10 P	12
Andover Dr	10 N	14
Andrea St	11 N	8
Andrews Av	10 M	13
Angelica Ct	11 N	7
Angelica St	10 P	14
Anita Ct	4 L	10
Anita Pl (AM)	5 G	6
Anita Pl	5 J	6
Ann Av	5 G	9
Ann Ct	10 O	10
Ann St	11 O	9
Anndom Ct	10 N	12
Annuskemunnica Rd	11 P	7
Antelope St	10 P	15
Anthony Ct	5 J	6
Anthony Dr	5 L	6
Araca Ct	11 P	7
Araca Rd	11 P	7
Arcadia Dr	10 N	14
Arch St	10 L	12
Archer Av	5 J	8
Arctic St	11 L	6
Ardmore St	11 N	8
Argyle Av	11 O	8
Arizona Rd N	4 L	11
Arizona Rd S	4 L	11
Arlington Av	4 M	13
Arlington Rd	11 M	9
Arnold Av	11 M	9
Arthur Av	11 N	10
Arthur Pl	10 N	14
Arthur St	5 H	8
Asbury St	9 P	15
Ash Pl	4 M	12
Ash St	5 L	7
Ashfield Pl	11 P	10
Atlantic Av	10 N	13
Atlantic St	11 M	6
Atlantic St (LI)	5 J	8
Atna Dr	5 H	8
Auburn St	11 N	8
Auburn St (LI)	5 L	8
Audley Ct	5 J	6
August Rd	10 N	12
Austin Av	5 H	7
Austin Pl	5 H	8
Austin Pl	5 J	6
Austin St	11 M	7
Autumn La	5 H	9
Autumn Pl	11 M	10
Ava Ct	10 O	11
Avelaine Ct	11 O	10
Avenue A	11 M	9
Avenue B	11 M	9
Avenue C	11 M	9
Avon Dr	5 H	8
Avon Dr E	5 H	8
Avon Pl	5 G	7
B Kay Pl	4 L	14
Babylon Farmingdale Rd	5 J	10
Babylon-Northport Expwy	11 P	9
Bacon La	11 N	8
Badger La	5 L	9
Bahama St	11 M	8
Bailey Av	11 N	9
Bailey St	4 L	11
Baiting Place Rd	5 F	9
Baker St	11 N	7
Baldwin Pa	10 O	15
Baldwin St	4 F	11
Baltic Pl	5 J	6
Banbury Pl	5 G	7
Banfi Plaza Blvd N	4 G	10
Banfi Plaza Blvd W	4 G	10
Banfi Plaza W	5 G	10
Bangor St	5 J	7
Banner Ct	10 O	11
Barbara La	4 F	11
Barberry Ct	5 H	6
Barclay St	10 M	11
Bark Ct	10 Q	13
Barnfield Pl	10 O	11
Barnfield Rd	5 J	6
Barnum St	10 M	11
Barrington Dr	4 L	14
Barry Rd	5 H	6
Baur St	10 M	11
Bay Blvd W	5 H	5
Bay Dr	5 K	5
Bay Pl (LI)	11 N	6
Bay Pl (LI)	5 L	6
Bay Point Ct	11 N	7
Bay Shore Rd	10 P	12
Bay St	11 P	7
Bay View Av (AM)	5 H	6
Bay View Av	5 H	8
Bay View Av E	11 M	6
Bay View Av W	5 L	6
Baylawn Av	5 J	5
Bayside Av (AM)	5 G	6
Bayside Av	5 H	8
Bayside Pl	5 H	5
Bayview Av	11 P	7
Bayview Av (AM)	5 H	5
Bayview Av E	5 M	6
Bayview La	5 H	6
Bayview Pl	5 H	6
Bayview Rd	5 H	6
Baywood St	5 M	10
Beach Av	5 J	6
Beach Promenade E	5 K	5
Beach St	11 M	6
Beach View St	5 H	6
Beach View St	5 H	7
Beacon Av	5 L	7
Beaver La	5 L	9
Bedell Pl	5 H	7
Bedell St	5 K	9
Bedford Av	11 N	10
Bedford St	5 H	8
Bedford St	10 M	12
Beebe Ct	10 P	12
Beech St	10 M	12
Beech St	10 P	12
Beecher Rd	10 P	11
Beechmont Av	11 M	7
Beechwood Dr	11 N	8
Beechwood St	4 E	12
Belinda Ct	10 P	11
Bell St	4 J	11
Belmont Av	10 O	13
Belmont Av	10 N	10
Belmont Pl	5 H	7
Belton Ct	11 O	8
Belton Rd	11 O	8
Belvedere Av	5 G	9
Benburb St	5 G	8
Bendix Pl	5 K	8
Benjamin Av	5 H	7
Benjamin Rd	10 P	11
Benjoe Dr	5 H	9
Bennett Ct	5 H	8
Bennett Pl	5 G	6
Bennington Pl	4 K	13
Bentley Rd	5 F	8
Bergen Av	11 N	7
Bergen Ct	5 K	6
Bergen Dr	9 Q	15
Berger Av	5 G	5
Berkshire Rd	11 N	9
Bermuda Rd	11 M	9
Berry St	5 J	9
Beta Dr	5 H	8
Bethpage Rd	5 J	8
Beverly Av	5 H	6
Beverly Rd	11 N	9
Bi-County Blvd	4 F	10
Biel Dr	5 H	8
Bingham Pl	5 G	5
Bioscience Park Dr	4 G	13
Birch Av	4 F	11
Birch Cir	4 F	11
Birch Cir N	4 F	11
Birch Cir S	4 F	11
Birch Ct	4 F	11
Birch Rd	5 G	9
Birch St (LI)	5 L	7
Birch St	10 M	12
Birchfield Av	11 O	9
Birs Av	5 K	9
Bishop Rd	10 M	10
Bismark Pl	5 G	8
Blanchard St	11 N	8
Bliss St	10 M	12
Bluebell La	10 P	12
Board Pl	11 N	10
Boening Plaza Blvd	4 G	10
Bolender Ct	10 P	10
Bolton St	5 J	9
Bond St (LI)	5 L	7
Bond St	10 M	11
Bonwit Pl	4 F	11
Booker Av	4 L	12
Booker Blvd	5 G	9
Blvd, The	5 G	9
Bourdette Pl	5 G	5
Bowling La	10 P	13
Boxwood La	4 E	12
Bradish La	11 N	8
Braham Av	5 G	5
Brandon Av	5 G	8
Brandy Vine Dr	10 Q	13
Brefni St	5 G	9
Brennan Pl	10 O	14
Brevoort Pl	10 N	14
Brewster La	5 G	8
Briarwood Rd	4 K	13
Brierly Ct	5 K	5
Bristol Ct	10 M	14
Bristol St	5 L	8
Broad Hollow Rd	4 G	11
Broadway	11 M	10
Broadway (LI)	5 K	7
Broadway	5 F	8
Broadway Rd	10 M	10
Brook Av	10 M	12
Brook Av	10 Q	12
Brook St (LI)	11 M	6
Brook St	11 M	9
Brookes Rd	10 P	11
Brooklyn Av	4 L	12
Brooklyn Av	10 M	12
Brooklyn St	10 P	15
Brookside Av	10 O	10
Brookside Ct	5 J	7
Brooktree Cir	5 K	6
Brookvale Av	11 N	8
Brookwood Dr	4 K	13
Broome St	10 N	11
Brown Blvd	10 L	14
Brown Pl	5 L	6
Brown St	11 N	8
Bruce St	11 N	8
Bruno La	10 N	14
Bryan Av	5 H	6
Bryant Pl	10 P	10
Buchanan Av	5 H	6
Buchanan Av	10 M	13
Budding Pl	5 J	7
Buena Vista Blvd	5 K	6
Buffalo Av	5 J	7
Bulger St	11 O	8
Bunker Ct	4 L	14
Bunnell Pl	11 N	9
Bunny La	5 H	6
Burch Av	5 G	7
Burgess Av	11 M	9
Burlington Av	10 P	14
Burnage La	11 O	10
Burndale Ct	4 J	13
Burr's La	10 M	14
Burt Dr	10 Q	13
Burton Pl	5 K	9
Byrd St	5 L	8
Byway Dr	10 Q	13
Cabot St	4 J	11
Caboto Av	5 J	8
Cadman Av	11 O	9
Cadman Dr	11 N	9
Cahill St	5 G	8
Caledonia Av	11 O	8
Calhoun St	10 O	10
Calvert Av	11 M	9
Cambridge Dr	11 O	7
Cambridge St	10 N	14
Cameron Av	11 O	8
Campagnoli Av	5 H	7
Campbell St	5 G	8
Canal St	5 L	6
Canary Pl	10 P	12
Canterbury La	10 P	10
Cantoni Ct	10 O	11
Cape Rd	5 H	6
Captain's Dr	11 N	7
Cardinal Ct	4 J	13
Carle La	4 F	10
Carljim Ct	10 O	12
Carll's Pa	10 P	12
Carlston Pl	11 O	8
Carlton Av	5 G	5
Carlton Rd	11 M	9
Carman Pl	5 G	6
Carmans Ct	4 F	11
Carmans Rd	4 F	10
Carnation Dr	4 F	12
Carolina St	11 M	8
Caroline Ct	10 P	12
Carolyn Blvd	4 G	10
Carrol St	5 G	9
Carto Cir	10 P	13
Cassata Ct	11 M	9
Catalpa St	4 L	12
Catalpa St	10 P	12
Catskill Av	5 J	7
Cayuga Av	10 P	14
Cedar Av	4 F	11
Cedar Ct	5 K	6
Cedar La (BV)	11 O	8
Cedar La (AM)	5 G	8
Cedar Pl	5 L	6
Cedar Rd	5 G	9
Cedar St (BV)	11 P	9
Cedar St (AM)	5 G	6
Cedar St	5 H	7
Cedar St	5 J	8
Cedar St (LI)	5 L	7
Cedar St	10 M	12
Cedarwood Rd	11 M	8
Celeste Ct	10 O	10
Center Dr	5 G	8
Center St	5 H	9
Centerwood St	4 L	11
Central Av	4 G	13
Central Av (AM)	5 G	5
Central Av	10 N	12
Central Av	10 P	12
Central Dr	4 H	13
Centre Av	5 L	9
Cesena St	5 J	7
Chadwick St	5 H	6
Chance Pl	11 N	10
Chapel Pl	10 P	11
Charles St (LI)	5 L	8
Charles St	10 M	12
Charleston Dr	5 H	6
Charlestown Pl	4 J	13
Chatham St	10 P	15
Chelmsford Dr	10 M	14
Chelsea Av	10 M	10
Chelsea Pl	10 N	13
Cheltenham Rd	10 N	10
Cherry St	4 L	12
Cherubina La	10 P	12
Cherwal St	11 M	8
Cheryl La	10 O	12
Chestnut Pl	5 J	7
Chestnut Rd	5 H	10
Chestnut St (LI)	5 L	7
Chestnut St	10 M	12
Chettic Av	5 J	7
Chevy Chase	5 H	8
Chichester Av	5 G	5
Christmas St	10 P	10
Christopher Ct (BV)	11 O	7
Christopher Ct	10 O	14
Chuck Blvd	10 N	12
Church Pl	5 H	7
Church St	10 O	13
Chyam St	10 O	12
Cindy Dr	11 M	10
Circle Dr	4 K	13
Citrus St	11 N	8
Claire Ct	11 N	9
Claremont Av	10 M	10
Claremont St	10 N	14
Clarence St	5 J	6
Clark St	10 M	11
Clearview Dr	4 J	13
Cleveland St	11 P	9
Clifton Ct	4 F	10
Clinton Ct	11 N	8
Clinton Pl (LI)	11 M	7
Clinton Pl	10 O	14
Clinton St	11 M	8
Clinton St (BV)	11 O	9
Cockenoe Av	11 P	9
Coles Av	5 G	6
Colfax La	10 P	11
Collins Av	10 N	14
Colombo Av	10 N	14
Colombo Dr	10 M	14
Colonial Rd	5 J	9
Colonial Rd	10 N	10
Colonial Springs Rd	4 J	14
Colt Av	11 P	9
Columba Av	5 G	9
Columbia St	10 M	11
Columbus Av	5 G	9
Columbus Av	10 M	10
Columbus Blvd	5 G	9
Commack Rd	10 P	12
Commack Rd (Bread & Cheese Hollow Rd)	8 R	20
Commander Av	4 L	11
Commerce Blvd	5 G	9
Commodore La	11 N	7
Common St	11 P	10
Common-Wealth Dr	10 M	13
Concord Av	5 K	6
Cone St	5 L	10
Conklin Av	4 L	14
Conklin St	4 H	12
Conklin St	10 O	12
Conklin St	10 O	14
Connor La	10 Q	12
Constance Ct	5 L	9
Conway Ct	4 L	14
County Route 1	5 F	9
County Route 2	4 M	14
County Route 3	4 H	12
County Route 4	10 Q	14
County Route 5	4 H	14
County Route 12	11 M	8
County Route 28	5 H	10
County Route 34	10 P	11
County Route 47	5 J	6
County Route 48	4 F	12
County Route 57	10 P	12
County Route 95	4 J	13
County Route 96	11 N	8
Coolidge Av	5 G	8
Coolidge Av	5 H	5
Cooper Av	5 G	6
Cooper Rd	10 P	10
Cooper St	11 P	8
Copiague Av	5 H	8
Copiague Pl	5 J	7
Copiague Rd	5 H	7
Coppertree La	11 O	8
Cord Av	11 M	8
Cormack Ct	11 P	8
Cornell Dr	4 L	14
Cornish Ct	10 M	14
Coronet Ct	4 L	14
Corral Dr	5 H	9
Corsica St	5 H	7
Cortland St	5 J	7
Cortland St	10 N	11
Cottage Pl	5 G	6
Cottage Row	11 P	8
Cottonwood Ct	10 Q	13
County Line Rd	5 F	9
County Pl	10 P	12
Court St	5 J	8
Court St	10 M	12
Coventry Ct	4 L	14
Crescent Av	11 P	8
Crescent Dr N	4 F	11
Crescent Dr S	4 F	11
Cricket Ct	10 Q	13
Crocus Ct	11 N	8
Crossway Dr	10 P	13
Crown St	10 P	12
Croydon Rd	5 H	8
Cumberbach St	4 L	12
Cumberland St	11 N	8
Curcio Ct	11 N	7
Current Pl	11 M	9
Cutter Pl	11 N	7
Cypress St	10 M	12
Cypress St	10 P	12
Daffodil Dr	4 F	12
Dahlia La	10 P	13
Daisy Ct	4 F	12
Dakota St	10 P	14
Dale St	4 J	11
Dallas St	5 M	7
Daly Pl	5 H	7
Daniel Dr	5 F	10
Daniel St	4 F	12
Daniel St (LI)	5 L	8
Dante Av	5 H	7
Dante Pl	5 J	6
Darerka St	5 G	9
Dartmouth Dr	10 N	14
Davenport St	5 M	7
Davidson St	4 L	12
Davis St	10 O	12
Dawn Ct	11 P	10
De Forest St (AM)	5 H	7
De Forest St	10 P	14
De Kalb Av	5 K	8
De Soto Rd	5 H	6
Dean St	10 O	10
Deauville Blvd	5 H	7
Deauville Pkwy	11 M	7
Debbie La	5 H	9
Decker St	5 H	8
Deer Lake Dr	10 Q	11
Deer Park Av	11 P	9
Deer Park Av Spur	11 P	11
Deer Park Blvd	10 N	14
Deer Park Rd	10 O	14
Deer St	10 M	12
Deerfield Ct	11 O	7
Deeringwood La	11 O	7
Defeo Ct	10 N	14
Dekay Pl	10 Q	12
Delamere Pl	10 N	14
Delano Pl	11 N	8
Delaware Av	5 G	8
Delaware Rd	4 L	11
Dell Dr	4 F	10
Delta St	5 L	7
Denise Dr	10 O	10
Densfield Rd	11 M	9
Denton Pl	4 F	11
Depot Pl	11 P	9
Devine Pl	5 G	8
Devon La	4 K	13
Dewey Av	5 H	5
Dewey Pl	11 M	7
Dewitt La	10 O	12
Dey Pl	4 K	13
Ditomas Ct	5 H	7
Dix Cir	10 M	14
Dix St	10 N	13
Dixon Av	5 H	7
Dock St	5 J	6
Doe St	10 N	14
Doges Promenade	5 K	6
Dogwood St	4 F	12
Dollard Dr	10 O	12
Dolphin Dr W	5 J	6
Dolphin La	5 J	6
Dolphin La E	5 K	5
Dolphin Lane W	5 K	6
Doolittle St	10 P	10
Dorset La	11 O	8
Douglas Av	11 O	8
Dover St	5 K	8
Dowsing Pl	5 H	6
Drake Av	10 N	13
Drakeford Av	10 P	12
Du Bois Av	5 G	9
Dubon Ct	4 G	13
Duke St	10 P	12
Dunbar St	5 G	9
Dundee Av	11 O	8
Dunkirk St	10 P	15
Durhamoc La	10 O	11
Dutchess St	10 N	11
Eads St	4 J	11
Earl Pl	5 J	6
Earl St	10 P	12
East 1st St	10 O	13
East 2nd St	10 O	13
East 3rd St	10 O	13
East 4th St	10 P	13
East 5th St	10 P	13
East 6th St	10 P	13
East 7th St	10 P	13
East 8th St	10 P	14
East Alhambra Av	5 K	6
East Belleterre Av	5 K	6
East Carmans Rd	4 F	11
East Clearwater Rd	5 K	6
East Ct	11 P	7
East Dr	5 J	6
East Dr	5 L	9
East Gate	5 J	7
East Gate Av	11 N	8
East Gates Av	5 L	7
East Granada Av	5 K	6
East Halycon Rd	5 K	6
East Hampton Rd	5 K	6
East Heathcote Rd	5 K	9
East Hoffman Av	5 L	7
East Hoffman Av (Angelini Av)	5 L	8
East Hollywood Av	5 K	6
East Industry Ct	10 R	13
East John St	5 K	8
East June St	5 J	9
East Kissimee Rd	5 K	6
East Lake Dr	5 G	6
East Lido Promenade Rd	5 K	6
East Main St	11 P	8
East Marine Av	5 K	6
East Merrit St	5 J	9
East Minerva Rd	5 K	6
East Neck Ct	11 N	8
East Neck Rd	11 O	8
East Neptune Av	5 K	6
East Riviera Dr	5 K	6
East Ronald Dr	5 G	8
East Saltaire Rd	5 K	6
East Seacrest Av	5 K	5
East Sherbrooke Rd	5 J	9
East Shore Dr	11 O	7
East St	5 H	10
Eastern Av	10 N	13
Eastern Concourse Emerson Av	5 J	5
Easton Av	10 P	12
Easton St	5 K	8
Eastwood Av	10 P	14
Eastwood Dr	10 O	11
Eaton Pl	10 M	14
Ecker Av	11 M	9
Edan Ct	5 H	6
Eddie Av	10 P	12
Edel Av	11 N	9
Edison Av	4 J	11
Edison St	5 H	7
Edison St E	5 H	7
Edith Ct	11 M	10
Edmunds Pl	5 H	8
Edmundton Dr	10 P	10
Edward Av	11 P	8
Elbert Rd	10 O	10
Elder St	4 L	12
Elgin Rd	5 H	5
Eliot Ct	5 G	6
Elise Pl	10 N	14
Elk St	10 M	13
Elkton La	10 O	11
Ellen Av	11 P	9
Ellen Ct	5 F	10
Ellensue Dr	10 N	14
Ellsworth Av	10 P	11
Elm Av	11 M	7
Elm Pl (AM)	5 G	7
Elm Pl	5 H	9
Elm St	5 H	7
Elm St	10 M	13
Elm St	10 N	13
Elmira St	10 P	11
Elmwood Rd	11 M	9
Elmwood Rd	10 P	13
Elwin Pl	5 H	6
Embargo Pl	10 P	10
Emerald La	5 H	8
Emerald La N	5 H	8
Emerald La S	5 H	8
Emerson Av	5 H	7
Emerson Av	10 P	11
Emerson St	10 N	14
Emmett Ct	10 M	10
Empire Av	10 M	11
Engineers La	4 H	13
Erickson Pl	5 G	8
Erie St	4 L	12
Erlanger Blvd	10 N	12
Ernest Pl	11 P	8
Espie La	10 O	10
Essen Dr	5 G	8
Essex Pl	10 P	14
Essex St	4 L	12
Essex St	10 N	11
Ethel Ct	4 L	14
Etna Ct	5 H	6
Euclid St	10 P	12
Evergreen Dr	5 J	9
Evergreen Pl	10 P	14
Evergreen St	11 O	8
Ewell St	11 O	9
Executive Blvd	4 F	10
Extension Totten Av	10 N	14
Eyre Pl	10 M	12
Fairchild Loop	4 G	12
Fairfield Dr	10 M	14
Fairhaven Dr	4 L	14
Fairlawn Dr	10 M	12
Fairview Av	10 O	12
Falls St	5 L	6
Falmouth Rd	11 O	10
Farber Dr	5 K	8
Farham La	10 O	11
Farm St	5 L	7
Farmers Av	5 K	9
Farmingdale Rd	4 G	10
Farragut Av	11 M	7
Farragut Pl	5 H	5
Farragut Rd	10 M	10
Faulkner Av	10 P	12
Federal Pl	5 G	7
Felix Pl	5 J	6
Fenimore Av	10 O	12
Fern Ter	11 N	8
Ferndale Ct	5 J	6
Ferraris St	5 H	7
Feustal St	5 K	9
Field St	4 J	11
Fillmore Av	10 Q	12
Finn Ct	4 H	13
Fir St	5 L	7
Fire Island Av	11 P	8
Fire Island Av S	11 P	7
Flanders Pl	11 M	10
Fleets Point Dr	11 N	8
Flint Rd	5 H	5
Floral Dr	5 G	9
Floral Pl	11 P	10
Florence Ct	11 P	9
Florida Av	5 H	7
Florida St	5 G	10
Florida St	10 P	14
Floyd St	10 P	12
Folkstone Rd	5 H	5
Foot Hill Pl	10 M	14
Fordham Rd	11 N	10
Forest Av	5 L	10
Forrest Pl	5 H	6
Forsyth Av	5 L	9
Forsythia La	10 Q	12
Foster Blvd	11 P	10
Foster Blvd N	11 P	10
Foster Blvd S	11 P	9
Foster La	11 O	8
Foxwood Dr	4 K	13
Frank St	5 K	8
Frankford Rd	11 M	9
Frankie La	10 O	11
Franklin Av	4 F	12
Franklin Av	11 P	8
Franklin St	5 G	6
Frederick Av	11 O	9
Freedom Ct	11 O	10
Freedom St	11 P	10
Fremont St	5 K	8
French Av	10 O	12
Friendly Ct	11 O	9
Frost La	5 G	6
Fuller Av	5 L	9
Fulton Pl	10 M	11
Fulton St	4 L	11
Fulton St	10 P	14
Gail Ct	10 P	13
Galvani St	5 H	7
Gamecock La N	11 O	8
Gamecock La S	11 O	8
Gamecock La W	11 O	7
Garden City Av	4 K	12
Garden Pl	5 K	8
Garden St	5 F	9
Garden St	5 J	6
Garfield Av	5 G	8
Garfield Av	5 J	7
Garfield Pl	11 M	7
Garibaldi Av	5 H	7
Garity Pl	4 F	11
Garnet St	10 O	12
Garrison Av	4 L	11
Gary Lagoon	5 J	5
Gary La	10 O	11
Gary St	5 K	8
Gateway Dr	5 J	6
Gaulton Dr	10 O	11
Gay-lore Dr S	5 H	6
Gay-lore Dr W	5 H	6
Gazza Blvd	4 G	12
Gear Av	5 J	10
Geiger Pl	10 M	13
Genoa St	10 M	11
Genova Ct	5 F	10
George Brown Plaza	5 H	6
George St (BV)	11 P	8
George St	4 F	12
Georgia Rd	5 J	6
Geraldine Av	5 F	9
Gibbs Rd	5 H	5
Gilbert Pl	5 H	8
Gladys St	5 J	9
Glasgow Av	10 O	14
Gleam St	4 J	11
Gleeland St	10 N	14
Glen La	5 J	6
Glen Rd	10 P	11
Glenda Dr	11 M	9
Glenda Rd	10 O	14
Glendale Rd	11 M	9
Glenmalure St	5 G	9
Glenn Ct	5 F	10
Gloucester Dr	4 L	14
Glynn St	10 N	11
Golden Av	10 O	13
Golding Av	5 L	9
Goodrich Av	10 O	12
Gordon Av	4 L	11
Goshen St	10 P	14
Governor Av	10 N	11
Grace Ct	5 G	6
Gracie Dr	10 P	12
Graham Pl	11 O	9
Granada Pkwy	11 M	7
Grand Av	5 G	10
Grand Av (LI)	5 L	9
Grand Blvd	10 M	13
Grand Central Av	5 H	5
Grant Av	5 G	8
Grant Av	5 J	6
Grant Av E	11 O	7
Grant Av W	11 O	7
Grant Pl	11 M	7
Grant St	5 G	9
Grant St	5 J	8
Great East Neck Rd	11 N	8
Great Neck Rd	5 G	9
Great Pl	11 M	6
Green Av	11 O	7
Green Lawn Ter	5 J	6
Green Wy S	11 N	8
Greene Av	5 G	7
Green-Meadow Dr	11 P	9
Greenmeadow Rd	10 Q	13
Greenway Ter	11 N	7
Greenwood Dr	10 P	11
Gregg Ct	10 N	13
Grenadon La	10 O	12
Grey Pl	4 L	11
Griffing Av	5 H	6
Grove Av	10 O	13
Grove Pl	11 O	8
Grove St	11 L	6
Guildford Park Dr	11 M	8
Guilette Pl	5 H	6
Gulf St	11 M	7
Gwynn St	11 O	9
Haab Av	11 N	9
Haas Av	10 P	13
Hadley Dr	4 L	14
Haight St	10 N	13
Hale Rd	10 P	11
Half Hollow Rd	10 N	14
Hall Ct	4 F	11
Halsey Pl	5 L	6
Hamilton Av	10 O	10
Hamilton St	5 G	6
Hamlin Av	4 L	11
Hampden Rd	5 J	6
Hampshire Dr	4 L	14
Hampton Pl	10 N	13
Hampton Rd	10 M	10
Hancock Pl	5 L	6
Harbor Ct	5 J	5
Harbor N	5 H	6
Harbor S	5 H	6
Harbour Rd	11 O	7
Harding Av	11 M	6
Harding Av	5 G	8
Harding Rd	5 J	5
Harding St	5 J	6
Harriet Rd	10 P	11
Harriman Av	10 M	13
Harrington Av	5 K	8
Harrison Av	5 G	8
Harrison Av	5 G	9
Harrison Av E	11 O	7
Harrison Av W	11 O	7
Harry St	4 L	12
Hartford St	5 K	8
Harvard Rd	11 O	10
Hatcher Ct	5 G	6
Havens Pl	10 P	10
Hawkins Blvd	5 J	7
Hawthorne Av	11 N	9
Hawthorne St	4 E	12
Hawthorne St	10 P	14
Hayes Rd	5 H	5
Heathcote Rd	5 K	9
Hedwig St	5 K	9
Hedwig St	5 L	9
Heling Blvd	5 L	8
Hemlock Av	10 N	13
Hemlock St	10 M	13
Hendel Cir	10 N	14
Henry Av	11 P	10
Henry St	11 M	8
Henry St	10 M	12
Herbert Av	5 L	7
Heritage La	10 M	14
Herman Av	10 P	12
Herzel Blvd	4 K	10
Hewlett Ct	11 P	8
Hiawatha Rd	11 P	7
Hickory St	4 F	12
Hickory St (LI)	5 L	7
Hickory St	10 M	12
Hickory St	10 P	12
Hicks St	5 H	10
Hidden Harbor Dr	11 O	7
Higgins St	10 N	11
Highland Pl	11 O	8
Highridge Rd	11 O	11
Highview Ct	4 K	13
Hildreth Ct	5 G	6
Hillside Rd	10 N	14
Hilltop Av	4 L	11
Hilltop La	4 L	14
Hinton Av	11 O	9
Hitherdell La	10 P	10
Hobart St	11 N	8
Hollings Dr	10 N	14
Holly Ct	10 O	12
Hollywood Av	5 H	7
Holmes Av	10 P	11
Holmes St	10 P	11
Holt St	5 H	10
Holy La	5 L	7
Homer Av	10 P	14
Homestead Av	5 G	6
Homestead Dr	4 K	13
Honeysuckle La	4 F	12
Hoover St	5 F	9
Hope St	11 N	8
Houston St	5 L	7
Howard Av	5 J	7
Howard St (BV)	11 P	9
Howard St	5 H	8
Howard St	10 M	13
Howell Av	10 M	13
Hoyt Pl	5 L	6
Hubbard's Pa	11 N	10
Hubbard's Path Av	10 N	10
Hudson St	5 J	8
Hughes La	10 O	11
Hughes St	10 N	11
Hunter Av	10 P	11
Hunter Ct	5 G	8
I Av	4 F	12
Ida Av	10 Q	14
Ida La	10 O	12
Idaho St	11 M	8
Iles Pl	5 H	8
Imola Pl	5 J	7
Independence Av	11 P	10
India Pl	5 J	5
Inlet Rd	5 K	6
Interlaken La	10 O	11
Ira Ct	5 G	8
Ireland Pl	11 N	9
Ireland Pl (AM)	5 G	7
Ireland Pl	5 H	6
Irene St	5 J	9
Irmisch Av	5 L	8
Iroquois St	10 P	15
Irving Av (LI)	5 L	7
Irving Av	10 M	13
Irving Av	10 P	11

Suffolk Co.

Town of Babylon / Town of Brookhaven

Suffolk Co.

STREET MAP GRID

David La (rk) 21 G1 18
David Overton Rd 27 Q1 21
David St 21 H1 18
David Terry St 32 F2 23
David Wy 28 S1 16
Davidia La 20 E1 25
Davids Wy 19 L1 30
Davidson Av 28 P1 15
Davidson Av (nb) 28 T1 15
Davis Av (PJ) 25 M1 27
Davis Av (bt) 28 N1 12
Davis Ct (sm) 20 E1 26
Davis Ct 25 P1 28
Davis La 25 O1 29
Dawn Dr (ya) 33 Z1 17
Dawn Dr (cr) 21 J1 22
Dawn Rd 25 W1 29
Dawnwood Dr 33 D2 18
Dawson Pl 26 R1 23
Day St 26 O1 25
Daylilly Ct 26 W1 24
Days Av 20 L1 22
Dayton Av (ps) 19 L1 27
Dayton Av (sm) 33 D2 21
Dayton Av (hv) 21 L1 18
Daytona Beach Pl 26 Q1 25
Dean La 20 E1 24
Dean St 20 L1 25
Dean St (mc) 33 C2 18
Dearborne Av 22 N1 15
Debbie Ct 20 G1 26
Debbie La 28 Q1 15
Debragga Av 38 L2 18
Decator Av 33 Y1 19
Deep Valley Dr 25 R1 30
Deepdale Dr 25 T1 29
Deer Av 26 S1 23
Deer Dr 25 S1 29
Deer La 38 J2 19
Deer La 20 K1 26
Deer Leep 32 Z1 24
Deer Meadow Run 34 W1 16
Deer Pa (BT) 19 K1 30
Deer Pa 34 A2 14
Deer Pa (co) 26 R1 24
Deer Pa 28 S1 16
Deera Ct 21 K1 19
Deerfield Ct (PJ) 19 M1 28
Deerfield Ct 38 J2 19
Deerfield Dr 31 B2 28
Deering Ct 28 R1 16
Deering St 19 G1 28
Defense Hill Rd 31 A2 28
Delaware Ct 26 P1 25
Dell Rd 34 C2 13
Delta Ct 27 L1 19
Dena Dr 23 M1 13
Denis La 26 R1 23
Denise Ct 20 M1 22
Denise Dr 28 S1 16
Dennis Dr 21 G1 18
Denton Pl 34 C2 17
Denton St 28 O1 15
Denver Ct 26 P1 24
Derbie Gate 21 L1 20
Derby Dr 20 E1 27
Dering Rd 25 R1 29
Derry St 28 S1 16
Detmer Rd 19 F1 27
Deville Dr 20 L1 24
Devoe Pl 33 B2 18
Devon Av (mf) 27 R1 19
Devon Av 21 K1 19
Devon La 26 R1 23
Devon Rd 25 R1 29
Dew Flag 32 Z1 24
Dewey St 25 M1 27
Dewitt Av 29 P1 12
Dexter St 33 B2 19
Dexter St (ns) 26 N1 23
Diamond St 21 F1 19
Diana Dr 34 B2 13
Diana Rd 34 B2 14
Diana Rd (sr) 31 W1 29
Diane Dr 33 F2 20
Diane La 38 L2 17
Dianne Av 21 G1 21
Dickerson Av 19 D1 27
Dickerson Ct 19 L1 28
Dickerson Dr 31 X1 29
Dietz Ct 29 N1 12
Dillon Av 20 M1 25
Diploma Pl 20 H1 24
Diplomat Dr 20 N1 22
Dipper Point Rd 29 Q1 13
Ditmas Av 34 D2 16
Division Av 20 M1 25
Division Av (PG) 23 N1 13
Division Rd (PG) 22 M1 14
Division Rd (rk) 21 G1 18
Division St (PJ) 19 K1 28
Division St (fv) 27 M1 19
Division St (pw) 24 F1 5
Division St 21 L1 19
Division St (PG) 28 O1 13
Dixie La 21 H1 20
Doane Av 26 O1 25
Doane Av (nb) 28 U1 15
Dock Ct 25 M1 29
Dock Rd 34 C2 13
Dock St 29 O1 12
Dockside Ct 34 D2 16
Dodge La 19 D1 28
Doe La 20 K1 24
Doe Pa 26 R1 24
Doe Pl 34 C2 13
Dogwood 38 G2 19
Dogwood Av 27 M1 19
Dogwood Dr 20 D1 27
Dogwood Dr (sn) 20 E1 25
Dogwood Hollow La 25 P1 29
Dogwood La 38 J2 19
Dogwood La (ps) 19 J1 28
Dogwood La (ya) 27 U1 21
Dogwood La (PG) 22 N1 14
Dogwood La (mp) 25 P1 29
Dogwood La (PG) 28 Q1 13
Dogwood Rd (PJ) 19 L1 28
Dogwood Rd (sn) 20 E1 27
Dogwood Rd (mb) 34 C2 13
Dogwood Rd (rp) 25 V1 29
Dogwood Rd W 34 B2 13
Dolphin Dr 20 K1 22
Domino Wa 21 K1 22
Domino Wy 26 Q1 26
Don La 20 L1 23
Don St 29 T1 13
Dona La 21 J1 20
Donack La 28 T1 14
Donald Av 27 V1 20
Donald Ct E 29 N1 11
Donald Ct W 29 M1 11
Donald St 20 K1 26
Donald St (hb) 21 H1 18
Donald St 38 L2 19
Donegan Av 29 T1 13
Donegan Av 28 T1 15
Donella Wk 30 P1 7
Dongan Blvd 33 D2 18
Donna Ct (sn) 20 G1 26
Donna Ct (ns) 20 L1 22
Donna Ct 21 L1 19
Donna La 21 H1 17
Donwood Av 20 K1 23
Doolings Pa 20 G1 27
Dor Wy 21 H1 20
Dora Rd 31 X1 28
Doradell Dr 21 J1 19
Dorado Ct 26 S1 22
Doral La 27 U1 19
Dorchester Ct 21 L1 20
Dorchester Dr 26 O1 23
Dorchester Rd 21 G1 20
Doris Av 19 M1 27
Doris Dr 34 B2 14
Doris Tr 32 C2 27
Dorm Ct 20 H1 25
Dorn Pl 20 K1 23
Dorothy St 20 J1 26
Dorset Dr 26 N1 26
Dorsett Pl 34 Z1 17
Dorwich 25 S1 29
Dougbeth Dr 21 H1 18
Douglas La 33 C2 20
Douglas St (mp) 25 S1 28
Douglas St (tv) 26 M1 26
Douglaston Ct 32 Y1 27
Douglaston Rd 25 S1 29
Douglaston St 34 D2 17
Dourland Rd 27 S1 21
Dove Pa 26 R1 24
Dove Rd 26 U1 24
Dover Av 34 C2 16
Dover Cir 32 Y1 25
Dover Dr 26 Q1 25
Dover Pl 33 C2 18
Dover St 33 C2 17
Down Ct 28 S1 16
Doyle Ct (BT) 19 M1 29
Doyle Ct (LG) 20 F1 22
Drake Av 28 T1 16
Drake Rd 20 H1 23
Dreamland St 33 B2 18
Dressel Dr 33 B2 17
Drew Dr 20 E1 23
Drew La 34 F2 16
Drexel St 27 M1 20
Drexelgate Ct 26 V1 24
Driftwood Ct 31 Y1 30
Driftwood La (ps) 19 H1 26
Driftwood La 38 L2 17
Driftwood Wk (fp) 24 K1 6
Driftwood Wk 30 P1 7
Drudy La 34 B2 14
Druid Hill Rd 19 K1 30
Drumlin Ct 28 O1 17
Drury Ct 21 L1 19
Dryad Rd 31 W1 28
Dryden Av 27 Q1 22
Duane Dr 21 G1 18
Dubon Rd 39 G2 16
Duchess St 31 Y1 29
Duck Rd 26 N1 23
Ducky La 34 B2 13
Duffield Rd 26 P1 23
Duke Ct 21 L1 20
Duke St 21 L1 20
Dumond Pl 26 Q1 22
Dunbar Av 27 T1 21
Duncan Av 21 H1 19
Dundalk Rd 33 D2 18
Dune Ct 19 D1 28
Dune Rd 39 N2 15
Dune Wk 30 Q1 7
Dunton Av (mf) 27 S1 18
Dunton Av 28 S1 15
Durkee La 29 R1 13
Durst Dr 21 L1 22
Duryea Wk 24 H1 5
Dusk Dr 20 H1 22
Dutch Ct 28 S1 16
Dyckes Ct 20 M1 26
Dyer's Ct 19 H1 29
Dyke Rd 19 F1 29
Dyke St 20 J1 24
Dynasty Dr 32 Y1 26
Eagle Av 27 R1 19
Eagle Dr 32 X1 23
Eagle Hill Ct 26 V1 24
Eagle La 33 E2 21
Eagle Rd 25 V1 28
Eagle St (sd) 27 W1 20
Eagle St 28 S1 13
Eagles Landing Rd 25 N1 29
Earl St 26 R1 27
Eason Dr 32 W1 22
East 2nd St (PG) 28 N1 14
East 2nd St (BP) 28 U1 13
East 3rd St (BP) 28 U1 13
East 3th St (PG) 28 N1 14
East 4th St (PG) 28 N1 14
East 4th St (BP) 28 U1 14
East 5th Av 33 C2 22
East 5th Av 32 A2 22
East 5th St (PG) 28 N1 14
East 6th St 28 N1 14
East Av 33 W1 18
East Bartlett Rd 26 T1 22
East Broadway 19 K1 28
East Carpenter Dr 27 T1 20
East Chapman Blvd 38 H2 19
East End Rd 25 U1 29
East Gate 19 L1 29
East Gate Dr 25 N1 28
East Gate La 19 E1 29
East Hope Ct 20 M1 23
East Kennedy Dr 20 K1 23
East Lake Ter 21 F1 19
East Locust Av 38 L2 18
East Loop Rd 20 F1 25
East Main St (PJ) 19 K1 28
East Main St (ya) 33 W1 19
East Main St 38 K2 17
East Main St (PG) 28 P1 14
East Margin Rd 32 B2 25
East Masem Sq 28 T1 14
East Midland Pond Ct 34 E2 16
East Moriches Sta 38 K2 17
East Moriches Sta (Railroad Av) 38 J2 17
East Moriches-Riverhead Rd 38 K2 18
East Moriches-Riverhead Rd 38 M2 21
East Shore Dr 28 N1 15
East Stonehurst Cir 20 J1 22
East St (nc) 20 J1 23
East St 33 Y1 22
East St (mi) 26 S1 23
East St (SR) 31 Y1 28
East St 31 Z1 27
East View Dr 25 R1 30
East Wk (cg) 24 H1 5
East Wk (wi) 30 N1 7
East Wk (dp) 30 P1 7
Eastbourne Cir 28 R1 15
Eastbourne Ct 32 Y1 26
Easterly Ct 38 G2 21
Easton St 21 F1 17
Eastport Dr 25 S1 29
Eastport La 38 L2 20
Eastport Manor Rd (mv) 32 F2 22
Eastport Manor Rd 38 H2 22
Eastport Manor Rd 38 J2 21
Eastwood Blvd 20 J1 23
Eastwood Rd 25 P1 29
Eaton La 20 H1 23
Eatondale Av 23 M1 13
Ebon La 26 O1 23
Echo Av 25 P1 28
Echo Rd 31 W1 29
Ecke Av 28 U1 14
Eden Dr 20 E1 26
Edenville-Patchogue Rd 28 M1 14
Edgar Av 34 W1 13
Edgewater Dr 34 E2 14
Edgewood Av (ps) 19 L1 27
Edgewood Av (ps) 19 M1 28
Edgewood Av (fv) 27 N1 19
Edgewood Rd (PJ) 19 M1 28
Edgewood St 34 D2 16
Edieann Ct 26 P1 24
Edinburgh Dr 32 Y1 25
Edith Ct 20 M1 24
Edna La 20 M1 24
Edward Av 28 R1 17
Edward St 21 H1 21
Edwards Dr 35 Z1 12
Edwards La 29 M1 11
Edwards La E 29 M1 12
Edwards Rd 34 B2 14
Edwards St (cm) 34 F2 16
Edwards St (PG) 28 P1 14
Edwin Av 28 Q1 16
Edwin St 20 H1 23
Egret Pa 26 R1 24
Egret Wy 34 E2 16
Eileen Ct (mf) 27 R1 18
Eileen Ct (co) 26 O1 22
Eileen Dr 21 H1 17
Eileen La 38 F2 19
Eisenhower Rd 20 K1 23
Elaine St 27 M1 20
Elan La 21 K1 18
Elberson Av 19 G1 28
El Camino Ct 26 P1 24
Elder Av 27 M1 20
Elder Dr 34 B2 13
Elder Duck Wk 30 O1 7
Eleanor Av 34 C2 16
Electric St 28 O1 13
Elfin Pl 34 C2 13
Elgin Pl 29 R1 12
Elgin St 33 B2 19
Elinor St 21 H1 21
Elizabeth Ct 20 M1 24
Elizabeth La 20 L1 25
Elizabeth Pl 39 G2 16
Elizabeth St 28 P1 13
Elizabeth Wy 32 A2 24
Elk La 20 K1 24
Elkin Dr 26 W1 23
Elkwood St 20 F1 22
Ellen Ct 20 G1 22
Ellen Dr 25 M1 28
Ellen La 38 H2 19
Elliot Av 20 G1 22
Elliot St 33 C2 18
Ellis Ct 26 O1 24
Ellsworth Av 28 N1 15
Elm Av 26 N1 24
Elm Ct 25 M1 28
Elm La 20 E1 25
Elm Pl 33 C2 17
Elm Rd (BP) 29 T1 13
Elm Rd (mb) 34 C2 13
Elm Rd (rp) 25 T1 28
Elm Rd (rp) 25 V1 29
Elm Rd W 34 A2 13
Elm St 20 J1 26
Elm St (ps) 20 L1 26
Elm St (PJ) 25 M1 27
Elm St (mp) 25 S1 27
Elm St (rk) 21 G1 17
Elm St (fc) 21 G1 20
Elm St (sc) 21 H1 19
Elm St (PG) 28 Q1 13
Elmer St 28 O1 16
Elmhurst Av 27 P1 17
Elmhurst Rd 25 S1 29
Elms La 31 B2 28
Elmwood Av 27 M1 21
Elsie St 28 O1 15
Elwood Rd 20 J1 23
Ely La 20 D1 27
Embasy Rd 26 N1 22
Emener Av 38 L2 18
Emerald Ct 34 D2 17
Emerald St 21 F1 19
Emerson Rd 35 A2 13
Emerson St 19 J1 28
Emery Av 21 G1 21
Emiley Av 27 N1 21
Emily Ct 34 E2 17
Emily Ct 28 Q1 17
Emily Dr 20 H1 23
Emlu Dr 21 L1 21
Enchanted Woods Ct 25 O1 29
Enfield Ct 32 Y1 26
Engineering Dr 20 E1 25
Engleke St 28 O1 16
English Ivy La 20 G1 23
Enterprise Ct 19 J1 27
Entrance Dr 20 F1 26
Eos Rd 31 W1 29
Epson Course 34 V1 14
Equestrian Ct (sn) 20 D1 26
Equestrian Ct 21 K1 20
Equestrian Wy 34 X1 17
Equity Ct 26 P1 25
Eric Dr 26 T1 23
Erica Dr 20 L1 25
Erie Ct 25 R1 28
Erie St (tv) 20 M1 25
Erie St (ob) 24 D1 4
Erie St 26 N1 22
Erik Dr 20 J1 26
Erin La 20 J1 25
Erland Av 13 D1 27
Ermine Rd 25 V1 29
Erna Dr 26 R1 22
Esplanade Dr 29 S1 13
Essex Cir 34 A2 16
Essex Dr (co) 26 O1 23
Essex Dr 21 K1 18
Estate Dr 34 D2 15
Estate Dr (mp) 25 S1 28
Estate La 34 F2 16
Estates Dr 26 O1 25
Estates La 31 Y1 28
Esther Ct (cr) 21 K1 22
Esther Ct 28 P1 15
Ethan Allen Ct 32 X1 24
Ethan Cir 26 T1 24
Ethan La 21 G1 19
Ethel La 27 R1 21
Ethel Pl 28 O1 16
Ethel St 28 Q1 15
Etna Pl 34 C2 17
Eton Dr 26 N1 26
Eton Rd 27 L1 20
Euclid Av 27 Q1 18
Euclid Rd 38 K2 18
Eva La 21 K1 19
Evans Ct 19 F1 30
Evans La (OF) 19 F1 30
Evans La 25 P1 28
Evans La (sc) 21 L1 20
Evans Pl 19 J1 28
Evans St (PG) 22 N1 15
Evans St 26 Q1 25
Eve Ann Dr 20 K1 25
Evelyn Ct 38 G2 21
Evelyn La 21 H1 21
Evelyn Rd 20 M1 25
Everett Dr (ya) 27 V1 20
Everett Dr 28 O1 15
Everett St 21 H1 21
Everglades La 26 P1 24
Evergreen Av (ns) 20 M1 23
Evergreen Av (mi) 26 S1 24
Evergreen Av (PG) 28 P1 14
Evergreen Av (em) 38 L2 17
Evergreen Av 28 R1 17
Evergreen Dr 38 H2 20
Evergreen La 29 R1 13
Evergreen Rd 25 V1 29
Executive Rd 20 L1 24
Exeter Dr 20 N1 26
Exeter Rd 28 R1 15
Exmore Ct 32 Y1 26
Express Dr N 21 J1 18
Express Dr S 27 M1 18
Faculty La 21 K1 18
Fair Harbor Dr 29 O1 13
Fairbanks St 26 P1 26
Fairfax Dr 26 O1 23
Fairfax Dr (sc) 21 K1 19
Fairfax Rd 28 R1 15
Fairfield Manor Dr 33 F2 19
Fairlane Dr 20 L1 23
Fairlawn Ct 35 A2 12
Fairlawn La 20 J1 23
Fairmont Av 27 P1 20
Fairview Av (co) 27 Q1 20
Fairview Av (np) 22 N1 16
Fairview Av (mp) 25 Q1 30
Fairview Cir 26 U1 23
Fairview Dr 35 A2 13
Fairview St 33 B2 18
Fairway Dr (BT) 19 L1 30
Fairway Dr (ss) 20 H1 23
Fairway Dr 20 K1 25
Fairway Dr (rp) 25 U1 28
Fairway Dr (mi) 26 T1 23
Fairway Dr 38 H2 20
Fairway Dr (nb) 28 T1 14
Fairwood La 26 O1 22
Falcon Av 20 L1 24
Falcon Av (mf) 27 R1 18
Falcon Ct 27 N1 20
Falcon Rd 25 V1 28
Falmouth Ct (ms) 25 P1 26
Falmouth Ct (ri) 31 Y1 26
Falmouth Dr 25 P1 26
Fannie Dr 21 M1 18
Fanny Landing Av 34 D2 17
Farah Ct 25 R1 28
Farber Dr 28 T1 16
Fargo Ct 26 P1 24
Farm Ct 21 M1 18
Farm House Ct 25 O1 28
Farm Rd (PJ) 19 M1 29
Farm Rd 31 Y1 29
Farmers Av 27 P1 22
Farmhouse Ct 33 F2 22
Farmingdale Av 25 S1 28
Farner Av 20 L1 23
Farnham Pl 20 N1 24
Farragut Ct 26 P1 25
Farrell St 38 K2 21
Farvo Ct 27 N1 19
Fawn Ct 20 M1 25
Fawn La 20 K1 24
Fawn La E 20 K1 25
Fawn La N 20 K1 25
Fawn La W 20 K1 24
Fawn Meadow Pa Rd 31 B2 28
Fawn Pl (sh) 34 A2 13
Fawn Pl (mb) 34 C2 13
Feather Pa 34 E2 16
Federal La 26 P1 25
Felway Dr 26 O1 24
Fenwick Av 21 K1 19
Fern Dr 21 H1 19
Fern Rd 25 V1 29
Ferndale Av (sd) 27 M1 21
Ferndale Av (sb) 25 R1 29
Ferndale Rd 25 T1 30
Ferret La 19 J1 27
Ferrick Av 27 Q1 17
Ficus Rd 31 W1 29
Ficus St 26 O1 26
Field Ct 25 Q1 28
Fieldhouse Av 20 H1 24
Fieldstone Ct 26 V1 24
Fiesta Ct 28 O1 16
Fiesta Dr 20 L1 24
Fife Dr 26 R1 22
Fife La 26 Q1 26
Filmore Av 26 O1 22
Fine Arts Dr 20 F1 26
Fine Arts Loop 20 F1 26
Firdale St 21 J1 20
Fire Av 27 R1 19
Fire Island Beach Rd 35 Z1 11
Fire Island Blvd 24 K1 6
Fire Place La 34 W1 14
Fireplace Av 28 U1 14
Fireplace Neck Rd 34 W1 15
Fireside La 20 J1 25
First Wk 30 P1 7
Firwood Dr 21 K1 20
Fish Rd 31 X1 28
Fish Thicket Rd 28 R1 16
Fishermans Cove 25 N1 28
Fishermans Pa 24 L1 6
Fitzgerald Rd 31 X1 29
Flagpole La 19 H1 27
Flair Wy 26 N1 22
Flamingo Rd 25 V1 29
Flanders Ct 32 Y1 27
Flanders Rd 25 S1 29
Flax Pond Woods Rd 19 E1 29
Fleet Rd 34 A2 16
Fleetwood Dr 27 O1 19
Flicker Dr 26 U1 23
Flint Ct 20 H1 26
Flint La 26 O1 22
Flintlock Dr 34 A2 15
Flintlock La 26 M1 24
Flora Dr 26 P1 25
Floradora Dr 33 A2 19
Floral Av 21 L1 18
Floral Ct 35 B2 12
Floral Rd 25 S1 30
Floral Rd 31 V1 29
Floral Wk 24 L1 6
Florence Ct 28 Q1 16
Florence Dr 38 F2 20
Florence Pl (PG) 29 S1 13
Florence Pl 39 G2 18
Florence Rd 20 K1 26
Florence St (cr) 21 G1 22
Florence St 28 Q1 15
Florence St 28 S1 13
Flores La 26 S1 22
Florida Av 27 Q1 18
Florida Rd 25 V1 29
Flower Av 27 N1 18
Flower Field Rd 25 S1 29
Flower Hill Dr 33 Y1 19
Flower Hill Dr E 33 Z1 19
Flower La 20 J1 23
Flower Pl 34 B2 13
Flower Rd 34 B2 13
Floyd Bennett Dr 25 R1 29
Floyd Rd 34 A2 16
Floyd Rd N 34 B2 16
Floyd Rd S 34 B2 14
Flushing Rd 25 S1 29
Flushing St 21 L1 18
Folsom La 26 O1 22
Fordham Av 27 P1 18
Fordham Rd 31 Y1 29
Fordham St 28 O1 13
Forest Av (LG) 20 F1 22
Forest Av 20 K1 26
Forest Av (fv) 27 M1 20
Forest Av (mf) 27 P1 18
Forest Av (sa) 34 X1 17
Forest Ct 20 H1 23
Forest Dr 20 F1 25
Forest La 26 R1 23
Forest Rd 20 H1 23
Forest Rd (mb) 34 D2 13
Forest Rd (rp) 25 V1 29
Forest Rd W 34 B2 13
Forest Tr 32 B2 26
Forest View Dr 21 F1 18
Foreston Cir 33 E2 20
Forge La 20 N1 22
Forest Ct 28 U1 15
Forrest Av (sa) 33 Z1 18
Forrest Av (fc) 21 G1 21
Forrestall Dr 33 A2 19
Forsythe Meadow La 20 D1 26
Forsythia Ct 28 N1 17
Forsythia Ct 25 R1 27
Forte Av 28 T1 17
Foster Ct 34 E2 17
Foster Rd 21 G1 18
Fountain Av 20 L1 23
Fountain Rd 31 W1 29
Four Winds Rd 19 F1 29
Fourth Wk 30 P1 7
Fowler Av 21 G1 18
Fowler La 25 N1 28
Fox Cir 33 E2 18
Fox Ct 33 F2 22
Fox Hill Pl 27 N1 21
Fox Hill Rd 19 E1 27
Fox Hollow Dr 34 A2 14
Fox Hollow La 32 W1 23
Fox Hollow Rd 20 G1 26
Fox Hunt La 27 T1 19
Fox La 31 Z1 28
Fox Pa 26 R1 24
Fox Pl 27 N1 18
Fox Rd (sn) 20 G1 26
Fox Rd (mi) 26 S1 23
Foxboro Av 27 N1 20
Foxcroft La 28 R1 15
Foxcroft St 33 B2 18
Foxdale La 19 J1 28
Foxglove Ct 27 O1 17
Foxhunt La 20 F1 25
Fradelos St 25 N1 27
Framingham Rd 31 X1 27
Fran La 21 L1 21
Frances Blvd 21 L1 19
Frances La 19 L1 29
Frances Pa 25 U1 29
Frances St 27 M1 19
Francine La 19 H1 27
Francine Pl 34 A2 17
Francis Landau Pl 34 B2 15
Francis Mooney 32 Z1 24
Francis St 20 H1 26
Franco Av 20 L1 23
Frank Av 27 V1 20
Frank Av (mi) 26 S1 23
Frank Ct 39 L2 17
Frank St 29 R1 13
Franklin Av (sn) 20 G1 25
Franklin Av (ns) 20 L1 23
Franklin Av (mf) 27 P1 18
Franklin Av (mr) 33 C2 17
Franklin Commons 33 X1 21
Franklin Ct 33 B2 17
Franklin Rd 25 S1 29
Franklin St (PJ) 19 L1 28
Franklin St 26 Q1 25
Franko La 20 H1 27
Fraternity La 20 E1 24
Frederick St 31 Y1 29
Fredericksburg Ct 26 P1 25
Fredrick Ct 20 L1 26
Freedom La 26 N1 22
Freemont La 26 N1 22
Freestate Dr 33 Z1 20
Fresh Pond Rd 25 S1 28
Freshman La 20 E1 24
Freya Rd 25 W1 29
Friar Cir 26 N1 22
Friar Tuck La 20 H1 26
Friends St 19 E1 28
Friendship Dr 31 W1 29
Frontier Tr 33 G2 21
Frost La 31 B2 28
Frost Valley Dr 28 S1 16
Frost Valley Rd 31 M1 28
Frowein Rd 34 F2 17
Fruita St 19 K1 27
Fry Blvd 28 N1 15
Fuller Dr 32 W1 22
Fulton Av (mc) 33 C2 18
Fulton St 19 M1 27
Fulton St 21 H1 21
Funard Ct 28 O1 13
Fuoco La 28 T1 14
Furman Av 29 S1 13
Furman La 29 O1 13
Furrow Pl 25 Q1 28
Fury Dr 20 L1 23
Gables Blvd 19 H1 27
Gabon La 26 O1 24
Gabriel Mills Rd 31 B2 28
Gaetano Ct 26 O1 23
Gaetano La 26 O1 23
Gail Dr 21 G1 18
Gaines Dr 21 K1 19
Galaxie La 27 M1 21
Gale Ct 29 P1 13
Gale La 28 Q1 15
Galleon La 20 H1 26
Gallo Ct 20 H1 26
Galloway Ct 20 G1 23
Game Ct 20 J1 25
Game La 20 J1 25
Garden Av (sn) 19 E1 27
Garden Av 25 Q1 30
Garden Ct 20 L1 26
Garden Gate Ct 26 V1 24
Garden La 20 J1 23
Garden La 27 U1 20
Garden Pl 34 B2 17
Garden Rd (sb) 25 S1 29
Garden Rd (rp) 25 V1 29
Garden St 21 H1 20
Gardenia Ct 28 O1 17
Gardenia Rd (rp) 25 V1 29
Gardenia Rd 26 P1 26
Gardiners Rd 25 R1 29
Garfield Av 27 O1 22
Garland Rd 31 W1 29
Garrity Av 21 G1 17
Garwood St 20 H1 22
Gary Dr 27 O1 19
Gary Pl 26 M1 23
Gary St 20 L1 25
Gaslight Rd 20 D1 26
Gate Dr 26 O1 24
Gate, The 38 L2 20
Gatelot Av 21 G1 19
Gates Av 26 O1 25
Gateway Blvd 28 M1 15
Gateway Ct 21 K1 22
Gateway Dr 31 B2 28
Gateway La 38 G2 20
Gaton Ct 26 O1 24
Gaton La 26 O1 24
Gauguin Ct 26 V1 23
Gaul Rd N 19 F1 29
Gaul Rd S 19 F1 29
Gayle Ct 20 L1 26
Gaymor La 21 K1 20
Gaymore Rd 20 L1 27
Gaynor St 20 G1 23
Gazebo Dr 27 M1 18
Gazzola Dr 28 S1 15
Geery Av 21 J1 19
General McLean Dr 29 U1 13
Georgann Rd 38 H2 19
George Av 31 Y1 28
George Ct 29 U1 13
George Ct (mp) 25 O1 29
George Dr 34 B2 17
George Hill Rd 25 P1 28
George St (PJ) 19 M1 27
George St 29 T1 13
George St (FC) 21 G1 20
George Link Cir 26 Q1 23
Georgia Av 21 G1 20
Georgian Ct 26 P1 25
Georgiapine Pl 28 R1 17
Gerald Dr 21 J1 19
Gerard St 29 U1 13
Gerard St (PG) 28 O1 14
Gerard Wk 24 H1 5
German Blvd 27 U1 20
Gerrard Rd (ya) 27 V1 19
Gerri La 28 R1 16
Gerta Ct 26 M1 23
Gettysburg Ct 26 Q1 25
Giant Oak Rd 32 X1 23
Gibbons St 28 N1 14
Gibbs Rd 26 P1 24
Gilbert St 29 O1 13
Gillespie Pa 34 W1 15
Gillette Av 28 O1 15
Gina Ct 28 Q1 15
Ginger Ct 21 G1 21
Ginny Ct 33 F2 20
Girald Dr 33 A2 19
Girard St 20 J1 24
Givin La 26 Q1 24
Glacier Lake Ct 26 Q1 25
Glades Rd, The 29 N1 12
Gladeview Ct 28 O1 17
Gladiola St 28 P1 15
Gladys St 27 N1 21
Glatter La 20 J1 23
Glen Ct 20 D1 26
Glen Dr (ey) 33 Z1 20
Glen Dr 32 Y1 27
Glen Dr (fc) 21 G1 20
Glen Hill Ct 31 Y1 29
Glen Hollow Dr (tv) 20 N1 25
Glen Hollow Dr (np) 22 M1 16
Glen St 20 J1 24
Glen Wy 20 M1 23
Glendale Av 28 O1 15
Glenmere La 26 O1 25
Glenn Av 21 K1 18
Glenn St 25 R1 27
Glenridge Av 20 F1 24
Glenwater La 19 E1 28
Glenwood Av 25 Q1 29
Glenwood La 19 J1 28
Glenwood Pl 20 E1 24
Glenwood Rd (sb) 25 S1 29
Glenwood Rd 25 T1 29
Glenwood St 29 Q1 13
Gloria Rd 38 H2 19
Glover St 33 W1 18
Gnarled Hollow Rd 19 G1 28
Gnarled Oak Dr 20 G1 26
Golden Gate Ct 34 Z1 13
Golden Gate Dr 34 Z1 13
Golden Gate La 34 Z1 13
Goldie La 26 O1 22
Golf Club Cir 38 H2 21
Golf Course Rd 29 T1 13
Golf La 27 P1 20
Goodwin La 26 O1 24
Gooseberry Rd 35 B2 13
Gooseberry Rd (rp) 25 V1 29
Gordal La 26 O1 24
Gordon Av 27 S1 21
Gordon St 38 K2 21
Gores Dr 33 B2 17
Gotham Ct 26 P1 27
Gothic Cir 33 F2 22
Gould Rd 21 H1 22
Grace Ct 39 G2 16
Grace Ct (sc) 21 J1 19
Grace Gate 32 B2 24
Grace La 26 O1 26
Grace St 20 K1 24
Grace's Wy 21 H1 22
Graduate Ct 20 H1 25
Grady La 26 P1 23
Graham Ct 25 O1 30
Granada Cir 26 Q1 26
Grand Av 34 A2 17
Grand Av (PJ) 25 M1 27
Grand Av (np) 28 O1 16
Grand Canyon La 26 P1 25
Grand Oak Av 33 Z1 18
Grand Offenbach St 21 G1 20
Grand Simth Rd 27 Q1 21
Grand View Dr (bt) 29 N1 12
Grand View Dr 34 Z1 12
Grandview Blvd 25 Q1 30
Granny Rd (hv) 27 N1 18
Granny Rd (co) 27 R1 21
Grant Av 27 O1 22
Grant Ct 27 Q1 22
Grant Pl 28 P1 14
Grant St (PJ) 19 K1 28
Grant St (mc) 33 B2 18
Grant St (PJ) 25 M1 27
Grant St (SR) 31 W1 28
Grapevine Wy 38 L2 20
Grassland Cir 25 O1 28
Grassmere Dr 34 D2 16
Grassy Knoll 31 C2 28
Gravin St 26 O1 24
Gray Av 27 S1 22
Great River Dr 25 R1 29
Green Av 28 N1 15
Green Ct (SR) 31 B2 29
Green Ct 38 G2 19
Green Pl 20 H1 23
Green Ter 32 W1 23
Green Wk 24 H1 5
Green, The 34 A2 15
Greenbriar Ct 27 S1 22
Greenbriar Ct (mp) 28 O1 17
Greenbrier Av 21 K1 19
Greencrest St 20 F1 23
Greendale La 21 G1 21
Greene Av 20 M1 25
Greenhaven Dr 20 L1 26
Greenlawn Pl 27 N1 19
Greenlawn Rd 25 R1 29
Greenleaf Rd 25 T1 29
Greenmist Dr 21 H1 18
Greenport Av 28 P1 17
Greentree Av 27 M1 20
Greentree Dr 27 T1 20
Greenvale Rd 25 S1 29
Greenway Dr 25 U1 28
Greenway Dr (mi) 26 T1 22
Greenway Ter 20 F1 22
Greenwich Ct 32 X1 27
Greenwood Blvd 38 G2 19
Greg St 28 S1 16
Gregg Dr 26 O1 24
Gregory Ct 21 K1 19
Gregory Dr 21 G1 18
Grendon La 21 K1 20
Grenville Av 29 O1 13
Gridley Rd 31 X1 29
Griffen Dr 26 P1 25
Griffin Ct 25 O1 29
Grist Ct 25 P1 30
Grist Mill La 25 P1 29
Grosvenor La 25 P1 28
Groton Dr 26 N1 26
Groton La 26 O1 24
Grouse La 20 H1 26
Grouse Pa 26 R1 24
Grove Av 29 P1 13
Grove Av (sr) 33 E2 20
Grove Av (co) 26 P1 24
Grove Dr 33 A2 18
Grove Rd (mb) 34 D2 14
Grove Rd (mb) 35 C2 13
Grove Rd 25 V1 29

Suffolk Co.

STREET	MAP	GRID
Grove St	20	K1 26
Grove St (cm)	34	F2 16
Grove St (PJ)	25	N1 26
Grove St (mp)	25	S1 27
Grove St	38	J2 19
Groveland Park Blvd	25	S1 29
Grover St	33	Z1 21
Grucci La	28	V1 17
Guardian Ct	26	P1 26
Guardian Dr	26	P1 26
Guilford Ct	32	Y1 26
Gulf La	26	P1 24
Gull Av	27	R1 19
Gull Dip St	32	A2 24
Gully Landing Rd	25	Q1 30
Gun Pa	19	G1 29
Gunter Pl	34	C2 17
Gymnasium Rd	20	E1 26
Hackberry La	21	J1 18
Hackensack Rd	35	A2 13
Haddon Ct	21	G1 21
Haddon Hollow Ct	32	V1 24
Hadley Ct	20	F1 24
Hagen Ct	26	R1 23
Hagerman Av (co)	27	S1 19
Hagerman Av	28	S1 13
Hagerman Landing Rd	25	T1 30
Haig Av	28	S1 16
Haiti La	26	O1 23
Hale La	26	O1 22
Hale St	26	O1 24
Halesite Dr	25	R1 29
Halewood Dr	34	A2 14
Half Hollow Rd	27	O1 22
Half Mile Rd	20	L1 25
Half Mile Rd (mi)	26	R1 24
Half Moon Rd	32	Z1 24
Halfcircle Dr	21	J1 18
Hall St	20	K1 25
Hallet Ct	29	N1 12
Hallett Av	19	K1 28
Halliday Rd	26	P1 23
Hallock Av (PJ)	19	M1 27
Hallock Av	32	F2 22
Hallock Ct	25	Q1 29
Hallock Landing Rd	25	U1 28
Hallock La (SR)	25	U1 30
Hallock La	39	G2 16
Hallock Meadow Ct N	20	E1 23
Hallock Meadow Ct S	20	E1 23
Hallock Meadow Ct W	20	E1 23
Hallock Rd (LG)	20	F1 22
Hallock Rd	28	P1 15
Hallowell La	26	O1 23
Halsey Av	26	N1 25
Halsey Manor Rd	38	H2 22
Halsey St	20	K1 25
Halston La	26	O1 21
Hamilton Ct	26	O1 23
Hamilton Rd	20	G1 25
Hamilton Rd (sn)	34	C2 14
Hamilton St (mc)	33	B2 18
Hamilton St	39	G2 17
Hamilton St (np)	28	N1 15
Hammond La	21	G1 22
Hammond Rd	20	K1 23
Hammond St	28	O1 14
Hampshire Wy	20	F1 23
Hampton Av	29	S1 12
Hampton Av (sh)	34	B2 16
Hampton Av (nb)	28	T1 15
Hampton Ct (mr)	34	E2 17
Hampton Ct (co)	26	P1 25
Hampton Ct	38	G2 20
Hampton Dr	34	E2 16
Hampton Rd (sh)	35	A2 12
Hampton Rd	26	R1 29
Hampton Vistas Dr	38	J2 19
Hampton Wy	25	Y1 25
Hancock Commons	33	X1 20
Hancock Ct	26	P1 25
Hancock Pl	25	P1 29
Hancock St	26	O1 25
Handsome Av	27	M1 22
Handy La	28	S1 16
Haney Ct	38	G2 21
Hannibal Ct	20	G1 25
Hanover Pl	27	R1 17
Hanrahan Av	27	M1 19
Hans Blvd	21	H1 19
Hansen Av	20	L1 25
Hansom La	19	H1 28
Hanson St	26	R1 24
Hanson Wy	26	O1 23
Happyacre Dr	34	A2 15
Harbor Beach Rd	25	M1 30
Harbor Ct	25	N1 29
Harbor Hill Rd	19	G1 28
Harbor Hills Dr	19	L1 29
Harbor Rd	13	D1 26
Harbor Rd (sb)	25	R1 29
Harbor View Rd	20	E1 26
Harbor Wk	24	K1 6
Harborside Ct	29	Q1 13
Harborview Av	19	K1 27
Harborview Ct	34	D2 17
Harborview Pl	39	G2 16
Harborview Rd	19	K1 29
Harding Rd	34	X1 15
Harding Rd (lr)	21	F1 19
Harding St	31	W1 29
Hare La	20	J1 27
Harford Dr	26	O1 23
Hargrave La	26	R1 23
Hargrove Dr	20	F1 24
Harlem Av	28	P1 16
Harmon Ct	20	F1 24
Harmony Dr	26	O1 25
Harmony La	19	J1 28
Harmony St	38	F2 22
Harness Ct	34	Y1 17
Harnett Dr	26	Q1 27
Harold Av	28	N1 14
Harold Rd	33	W1 20
Harper St	28	O1 16
Harriet St	21	G1 22
Harris St	28	O1 15
Harrison Av (nc)	20	K1 23
Harrison Av (mp)	25	S1 28
Harrison Av (co)	26	O1 22
Harrison Av	28	T1 16
Harrison Commons	33	X1 21
Harrison Ct	27	Q1 21
Harrison Dr	35	A2 13
Harrison St (PG)	29	P1 13
Harrison St (fc)	21	H1 19
Harrison St (SR)	31	W1 28
Hart La	20	K1 24
Hart Pl	33	C2 17
Hart St	20	L1 25
Harts Rd	38	J2 18
Hartsdale La	26	O1 23
Hartwell Dr	26	O1 27
Harvard Pl	29	S1 13
Harvard Rd	31	Y1 29
Harvard St	20	L1 25
Harvey La (BT)	19	K1 30
Harvey La	21	H1 18
Harwick La	20	F1 24
Harwood Wy	26	O1 23
Haskel Ct	20	F1 25
Haskel La	20	F1 25
Haspel La	27	M1 18
Hastings Dr (sn)	20	F1 25
Hastings Dr	32	Y1 26
Hatteras Wy	25	O1 28
Hattie La	20	J1 24
Haug Dr	21	F1 19
Haven Ct	20	F1 22
Haven Pl	34	B2 17
Havendale Gate	32	Z1 25
Havens Av	28	O1 14
Havenwood Dr	34	A2 13
Haverford La	26	O1 23
Hawk Dr	20	L1 23
Hawk Rd	25	V1 28
Hawkins Av (gh)	27	S1 21
Hawkins Av	39	H2 17
Hawkins Av (lr)	21	G1 19
Hawkins La	34	X1 14
Hawkins Pa	26	N1 23
Hawkins Rd	20	D1 26
Hawkins Rd (cr)	20	G1 23
Hawkins Rd	20	M1 23
Hawkins Rd E	26	N1 23
Hawkins Rd W	26	N1 23
Hawkins St	19	G1 28
Hawkins St (PJ)	19	K1 28
Hawks Nest Rd	19	D1 27
Hawley La	20	F1 24
Hawser Pl	26	O1 23
Hawthorn Rd	34	D2 14
Hawthorn Rd (rp)	25	V1 29
Hawthorne La	38	K2 18
Hawthorne St (ek)	19	J1 28
Hawthorne St (nc)	20	L1 23
Hawthorne St (mc)	34	B2 17
Hawthorne St (ns)	26	M1 23
Hawthorne St	26	Q1 25
Hay Rd	34	Z1 13
Hayden Ct	26	R1 23
Hayes La	26	P1 23
Hayuta Ct	21	L1 18
Hayward Av	25	O1 28
Hayward St	28	M1 15
Hazel Av	27	M1 20
Hazel Rd	31	W1 29
Hazel St	25	V1 29
Head of the Neck Rd	38	J2 19
Head of the Neck Rd (BP)	28	T1 14
Hearth Ct	26	N1 23
Hearth La	34	W1 15
Heartside Dr	25	P1 26
Heath Ct	20	F1 24
Heathcote Ct	35	A2 12
Heather Av	27	R1 19
Heather Ct (nc)	20	K1 22
Heather Ct	27	O1 17
Heather Ct (mi)	26	U1 24
Heather Dr	34	E2 15
Heather La (mp)	25	Q1 29
Heather La	31	Y1 27
Heatherwood Ct	38	K2 19
Hedda Rd	20	L1 26
Hedge La	20	J1 23
Hedge Rd	28	S1 14
Hedges Av	28	S1 13
Heidi La	19	M1 28
Helen St (ms)	25	O1 27
Helen St (rp)	25	V1 29
Helen St	21	H1 21
Helene Av	33	Y1 19
Helene Dr	34	A2 15
Helm Pl	20	F1 24
Helme Av	25	Q1 27
Hemlock Dr (mb)	34	C2 14
Hemlock Dr (mp)	25	Q1 29
Hemlock Dr	31	B2 28
Hemlock Pa	19	K1 30
Hemlock Rd (mp)	25	P1 26
Hemlock Rd	25	V1 29
Hemlock St	20	L1 23
Hempstead Av	25	R1 28
Hempstead Dr	25	S1 28
Hempstead Rd	35	B2 13
Hempstead St	21	L1 19
Henearly Dr	26	R1 27
Henry Av (ns)	20	L1 22
Henry Av	26	R1 26
Henry Av (rk)	21	G1 17
Henry Pl (ns)	26	N1 23
Henry Pl	28	Q1 16
Henry Rd	21	H1 22
Henry St (cr)	20	G1 22
Henry St (fv)	27	M1 19
Henry St (mr)	33	C2 17
Henry St	39	G2 16
Hepburn Ct	20	F1 24
Herbert Cir	28	O1 15
Herbert Ct	34	B2 17
Herd La	20	J1 25
Herdman Ct	32	W1 23
Heritage Ct	21	G1 20
Heritage La (sg)	19	F1 29
Heritage La	25	R1 27
Heritage La N	25	R1 27
Herkimer St	34	C2 17
Hermann Av	38	F2 17
Hermart La	21	J1 20
Hermitage St	31	B2 28
Heron Hill	20	D1 26
Heron Pa	26	R1 24
Hester La	21	H1 18
Heston Rd	34	A2 15
Hettys Pa	21	K1 20
Hewes St	20	K1 24
Hewitt Blvd	34	F2 16
Hewlett Av	28	Q1 15
Hewlett Rd	25	S1 27
Hiawatha La	19	E1 28
Hickory Av (rk)	21	G1 18
Hickory Av (fv)	21	M1 20
Hickory Ct	31	C2 29
Hickory Hill Dr	28	N1 17
Hickory La	33	F2 19
Hickory La (em)	38	K2 18
Hickory Rd	34	B2 13
Hickory Rd (rp)	25	V1 29
Hickory St	26	O1 25
High Ct	25	O1 29
High Gate Dr	20	G1 26
High Hill	26	H1 27
High Hill Dr	25	R1 29
High Hill Rd	25	O1 28
High Hollow La	25	P1 29
High Pa	19	K1 29
High St	19	K1 28
High St (PJ)	19	L1 28
High St (lr)	21	G1 18
High St	39	J2 16
High View Dr	21	L1 21
High View La	32	Z1 25
Highland Av (sk)	19	G1 28
Highland Av (ms)	25	O1 27
Highland Av	28	N1 14
Highland Blvd	25	L1 27
Highland Ct (mr)	34	E2 17
Highland Ct	39	K2 16
Highland Down	31	Y1 29
Highland Pl	21	L1 20
Highland Rd	31	W1 29
Highview Av (ek)	19	H1 28
Highview Av	27	N1 20
Highview Blvd	34	V1 14
Highview Rd	20	D1 26
Highwood Rd	19	E1 28
Hilda Ct	20	L1 26
Hill Dr	19	M1 28
Hill St (PG)	29	N1 13
Hill St (PG)	22	N1 15
Hill St (cr)	21	J1 20
Hillberry Cir	21	J1 18
Hillberry La	21	J1 18
Hillcrest	25	M1 29
Hillcrest Av (PJ)	19	L1 28
Hillcrest Av (PJ)	25	M1 28
Hillcrest Av	25	T1 30
Hillcrest Dr (SR)	31	W1 29
Hillcrest Dr	31	X1 29
Hillcrest La	32	W1 23
Hillcrest Pl	25	N1 28
Hillcrest Rd	19	M1 29
Hillcrest St	21	G1 19
Hilldale Av	25	O1 29
Hilldown Rd	27	U1 20
Hills Dr, The	19	G1 27
Hills La	20	G1 25
Hillsdale La	26	Q1 23
Hillside Av	25	T1 30
Hillside Av (PG)	28	N1 14
Hillside Rd (sd)	27	M1 21
Hillside Rd	13	D1 28
Hillside Rd (sb)	25	S1 29
Hillsview Rd	19	D1 27
Hilltop Ct	27	P1 21
Hilltop Dr (sn)	19	E1 27
Hilltop Dr (ms)	25	N1 27
Hilltop Dr (sb)	25	R1 30
Hilltop Dr (rp)	25	T1 29
Hilltop La (ek)	19	G1 27
Hilltop La	38	H2 20
Hilltop La (ri)	32	Z1 25
Hilton Ct	20	F1 24
Himmel Ct	26	O1 23
Hines Rd	26	S1 23
Hingle Pl	26	O1 23
Hirsch Av	26	O1 24
Hock Ct	21	L1 18
Hockey Rd	34	C2 14
Hoffman Av	28	U1 15
Hofstra Ct	27	M1 20
Hofstra Dr	27	M1 20
Hogan La	38	H2 20
Holbrook Av	21	J1 19
Holbrook Rd (hb)	21	J1 18
Holbrook Rd	28	O1 14
Holbrook St	28	O1 15
Holbrook Blvd	34	F2 16
Holiday Pk Dr	20	K1 23
Holland Av	27	P1 18
Hollingsworth Pl	21	H1 22
Hollingwood Dr	26	P1 23
Hollis Dr	25	S1 29
Hollis Pl	35	B2 13
Hollo Dr	21	J1 19
Hollow Ct (ek)	19	H1 27
Hollow Ct	28	T1 16
Hollow Oak Dr	28	S1 16
Hollow Rd (sn)	20	D1 26
Hollow Rd	20	H1 27
Holly Ct	25	R1 27
Holly Ct	34	F2 17
Holly Ct (mi)	26	U1 24
Holly Hill Ct	27	N1 17
Holly Hill Ct (np)	22	M1 17
Holly Hill La	26	N1 23
Holly Hock Ct	21	L1 19
Holly La (OF)	19	D1 29
Holly La	34	Z1 16
Holly La (PG)	22	N1 14
Holly La (PJ)	25	M1 28
Holly La (ep)	28	R1 13
Holly Rd (lr)	21	H1 19
Holly Rd (cr)	20	J1 20
Holly St	33	C2 17
Holly St (cr)	21	G1 21
Holly Wk (cg)	24	H1 5
Holly Wk (fp)	24	K1 6
Hollywood Av	27	M1 21
Hollywood Dr	34	A2 14
Holmes Wy	26	O1 23
Holyoke La	20	F1 24
Holzer Ct	28	P1 13
Homan Av	22	N1 13
Home Dr	27	R1 17
Homecoming Pl	20	H1 24
Homecreek Dr	34	D2 15
Homestead Av	19	L1 27
Homestead Dr	27	R1 22
Honey La	25	P1 29
Honey La W	25	O1 29
Honeysuckle La	21	L1 19
Hooper St	20	K1 25
Hope Ct (ns)	20	M1 23
Hope Ct (mf)	27	S1 19
Hopes Av	27	M1 18
Hopewell Dr	20	F1 24
Hopkins Commons	33	X1 21
Horizon Gate	28	U1 16
Horizon La	28	U1 16
Horizon View Dr	27	O1 21
Hornleaf La	21	J1 18
Horse Block La	21	L1 20
Horse Block Rd (fv)	27	M1 19
Horse Block Rd (ya)	34	X1 16
Horse Block Rd (cr)	21	J1 21
Horse Block Rd	28	U1 17
Horseshoe Dr	21	J1 18
Horseshoe La	38	H2 18
Hospital Rd	28	R1 15
Hot Water St	38	G2 21
Hot Water St	38	J2 21
Houghton Blvd	19	E1 27
Hounslow Rd	34	A2 16
Howard Av	28	O1 15
Howard Ct	33	B2 17
Howard Dr	26	R1 23
Howard St (tv)	20	K1 26
Howard St (sd)	27	N1 21
Howard St (SR)	31	X1 28
Howe Ct	26	O1 23
Howe Rd	26	O1 23
Howell Av	28	O1 15
Howell Pl	39	G2 16
Howell's Ct	29	M1 12
Hoyt La	19	J1 28
Hub Rd	20	G1 25
Hubbard Ct	28	M1 12
Hubbard Rd	33	X1 18
Huck Finn La	31	Z1 28
Huckleberry La	20	G1 26
Hudson Av	20	K1 22
Hudson St	26	Q1 25
Huguenot Dr	35	B2 13
Hulse Pl	29	P1 13
Hulse Rd	19	J1 27
Hulse St	29	V1 13
Humming La	26	R1 24
Humphrey La	29	M1 12
Hunt Club Dr	26	Q1 24
Hunter Av	25	S1 28
Hunter La	20	J1 23
Hunters Ct	20	F1 25
Hunter's Tr	31	B2 29
Hunting Hill Dr	28	N1 13
Huntingdale Way Dr	27	S1 22
Huntington Commons	33	X1 21
Huntington Ct	32	Y1 27
Huntington Dr	35	B2 13
Huntington Rd	25	S1 29
Huron Ct	25	R1 28
Huron Rd	34	Z1 21
Huron Rd	24	D1 4
Huron St	33	Z1 16
Huron St	26	M1 25
Hurstwood Dr	34	Z1 14
Hurtin St	20	K1 24
Huxley La	21	H1 19
Huyler Ct	19	E1 27
Huyler Rd	19	E1 27
Hyacinth Ct	27	M1 17
Hyacynth La	21	J1 18
Hyanis St	25	O1 28
Hyde La	26	Q1 23
Hysler Ct	26	O1 23
Hyson Wy	26	N1 23
Illinois Av	27	Q1 18
Impala Dr	20	L1 23
Imperial Dr	26	Q1 27
Imperial Dr (nc)	21	L1 22
Independence Ct	32	X1 23
Independence Hill	27	O1 20
Independence Wy	25	Q1 27
Indian Field Rd	19	G1 30
Indian Pa	19	E1 28
Indian Ridge La	32	W1 23
Indian Valley Rd	19	H1 29
Industrial Blvd (Scouting Blvd)	27	T1 18
Industrial Rd	26	N1 25
Infirmary Rd	20	F1 26
Ingrid Rd	19	E1 28
Inlet View Pa E	38	L2 18
Inlet View Pa W	38	L2 18
Inletview Pl	39	G2 15
Innis Av	21	G1 18
Interstate 495 (hv)	21	M1 18
Intervale Rd (sk)	19	E1 28
Intervale Rd (BT)	19	K1 29
Inwood Av	27	P1 18
Inwood Av (sd)	21	M1 21
Inwood Rd (PJ)	19	L1 28
Inwood Rd (sb)	25	S1 29
Inwood Rd (cm)	39	G2 16
Iowa Av	26	N1 26
Iowa Ct	26	P1 24
Iowa St	26	N1 23
Ira Ct	38	L2 20
Iran Ct	21	G1 18
Irene Ct	20	H1 22
Iris Av	21	K1 18
Iris Rd	35	B2 12
Iris Rd (rp)	25	V1 29
Irma La	25	P1 29
Iroquois Av	27	N1 21
Iroquois Tr	32	B2 27
Irving Av	28	S1 13
Irving Pl	24	E1 5
Irving St (PJ)	25	N1 26
Irving St (mp)	25	S1 27
Isis Rd	31	W1 29
Island Bay Av	26	U1 23
Island Rd	25	R1 29
Island St	29	S1 13
Island View Av	27	O1 20
Islander Ct	25	R1 27
Islip Dr	25	S1 29
Islip Rd	35	B2 12
Islip St	21	L1 18
Ivory St	20	G1 22
Ivy Av	24	D1 4
Ivy Covered Wy	26	Q1 26
Ivy La (sg)	19	F1 30
Ivy La	21	G1 21
Ivy Leaf Ct	27	N1 18
Ivy League La	20	E1 24
Ivy Meadow Ct	32	V1 24
Ivy Rd	34	D2 14
Ivy Rd	31	V1 29
Ivy Wk	24	J1 5
Jackson Av (nc)	20	K1 23
Jackson Av (sb)	25	S1 29
Jackson Dr	20	G1 25
Jackson St	31	W1 28
Jackwill Rd	28	R1 13
Jacob's La	31	B2 29
Jacobsen Ct	27	P1 18
Jacqueline Ct	26	O1 25
Jacqueline Dr	38	G2 20
Jacqueline La	21	J1 21
Jamaica Av (ps)	19	M1 27
Jamaica Av (mf)	27	Q1 18
Jamaica Av (Bellmore Av)	27	N1 17
Jamaica Av (Chapman Blvd)	38	H2 19
Jamaica Dr	25	S1 30
Jamaica St	21	L1 18
Jamar Dr	26	O1 25
Jamar La	21	H1 19
James Annex	31	Y1 28
James Hawkins Rd	34	E2 16
James St (ps)	19	M1 27
James St (nc)	20	J1 22
James St (PG)	28	P1 14
James St (SR)	31	Y1 28
James Wy	19	L1 28
Jamestown Ct	32	X1 23
Jamie St	32	W1 22
Jan Ct	21	G1 18
Jane La	27	N1 21
Jane St (ns)	26	N1 23
Jane St	26	R1 26
Janell La	21	K1 20
Janet Ct	25	R1 28
Janet La	21	J1 20
Janet St	20	K1 25
Janice La	27	N1 20
Janis La	25	U1 28
Jared's Pa	34	X1 14
Jarvin Rd	19	L1 27
Jarvis La	39	H2 16
Jasmine Ct	28	N1 17
Jasper Av	28	P1 16
Jay Pl	21	F1 19
Jay Rd	21	J1 22
Jay St	21	F1 19
Jayne Av (PJ)	19	J1 28
Jayne Av (PG)	28	O1 15
Jayne Blvd	19	M1 27
Jayne Rd	20	L1 29
Jaynes Wy	31	C2 28
Jean Ct	27	V1 20
Jean Ct	20	G1 26
Jeanatta Av	34	C2 14
Jeanne Av	20	K1 26
Jeanne Rd	20	F1 22
Jeff Ct	28	S1 16
Jeff St	27	S1 19
Jefferson Av (PG)	22	N1 16
Jefferson Av (PJ)	19	J1 28
Jefferson Av (nc)	20	K1 23
Jefferson Av (tv)	26	N1 26
Jefferson Av (np)	28	N1 16
Jefferson Blvd	19	L1 27
Jefferson Commons	33	X1 21
Jefferson Ct (sn)	20	G1 25
Jefferson Ct (co)	27	Q1 22
Jefferson Dr (mb)	34	C2 14
Jefferson Dr	26	M1 25
Jefferson Ferry Dr	20	J1 24
Jefferson Landing Cir	19	M1 28
Jefferson St (LG)	21	G1 22
Jefferson St	31	W1 28
Jeffrey La	19	G1 28
Jennifer Ct	34	E2 16
Jennifer La	26	T1 24
Jenning Pl	28	O1 15
Jennings Av	39	F2 16
Jennings Av (PG)	28	O1 15
Jenny Path Dr	27	O1 17
Jeremy Ct	21	H1 20
Jerome Rd	25	R1 29
Jersey Av (mp)	25	Q1 28
Jersey Av (BP)	28	U1 14
Jerusalem Hollow Rd	33	E2 18
Jesse Ct	26	N1 25
Jesse Wy	25	P1 27
Jessica La	26	R1 25
Jewel Dr	21	L1 19
Jillian La	26	T1 24
Joan Av	21	L1 21
Joan Ct	27	M1 18
Joann Ct	38	L2 20
Joanna Pl	20	M1 26
Jocelyn La	33	X1 18
Jodi Dr	38	L2 20
Jody Ct	31	Y1 28
Joel Ct	21	K1 19
Joe's Wy	21	H1 22
John Ct (sr)	33	D2 20
John Ct (ya)	33	X1 17
John Dr	27	N1 19
John O'Hara Dr	35	Z1 12
John Roe Smith Av (mf)	27	S1 17
John Roe Smith Av	27	S1 19
John St (ps)	19	M1 27
John St	20	K1 24
John St (ns)	26	M1 23
John St	26	N1 24
John St	28	P1 14
John St (PG)	31	Y1 28
John Vincent Ct	21	J1 22
Johns Hollow Rd	19	D1 29
Johns Hopkins St	33	D1 22
Johns Neck Rd	35	A2 12
Johns Rd	19	G1 29
Johnson Av	38	K2 18
Johnson Ct	26	N1 26
Johnson St (PJ)	19	M1 27
Johnson St	28	M1 15
Joline Rd	19	M1 26
Jomarr Rd	31	Y1 29
Jonah Rd	26	T1 25
Jonas Blvd	21	K1 21
Jonathan's Pa	25	U1 29
Jones Av (PJ)	19	K1 28
Jones Av (tv)	26	O1 26
Jones St (sk)	19	G1 28
Jones St (PG)	28	O1 13
Jones St	28	O1 15
Jones St	28	P1 14
Jones Wk	30	N1 6
Joni Dr	26	O1 26
Jordan Dr	21	G1 21
Joseph Ct	21	L1 20
Joseph Rd	20	K1 26
Joseph St	19	M1 27
Josephine Blvd	31	Y1 29
Josephine St	21	M1 19
Josiah's Pa	25	U1 29
Joy Pl	21	J1 19
Joy Rd	21	L1 21
Judith Ct	25	T1 29
Judith Dr	26	R1 22
Julia Cir (ps)	19	J1 27
Julia Cir (mi)	26	T1 24
Julian Ct	26	Q1 26
Julie La	20	M1 23
Julius St	21	H1 19
Junard Blvd	20	N1 27
Junior Dr	21	G1 19
Juniper Av (ob)	24	D1 4
Juniper Av (PG)	28	O1 15
Juniper Ct	26	P1 24
Juniper Ct (mf)	27	N1 17
Juniper Ct (mi)	26	V1 24
Juniper Rd (mb)	34	D2 14
Juniper Rd (rp)	25	V1 28
Jupiter Rd	31	V1 29
Justin Cir	20	L1 24
Justin Dr	28	Q1 17
Jute Pl	35	B2 12
Jute Rd	25	U1 29
Kale Rd	25	U1 29
Kaler Dr	39	J2 17
Kamio Dr	33	B2 18
Kane Av (mf)	27	R1 19
Kane Av (hg)	28	S1 14
Kara Ct (sb)	25	T1 28
Kara Ct (cr)	21	J1 21
Karl Ct	28	R1 17
Karls Rd	27	U1 20
Kasper Ct	19	J1 27
Kastal Ct	32	Y1 25
Kastal Dr	32	X1 25
Kate Cir	26	T1 24
Katherine Pa	33	W1 22
Katherine St	20	K1 26
Kathleen Ct	27	O1 21
Kathleen Cres	26	O1 25
Kathryn La	21	H1 18
Kathryn St	28	Q1 15
Katie Dr (er)	31	C2 28
Katie Dr (np)	28	O1 17
Katie Wy	34	F2 17
Katy St	28	P1 16
Kay St	21	G1 20
Kayla La	20	L1 25
Kayron Dr	21	K1 19
Keewaydin Ct	19	K1 27
Kejaro Ct	20	K1 22
Keller Dr	33	B2 19
Kelp Av	24	D1 4
Kelsey Av	20	N1 26
Kempster St	19	M1 27
Kemswick Dr	20	D1 26
Ken Pl	20	L1 25
Kendra Sea Ct (ya)	27	W1 20
Kenmare St	38	J2 18
Kennedy Av (mf)	27	P1 20
Kennedy Av (PG)	22	M1 13
Kennedy Ct	27	Q1 18
Kennedy Rd	20	K1 26
Kensington Av	27	N1 18
Kensington Gate	26	O1 23
Kensington Wy	26	N1 26
Kent Commons	33	X1 20
Kent Dr	35	Z1 12
Kent La	20	J1 23
Kent Pl	33	C2 17
Kent Rd	26	M1 25
Kent St	28	N1 15
Kentucky Av	26	O1 25
Kenwood St	19	G1 27
Kern St	27	Q1 22
Kerry Ct	20	H1 23
Ketcham Av	28	O1 15
Kettle Hole Rd	38	G2 21
Kettle Knoll Pa	25	P1 28
Kew Dr	25	S1 29
Keystone Ct	21	K1 22
Kilroy Dr	33	B2 18
Kim Ct	20	M1 23
Kim St	26	R1 27
Kimberly Av	21	K1 19
Kimberly Ct	38	J2 21
King Arthur's Ct	20	H1 26
King Av	20	L1 22
King Rd (mb)	34	D2 14
King Rd (sb)	25	S1 29
King Rd (rp)	25	V1 28
King Rd W	35	B2 13
King St (ss)	20	J1 24
King St (tv)	20	K1 24
King St	25	S1 27
Kings Wk	25	T1 29
Kingsland Av	33	Y1 19
Kingston Ct	32	Y1 26
Kingston Dr	32	Y1 25
Kingston Rd	26	P1 26
Kinn St	29	N1 13
Kirby La	21	F1 19
Kirk Dr	21	H1 18
Kismet Ct	32	Y1 27
Kismet St	21	J1 20
Knapp Rd	34	B2 14
Knickerbocker Av (co)	27	R1 19
Knickerbocker Av	21	H1 18
Knight St	31	Z1 28
Knoll Crest Av	25	O1 29
Knoll Pa	25	P1 29
Knoll Rd	25	V1 29
Knoll St	25	T1 30
Knoll Top Rd	20	D1 26
Knollcrest Av	27	N1 20
Knolls Dr	20	F1 24
Knot St	28	S1 16
Knox Av	26	N1 26
Kocsis St	21	J1 17
Kool Pl	26	M1 26
Kreamer St	28	U1 13
Krispin La	20	H1 24
Kristal Ct	26	O1 23
Kristi St	20	K1 24
Kristina St	28	S1 16
Kristina Wy	31	Z1 27
Kroll Wy	20	K1 25
Kross Ct	27	Q1 19
Kuebler St	28	N1 13
Kyla Ct	26	M1 26
Kyle St	28	T1 16
La Bonne Vie Dr	28	R1 16
La Bonne Vie Dr W	28	R1 16
Lacebark La	28	S1 17
Lacrosse Rd	34	C2 14
Lacy Ct	28	N1 13
Lad Av	27	Q1 19
Lafayette Av (mc)	33	C2 18
Lafayette Av	34	D2 17
Lafayette Dr (mb)	34	C2 13
Lafayette Dr	35	A2 13
Lafayette Pl	26	N1 26
Lagoon Ct	23	M1 11
Lake Av	39	F2 16
Lake Av (rk)	21	H1 18
Lake Ct (mi)	26	V1 23
Lake Ct (PG)	28	O1 14
Lake Dr (sn)	20	F1 26
Lake Dr (mi)	26	V1 23
Lake Dr (ep)	28	Q1 14
Lake Grove Blvd	21	G1 21
Lake Grove St	20	K1 23
Lake Pk St	21	G1 19
Lake Placid Ct	26	Q1 24
Lake Point Cir	26	V1 23
Lake Point Dr	26	V1 23
Lake Promenade	21	F1 17
Lake Shore Rd	21	F1 18
Lake St (BP)	29	S1 13
Lake St (sk)	19	F1 28
Lake St (PG)	28	O1 14
Lake Ter	26	S1 24
Lake Ter (lr)	21	F1 18
Lake View Dr	28	N1 16
Lake View St	38	M2 19
Lakeland Av	28	N1 14
Lakeland Pl	21	L1 20
Lakeland St	21	F1 17
Lakeshore Rd	21	F1 19
Lakeside Av	20	F1 22
Lakeside Dr	26	S1 24
Lakeside Dr (hv)	21	K1 18
Lakeside Tr	32	B2 26
Lakeview Av	28	O1 16
Lakeview Blvd	27	U1 20
Lakeview Dr (mb)	34	C2 14
Lakeview Dr	35	D2 13
Lakeview Dr (mi)	26	S1 24
Lakeview Dr	26	V1 24
Lakeview Dr	38	J2 20
Lakeview Dr E	39	F2 16
Lakeview Dr W	39	F2 16
Lakeview Pl	39	G2 16
Lakeview Rd	21	F1 18
Lakeview Ter	26	U1 23
Lakeview Tr	32	C2 26
Lakewood Av	21	G1 18
Lakewood Ct	33	E2 18
Lakewood Rd	21	F1 18
Lakewood St	28	O1 14
Lama Dr	34	A2 15
Lambert Av	33	B2 18
Lamont Ct	32	X1 26
Lamont La	20	E1 27
Lamont Rd	32	X1 26
Lamport Av	19	M1 26
Lancaster Ct	32	Y1 25
Lancaster Pl	20	F1 23
Lancelot La	20	G1 26
Lancer Rd	20	L1 23
Landing La (PJ)	19	L1 29
Landing La (PG)	28	Q1 13
Landing Rd	25	P1 30
Lands End Ct	34	D2 16
Landsberger St	27	U1 20
Lane, The	25	T1 29
Lanes End	23	N1 12
Lanes Rd	32	F2 23
Langley Ct	26	N1 24
Langley La	28	V1 14
Lanier Pl	34	A2 17
Lansing St	25	R1 28
Lantern Ct	20	D1 26
Larch Rd	25	T1 28
Larch St	21	H1 18
Larchmont Ct	32	Z1 26
Lark Dr	20	L1 23
Larry Ct	38	H2 21
Larry Rd	21	L1 22
Latimer Av	26	Q1 25
Laura Av	29	R1 13
Laura Ct	25	P1 27
Laura Dr	21	K1 22
Laura La	20	H1 26
Laura Lee Dr	39	G2 15
Laurel Av (sn)	19	E1 27
Laurel Av (PJ)	19	M1 28
Laurel Av (ob)	24	D1 4
Laurel Cres	19	M1 29
Laurel Dr (PJ)	19	M1 28
Laurel Dr (sn)	20	D1 26
Laurel Dr	31	Y1 27
Laurel La (OF)	19	E1 29
Laurel La (PJ)	19	K1 28
Laurel La (mf)	27	N1 17
Laurel La (sg)	34	Z1 16
Laurel Ledge	25	N1 28
Laurel Pa	19	K1 29
Laurel Pl	27	M1 21
Laurel Rd	34	D2 14
Laurel Rd (rp)	25	T1 29
Laurel Rd (rp)	25	U1 29
Laurel Rd (rk)	21	H1 19
Laurel Rd W	35	B2 13
Laurel St	34	C2 14
Laurel St (mp)	25	S1 27
Laurel St (rk)	21	G1 18
Laurel St (LG)	21	G1 22
Laurel St (rk)	21	J1 18
Laurel St	28	O1 13
Laurelton Av (sd)	21	N1 21
Laurelton Dr (mb)	34	B2 13
Laurelton Dr	35	B2 13
Laurelton Rd	25	S1 29
Laurence La	32	Y1 25
Laurie Blvd	21	G1 21
Laurita Gate	19	M1 27
Lavender La	28	N1 11
Lavender Rd	31	W1 29
Lavern Dr	26	T1 24
Lawrence Av (PJ)	19	M1 27
Lawrence Av	21	H1 19
Lawrence Dr	32	Z1 22
Lawrence Rd	34	A2 15
Lawrence Rd (sb)	25	R1 29
Layton La	21	G1 21
Lea Av	38	J2 19
Leather Stocking La	19	E1 27
Lebrun St	20	K1 21
Ledgewood Cir	20	G1 25
Ledgewood Ct	25	T1 29
Lee Av	29	P1 13
Lee Pl	33	C2 17
Leeana Ct	29	S1 13

Suffolk Co.

Index

Suffolk Co.

Town of Brookhaven

STREET	MAP	GRID
Rose Av	28	P1 14
Rose Ct (ya)	33	Y1 19
Rose Ct	38	G2 18
Rose La (ps)	19	M1 26
Rose La	27	S1 21
Rose Pl	27	N1 22
Rose St	25	S1 26
Rose St (ep)	28	Q1 14
Rosedale Av	28	O1 16
Rosedale Rd	25	S1 29
Roseland La	28	T1 12
Roseland Pl	28	T1 13
Rosemary Ct	38	G2 21
Rosemary La	21	L1 21
Rosemont Av	27	N1 19
Rosewood Ct	20	H1 26
Rosewood La	33	D2 21
Rosewood Rd (sn)	19	D1 27
Rosewood Rd (mb)	34	C2 13
Rosewood Rd (RP)	25	V1 29
Rosita La	19	M1 29
Roslyn Av	21	N1 22
Roslyn Ct (PJ)	19	M1 28
Roslyn Ct (sm)	28	Q1 16
Roslyn Pl	34	B2 13
Roslyn Rd	25	S1 30
Ross Ct (mp)	25	P1 27
Ross Ct	38	G2 21
Ross La	25	P1 26
Ross St	20	K1 24
Roswell Av	31	X1 28
Round Pond Rd	21	H1 19
Rowe St	26	Q1 23
Rowing St	29	S1 12
Rowland Av	28	N1 13
Rowland St	33	Z1 22
Rowland St (PG)	28	O1 15
Rowley La	34	F2 15
Rowlinson Dr	33	A2 20
Roxborough Av	28	N1 15
Roxbury Ct	21	M1 19
Roxbury Rd	25	Q1 29
Royal Dr	26	O1 24
Royal Oaks La	21	H1 21
Royal Wy	32	Z1 29
Royal Wood Ct	27	Q1 18
Royalston La	20	K1 24
RSVT St	28	O1 13
Ruby La	20	F1 22
Ruby Pl	21	F1 19
Rudy's La	26	O1 24
Rugby Dr	34	Z1 12
Ruland Rd	20	L1 24
Runs Rd	19	G1 28
Rupolo Ct	28	Q1 14
Rush St	20	K1 24
Russell Dr	31	B2 28
Russell La (ep)	28	Q1 15
Russell La	28	R1 17
Russell St	38	G2 19
Russet La	20	F1 22
Rustic Av	28	T1 16
Rustic Gate	32	Z1 25
Rustic Rd (ps)	19	K1 27
Rustic Rd (ya)	27	U1 21
Rustic Rd (mp)	25	Q1 29
Rustic Rd (cr)	21	H1 21
Rutgers Rd	27	L1 20
Ruth La (ns)	20	M1 23
Ruth La (ri)	32	Y1 24
Rutherford Dr	32	Z1 22
Rutland Rd (mr)	33	C2 17
Rutland Rd	34	D2 17
Rutledge Commons	33	X1 21
Ruxton Rd	25	Q1 28
Ryan Ct	32	X1 25
Ryan La	25	R1 27
Ryder Pl	21	G1 18
Ryerson Av	32	F2 22
Saber La	20	G1 24
Sabre Dr	27	O1 21
Sachem Ct	27	P1 20
Sachem Dr	33	B2 18
Saddle Brook La	38	G2 20
Saddle La	20	J1 23
Saddle Rd (sn)	20	D1 25
Saddle Rd (co)	26	Q1 25
Saddle Rock Rd	20	Q1 26
Saddlebrook Ct	27	S1 22
Saddler La	20	G1 25
Sagamore Hills Dr N	26	N1 25
Sagamore Hills Dr S	26	N1 25
Sage Brush Ct	19	G1 28
Sage La	20	G1 24
Sage Rd	20	K1 26
Sagewood Dr	34	Z1 13
Sagoponak Ct	31	Y1 27
Sail Wk	24	L1 6
Sailor's Ct	25	P1 30
St Charles Pl	20	J1 24
St Francis Blvd	26	U1 23
St George Dr	34	Z1 12
St George Glen Dr	20	G1 27
St James Rd	25	S1 30
St John	39	G2 16
St John Pl	34	C2 17
St Joseph Av	21	G1 18
St Margaret's Blvd	26	T1 23
St Mark's Av	19	E1 27
St Nicholas Av	20	F1 22
St Orchard Rd	19	K1 29
St Paul Av	20	E1 26
St James Av	25	R1 28
Salem Dr	20	E1 26
Salem La	26	L1 24
Salem Rd (cr)	20	J1 23
Salem Rd (tv)	20	M1 25
Salem St	28	N1 15
Salisbury Run	26	Q1 25
Saljon Ct	20	G1 22
Sally La	32	Y1 23
Salt Meadow Ct	31	B2 28
Salt Meadow La	19	E1 29
Salt Meadow Rd	29	R1 13
Saltaire Rd	25	R1 29
Salty Wy	31	Y1 29
Samantha Dr	26	P1 23
Sambi Ct	21	L1 19
Sam's Pa	25	U1 29
Samuel St	21	G1 19
Samuels La	20	M1 24
Samuels Pa	25	P1 29
Sand St	20	D1 26
Sandie Ct	22	N1 15
Sandie La	38	H2 21
Sandpiper Ct	31	Y1 29
Sandpiper La (ns)	26	N1 23
Sandpiper La (sc)	21	K1 20
Sandpiper Wk	30	Q1 8
Sander Ct	32	W1 22
Sandra Ct	27	S1 19
Sandra Ct (fc)	21	G1 19
Sandra Dr	28	S1 16
Sands La	19	L1 29
Sands La (PJ)	34	V1 15
Sands La (BP)	28	V1 14
Sands Rd	38	G2 22
Sandstone La	20	G1 24
Sandy Ct (LG)	20	F1 22
Sandy Ct (fv)	27	M1 20
Sandy Hill Rd	25	N1 28
Sandy Hollow La	32	Z1 25
Sandy La	20	M1 24
Sandy Wk	24	J1 6
Sanford La	20	G1 24
Sanford Rd	21	J1 21
Sara Cir	20	K1 25
Sara La	26	T1 24
Sarah Ct	21	J1 19
Saratoga Av	28	P1 16
Saratoga Ct	32	X1 23
Sari La	26	O1 25
Satinwood La	19	J1 28
Satinwood Rd	25	U1 29
Satterly Rd	19	H1 27
Saunders Av	38	G2 17
Savannah Blvd	28	N1 15
Savoy Ct	20	L1 23
Sawtooth Cove	25	L1 28
Sawtooth Cove Dr	19	L1 28
Sawyer Ct	20	G1 26
Sawyer St	34	B2 17
Saxon Rd	20	J1 22
Saxton St	28	P1 15
Saybrook Ct	26	O1 25
Sayville Ct	31	Y1 27
Sayville Rd (mb)	34	B2 13
Sayville Rd (sb)	25	S1 29
Saywood La	20	G1 24
Scenic Hills Dr	32	W1 23
Schenk Dr	34	A2 15
Scherger Av	28	T1 15
Schiller Ct	27	U1 20
Schiller St	38	J2 18
Schmeelk Pl	19	F1 27
Schoenfield Blvd	28	Q1 14
Scholar La	20	E1 24
Scholar Pl	20	H1 25
School Ct (co)	26	Q1 23
School Ct (SR)	31	Y1 28
School Dr	20	M1 26
School House Rd	21	F1 19
School St (fc)	21	G1 19
School St (cr)	21	J1 22
Schooner Cove	19	H1 28
Schroeder La	28	P1 13
Scotch Pine Dr	28	S1 17
Scotch Pines La	20	G1 23
Scott Av	26	N1 23
Scott Ct (ek)	19	H1 28
Scott Ct (LG)	20	G1 22
Scott Ct (fv)	21	M1 20
Scott La (sf)	38	J2 21
Scott La	28	R1 16
Scott St (cr)	20	J1 23
Scott St (PG)	28	N1 13
Scotts Cove Rd	19	H1 28
Scotty La	20	K1 22
Scout Tr	31	C2 27
Scraggy Hill Rd	19	L1 28
Scranton Av	26	M1 26
Scranton Rd	20	M1 26
Scrup Wk	24	K1 6
Scudder Av	32	F2 22
Scudders Pl	26	Q1 23
Scully Wy	26	O1 27
Sea Breeze Ct	34	D2 17
Sea Court La	19	L1 27
Sea Wk	24	H1 5
Seabreeze Pl	39	G2 15
Seabrook Ct	20	G1 25
Seabrook La	20	G1 25
Seacliff Av	25	Q1 30
Seacliff La	25	P1 30
Seacliff Rd	25	S1 29
Seafoam Wk	30	Q1 7
Seaford Av (mf)	27	Q1 18
Seaford Av (mc)	33	B2 17
Seaford Av (mc)	33	B2 18
Seaford Rd (mb)	34	B2 13
Seaford Rd (mp)	25	Q1 29
Seajay Wk	30	P1 7
Sean La	25	O1 28
Seaside Av	28	N1 16
Seaside Dr (BT)	19	K1 30
Seaside Dr (sb)	25	T1 29
Seatuck Av	38	L2 19
Seatuck Cove Cir	38	M2 18
Seatuck Cove Ct	38	M2 18
Seaview La (cm)	34	F2 15
Seaview La (ms)	25	O1 29
Seaview Ledge	31	X1 29
Seaview Wk	24	J1 6
Second Wk	30	P1 7
Sedgemere Rd	39	G2 16
Sedgewick La	20	G1 24
Seeley St	34	W1 15
Segatogue La	20	K1 23
Seifert Av	25	Q1 30
Seitz Ct	28	O1 14
Selden Blvd	20	L1 22
Selden Ct (sb)	25	S1 29
Selden Ct (sd)	21	M1 22
Selden Rd	34	B2 13
Selden Stage Rd	20	M1 24
Selvia Ct	26	Q1 24
Seminole St	21	L1 21
Seneca Ct	20	M1 25
Seneca Pl	27	N1 21
Seneca St	24	E1 5
Seneca Tr	31	B2 27
Senix Av	34	F2 16
Sephton St	28	O1 16
September St	26	Q1 25
Sequoia Dr (co)	26	Q1 25
Sequoia Dr	26	Q1 24
Service Rd	20	E1 26
Serviceberry Ct	25	R1 27
Setalcott Pl	19	F1 27
Setalcott Pl N	19	F1 27
Setalcott Pl S	19	F1 27
Setauket Tr	32	C2 26
Settler Dr	20	F1 26
Settlers Wy (sk)	19	E1 28
Settlers Wy (PJ)	19	L1 29
Sevilla Wk	26	Q1 26
Seville La	20	G1 25
Seward Ct	20	G1 24
Seward La	20	G1 24
Seymour Dr	35	Z1 12
Seymour La	27	R1 21
Shaber Rd	28	O1 15
Shadetree Ct	20	G1 24
Shadetree La	20	G1 24
Shady La	27	P1 21
Shady Pa	19	M1 29
Shady Tree La (PJ)	19	M1 28
Shady Tree La (sf)	28	S1 16
Shady View Crossing	38	J2 21
Shady Wk	24	L1 6
Shagwong Dr	25	R1 29
Shaker Hollow Rd	19	E1 28
Shamrock Ct	26	O1 25
Shamrock La	20	K1 22
Shamrock Rd	31	W1 29
Shang Lee Dr	38	J2 19
Shannon Blvd	27	V1 20
Shannon Ct	34	E2 16
Shari La	38	G2 20
Sharon Av	19	H1 28
Sharon Ct (mf)	27	P1 17
Sharon Ct (ri)	32	X1 24
Sharon Dr (mi)	26	P1 25
Sharon Dr (ep)	28	Q1 15
Sharon St	19	K1 26
Sharp St	28	O1 15
Sharpsburg Ct	26	Q1 25
Shaw Av	28	U1 14
Shawmont La	20	G1 24
Shearwater Ct	21	K1 20
Sheep Pasture Rd	19	J1 27
Sheffield Ct	32	Z1 26
Sheffield Dr	32	Y1 26
Sheffield La	38	L2 17
Sheila Ct	38	G2 20
Sheldon Av	28	Q1 14
Shell Rd	25	W1 29
Shell St	19	J1 28
Shell Wk	24	L1 6
Shellbourne La	20	G1 24
Shelldrake Av	19	J1 28
Shelley Dr	32	W1 23
Shelley Gate	26	W1 23
Shelter Dr	25	R1 29
Shelter Harbor Ct	31	B2 28
Shelton Ct	21	H1 20
Shen Ct	19	H1 29
Shenandoah Blvd (ps)	19	N1 27
Shenandoah Blvd (co)	26	Q1 25
Sheppard La	20	G1 24
Sherbrook Ct	34	A2 12
Sheri Ct	21	K1 20
Sheridan Rd	34	A2 13
Sheridan Wy	21	G1 21
Sherman St	28	N1 15
Sherrill La	20	L1 25
Sherry Ct	38	K2 20
Sherry Dr	19	G1 27
Sherry La	27	O1 22
Sherwood Ct	21	J1 19
Sherwood Dr	34	A2 14
Sherwood La	20	H1 26
Shetland Ct	20	G1 24
Shetland La	20	G1 24
Shields Ct	28	V1 13
Shiloh Ct	26	P1 25
Shinnecock Av	34	C2 16
Shinnecock Dr	25	R1 29
Shipman La	19	D1 27
Ships Point La	19	K1 30
Shipyard La	19	G1 28
Shirley La	27	S1 21
Shirley St	39	H2 16
Shoestring La	34	Y1 17
Shore Dr (OF)	19	D1 29
Shore Dr (mb)	34	E2 14
Shore Dr (sb)	25	S1 30
Shore Dr (mi)	26	V1 23
Shore Dr (PG)	28	O1 14
Shore Haven Blvd	21	F1 19
Shore Oaks Dr	19	D1 27
Shore Rd (sk)	19	G1 28
Shore Rd (sn)	20	D1 26
Shore Rd (ms)	19	N1 28
Shore Rd (em)	39	K2 17
Shore Rd (PG)	28	O1 15
Shore Rd (ep)	28	R1 12
Shore Rd (BP)	28	V1 13
Shore Rd W	25	N1 28
Shore Wk	24	J1 6
Shoreham Av	25	R1 28
Shoreham Rd	25	S1 30
Short Av	28	Q1 16
Short La	25	U1 29
Short St (LG)	20	F1 22
Short St (mi)	26	V1 24
Short St	38	L2 20
Short Wy	31	X1 29
Shortwood La	19	E1 28
Sidney Av	27	M1 20
Siegfried Park Blvd	27	U1 20
Silas Carter Rd	33	F2 21
Silas Woods Rd	33	E2 21
Sills Rd (wy)	27	U1 20
Silver Beech Ct	19	H1 29
Silver Ct	32	A2 24
Silver Dr	21	M1 21
Silver Pine Dr	28	S1 17
Silver Ponds Blvd	33	F2 22
Silver Rd	34	B2 14
Silver St (ns)	27	M1 22
Silver St (PG)	28	P1 14
Silverspruce La	20	G1 24
Simon Av	21	K1 21
Simon Ct	21	L1 20
Simpson Gate	38	K2 20
Simpson Pl	20	E1 26
Sims St	22	M1 15
Sinclair St	34	B2 17
Singingwood Dr	20	E1 23
Singingwood La	19	H1 29
Sinn St	28	O1 15
Sinnickson Rd	39	G2 15
Sipp Av (mf)	27	R1 19
Sipp Av (hg)	28	S1 16
Sky Rd	31	W1 29
Sky View La	20	D1 26
Sky Wk	24	L1 6
Skyhaven Dr	29	Q1 13
Skylark La	20	G1 24
Skyline Dr	27	O1 21
Skyview Ct	20	K1 23
Sleepy Hollow	21	H1 20
Sleepy Hollow Dr	33	A2 20
Sleepy Hollow La	25	P1 29
Sloan Dr	21	H1 17
Small La	20	K1 23
Smith Av	21	J1 19
Smith Commons	33	X1 21
Smith Ct (sn)	20	E1 26
Smith Ct (mc)	34	B2 17
Smith Ct (BP)	29	U1 13
Smith La (ch)	27	S1 21
Smith La (cr)	21	H1 21
Smith Rd (sh)	34	Z1 16
Smith Rd (sh)	35	A2 13
Smith Rd (mi)	32	X1 22
Smith Rd	21	G1 20
Smith St (mc)	34	B2 17
Smith St (cm)	34	F2 16
Smith St (bt)	23	N1 12
Smith St (cr)	21	H1 21
Smith St (em)	39	J2 15
Smith St (PG)	28	P1 12
Smithtown Blvd	20	K1 23
Smyth Ct	28	U1 13
Snapper Wk	24	L1 6
Snowcrest Ct	25	N1 28
Snyder St	28	O1 15
Soccer Rd	34	C2 14
Sohmer St	33	E2 21
Solitaire Rd	31	X1 29
Somers Ct	21	K1 20
Somers La (sc)	21	K1 20
Somers Pl	33	C2 17
Somerset Av	34	B2 16
Somerset Ct	20	G1 26
Somerset La	20	G1 26
Somerset Rd	25	V1 29
Somerset St	21	J1 21
Songsparrow Ct	21	K1 20
Sophia Dr	26	T1 24
Sophomore La	20	E1 24
Sorrel Dr	34	Z1 13
Sorrento Ct	25	R1 28
Sound Beach Blvd	25	S1 29
Sound Lower Rocky Point Rd	25	S1 29
Sound View Dr (PJ)	19	J1 29
Sound View Dr (mp)	25	O1 30
Sound View Dr (rp)	25	T1 30
Soundbreeze Dr	25	P1 29
Soundview Ct	20	D1 26
Soundview Dr (PJ)	19	L1 29
Soundview Dr (SR)	31	Y1 29
Soundway Dr	25	T1 29
South 3rd St	24	E1 4
South 4th St	24	E1 5
South 8th St	24	E1 5
South 9th St	24	E1 5
South 11th St	24	E1 5
South 13th St	24	F1 5
South 14th St	24	F1 5
South Alabama St	26	N1 25
South Bicycle Path Dr	27	N1 22
South Breeze Dr	27	P1 21
South Coleman Rd	21	K1 21
South Country Rd (BP)	29	T1 13
South Country Rd (ep)	28	R1 14
South Country Rd (BP)	28	U1 13
South Cozine Rd	38	G2 18
South Dr	20	E1 24
South Dunton Av	29	S1 12
South Gate (mp)	25	P1 29
South Gate (SR)	31	Y1 29
South Haven Av	34	B2 16
South Hickory St	26	O1 25
South Hope Ct	20	M1 23
South Howell Av	21	K1 21
South Howells Point Rd	29	T1 12
South Jersey Av	19	G1 28
South Kennedy Dr	20	K1 23
South Larry Rd	21	L1 22
South Locust Av	27	S1 19
South Loop	20	F1 25
South Mallard Av	21	L1 22
South Masem Sq	28	T1 13
South Newton Av	21	L1 22
South Ocean Av	28	O1 14
South Orchard Rd	28	S1 13
South Pine Lake Dr	22	N1 14
South Pond Tr	32	B2 26
South Prospect Av	28	N1 13
South Rd	28	U1 15
South Ruland Rd	21	L1 22
South Stonehurst Cir	20	J1 22
South St (PJ)	19	K1 28
South St (ps)	19	N1 27
South St (sr)	33	C2 21
South St (mi)	26	S1 23
South St (cm)	39	H2 15
South St (PG)	28	O1 14
South Summit Av	28	N1 13
South Tr	31	Z1 28
South Village Dr	28	U1 16
South Washington Av	21	H1 21
South Wind Rd	29	T1 12
Southaven Av	28	P1 17
Southern Blvd	28	R1 13
Southern Pine Av	28	S1 17
Southfield La	26	R1 23
Southgate Rd	19	E1 28
Southold Rd	25	T1 29
Southview Ct	33	W1 17
Southwood Dr	25	P1 29
Space Av	21	K1 19
Spar Dr	34	D2 14
Sparrow Dr	26	R1 25
Sparrow La	38	J2 19
Spencer La	20	G1 24
Speonk Rd	25	R1 29
Spindrift Wk	30	Q1 7
Spinning Wheel Cir	26	P1 26
Split Pine Cir	27	R1 18
Split Rail La	20	G1 26
Sportsman Dr	34	A2 13
Sprague Dr	39	G2 15
Sprat St	28	T1 17
Spring Ct	26	O1 26
Spring Garden Rd	25	T1 29
Spring La	19	H1 27
Spring St (PJ)	19	K1 28
Spring St (mp)	25	S1 26
Springbriar La	21	K1 21
Springfield Rd	25	S1 29
Springlake Dr	26	T1 24
Springview Ct	28	S1 13
Spruce Cir	21	K1 20
Spruce Dr (PG)	29	R1 13
Spruce Dr (PG)	22	M1 14
Spruce La	25	R1 27
Spruce St (LG)	20	G1 22
Spruce St (ns)	20	M1 23
Spruce St (np)	28	N1 16
Spruce St (PG)	28	Q1 13
Spruceton St	21	L1 21
Spur La	20	J1 23
Spurwoods La	21	N1 19
Spyglass La	20	H1 26
Squaw La	34	D2 16
Squires Av	20	M1 25
Stacey Ct	34	Z1 17
Stackyard Dr	34	D2 15
Stacy Ct	19	J1 28
Stacy Dr	26	O1 25
Stadium Blvd	20	H1 24
Stafford La	20	G1 24
Stagecoach Rd	20	M1 23
Stalker La	20	J1 25
Standish Dr	25	P1 26
Standish La	20	G1 24
Stanley Av	28	S1 14
Stanley Ct	21	H1 18
Stanley Dr (cr)	20	H1 22
Stanley Dr (sh)	34	A2 13
Stanton Av	27	Q1 22
Star Ct	28	S1 16
Star Rd	31	W1 29
Starboard La	28	O1 13
Starfire Dr	20	L1 24
Stark Dr	39	G2 16
Starlight Dr	33	A2 20
Starling Ct	26	R1 24
Starling Pl	21	N1 19
Starr St	20	K1 25
State Hwy 25 (cr)	21	J1 21
State Hwy 25A (sk)	19	F1 27
State Hwy 25A (SR)	31	W1 28
State Hwy 27 (PG)	22	M1 14
State Hwy 112 (tv)	20	N1 25
State Hwy 347 (sn)	20	G1 23
State St (LG)	20	F1 22
State St (mc)	33	C2 17
State St (ps)	26	M1 26
Station Av	28	N1 15
Station Rd (mi)	27	T1 22
Station Rd (nb)	28	U1 15
Steels Wk	24	N1 7
Steep Hill Rd	19	H1 27
Steeple La	20	G1 24
Stem La	20	G1 25
Stephani Av (ep)	28	S1 13
Stephanie Ct	21	L1 21
Stephanie La (sn)	20	G1 25
Stephanie La	38	G2 20
Stephano Av	28	S1 14
Stephen Av	20	K1 22
Stephen Dr	32	C2 22
Stephen St	21	M1 19
Stephen's Pa	19	L1 30
Sterling Av	22	N1 15
Sterling Av	28	R1 13
Sterling Ct	28	Q1 16
Sterling Pa	33	X1 18
Sterling Pl	34	C2 17
Sterling St	20	K1 26
Stern Dr	19	M1 29
Sthem Rd	21	H1 20
Steven Ct (PG)	22	N1 15
Steven Ct (ms)	25	O1 28
Stewart Cir	20	J1 22
Stewart Rd	25	S1 29
Sierra Ct	26	P1 24
Stillhunter La	26	M1 24
Stillwood Rd	34	X1 15
Stiriz Rd	28	V1 14
Stirrup La (ps)	19	J1 28
Stirrup La (cr)	20	J1 23
Stockton Commons	33	X1 20
Stockton La	20	G1 24
Stone Commons	33	X1 21
Stone Ridge Ct	19	F1 27
Stonegate Ct	19	F1 27
Stoney Hollow La	32	Z1 25
Stonington Wy	20	K1 26
Stony Brook Av	19	D1 26
Stony Brook Rd	20	D1 25
Stony Hill Rd	19	L1 28
Stony Rd	19	E1 27
Stony Wood Rd	19	G1 26
Storybook La	20	G1 26
Storyland La	20	G1 26
Stratford St	34	B2 16
Stratford Av	26	Q1 25
Stratford La	32	Y1 25
Stratford Rd (mp)	25	Q1 29
Stratford Rd (fv)	21	M1 19
Strathmore Court Dr	26	P1 25
Strathmore Gate Dr	20	F1 23
Strathmore on the Green Dr	27	S1 22
Strathmore Ridge Dr	32	X1 23
Strathmore Village Dr	20	J1 24
Stratler Dr	33	Z1 20
Stratton Ct	20	G1 24
Stratton La	20	G1 24
Strauss Av	20	L1 23
Strawberry La	34	X1 17
Stonegate Wy	26	R1 24
Strongs La	28	S1 14
Strongs Rd	28	R1 14
Stuart Dr	26	P1 24
Stuart Pl	33	B2 18
Stuart Rd	34	A2 16
Stuarts Ct	19	L1 30
Sturbridge Ct	31	X1 27
Sturrock Wy	20	G1 23
Stuyvesant Av	33	C2 18
Stuyvesant Cir E	20	H1 24
Stuyvesant Cir W	20	H1 24
Stuyvesant Ct	20	M1 24
Stuyvesant Dr	20	L1 24
Stuyvesant Rd	20	L1 24
Suffolk Av	19	E1 26
Suffolk Av (ya)	33	W1 18
Suffolk Blvd	35	A2 11
Suffolk Down	31	X1 29
Suffolk Dr	25	T1 28
Suffolk St	28	N1 15
Suffolk Traction Blvd	22	M1 17
Sugar Bush La	26	Q1 24
Sugar Pine Cir	27	R1 17
Sullivan Ct	26	P1 25
Sullivan St	21	H1 19
Summer St	25	P1 26
Summer Wk	24	J1 5
Summercress La	26	Q1 24
Summerfield Dr	28	N1 17
Summerfield Gate	27	O1 17
Summersweet Dr	26	W1 24
Summerwood Ct	32	Z1 26
Summit Av	19	G1 27
Summit Pl	27	N1 20
Summit St (sk)	20	J1 24
Summit St (ep)	28	R1 13
Sun Rd	31	W1 29
Sun Valley Dr	26	P1 24
Sun Valley La	28	T1 16
Sun Wk	24	K1 6
Sunbonnet La	28	T1 16
Sunburst Dr	25	V1 29
Sunburst La	28	U1 16
Sunburst Wk	24	K1 6
Sunbury La	20	G1 24
Sundial La	28	U1 16
Sundown Dr	28	T1 16
Sunflower Ct (mf)	27	O1 17
Sunflower Ct (co)	26	Q1 24
Sunflower La	38	K2 20
Sunflower La	25	U1 30
Sunflower Ridge	20	G1 23
Sunken Valley Dr	19	M1 28
Sunny Dr	28	T1 16
Sunny Rd	21	F1 19
Sunnydale	25	M1 29
Sunnydale Rd	19	M1 29
Sunnyside Dr (sb)	25	S1 29
Sunnyside Dr (rk)	21	H1 18
Sunray Ct	28	T1 16
Sunreigh Ct	25	S1 28
Sunrise Ct	33	E2 18
Sunrise Dr	25	S1 29
Sunrise Hwy	22	J1 14
Sunrise Pl	27	N1 20
Sunrise Tr	32	C2 26
Sunset Av (co)	26	Q1 23
Sunset Av (rk)	21	J1 17
Sunset Av (fv)	21	M1 21
Sunset Dr (cr)	20	H1 22
Sunset Dr (ey)	33	Z1 18
Sunset Dr (cr)	21	J1 22
Sunset Dr (hg)	28	T1 16
Sunset La (mp)	25	Q1 29
Sunset La (PG)	28	O1 12
Sunset Pa	19	K1 29
Sunset Tr	32	B2 26
Sunwood Dr	25	R1 28
Superior St (tv)	20	M1 25
Superior St (ob)	24	D1 4
Superior St (mp)	25	Q1 28
Surf Rd	25	W1 29
Surf Wk	24	H1 5
Surrey Cir	34	A2 16
Surrey Dr	34	F2 16
Surrey La (ek)	19	H1 28
Surrey La	38	G2 20
Susan Ct	19	E1 28
Susan Dr	28	U1 14
Susan Rd	20	M1 25
Susan La	33	W1 22
Susan Wk	24	J1 5
Sussex La	20	G1 25
Sutton Pl	21	H1 18
Swain St	21	G1 20
Swan Ct	28	Q1 15
Swan Creek Rd	28	P1 14
Swan Lake Dr	28	Q1 14
Swan River St	28	P1 13
Swan Rd	25	V1 28
Swan View Ct	28	Q1 15
Swan View Dr	28	Q1 15
Sweet Briar Pa	20	G1 23
Sweetbriar Ct	21	K1 19
Sweetbriar Dr	33	A2 18
Sweetgum La	25	R1 27
Swezey La	26	R1 24
Swezey St	28	P1 14
Swezey Town Rd N	26	S1 24
Swezey Town Rd S	26	S1 24
Swindow Row	26	Q1 25
Swiss Stone St	27	S1 17
Sycamore Av (LG)	21	F1 20
Sycamore Av (fv)	21	M1 20
Sycamore Cir	20	G1 24
Sycamore Dr	38	J2 18
Sycamore Dr	20	G1 24
Sycamore Rd (mb)	34	C2 13
Sycamore Rd (rp)	25	V1 29
Sycamore St (PJ)	19	N1 27
Sycamore St (cr)	21	G1 22
Sycamore St	25	R1 27
Sycamore St (PG)	28	P1 14
Sylvan Av	25	P1 29
Sylvan Dr	21	N1 18
Sylvan La	25	P1 29
Sylvan Rd	25	T1 29
Sylvester Av	21	G1 19
Sylvester Rd	31	B2 29
Sysoset Rd	25	R1 29
Syracuse Av	27	P1 18
Taber St	28	P1 14
Taft St	25	W1 28
Tagliabue Rd	31	X1 29
Tahoe Ct	26	Q1 24
Taj Ct	21	G1 21
Taj St	21	G1 21
Talbot La	20	M1 24
Tall Oak Cir	33	E2 18
Tall Oaks Ct	33	C2 21
Tall Tree La	25	T1 29
Tallmadge Gate	19	E1 27
Tallow La	20	F1 22
Tallwood Rd	34	Z1 13
Talmadge Tr	25	Q1 28
Tamara Ct	21	H1 20
Tamarack Rd	20	H1 24
Tami Ct	28	T1 16
Tammy Dr	25	N1 27
Tan La	19	G1 29
Tangier Dr	25	P1 29
Tap Rd	28	O1 15
Tap St	19	K1 26
Tara Ct	27	Q1 17
Tarkill Rd	31	B2 27
Tarkill Tr	32	C2 26
Tarkington Rd	21	H1 18
Tarn Rd	31	W1 29
Tarpon Av	28	T1 16
Tarpon La	20	K1 22
Tarpon Rd	31	W1 29
Tarpon Wk	24	L1 6
Taurgo La	20	K1 22
Tavern Wy	19	F1 28
Tawny Pass	20	K1 23
Taylor Av (nc)	20	K1 23
Taylor Av (hg)	28	T1 15
Taylor Commons	33	X1 21
Taylor Ct	21	F1 18
Taylor La	28	P1 14
Taylor St	20	K1 24
Teaberry Ct	20	K1 23
Teak Ct	20	F1 23
Teal Wk	24	K1 6
Technology Dr	20	H1 24
Technology St	32	Z1 22
Ted Ct	26	P1 24
Tee Ct	20	H1 23
Tee Dr	19	E1 27
Tee La	20	L1 25
Teele Dr	26	R1 23
Teepee Rd	25	W1 29
Teller Av	27	R1 21
Tempest Rd	20	L1 23
Temple Rd	19	G1 30
Tennessee Ct	26	N1 25
Tenpoint La	20	J1 26
Terapin St	34	B2 16
Terillium Wy	19	E1 29
Terrace Ct	27	U1 20
Terrace Rd	25	N1 28
Terrell La	19	D1 27
Terrell St	28	P1 13
Terry Dr	34	B2 17
Terry or Whitman Av	25	S1 29
Terry Pl	39	G2 16
Terry Rd	28	P1 15
Terry St	28	O1 14
Terryville Rd	19	L1 27
Tesla St	31	Y1 28
Teton Pl	20	F1 22
Texaco Av	19	L1 27
Texas St	20	N1 23
Thames St	20	K1 26
Theodore Dr	27	O1 22
Theresa Ct	28	Q1 16
Thicket Rd	27	O1 17
Thies Dr	28	S1 16
Third Wk	30	P1 7
Thomas Dr	31	B2 28
Thomas La	20	J1 26
Thomas Rd	25	S1 30
Thomas St (mp)	25	S1 26
Thomas St (co)	26	Q1 23
Thomas St (fv)	21	M1 19
Thompson Av (ob)	24	D1 4
Thompson Av	38	K2 18
Thompson Rd	32	Z1 23
Thompson St (PJ)	19	K1 28
Thompson St (ep)	28	R1 13
Thompson St (rp)	31	W1 29
Thompson's Hay Pa	19	E1 28
Thor Rd	31	W1 29
Thorburn Av	28	P1 13
Thorn Hedge Rd	29	U1 12
Thorne La	19	L1 28
Thorne St (rk)	21	G1 18
Thorne St (PG)	28	O1 14
Thornewood La	38	K2 18
Thornridge La	21	K1 23
Thornton Commons	33	X1 21
Thornton St	28	N1 15
Thornwood Cir	19	G1 26
Thornwood Ct	19	G1 26
Thornwood Dr	34	A2 13
Thornwood Rd	20	J1 22
Thornwood Wy	19	G1 26
Thoroughbred Ct	38	K2 17
Thrasher Av	28	T1 16
Three Village La	19	F1 27
Thrush Pa	26	R1 24
Thunder Rd	25	S1 27
Thunderbird Ct	31	Z1 27
Ticonderoga Ct	32	X1 23
Tie St	28	T1 16
Tiger Ct	27	U1 19
Tiger La	34	F2 16
Tilden Av	20	L1 22
Tilden St	20	L1 22
Tilney Av	27	S1 20
Timber Ridge Dr	26	Q1 23
Timber Ridge Dr	21	M1 18
Timber Rd	32	Y1 23
Timber Tr	38	K2 20
Timber Trail Dr	27	T1 19
Timbercrest La	20	K1 24
Timberidge Ct	26	P1 24
Timberidge Dr	26	P1 23
Timberline Cir	19	M1 29
Timberpoint La	39	L2 17
Tina La	21	K1 18
Tina Rd	25	R1 29
Tinder La	20	F1 22
Tinker Bluff	19	H1 29
Tinker La	19	H1 29
Tipton Dr E	34	A2 15
Tipton Dr W	34	A2 15
Titmus Dr	33	B2 19
Titus La	28	U1 12
Tobi La	19	G1 27
Todd Ct	20	M1 25
Togerson Dr	22	M1 16
Toledo Av (sb)	25	R1 28
Toledo Av (em)	39	L2 16
Tom Ct	19	K1 26
Tomahawk Ct	25	P1 27
Tonopan St	34	B2 16
Topaz Dr	21	J1 19
Toppings Pa	38	L2 20
Torquay Ct	32	X1 26
Torreypine La	27	S1 18
Torrington La	31	X1 27
Tower Hill Av	21	N1 20
Tower Hill Rd	31	X1 29
Tower St	20	F1 22
Town Av	25	S1 27
Towne Ct	26	O1 23
Towne Dr	26	O1 23
Towne House Dr	26	O1 23
Towne La	20	J1 22
Towne Woods Rd	26	O1 23
Townsend Ct	19	E1 27
Townsend St	26	N1 26
Tracker La	20	K1 24

Index

Suffolk Co.

Town of Brookhaven / Town of East Hampton

STREET	MAP	GRID
Tracie La	26	T1 24
Traction Blvd	28	N1 16
Traders Cove	19	K1 28
Trafalgar Dr	34	Z1 12
Traffic Av	24	D1 4
Trailblazer Ct	21	K1 17
Trainor Av	38	G2 19
Trapper La	20	K1 24
Trapper's Path	31	B2 28
Travis Rd	28	T1 12
Treasure La	19	H1 26
Tree Ct	20	H1 24
Tree Rd (cr)	20	J1 23
Tree Rd (mp)	25	Q1 28
Tremont Av (mf)	27	P1 18
Tremont Av (msm	28	P1 17
Trent Ct	32	Y1 26
Trenton St	25	R1 27
Triangle Dr	19	E1 28
Trim La	20	G1 23
Triton Rd	31	W1 29
Troon Rd	20	D1 23
Trout Ponds Ct	34	W1 15
Truburg Av	28	O1 16
Truman Dr	27	P1 20
Trustees Rd	19	D1 27
Trustees Wk	30	P1 7
Tuckahoe Rd	25	R1 29
Tucker La	21	G1 21
Tudor Dr	19	E1 27
Tudor Dr	20	G1 25
Tudor La	26	U1 23
Tudor Rd (sh)	34	A2 16
Tudor Rd (cr)	21	J1 21
Tulip Av	21	M1 20
Tulip Ct	28	N1 17
Tulip Ct	34	E2 17
Tulip Dr	20	L1 25
Tulip Grove Dr	20	F1 22
Tulip Hill La	20	K1 23
Tulip Rd	34	C2 12
Tulip Rd (rp)	25	V1 29
Tuna Wk	24	J1 6
Tupelo St	33	E2 20
Tupper Av	28	P1 16
Turin St	28	S1 13
Turnberry Ct	27	S1 22
Turnberry St	20	G1 23
Turnpike Blvd	26	V1 24
Tuscala St	21	L1 21
Tuthill Creek Dr	28	N1 15
Tuthill Ct	25	P1 29
Tuthill La	39	K2 15
Tuthill Point Rd	39	J2 16
Tuthill St (PJ)	19	K1 28
Tuthill St (BP)	28	V1 13
Twig Ct (LG)	20	F1 22
Twig Ct	20	J1 25
Twilight Rd	25	W1 29
Twin Dr	26	T1 25
Twin Pine La	34	E2 16
Twisting Dr	20	F1 23
Two Rod Rd	19	M1 27
Tyburn La	20	K1 23
Tyler Av (mp)	25	S1 28
Tyler Av (co)	26	O1 22
Tyler St	25	W1 28
Tyne Rd	34	B2 15
Uhl St	21	F1 19
Ulrich Rd	21	H1 21
Underhill Ct	26	P1 26
Underwood St	28	O1 13
Undine Rd	31	W1 29
Union Av (hv)	27	M1 18
Union Av (ep)	29	S1 12
Union Av (cm)	39	G2 15
Union Av (hv)	21	L1 18
Union Av (PG)	28	O1 14
Union Av (rk)	21	G1 17
Union Square Av	21	G1 17
Union St (ps)	19	L1 27
Union St (mp)	26	S1 26
Union St	38	M2 19
Union St (rk)	21	H1 18
Unity Rd	20	J1 22
Universe Wy	25	P1 26
University Dr (sn)	20	F1 25
University Dr (tv)	20	L1 26
University Dr (sc)	21	K1 19
University Heights Ct	20	E1 24
University Heights Dr	20	E1 24
University Rd (mb)	34	C2 12
University Rd (rp)	25	U1 29
Upham Down	31	X1 29
Upper Cross Wy	31	X1 29
Upper Devon Rd	19	K1 29
Upper Midland Pond Ct	34	E2 16
Upper Sheep Pasture Rd	19	H1 26
Upton Dr	25	R1 29
Upton Rd	33	Z1 20
Upton Rd	32	Z1 22
Uranus Rd	25	V1 29
Urban Dr	21	L1 21
Urbans Rd	25	S1 30
Utah Av	25	Q1 27
Uva Way	19	K1 29
Vacation Ct	21	J1 18
Vailey St	26	M1 26
Vale Ct	19	N1 28
Valencia Ct	28	S1 13
Valentine Rd	31	Z1 29
Valerie Ct	27	W1 20
Valerie St	28	P1 16
Valhalla Rd	31	W1 29
Valiant Ct	25	P1 26
Valiant Dr	20	K1 23
Valkyrie Rd	31	W1 29
Valley Cir	25	P1 29
Valley Ct (PJ)	25	N1 27
Valley Ct (fv)	21	L1 19
Valley Dr	38	L2 18
Valley Forge Ct	32	X1 23
Valley Rd (sn)	19	D1 27
Valley Rd (BT)	19	K1 29
Valley Rd (sb)	25	S1 30
Valley Rd (sm)	28	Q1 16
Valley St	21	J1 20
Valley Wy	31	X1 29
Van Bergen Blvd	21	H1 21
Van Brunt Av (ns)	27	M1 22
Van Brunt Manor Rd	19	H1 29
Van Buren Av (nc)	20	K1 23
Van Buren St (nc)	34	B2 16
Van Buren St (tv)	26	O1 25
Van Buren St (SR)	31	X1 28
Van Cleve La	28	T1 13
Van Dyke Pl	19	F1 27
Van Horne Ct	19	G1 29
Vantage Ct	19	L1 27
Varsity Blvd	20	H1 24
Vautrin Av	21	M1 18
Vautrin La	21	M1 18
Vee Jay Dr	31	Z1 28
Vega Dr (rk)	21	H1 17
Vega Dr (sr)	31	Z1 27
Vehslage St	28	O1 16
Veith Av	33	D2 18
Ventry Ct	31	Y1 26
Vera Ct	21	H1 21
Vera Pl	28	Q1 14
Vernon Av (mc)	33	C2 17
Vernon Av (sf)	28	P1 15
Vernon La	20	K1 23
Versa Pl	34	A2 17
Viburnum Ct	25	R1 27
Viceroy Pl	20	L1 25
Vickey Ct	38	L2 20
Vicki Ct	19	G1 27
Vicksburg Ct	26	P1 25
Victor Av	20	L1 23
Victor Ct	26	Q1 23
Victor Pl	20	G1 22
Victoria Cir	28	S1 16
Victoria Dr	33	C2 20
Victoria La	27	Q1 18
Victoria Pl	34	B2 13
Victory Av	25	P1 28
Victory Av	34	Y1 17
Victory Pl	28	Q1 14
Vidoni Dr	25	N1 28
View Ct	20	G1 22
View Dr	25	Q1 29
View Rd	19	G1 28
Viking Pl	20	H1 22
Vilandya Ct	31	Y1 27
Villa Dest Dr	26	P1 22
Villa St	31	X1 28
Village Beach Rd	19	L1 29
Village Cir E	38	G2 19
Village Cir N	38	G2 19
Village Cir S	38	G2 19
Village Cir W	38	G2 19
Village Ct	26	N1 23
Village Dr (mf)	27	R1 17
Village Dr (ri)	32	Y1 24
Village Dr (ep)	28	R1 14
Village Gate	21	M1 20
Village Gate	20	K1 23
Village La	21	L1 22
Village Manor Ct	19	L1 28
Village St	21	H1 17
Village Woods Dr	27	O1 22
Village Woods Rd	19	L1 28
Villet Dr	19	H1 27
Vine Ct	20	J1 23
Vine Rd (mb)	34	C2 14
Vine Rd (rp)	25	V1 29
Vine St (mf)	27	Q1 17
Vine St (co)	26	S1 26
Vine St (cr)	21	G1 22
Vineyard Pl (PJ)	19	K1 28
Vineyard Pl	38	K2 20
Vineyard Wy	26	Q1 23
Vineyard Wy (co)	26	P1 24
Vineyard Wy (ms)	25	O1 28
Vingut La	19	G1 28
Vintage Ct	26	P1 24
Viola La	21	L1 19
Violet La	29	S1 12
Violet Rd (sh)	35	B2 12
Violet Rd (rp)	25	V1 29
Virginia Av	21	G1 20
Virginia Dr	28	Q1 17
Virginia Pl	28	O1 16
Virginia Rd	21	J1 22
Virginia St	21	H1 21
Virginiapine Dr	27	S1 18
Vista La	38	K2 20
Vista Pl	34	E2 15
Vista View Dr	27	O1 20
Vita Dr	33	A2 19
Vivian La	20	F1 22
Von Hagen Av	20	E1 22
Voyages Ct	27	N1 18
Wabil Rd	25	R1 27
Wading River Av	25	Q1 29
Wading River Hollow Rd	27	V1 22
Wading River Rd (sm)	33	E2 22
Wading River Rd (rp)	32	W1 26
Wading River Rd (ri)	32	Z1 26
Wading River Rd (mv)	32	D2 23
Wading River Rd	38	F2 18
Wadleigh Av	33	F2 22
Wadsworth Av	26	O1 25
Wagner Dr	26	Q1 23
Wagner Rd	27	T1 21
Wagon La E	20	J1 23
Wagon La S	20	J1 22
Wagon La W	20	J1 22
Wagon Wheel La	38	H2 17
Wainscott Ct	31	Y1 27
Wainscott Dr	25	R1 29
Wainscott La	19	H1 28
Wakefield Av	26	Q1 25
Walbash Ct	26	Q1 26
Walcott Ct	25	O1 27
Waldorf Dr	33	Z1 20
Waldrow Pl	28	O1 15
Walker Av (hg)	28	S1 14
Walker Av (nb)	28	U1 15
Wall St (tv)	26	O1 23
Wall St (ep)	28	R1 13
Wallace St	21	H1 21
Walnut Av (PQ)	19	J1 29
Walnut Av (sn)	20	E1 26
Walnut Av (fv)	21	M1 20
Walnut Av (sf)	28	P1 15
Walnut Dr	31	Y1 29
Walnut Rd (sh)	35	B2 12
Walnut Rd (rp)	25	T1 28
Walnut Rd (rp)	25	T1 29
Walnut Rd (rp)	25	V1 29
Walnut St (ps)	19	L1 27
Walnut St (co)	26	P1 24
Walnut St (fc)	21	G1 20
Walnut St (cr)	21	G1 21
Walnut St	21	H1 18
Walnut St (sd)	21	M1 22
Walter Ct	20	M1 24
Walter St	21	H1 19
Walters Rd	21	G1 18
Walters St	27	V1 20
Walton Wy	20	N1 25
Wampum Tr	32	C2 26
Wanda Pl	20	M1 22
Wanda Ter	21	K1 20
Warden-Cliff Rd	31	X1 29
Wards La	28	U1 14
Warner La	21	F1 19
Warren Av	21	K1 19
Warren Ct	21	K1 19
Washburn Av	21	G1 21
Washington Av (PQ)	19	J1 28
Washington Av (ps)	19	K1 26
Washington Av (ps)	19	M1 27
Washington Av (sn)	20	G1 26
Washington Av (nc)	20	K1 23
Washington Av (ns)	20	L1 23
Washington Av (tv)	20	N1 26
Washington Av (mb)	34	B2 14
Washington Av (mc)	34	D2 17
Washington Av (mp)	25	R1 28
Washington Av (fv)	21	L1 19
Washington Av (ep)	28	Q1 14
Washington Av N	20	H1 23
Washington Ct	26	Q1 22
Washington Dr	34	D2 14
Washington Heights St	20	L1 22
Washington Pl	28	Q1 15
Washington St (ps)	19	J1 28
Washington St (np)	22	N1 15
Washington St (fc)	21	G1 20
Washington St (hv)	21	N1 18
Watch Hill Av	27	R1 19
Watchogue Av	38	K2 17
Water Rd (rp)	25	T1 29
Water Rd	31	X1 28
Water View Dr	25	R1 30
Water Works Rd	28	N1 14
Watergate La	28	O1 13
Waterloo La	19	G1 27
Watermill Wy	31	Y1 26
Waters Edge La	25	O1 29
Watersedge Wy	19	M1 29
Waterview Dr	19	M1 29
Waterview La	19	D1 28
Waterview Rd	26	V1 24
Waterville Dr	25	R1 29
Waterway Dr	26	T1 25
Watson La (sk)	19	F1 28
Watson La (rk)	21	H1 18
Wauwepex Tr	32	C2 26
Wave Av	27	Q1 19
Wavecrest Dr	34	C2 15
Waverly Av (mf)	27	P1 18
Waverly Av (co)	27	R1 18
Waverly Av (np)	22	M1 17
Waverly Av (PG)	22	N1 15
Waverly Av (fv)	21	L1 20
Waverly Av (fv)	21	M1 19
Waverly Rd	34	A2 12
Wayne St	25	R1 27
Wayside La	20	M1 24
Weaver Av	28	T1 14
Weaver Dr	33	Z1 21
Webster Av	21	G1 20
Wedge Ct	27	O1 22
Wedge La	27	N1 22
Wedgewood Ct (mp)	25	R1 28
Wedgewood Ct	21	G1 19
Wedgewood Dr	20	N1 23
Wedgewood La (mp)	25	R1 28
Wedgewood La (nb)	28	V1 15
Weede St	26	R1 23
Weeks Av	33	C2 20
Weeks Ct	25	P1 29
Weeks St	28	N1 13
Weeler Ct	20	E1 26
Weeler Rd	21	H1 21
Weicher St	21	F1 18
Weidners La	28	P1 16
Weldon La (ps)	19	L1 27
Weldon La (sc)	21	K1 20
Wellbourn La	26	N1 25
Wellington Ct	21	G1 19
Wellington Dr	20	D1 25
Wellington Rd	26	R1 23
Wells La	19	D1 27
Wellsley Ct	20	N1 25
Wellsley La	20	N1 25
Wellwood Dr (ey)	33	Z1 20
Wellwood Dr (sh)	34	Z1 13
Wels La	19	H1 28
Wendover Dr	19	H1 28
Wendy Ct	26	P1 25
Wendy Dr	21	N1 19
Wendy La	21	H1 18
Wendy Rd	26	R1 24
Wenmore La	20	L1 25
Wesley St	39	H2 16
Wesleyan La	32	Z1 26
Wessel La	27	O1 17
West 2nd St	28	N1 14
West 3rd St	28	N1 14
West 4th St	28	N1 14
West 5th Av	32	Z1 23
West 5th St (PG)	28	N1 14
West Aspen Rd	34	B2 14
West Av	28	O1 13
West Bartlett Rd	27	T1 21
West Broadway (tv)	20	K1 25
West Broadway (PJ)	19	J1 28
West Carpenter Dr	27	T1 20
West Cedar Rd	34	C2 13
West Ct	32	Y1 25
West Court Dr	20	H1 23
West Denis La	26	Q1 23
West Dogwood Rd	34	C2 13
West Elfin Pl	34	C2 13
West End Av	34	Z1 17
West End Dr	27	P1 19
West Fawn Pl	34	C2 13
West Forest Rd	34	C2 13
West Gate	25	N1 27
West Gate Av	27	S1 19
West Gate La	19	D1 29
West Giant Oak Rd	32	X1 24
West Hope Ct	20	M1 23
West Lake Dr	28	N1 14
West La (sh)	27	S1 21
West La	38	J2 17
West Main St	22	N1 13
West Masem Sq	28	T1 14
West Meadow La	19	D1 27
West Meadow Rd	19	D1 28
West Miland Pond Ct	34	E2 16
West Parsons Ct	19	H1 27
West Princeton Av	33	Y1 22
West Riviera St	34	B2 14
West Rd	19	E1 28
West Shore Ct	34	D2 17
West Shore Dr	28	N1 15
West St (np)	22	N1 16
West St (pw)	24	E1 5
West St (mi)	26	S1 23
West View Dr	25	R1 29
West Wk	24	N1 7
West Yaphank Rd	26	R1 22
Westbrook Rd	26	N1 25
Westbury Rd	25	S1 29
Westchester Ct	27	S1 22
Westchester Dr	25	T1 29
Westcliff Dr	25	O1 27
Westend Av	33	Y1 19
Westfield Rd	26	R1 24
Westminster Dr	34	Z1 13
Westmoylan La	26	N1 24
Wests Rd	19	G1 27
Westside Ct	25	S1 29
Westview Av	19	L1 28
Westwood Av	20	E1 23
Westwood Ct	21	G1 19
Westwood Dr	34	A2 15
Weymouth Ct	32	X1 26
Whalebone Wk	30	Q1 8
Wheat Path Rd E	25	O1 27
Wheat Path Rd W	25	P1 27
Wheeler Rd	19	E1 30
Whinstone St	26	N1 24
Whippoorwill La	28	Q1 15
Whiskey Rd (ri)	32	X1 25
Whiskey Rd (co)	26	S1 25
Whispering Pines Ct	21	G1 21
Whistler's Ct	26	V1 23
Whitcomb Av	25	O1 27
White Birch Cir	25	Q1 28
White Birch Dr	21	H1 20
White Oak St	26	S1 24
White Pine Dr	29	R1 13
White Pine La	19	H1 29
White Pine Way	27	S1 18
White Tail La	26	T1 26
Whitestone Rd	25	S1 29
Whitetail Ct	34	E2 15
Whitewood Dr	25	T1 29
Whitfield La	26	N1 24
Whitford Rd	20	E1 26
Whitman Dr	27	P1 20
Whitmore La	26	N1 24
Whitney La	26	N1 24
Whittier Av	27	P1 20
Whittier Dr	34	C2 15
Whittier Pl	19	J1 28
Wicket St	26	N1 23
Widgeon Rd	39	H2 15
Widgeon Wk	24	K1 6
Wiggins Av	28	P1 13
Wiggins St	21	G1 18
Wigim Ct	25	S1 29
Wigtel La	28	V1 13
Wilcox Av	39	F2 17
Wildbriar Ct	25	O1 29
Wilderness Ct	33	G2 22
Wilderness Pa	13	D1 28
Wilderness Path Rd	19	D1 28
Wildflower Ct (mc)	33	E2 18
Wildflower Ct (SH)	31	Y1 27
Wildwood Dr	25	R1 29
Wildwood Rd	25	U1 30
Wildwood St	21	G1 22
Willa Wa	21	L1 19
William Floyd Pkwy (sh)	35	A2 12
William Floyd Pkwy (up)	32	Y1 22
William La	21	J1 21
William Penn Dr	19	E1 27
William St (ps)	19	K1 28
William St (ps)	19	M1 27
William St (mc)	34	D2 17
William St (co)	26	N1 24
William St	38	G2 18
William St (fv)	21	M1 19
William St (PG)	28	N1 15
William St (ep)	28	R1 13
Williams Av	21	M1 18
Williams La	26	S1 23
Williams St	21	H1 21
Williamsburg Ct	32	X1 23
Willis Av	19	K1 28
Willis Av Ext	19	K1 27
Williston Dr	25	S1 29
Willmarth Av	28	O1 15
Willoughby Av	26	Q1 25
Willoughby St	19	N1 27
Willow Av (fv)	21	M1 20
Willow Av (nb)	28	U1 14
Willow Ct (fc)	21	G1 19
Willow Ct	38	G2 19
Willow Ct (sf)	28	S1 17
Willow Ct (SR)	31	X1 29
Willow Pl	21	G1 19
Willow Pond La	25	P1 30
Willow Rd	25	Q1 29
Willow St (mc)	33	C2 17
Willow St (cr)	21	G1 22
Willow St (sd)	21	M1 21
Willow St (sf)	28	T1 17
Willow Wk	28	O1 13
Willow Wy	19	M1 28
Willowbend La	27	N1 17
Willowood Ct	20	N1 23
Wills Av (mc)	34	C2 16
Wills Av (rk)	21	G1 18
Willyn Rd	23	M1 12
Wilma Dr	20	M1 24
Wilmington St	25	R1 26
Wilmont Turn La	20	N1 24
Wilmot Rd	19	L1 28
Wilson Av (sd)	27	N1 21
Wilson Av (sr)	33	E2 21
Wilson Av (mb)	34	B2 14
Wilson Av (gh)	26	R1 22
Wilson Av	38	K2 18
Wilson Av (np)	22	N1 16
Wilson Commons	33	X1 21
Wilson Dr	19	K1 27
Wilson St (ps)	19	L1 27
Wilson St (tv)	20	K1 24
Wilson St (PG)	22	N1 13
Wilson St (ep)	28	R1 13
Wilstan Av	22	N1 14
Wiltshire Ct	33	G2 18
Winchester Rd	21	H1 17
Windcrest Dr	38	J2 20
Windham La	21	H1 18
Windham La S	21	H1 17
Windmar Wy Ct	21	J1 22
Windmill La	19	N1 27
Windover La	20	N1 24
Windsor Ct	26	O1 24
Windsor Dr	20	L1 24
Windsor Pl (mc)	34	C2 17
Windsor Pl (sa)	34	Z1 17
Windsor St	21	J1 20
Windus Dr	34	A2 15
Windward Ct N	19	M1 27
Windward Ct S	19	M1 27
Windward Dr	19	M1 27
Windward Wk	30	P1 7
Winfield Davis Dr	26	Q1 22
Winfield Dr	25	R1 30
Winged Foot Dr	27	T1 19
Winges Av	28	O1 16
Winne Rd	39	G2 15
Winside La	26	N1 24
Winston Dr (PJ)	19	M1 29
Winston Dr (mc)	33	A2 17
Winston La	20	M1 25
Winston Rd	20	J1 22
Winter La	25	P1 26
Winter Wy	26	O1 24
Winterberry Dr	32	W1 24
Winterberry La	25	R1 27
Wintergreen Ct	32	Z1 26
Wintergreen Dr	26	O1 24
Winterling St	26	O1 23
Winters Dr	33	B2 18
Winthrop Ct	23	M1 12
Wireless Rd	20	J1 24
Wisconsin Av (mp)	25	Q1 26
Wisconsin Av (tv)	26	N1 26
Wisteria Cir	28	U1 17
Wisteria Dr	20	G1 23
Wittridge Rd	21	F1 18
Wolf Hollow Rd	21	J1 21
Wood Acres Rd	28	T1 12
Wood Av (mc)	34	B2 17
Wood Av (PG)	28	P1 14
Wood Fern La	38	L2 18
Wood Lot Rd	32	X1 25
Wood Pa	25	T1 29
Wood Rd	20	G1 23
Wood Thrush Ct	25	O1 29
Woodberry Rd	29	T1 12
Woodbine Av	19	D1 27
Woodbine La	38	L2 18
Woodbine St	26	N1 24
Woodbridge Ct	25	T1 29
Woodbridge Dr	32	X1 26
Woodbrook Cir	22	M1 16
Woodbrook Dr	32	Z1 25
Woodburn St	28	P1 13
Woodbury Rd	21	M1 19
Woodchuck Ct (ek)	19	J1 26
Woodchuck Ct (mp)	34	A2 14
Woodchuck La	19	J1 26
Woodchuck Tr	26	R1 24
Woodcock La	19	C1 30
Woodcrest Dr	38	L2 18
Woodcut Dr	34	D2 15
Woodfield Rd	19	D1 27
Woodhaven Dr	25	S1 29
Woodhill Cir	29	S1 13
Woodhollow Ct	27	O1 18
Woodhull Av	19	L1 27
Woodhull Cove La	19	D1 28
Woodhull Landing Rd	25	R1 29
Woodhull La	21	M1 18
Woodhull Rd	19	H1 28
Woodland Av (sr)	33	D2 20
Woodland Av (bp)	23	N1 12
Woodland Av (hv)	21	M1 18
Woodland Av (nb)	28	V1 14
Woodland Blvd	21	G1 21
Woodland Ct (co)	27	P1 21
Woodland Ct (gh)	26	T1 22
Woodland Dr	34	C2 14
Woodland Rd (BT)	19	K1 29
Woodland Rd	25	Q1 28
Woodland Rd (cp)	21	H1 21
Woodland Rd (nb)	28	U1 14
Woodland St	21	F1 19
Woodlawn Av	38	K2 17
Woodlawn Av (sd)	21	N1 21
Woodlawn Rd	25	V1 29
Woodmere Dr	34	E2 15
Woodmere Pl	21	M1 22
Woodmere Rd	25	S1 30
Woodmont Pl	21	N1 19
Woodridge La	26	N1 23
Woodruff Av	29	U1 13
Woods Corner Rd	19	F1 27
Woods Dr	20	K1 25
Woods La	20	J1 23
Woods Rd	32	Y1 22
Woodscreek Ct	34	E2 17
Woodside Av (ps)	19	M1 27
Woodside Av (np)	28	N1 16
Woodside Ct	28	N1 16
Woodside Rd	34	B2 13
Woodspath La	38	L2 18
Woodview La	21	H1 21
Woodville Landing Rd	31	X1 29
Woodville Rd (mi)	26	V1 24
Woodville Rd (SR)	31	X1 28
Woodward Av	28	N1 16
Woody Pl	19	N1 27
Woodycrest Dr	27	N1 19
Wrana La	27	O1 17
Wrana St	27	O1 17
Wren Pa	26	R1 24
Wright Rd	33	D2 19
Wyandanch La	23	M1 12
Wyandanch Tr	26	O1 23
Wyandotte La	29	V1 13
Wyandotte St	20	M1 22
Wyanet St	21	L1 21
Wyant Av	21	G1 18
Wyckoff Av	19	M1 27
Wycomb Ct	26	N1 24
Wycomb Pl	26	N1 25
Wyeth St	26	N1 23
Wylde Rd	25	P1 28
Wyman Ct	26	N1 25
Wyngate La	26	O1 24
Wynn La	19	K1 28
Wynville Ct	26	O1 24
Wyoming St	26	N1 23
Wyona Av	26	N1 22
Wyona Ct	21	G1 20
Xenia Ct	25	P1 27
Xylo Rd	25	V1 29
Xyris Rd	25	V1 29
Yacht St	29	S1 12
Yale Ct	20	G1 25
Yale Rd (ya)	33	Y1 21
Yale Rd (ep)	28	Q1 15
Yale St	20	L1 25
Yaphank Av	33	W1 18
Yaphank Middle Island Rd	26	U1 23
Yaphank Rd (ya)	33	Y1 21
Yaphank Rd (mb)	34	B2 13
Yaphank Rd (sb)	25	S1 30
Yaphank Rd (ep)	28	R1 15
Yaphank Woods Blvd	33	X1 20
Yarmouth La	33	G2 17
Yarror Cir	28	U1 17
Yava St	20	K1 25
Yellow Pine Cir	27	R1 17
Yellowstone Ct	26	P1 24
Yeoman La	20	H1 25
Yeoman Rd	25	V1 29
Yerk Av	21	G1 18
Yonkers Av	27	P1 18
York Dr	26	Q1 26
York La	33	Y1 22
Yorkshire Av	19	E1 27
Yorktown Ct	26	P1 25
Yorktown Dr	20	G1 26
Yosemite La	26	Q1 24
Young Rd	26	Q1 23
Youngs La	19	G1 29
Yucca Rd	25	V1 29
Yule La	33	Y1 21
Zebra Rd	25	V1 29
Zenith Rd	25	V1 29
Zophar Mill's Rd	31	B2 29
1st Av (PJ)	19	L1 28
1st Av (mc)	33	D2 18
1st Av (rp)	25	U1 29
1st Av (np)	28	O1 16
1st Av (sf)	28	P1 16
1st Pl	34	C2 17
1st St (co)	27	P1 21
1st St (co)	27	P1 22
1st St (PG)	22	N1 14
1st St (pw)	24	E1 5
1st St (mp)	25	S1 28
1st St (sb)	25	S1 29
1st St (lr)	21	F1 17
1st St (rk)	21	H1 17
1st St (sc)	21	J1 20
1st St (hv)	21	M1 19
1st St (PG)	28	Q1 13
2nd Av	19	M1 28
2nd Av (PG)	25	M1 28
2nd Av (np)	25	U1 29
2nd Av	28	O1 17
2nd Av (sf)	28	P1 16
2nd St (co)	27	P1 21
2nd St (mc)	33	D2 18
2nd St (sr)	33	F2 19
2nd St (sa)	34	W1 14
2nd St (pw)	24	E1 5
2nd St (mp)	25	S1 28
2nd St (sb)	25	S1 29
2nd St (lr)	21	F1 17
2nd St (lr)	21	F1 19
2nd St (nb)	21	H1 18
2nd St (sc)	21	J1 19
2nd St (em)	38	L2 18
2nd St (fv)	21	M1 19
3rd Av (rp)	25	U1 29
3rd Av (np)	28	O1 17
3rd St (co)	27	P1 22
3rd St (mc)	33	D2 18
3rd St (mp)	25	S1 28
3rd St (sb)	25	S1 29
3rd St (co)	26	Q1 25
3rd St (lr)	21	F1 17
3rd St (hb)	21	H1 18
3rd St (hb)	21	J1 19
4th Av (up)	32	Z1 22
4th Av (ri)	25	U1 28
4th Av (np)	28	O1 17
4th St (ps)	19	L1 26
4th St (co)	27	P1 22
4th St (mc)	33	D2 18
4th St (lk)	21	F1 17
4th St (sc)	21	J1 19
4th St (fv)	21	M1 20
5th Av (np)	28	O1 17
5th St (ps)	19	L1 26
5th St (mc)	33	D2 18
5th St (sb)	25	S1 29
5th St (lr)	21	F1 17
5th St (hb)	21	J1 18
5th St (hb)	21	K1 18
6th Av (np)	28	O1 17
6th St (up)	33	A2 22
6th St (mc)	33	D2 18
6th St (PG)	22	N1 14
6th St (sb)	25	S1 29
6th St (hb)	21	J1 18
7th Av (np)	28	N1 17
7th St (up)	33	A2 22
7th St (mc)	33	F2 18
7th St (mp)	25	S1 28
7th St (hb)	21	J1 18
7th St (PG)	28	N1 14
8th Av (np)	28	N1 17
8th St (lr)	21	F1 18
8th St (fv)	21	M1 20
8th St (PG)	28	N1 14
9th Av (np)	28	N1 17
9th St (ps)	19	L1 26
9th St (lr)	21	F1 18
9th St (PG)	28	N1 14
10th Av (np)	28	N1 17
10th St (lr)	21	F1 18
11th Av (np)	28	N1 17
11th St (lr)	21	F1 18
12th Av (np)	22	N1 17
12th St (lr)	21	F1 18
13th Av (np)	22	N1 17
13th St (ps)	19	L1 27
13th St (mp)	25	S1 28
14th Av (np)	22	N1 17
14th St (mp)	25	S1 27
15th St (ns)	20	M1 24
15th St (mp)	25	S1 27
18th St (sk)	20	H1 24
23rd St (sk)	20	H1 24
25th St (sk)	20	H1 24
28th St (sn)	20	G1 24
31st St (sn)	20	G1 24
34th St (sn)	20	G1 25
34th St (tv)	20	N1 27
34th St (ps)	25	N1 27
43rd St	20	H1 22
57th St	21	H1 22

EAST HAMPTON

STREET	MAP	GRID
Abigails Pa	55	C4 35
Aborigine Wy	55	E4 34
Abrahams Pa	60	F4 32
Abrams Landing Rd	60	K4 31
Accabonac Rd	59	H4 33
Ackerley St	55	W3 32
Acorn Pl	60	K4 32
Adams Dr	61	X4 35
Agnew Av	62	B5 36
Albertines La	55	E4 33
Alberts Landing Rd	60	K4 32
Alewive Brook Rd	55	B4 35
Alexis Ct	60	K4 32
Alpine Av	63	T4 53
Amagansett Dr W	60	G4 31
Amagansett Pl	60	H4 30
Amys La	60	G4 30
Ancient Hwy	56	A4 31
Angiedon Ct	55	C4 35
Anvil Ct	56	C4 30
Apaquogue Rd	57	C4 28
Arbor Pa	60	K4 32
Ardsley Rd	56	Z3 28
Argyle La	59	H4 36
Arnold Ct	61	W4 34
Arthur Rd	61	X4 35
Asa's Pa	60	H4 31
Ashwood Ct	60	K4 31
Astor Pl	59	H4 34
Astor St	59	G4 33
Athol Cres	63	T4 54
Atlantic Dr	61	Q4 32
Atlantic Av	55	W3 32
Atlantic Av (SH)	60	K4 31
Atlantic St	56	D4 31
Audibon St	59	F4 33
Augie's Pa	55	D4 33
Av B	63	T4 54
Ayrshire Pl	59	H4 36
Babes La	59	F4 35
Bailow La	56	D4 29
Baiting Hollow Rd	56	D4 28
Banks Ct	60	G4 31
Barcelona Neck Rd	55	Z3 33
Barclay Ct	55	D4 33
Barclay Rd	56	Z3 28
Bark Ct	56	Z3 30
Barnes Av	55	C4 32
Barnes Hole Rd	59	L4 33
Barns La	60	E4 30
Barry La	59	F4 35
Barsdis La	60	F4 34
Bathgate Rd	56	Z3 28
Bay Colony Ct	55	C4 35
Bay Inlet Rd	59	G4 36
Bay St	55	W3 33
Bay View Av	60	F4 32
Bayberry La	60	L4 31
Bayberry Rd	62	Y4 38
Bayview Av	55	C4 32
Bayview Av	60	P4 33
Beach Av (SH)	55	X3 32
Beach Av	63	T4 53
Beach Av	60	L4 30
Beach Plum Ct	61	R4 32
Beach La	57	A4 27
Beach Plum Rd	62	Y4 38
Beach Rd	55	X3 32
Beachway	59	K4 33
Bearing East Rd	55	B4 35
Beech Hollow ST	61	U4 34
Beech Hollow Ct	62	Y4 37
Beechwood Ct	55	C4 35
Bell Hill Av	63	T4 53
Bell Pl	60	K4 32
Bell Rd	59	G4 33
Bendigo Rd	60	M4 32
Benson Dr	62	B5 36
Berryman St	55	E4 31
Between La	59	G4 34
Beverly Rd	59	G4 33
Bianco Rd	55	D4 35
Big Reed Pa	62	B5 38
Birch Dr	61	V4 34
Birch St	60	F4 32
Birdie La	60	G4 32
Bittersweet La	60	L4 32
Blackberry Dr	62	Y4 38
Blacksmith Pl	56	C4 29
Blue Jay Wy	56	C4 29
Blueberry Knolls La	55	C4 33
Blueberry La	56	D4 29
Bluff Rd	60	J4 30
Boat Yard Rd	56	E4 30
Boatheaders La	56	E4 31
Boatsteerers Ct	60	F4 31
Bob White Ct	56	D4 31
Bon Pinck Wy	59	H4 37
Bonac Ct	60	H4 33
Bonac Woods La	60	H4 33
Borden Pl	59	H4 33
Boulder La	55	C4 35
Bowling Green Pl	59	G4 34
Bow-Oarsman's Rd	56	E4 31
Boxwood St	60	E4 30
Brandywine Dr	55	X3 32
Breeze Hill Rd	59	F4 33
Briar Patch Rd	56	C4 32
Briarcroft Dr	59	G4 35
Briarsweet La	60	E4 34
Brisbane Av	62	B5 36
Broadview Rd	60	L4 32
Broadway	59	G4 35
Broadwood Ct	56	Z3 29
Bruce La	59	F4 35
Bryan Rd	61	X4 35
Bryant St	59	G4 33
Bucks Pa	55	E4 32
Buckskill Rd	56	B4 30
Buells La	56	D4 29
Buells La Ext	56	D4 29
Buffalo Pa	55	D4 34
Bull Pasture La	59	H4 36
Bull Pa	55	A4 32
Bull Path Cl	55	B4 32

Index

Suffolk Co.

Town of East Hampton

STREET	MAP	GRID	
Bull Run	55	B4	32
Bunker Hill Rd	60	K4	31
Burke St	55	W3	33
Butternut Dr	62	Y4	38
Buxton Rd	57	C4	28
Cadmus Rd	55	X3	32
Camberly Rd	59	H4	35
Camp Hero Rd	62	E5	38
Canvas-Back La	60	L4	31
Captain Belfour Wy	62	Y4	38
Captain Kidd's Pa	62	Y4	38
Captains Wk	59	K4	33
Carriage La	59	K4	33
Carver St	55	X3	32
Castle Ct	60	M4	31
Caswell Rd	62	C5	36
Catalpa Pl	60	K4	32
Cattalo Cir	55	D4	34
Cattle Wk	55	B4	33
Cedar Ct	56	E4	30
Cedar Dr	59	H4	36
Cedar Dr	60	G4	31
Cedar Point Rd	55	B4	35
Cedar Ridge Dr	59	F4	33
Cedar St	60	G4	33
Cedar St	56	E4	30
Cedar St	61	U4	34
Cedar Tr	56	C4	31
Cemetery Rd	61	T4	33
Central Av	63	T4	54
Central Av	60	G4	31
Central Av	60	L4	31
Centre Wy	55	D4	34
Chapel La	60	K4	33
Charter La	55	D4	34
Chatfield Ridge Rd	56	B4	31
Chatfields La	55	A4	32
Cherry St	60	H4	32
Chestnut Wy	56	C4	29
Church La	59	G4	33
Church La (EV)	56	E4	29
Circle, The	60	F4	30
Clamshell Av	55	D4	34
Claremont St	59	F4	34
Clearview Dr	62	X4	35
Cleveland Dr	61	W4	35
Cliff Rd	60	L4	31
Clinton Academy La	60	L4	30
Clinton St (SH)	55	W3	32
Clinton St	59	F4	33
Close Ct	60	G4	31
Clover Leaf La	56	C4	29
Clyden Rd	56	Z3	28
Cobblers Ct	55	C4	32
Cobblers La	56	Z3	30
Collins St	60	F4	30
Colony Ct	55	B4	33
Conklin Ter	60	E4	30
Coolidge Rd	61	W4	34
Cooper La	56	E4	30
Copeces La	59	F4	33
Cora Rd	60	F4	32
Corbin Av	59	G4	35
Cordwood La	55	C4	33
Coronet La	56	C4	30
Cosorew La	56	A4	31
Cottage Av	56	D4	28
Coultes Wy	56	A4	30
Country La	55	C4	31
County Route 30	62	A5	38
County Route 33	60	G4	30
County Route 40	59	G4	36
County Route 41	59	H4	34
County Route 45	59	H4	35
County Route 45	59	K4	33
County Route 49	62	Z4	38
County Route 59	55	A4	31
County Route 59	60	E4	30
County Route 74	60	M4	31
County Route 77	62	Z4	39
County Route 81	55	W3	33
County Route 113	56	B4	29
Cove Hollow Farm Rd	56	C4	28
Cove Hollow Rd	56	C4	28
Cowhill La	56	Z3	28
Cranberry Hole Rd	60	L4	31
Cranberry La	60	M4	31
Cranberry Rd	62	Y4	38
Crandall St	59	G4	35
Crassen Blvd	61	P4	33
Creek Rd	55	D4	34
Crescent Av	63	T4	54
Crooked Hwy	55	A4	32
Cross Dr	62	C5	36
Cross Hwy (EV)	60	F4	31
Cross Hwy	60	G4	30
Cross Hwy	60	H4	30
Cross Hwy	60	M4	31
Cross Hwy	60	M4	32
Cross Hwy to Devon	60	L4	32
Cross St	55	W3	33
Cross Wy Rd	56	D4	28
Crossway, The	56	Z3	29
Crossways	56	E4	28
Crows Nest La	55	D4	34
Crystal Dr	60	F4	32
Cuffee Dr	55	X3	32
Culloden Pl	62	Z4	38
Cutter Ct	56	C4	30
Cynthia's Pa	60	M4	32
Daniel's Hole Rd	56	Z3	30
Darley Rd	56	Z3	28
David Darby Pass	56	D4	29
Davids La	60	F4	29
Davis Dr	61	V4	34
Davis Av	62	X4	36
Dayton La	56	E4	29
Dayton La Ext	56	D4	29
Den Tree Pa	55	D4	33
Debra's Wy	56	Z3	29
Deep La	60	J4	31
Deep Six Dr	59	H4	34
Deep View Ct	56	Z3	30
Deep Wood La	60	K4	32
Deer Haven Ct	56	Z3	31
Deer Pa	59	G4	35
Deer Pa	56	Z3	31
Deer Wy	62	B5	38
Deerfield Dr	55	X3	32
Deerfield La	60	L4	30
Deerfield Wy	60	L4	30
Deforest Rd	62	B5	36
Delavan St	59	G4	33
Dennistown Dr	60	K4	33
Dering Rd	55	W3	32
Devon Rd	60	M4	31

STREET	MAP	GRID	
Devon Woods Cl	60	L4	32
Devonshire La	60	L4	31
Dewey Pl	62	Y4	35
Diane Dr	55	D4	32
Discovery La	55	D4	34
Ditch Plains Rd	62	B5	36
Division St	55	W3	32
Dogwood St	61	V4	34
Dogwood Dr	59	H4	35
Dolphin Dr	61	Q4	32
Dominy Ct	60	G4	30
Dongans Wy	55	D4	33
Dorset Rd	59	H4	35
Downer Pl	55	X3	32
Downey La	60	F4	30
Drew La	57	D4	28
Driftwood La	59	H4	36
Du Val Pl	62	B5	36
Duke Dr	55	D4	33
Dune Alpin Dr N	56	C4	29
Dune Alpin Dr S	56	C4	29
Dune Crest Wy	60	L4	31
Dune Hill Rd	60	L4	30
Dune La	60	M4	31
Dune Wy	60	M4	31
Dunemere La	60	E4	29
Dunes La	61	Q4	32
Duryea Av	62	Z4	38
East Dune La	60	F4	29
East End Av	62	C5	36
East End Rd	63	W4	54
East Flamingo Av	62	Z4	38
East Gate Rd	56	Z3	29
East Hampton Dr E	60	G4	31
East Hampton-Sag Harbor Tpke	56	Z3	31
East Hollow Rd	56	D4	28
East Lake Dr	62	B5	38
East Wy	55	E4	34
Easton Rd	61	X4	34
Eastside Ct	59	J4	33
Eastville Av	55	X3	32
Eastwood Ct	60	K4	32
Eau Claire St	59	H4	35
Ed Hults La	59	H4	34
Edgewater Dr	62	C5	36
Edin St	62	Z4	36
Edison Dr	61	W4	35
Edison Dr	62	E5	38
Edwards Av	60	H4	30
Edwards Cl	60	L4	33
Edwards Hole Rd	55	Z3	32
Edwards La	59	F4	35
Edwards La	56	E4	29
Egypt Cl	60	F4	30
Egypt La	60	F4	30
Eileen's Pa	60	H4	30
Eli Cir	55	D4	35
Elisha's Pa	56	A4	28
Elizabeth St	55	W3	32
Elliot Pl	62	Y4	36
Elm La	61	V4	34
Elm Pl	62	Z4	36
Elvira St	60	G4	32
Elwell St	62	Z4	36
Ely Brook to Hands Creek Rd	55	C4	34
Ely Brook Rd	55	C4	34
Endicott Ter	62	Y4	35
Equestrian Av	63	T4	53
Essex St	62	Z4	36
Esterbrook Rd	56	Z3	29
Ettrick Av	63	T4	53
Exeter La	56	Z3	28
Fair Pl	60	H4	30
Fair View Rd	62	X4	35
Fairfield Dr	62	Z4	36
Fairfield La	56	Z3	29
Fairlawn Dr	62	Z4	36
Fairmont Av	62	Y4	37
Fairview Av	62	Z4	36
Fairview Pl	62	Z4	37
Fairway Dr	60	F4	32
Falcon Pl	62	Y4	37
Falcon Rd	56	Z3	29
Fanning Av	59	F4	35
Farm House La	59	H4	35
Farm La	60	G4	30
Farragut Rd	62	Y4	37
Farrington Pl	62	Z4	37
Farrington Rd	62	Z4	37
Federick Ct	62	Z4	37
Fenmarsh Rd	59	G4	36
Fenwick Pl	62	Y4	37
Fenwick Rd	62	Z4	36
Fernald Rd	62	Y4	36
Ferndale Dr	62	Z4	37
Fernwood Rd	56	A4	28
Fetlock Ct	56	C4	30
Fieldview La	56	D4	30
Fireplace Rd	59	H4	36
Firestone Rd	62	Y4	37
Fir La	61	U4	34
Fithian La	60	F4	30
Five Rod Rd	57	A4	27
Flagg Av	62	B5	36
Flaggy Hole Rd	59	F4	36
Flamingo Av	62	Y4	36
Flamingo Ct	62	Z4	38
Flanders Rd	62	Z4	38
Fleming Rd	62	Y4	37
Flintlock La	55	D4	35
Florence St	59	H4	35
Florida Rd	62	Y4	37
Floyd St	60	F4	31
Folkstone Dr	59	F4	35
Forest Ct	55	E4	33
Fort Pond Blvd	59	G4	35
Fort Pond Rd	62	Y4	36
Founders La	55	D4	34
Fox Av	63	T4	54
Fox Hunt La	60	M4	32
Fox La	63	S4	53
Foxboro Rd	62	Z4	37
Foxcroft La	57	A4	28
Foxgrove Rd	55	D4	35
Franklin Av	55	W3	32
Franklin Dr	61	X4	35
Franklin St	62	Z4	36
Fredericka La	60	F4	30
Freemont Rd	62	Z4	37
Fresh Pond Rd	60	K4	31
Fresno Pl	56	E4	30
Front St	59	G4	34
Fulton Dr	62	A5	36
Further Ct	60	J4	30
Further La	60	G4	29
Gainsborough Ct	62	A5	37

STREET	MAP	GRID	
Gaiton Pl	62	A5	37
Gann Rd	59	F4	35
Gannet Dr	62	Z4	38
Gansett La	60	J4	30
Garden Wy	60	J4	30
Gardiner Av	59	G4	34
Gardiner Cove Rd	60	F4	32
Gardiner Dr	60	M4	31
Gardiners La	59	F4	34
Gates Av	62	A5	37
Gay Rd	60	F4	30
Georgia Pl	62	A5	37
Georgica Association Rd	57	B4	28
Georgica Close Rd	56	B4	29
Georgica Dr	56	A4	29
Georgica Rd	56	C4	28
Georgica Woods La	56	A4	29
Gerard Dr	59	J4	36
Gilbert Pa	60	M4	31
Gilbert Rd	62	A5	37
Gingerbread La	56	E4	30
Githian La	59	F4	34
Glade Rd	59	G4	34
Gladstone Pl	62	Z4	37
Glen Oak Ct	57	A4	28
Glen The	61	W4	35
Glenmaine Av	63	T4	54
Glenmore Av	62	Z4	37
Glenway	59	K4	33
Gloaming The	63	U4	53
Gloucester Av	62	Z4	37
Golf Club Dr	60	K4	31
Goodfriend Dr	56	A4	30
Goodridge Pl	62	B5	36
Gordon St	60	F4	32
Gould St	56	E4	30
Grace La	57	D4	28
Grand St	55	W3	32
Grant Av	60	G4	33
Grant Dr	61	X4	34
Grape Arbor La	56	D4	31
Grassy Hollow Dr	55	C4	33
Gravesend Av	62	Z4	37
Great Oak Wy	55	C4	34
Green Hollow Rd	56	C4	29
Greentree Ct	60	J4	33
Greenway	60	K4	33
Greenway Dr	56	D4	29
Greenwich St	62	A5	37
Greenwood Rd	63	S4	53
Grove St	60	H4	31
Guernsey La	59	G4	36
Gull Rd	62	Z4	38
Gull Rock Rd	55	X3	32
Gun Powder La	55	D4	35
Halcyon Av	63	T4	53
Hamilton Dr	61	W4	34
Hamilton St	55	W3	32
Hamlin La	60	J4	32
Hampton La	60	M4	31
Hampton Pl	60	H4	30
Hampton St	55	W3	32
Hand La	60	K4	31
Hands Cir	56	C4	30
Hands Creek Rd	55	D4	32
Hands Creek Rd	55	D4	34
Hands Pa	55	C4	32
Handy La	60	H4	30
Harbor Av	55	X3	32
Harbor Blvd	59	F4	35
Harbor Blvd	59	G4	33
Harbor Hill La	59	K4	33
Harbor La	59	H4	34
Harbor Rd	61	Q4	33
Harbor St	55	C4	32
Harbor View Av	60	F4	32
Harbor View Dr	59	F4	33
Harbor View La	59	F4	35
Harboy Pl	55	X3	32
Harding Rd	61	W4	35
Harding Ter	55	Y3	33
Hardscrabble Cl	56	B4	30
Hardscrabble Ct	56	D4	30
Harness La	56	C4	30
Harrison Av	60	G4	33
Harrison Rd	61	X4	35
Harrison St	55	W3	32
Hartley Blvd	60	F4	33
Harvest La	55	D4	33
Hawk's Nest La	60	L4	31
Hawthorne Av	60	F4	33
Hawthorne St	59	G4	35
Hayes Rd	61	X4	35
Haynes La	59	H4	35
Hayseed Wy	56	C4	29
Heatherwood La	60	M4	32
Heathulie Av	63	T4	53
Hedge Banks Dr	55	C4	36
Hedge St	63	T4	53
Hedgerow La	56	E4	30
Hedges Av	56	E4	31
Hedges La (EV)	56	D4	28
Hedges La	60	J4	30
Hedges Rd	56	A4	29
Heller La	60	G4	29
Hempstead St	55	X3	32
Heritage Farm La	56	C4	31
Hickory Ct	55	C4	35
Higbee Pl	59	G4	33
High Point Rd	55	D4	35
High Ridge Rd	56	A4	31
High St (SH)	55	W3	32
High St	60	G4	32
Highland Blvd	60	G4	32
Highland La	55	A4	33
Highway Behind the Lots	56	D4	29
Highway Behind the Pond	60	F4	29
Highway to Phoebe Van Scoys	55	A4	34
Highwood La	59	H4	33
Hildreth Pl	59	H4	33
Hill Rd	60	F4	33
Hillcrest Dr	55	X3	32
Hillside Dr E	55	Y3	32
Hillside Dr W	55	Y3	32
Hilltop La	56	A4	31
Historical Wy	55	E4	33
Hither La	60	F4	29
Hodder Av	59	F4	35
Hog Creek La	59	H4	37
Hog Creek Rd	59	H4	36
Hollow Oak Ct	60	H4	30
Hollow Tree La	55	D4	33
Holly Hill Rd	60	L4	32
Holly Pl	60	H4	30

STREET	MAP	GRID	
Holly Wy	60	K4	30
Hollyoak Av	59	H4	33
Homestead La	59	H4	36
Homeward La	62	C5	38
Hook Nell La	60	F4	30
Hook Pond Rd	56	E4	29
Hoover Ct	61	W4	35
Hopkins Av	62	A5	35
Hoppin Av	62	B5	36
Horizon Dr	55	X3	32
Horse Meadow La	56	C4	29
Horseshoe North Dr	56	C4	29
Houston Dr	62	W4	35
Howard St	60	F4	32
Hoyt Pl	62	B5	36
Huckleberry La	56	B4	29
Hudson Rd	62	W4	34
Hull Dr	61	W4	34
Hunting La	60	E4	30
Hunting La	60	F4	29
Hunting Pl	60	E4	32
Indian Hill La	60	F4	30
Indian Wells Plain Hwy	60	J4	30
Industrial Rd	56	Z3	29
Industrial Rd	62	Y4	36
Inkberry St	60	E4	30
Irma Ct	56	E4	30
Isaac's Gate	55	C4	34
Isaacs Pa	60	G4	31
Island Rd	60	E4	33
Isle of Wight Rd	59	G4	36
Jackson Rd	61	X4	35
Jackson St	60	F4	31
Jacqueline Dr	60	M4	31
James La	56	E4	29
James St	56	C4	31
Jasons Ct	55	B4	32
Jasons La	55	B4	31
Jay Rd	61	W4	34
Jefferson Av	62	F5	38
Jefferson Rd	61	X4	35
Jefferys La	56	E4	29
Jenny's Pa	60	G4	31
Jericho Close La	56	C4	28
Jericho La	56	D4	28
Jericho Rd	56	C4	29
Jermain Av	55	W3	32
Jody's Pa	55	D4	33
Jonathan Dr	55	E4	32
Jones Cove Rd	56	B4	29
Jones Rd	57	D4	28
Joshua Edwards Ct	60	F4	31
Joshuas Hole Rd	55	B4	32
Joshua's Pa	56	B4	31
Kalman Ct	55	B4	33
Karin Dr	55	D4	32
Karlsruhe Cross Hwy	60	F4	32
Katie La	60	L4	31
Kembell Av	56	E4	31
Kent Pl	59	H4	36
Kettle Ct	55	E4	32
Kettle Hole Rd	62	Y4	37
King Ct	59	H4	34
King St	55	D4	32
Kings Point Rd	59	G4	37
Kingston Av	59	F4	34
Kirk Av	62	Z4	38
Kirk's Pl	55	A4	35
Knoll La	56	Y3	31
Koala La	55	B4	32
La Foret La	60	J4	32
Lafayette Pl	59	F4	33
Lakeside Ct	62	A5	37
Landfall Cir	55	B4	35
Landfall Rd	55	C4	35
Landing La	59	J4	34
La Forest La	57	C4	28
Lantern La	59	K4	33
Laura's La	60	G4	31
Laurel Dr	61	W4	35
Laurel Hill La	60	H4	32
Lazy Point Rd	60	P4	32
Lee Av	56	D4	28
Lee Ct	61	X4	35
Lee La	56	A4	28
Leeton Rd	61	Q4	32
Leon Ct	62	C5	37
Liberty St	55	X3	32
Light House La	55	X3	32
Lighthouse Rd	55	A4	35
Lilla La	59	J4	33
Lily Pond La	57	D4	28
Lincoln Av	59	G4	35
Lincoln Rd	61	X4	35
Lincoln St (SH)	55	Y3	32
Lincoln St	59	G4	33
Lion Head Rock Rd	59	H4	36
Little Ct	55	C4	35
Livery La	56	C4	30
Lockwood La	56	E4	28
Locust Dr	59	H4	35
Long Hill Rd	55	C4	32
Long La	56	C4	30
Long Ridge La	56	D4	31
Long Woods La	55	X3	33
Longboat La	55	C4	35
Lookout Point La	59	K4	34
Loop, The	62	Y4	36
Lotus Av	59	H4	33
Louse Point Rd	59	K4	33
Love La	55	W3	32
Lumber La	56	E4	30
Lyme La	55	B4	32
Lynda Ct	56	E4	30
Lynda La	56	E4	30
Madeline Av	63	T4	54
Madison Av	63	T4	35
Madison Dr	61	X4	35
Madison Hill Dr	62	E5	38
Maidstone Av	56	E4	29
Maidstone La	56	E4	29
Maidstone Park Rd	59	F4	35
Maidstone Rd	60	M4	31
Main St	55	C4	32
Main St (SH)	56	E4	29
Main St	60	J4	30
Mako La	60	L4	31
Malcolm Av	55	B4	32
Mallard Ct	55	D4	33
Malone St	59	H4	34
Mane La	56	C4	30
Manor La	59	G4	35
Manor La N	59	G4	35
Manor La S	59	G4	34
Mansion House Dr	63	T4	54
Maple St	61	V4	34

STREET	MAP	GRID	
Maple St	60	H4	32
Marina La	56	D4	28
Marine Blvd	60	L4	30
Marion La	55	C4	32
Maritime Wy	59	H4	34
Mark Twain La	56	C4	29
Marlin Dr	61	Q4	33
Marlin Dr	62	C5	36
Mary St	59	F4	35
Mashie Dr	60	F4	32
Masthead La	55	C4	36
McElena St	60	F4	32
McGuirk St	56	E4	30
Mckinley Rd	61	W4	35
Meadow Wy	56	D4	29
Medway	56	E4	29
Meeting House La	60	K4	31
Melchionna Rd	62	C5	38
Melissa Wy	60	K4	30
Merchant's Pa (Slough Hwy)	56	Y3	31
Meredith Av	55	X3	32
Merriwood Dr	56	A4	28
Methodist La	60	F4	30
Miankoma La	60	J4	31
Middle Hwy	55	D4	33
Middle Hwy	55	E4	32
Middle La	60	G4	29
Midland Hwy	55	C4	32
Midland Rd	62	X4	35
Midlothian Av	63	T4	53
Midway	62	C5	36
Mile Hill Rd	55	A4	34
Milina Dr	55	D4	35
Mill Hill La	56	D4	29
Miller Av	62	B5	36
Millers Ct	60	F4	30
Millers La	60	F4	30
Millers La E	60	F4	30
Millers Lane Ter	60	F4	30
Millers La W	60	F4	30
Mitchell Dunes La	60	M4	31
Monroe Dr	61	X4	35
Montauk Av	55	D4	32
Montauk Av	55	X3	32
Montauk Av	63	T4	53
Montauk Blvd	59	H4	33
Montauk Blvd	56	B4	30
Montauk Hwy	57	U3	27
Montauk Hwy (EV)	60	G4	30
Montauk Hwy	60	K4	31
Montauk Hwy	56	Y3	28
Montauk Point State Pkwy	62	X4	35
Montauk Point State Pkwy (Montauk Point State Blvd)	62	D5	37
Montgomery Av	59	F4	33
Monument La	55	D4	35
Morell St	60	F4	32
Morris Park La	60	F4	31
Muchmore La	56	E4	30
Mudford Av	59	F4	35
Muir Blvd	60	F4	32
Mulford Av	55	C4	32
Mulford Av	55	D4	31
Mulford Av	62	Z4	38
Mulford La (SH)	55	W3	32
Mulford La	60	P4	33
Munnatawket Av	63	U4	54
Musket La	55	D4	34
Napeague La	60	M4	31
Napeague Harbor Rd	61	S4	33
Napeague Meadow Rd	60	O4	32
Navahoe Rd	61	S4	33
Navy Rd	61	X4	35
Neck Pa	59	J4	33
Neighborhood House Dr	60	F4	31
Nevins Pl	59	H4	33
Newtown La	56	E4	30
Nichols La	57	D4	28
Ninevah Pl	55	X3	32
Norfolk Dr	59	G4	36
Norfolk St	59	G4	35
North Bay La	55	A4	34
North Cape La	55	C4	34
North Cir	60	F4	30
North Farragut Rd	62	Z4	37
North Ferndale Pl	62	Z4	37
North Fernwood Rd	62	Z4	38
North Filmore Rd	62	Z4	38
North Fleming Ct	62	Z4	37
North Greenwich St	62	Z4	38
North Hollow Dr	55	C4	35
North Hopkins Av	62	Z4	36
North Main St	60	F4	30
North Neck La	62	Y4	37
North Pass Rd	55	C4	35
North Seaside Av	62	A5	36
North Shore Rd	61	X4	35
North Surfside Av	62	A5	36
North Woods La	55	C4	35
Northwest Landing Rd	55	A4	33
Oak Hill La	55	B4	32
Oak La	60	H4	31
Oak La	61	V4	34
Oak Ledge La	59	G4	33
Oak St	60	G4	32
Oak View Hwy	56	E4	31
Oakwood Ct	56	A4	28
Ocean Av	56	E4	28
Ocean Blvd	60	G4	31
Ocean La	60	L4	31
Ocean Pkwy	60	G4	31
Ocean View	59	H4	33
Ocean View Av	63	T4	53
Oceanic Av	63	T4	53
Oceanview La	60	M4	32
Oceanview Ter	62	Z4	35
Old Accabonac Rd	60	F4	30
Old Beach La	60	G4	29
Old Fireplace Rd	59	J4	36
Old Fireplace Rd	60	G4	32
Old Hedges La	56	E4	31
Old Hedges La	60	E4	31
Old Hollow La	55	C4	34
Old House Landing Rd	55	C4	34
Old West Lake Dr	62	B5	37
Old Lazy Point Rd	61	P4	33
Old Montauk Hwy	56	A4	28
Old Montauk Hwy	62	D5	37
Old Montauk Hwy	60	K4	31
Old Montauk Hwy	62	X4	35

STREET	MAP	GRID	
Old Northwest Rd	55	B4	33
Old Orchard La	56	D4	31
Old Pine Dr	55	B4	32
Old Sag Harbor Rd	55	Z3	32
Old School House La	55	C4	34
Old Station Pl	60	K4	31
Old Stone Hwy	59	H4	34
Olive St	60	G4	33
Orchard La	59	H4	36
Oriental Av	63	T4	53
Orkney Rd	59	G4	36
Osborn Farm La	57	Z3	28
Osborne La	56	E4	30
Osprey Rd	61	Q4	33
Otis Av	62	B5	36
Outlook Av	59	F4	35
Owl's Nest Rd	56	C4	31
Oyster Pond La	55	E4	33
Oyster Shores Rd	55	E4	33
Palma Ter	56	E4	30
Pantigo Pl	60	G4	30
Pantigo Rd	60	F4	30
Park Pl	60	E4	29
Park St	55	D4	32
Park St	59	G4	33
Park Av	61	Q4	33
Parsons Cl	59	H4	34
Parsons Pl	59	H4	34
Passing Rd	55	Z3	32
Patriots La	55	D4	34
Pebble Ct	55	C4	34
Pembroke Dr	59	G4	36
Peninsula Rd	63	U4	54
Peninsula The	63	U4	53
Pepperidge La	60	L4	32
Perigee Pa	55	C4	33
Peters Pa	55	E4	33
Pheasant Woods La	56	C4	31
Phelan Ct	60	K4	33
Pine Way	60	M4	31
Pine St	56	D4	30
Pinetree Dr	62	Z4	38
Pintail La	60	L4	31
Pioneer La	55	D4	34
Plank Rd	56	A4	30
Plaza, The	62	Z4	35
Pleasant La	56	E4	30
Plover Wy	55	D4	35
Pocahontas La	62	C5	38
Pond La	59	G4	36
Pond Pk Pl	60	K4	32
Pond View La	60	E4	29
Pony Ramble	56	C4	29
Poplar St	60	H4	32
Post St	56	D4	31
Potters La	56	B4	29
Powder Hill Dr	55	A4	33
Prentice Pl	62	C5	36
President St	59	G4	33
Presidio Pl	59	G4	33
Private	59	H4	34
Private Rd	55	A4	33
Promised Land Rd	60	N4	32
Prospect Av	55	W3	32
Prospect Blvd	56	C4	31
Prospect Hill La	62	B5	38
Prospect St	59	F4	33
Pudding Hill La	56	E4	29
Quadrant Hill Rd	55	B4	35
Quail La	59	G4	33
Quality Row	60	K4	33
Quarty Cir	55	D4	32
Quarty Ct	55	D4	32
Queens La	60	G4	31
Race La	56	E4	30
Railroad Av	56	E4	30
Ranch Ct	62	C5	37
Ranch Rd	62	D5	37
Ranger Pa	55	D4	34
Rector St	55	W3	33
Red Dirt Rd	60	H4	33
Red Fox La	56	Z3	31
Rehan Av	62	B5	36
Renee's Wy	59	G4	33
Renfrew La	59	G4	36
Reservoir Rd	63	S4	53
Reuter Pl	62	B5	36
Richards Dr	55	X3	32
Revere Rd	61	W4	34
Richardson Av	59	F4	35
Richardson Av Ext	59	G4	35
Ridge Rd	56	Z3	31
Ridge The	61	W4	35
Rivers Rd	55	E4	32
Roberts La	56	D4	30
Robeson Blvd	55	X3	32
Robins Wy	60	K4	33
Rolling Wood La	55	B4	32
Rolling Woods Ct	56	Z3	30
Roosevelt Av	59	F4	35
Roosevelt Rd	61	X4	35
Roosevelt St	59	G4	33
Rose Hill Rd	55	A4	32
Rosemarch La	59	F4	33
Rosemarie's La	60	H4	33
Rowman Ct	59	F4	34
Roxbury La	57	A4	28
Royal Oak Wy	62	Y4	38
Royal St	60	G4	31
Ruffed Grouse Ct	56	D4	31
Runnymeade Dr	59	G4	36
Rutland Dr	59	H4	35
Ryson St	55	W3	33
Sachems Pa	56	Z3	29
Saddle La	55	C4	30
St Mary's La	60	J4	30
St Regis Ct	55	A4	34
Sally Ct	56	E4	30
Sally's Pa	55	A4	33
Salt Marsh Pa	59	F4	35
Sammys Beach Rd	55	C4	35
Sand Castle La	60	M4	31
Sand Hill La	55	B4	36
Sand Lot Rd	59	H4	33
Sandown Ct	56	Z3	29
Sandpiper La	60	L4	30
Sandra Rd	59	F4	34
Sanger Pl	62	B5	36
Sappho Rd	63	T4	54
Sarah's Pa	60	K4	31
Sara's Way	60	F4	29
Sawmill La	56	D4	31
Sayres Pa	56	Z3	28
Scallop Av	55	D4	34
Schellinger Rd	60	H4	31
School La	62	Y4	35

STREET	MAP	GRID	
School St	59	H4	34
Scoy La	55	B4	32
Scrimshaw La	60	L4	31
Sea Bright Av	59	H4	33
Seabreeze La	60	L4	30
Seaside Av	62	A5	36
Seaton St	56	C4	31
Seaview Av	62	A5	35
Second House Rd	62	Y4	36
Semaphore Rd	55	C4	36
Settlement Ct	55	A4	34
Settlers Landing La	55	D4	34
Shadbush Rd	62	Y4	38
Shadom La	60	F4	32
Shadow La	59	K4	33
Shaw Rd	55	X3	32
Sheep Fold La	59	G4	36
Shellfish La	55	E4	33
Shepherds Pa	60	L4	31
Sherman Rd	61	W4	34
Sherrill Rd	56	E4	30
Sherwood La	59	H4	35
Ship Wreck Dr	60	N4	31
Shipyard La	59	H4	34
Shore Rd	61	P4	33
Shore Rd	61	Q4	32
Shore Ridge Rd	59	K4	33
Shorewood Ct	55	D4	33
Shorewood Dr	55	C4	33
Short La	55	Z3	33
Side Hill Rd	60	J4	31
Skidmore Wy	60	G4	31
Skimhampton Rd	60	H4	30
Snapper Av	62	C5	36
Soak Hides Rd	60	F4	32
Sound View Dr	55	X3	32
Soundview Dr	62	Y4	38
South Etna Av	62	Z4	35
South Breeze Dr	56	Z3	30
South Davis Av	62	Y4	35
South Dearborn Pl	62	Y4	35
South Debusy Rd	62	Y4	35
South Delphi St	62	Y4	35
South Delrey Rd	62	Y4	35
South Devon Pl	62	Y4	35
South Dewey Pl	62	Y4	35
South Dewitt Pl	62	Y4	35
South Dorsett Dr	62	Y4	35
South Dubois Pl	62	Y4	35
South Duncan Dr	62	X4	35
South Durham Rd	62	Y4	35
South Eagle St	62	Y4	35
South Easton Pl	62	Y4	36
South Edgemere St	62	Y4	36
South Edgewater Av	62	Z4	35
South Edison St	62	Z4	36
South Egmont Pl	62	Y4	36
South Elder St	62	Z4	35
South Eldert La	62	Y4	35
South Eliau Pl	62	Y4	35
South Elizabeth Pl	62	Y4	36
South Elmwood Av	62	Z4	35
South Elroy Dr	62	Y4	35
South Embassy St	62	Z4	35
South Emden Rd	62	Y4	36
South Emerson Av	62	Z4	35
South Emery St	62	Z4	35
South Endicott Pl	62	Y4	35
South Erie Av	62	Z4	35
South Essex St	62	Z4	35
South Etna Pl	62	Z4	35
South Eton St	62	Y4	35
South Euclid Av	62	Z4	35
South Faber St	62	Z4	36
South Fairbanks St	62	A5	36
South Fairmont St	62	A5	36
South Fairview Av	62	A5	36
South Federal St	62	A5	36
South Fenimore Dr	62	A5	36
South Ferincroft Pl	62	A5	36
South Ferris St	62	Z4	36
South Fish St	62	Z4	36
South Flagler St	62	A5	36
South Flint St	62	A5	36
South Forbes St	62	Z4	36
South Forrest St	62	Z4	36
South Fox St	62	A5	36
South Fran St	62	A5	36
South Front St	62	A5	36
South Fuller St	62	A5	36
South Fulton Dr	62	B5	36
South Genesee Ct	62	B5	36
South Geneva Ct	62	A5	36
South Gibson Pl	62	B5	36
South Greenbriar Rd	62	B5	36
South Greenfield Dr	62	B5	36
South Greenwich St	62	A5	37
South Lake Dr	62	C5	36
South Pond Rd	60	E4	33
Southview Rd	60	J4	30
Southwood Ct	60	K4	32
Spaeth La	60	G4	29
Spencer La	56	C4	30
Spread Oak La	55	D4	33
Spring Close Hwy	60	G4	30
Spring Close La	60	G4	30
Spring-Amagansett Rd	60	K4	32
Springs Fireplace Rd	59	G4	33
Springwood Wy	55	E4	34
Springwoods La	55	D4	33
Springy Banks Rd	55	D4	33
Spruce St	60	G4	32
Spy Glass La	55	D4	34
Squaw Rd	59	F4	34
Squires Pa	56	C4	30
Star Island Rd	62	A5	38
Startop Dr	62	C5	38
State Hwy 27	56	C4	29
State Hwy 114	55	Y3	32
Stephen Hands Pa	56	B4	29
Sterling St	63	U4	53
Stirrup Ct	56	C4	30
Stokes Ct	60	G4	31
Stonewall Ct	56	A4	30
Stony Hill Rd	60	H4	32
Stratton Sq	56	E4	30
Stuyvesant Dr	61	W4	35
Sulky Cir	56	C4	30
Summit Av	60	F4	32
Sunburst La	59	J4	33
Sunset La	56	E4	30
Surf Dr	60	M4	31
Surfside Av	62	A5	36
Surfside Pl	62	Z4	35
Surrey Ct	56	C4	29
Swamp Rd	55	A4	32

Suffolk Co.

Suffolk Co.

Town of Huntington

STREET	MAP	GRID
Larkin St	3	K 18
Larry Dr	8	R 20
Lattice Ct	3	F 15
Laurel Av	7	N 24
Laurel Ct	7	N 24
Laurel Ct (LH)	1	D 27
Laurel Dr	1	J 25
Laurel Hill Rd	2	M 23
Laurel Rd	7	O 24
Laurel St	7	O 25
Laurelwood Ct	9	P 17
Lauren Av	9	Q 17
Lauren Av S	9	R 16
Laurinda Dr	9	R 19
Lawn St	2	L 21
Lawrence Hill Rd	2	D 21
Lawrence St	2	L 22
Lawson Pl	9	Q 17
Layne Wy	7	O 25
Leaf Ct	3	F 16
Leatrice Ct	9	N 17
Lebkamp Av	2	L 20
Ledgewood Dr	2	E 19
Lee St	3	E 19
Leeds St	3	H 18
Leefield Gate	3	H 17
Leeward La	8	Q 20
Lefferts Av	8	O 20
Lefferts Pl	8	O 20
Leghorn Ct	2	J 20
Legion Dr	2	H 23
Leigh St	2	L 20
Leighton Ct	4	J 14
Leland St	8	P 23
Lemington Ct	1	J 27
Lendale Pl	2	H 22
Lenisue Ct	9	N 15
Lenox Rd	2	H 21
Leroy St	9	Q 16
L'escluse Dr	1	J 25
Leslie La	2	H 22
Lester Ct	8	Q 22
Leverich Pl	2	F 23
Lewis Av	8	R 22
Lewis Ct	8	R 22
Lewis Rd	7	M 25
Lexington Ct	8	O 23
Leyden St	2	H 20
Liberty La	7	Q 24
Liberty St	3	J 18
Lido Ct	8	P 22
Lieper St	3	H 19
Lighthouse Point	1	E 25
Lighthouse Rd	1	J2 9
Lilac Ct	3	D 19
Lilan Ct	7	O 24
Lincoln Av (NP)	7	N 24
Lincoln Av	9	Q 16
Lincoln Dr	8	R 23
Linda Ct	7	Q 25
Linda Pl	2	H 22
Lindberg Ct	7	N 24
Lindbergh Cir	2	L 20
Linden St	3	L 19
Lindsay St	2	L 19
Linford La	3	J 17
Links Ct	3	E 18
Linwood Av	2	L 20
Lipson Ct	8	O 22
Lisa Ct	2	E 21
Lisa Dr	2	M 24
Lisa Dr	3	L 17
Little Bull Ct	2	K 23
Little Dr	1	F 24
Little East Neck Rd	4	J 13
Little Neck Rd	1	K 25
Little Plains Ct	2	M 21
Little Plains Rd	2	K 21
Livingston	3	G 18
Livingston Pl	3	L 18
Lloyd Av	2	H 21
Lloyd Cove Ct	1	A 27
Lloyd Harbor Rd	1	B 26
Lloyd La	1	A 27
Lloyd Point Dr	1	B 27
Lloydhaven Dr	1	D 25
Lobster Wy	1	L 27
Locksley Ct	8	Q 20
Lockwood Av	3	G 19
Locust Av	7	N 26
Locust Ct	2	F 21
Locust La (HB)	1	F 25
Locust La (HB)	1	H 25
Locust La	1	J 28
Locust Pl	7	O 23
Locust Pl	3	H 18
Lodge Av	2	J 20
Loft La	9	O 18
Logan Hill Rd	7	N 24
Logan Pl	2	H 23
Logwood Ct	3	G 17
Loma Pl	2	H 23
Londel Ct	8	O 20
London Ct	1	J 27
Lone Hill Pl	3	L 16
Lone Oak Ct	2	K 23
Lone Oak Dr	2	K 24
Long Island Expwy	9	O 17
Long St	3	H 18
Longacre La	2	J 21
Longacre La	9	R 17
Longfellow Dr	2	K 19
Longfield Dr	8	Q 23
Longford St	3	F 19
Longhill La	2	M 20
Longley Pl	3	G 19
Longview Ct	1	H 24
Longwood Dr	3	J 18
Longworth Av	9	N 15
Lord Joe's Landing	7	M 25
Loret La	8	P 23
Loretta Ct	2	G 22
Lori Ct	8	Q 23
Lorijean La	8	O 21
Lorraine Ct	7	O 24
Lost Pond Ct	3	K 18
Lou Ct	3	H 17
Louis Ct	2	M 20
Louis Dr	3	E 16
Louisa Ct	7	N 23
Lovers La	2	F 24
Lowell Av	2	L 21
Lower Dr	1	H 25
Lowick Pl	3	J 18
Lowndes Av	2	H 21
Lucille La	3	M 17
Lucille La	9	Q 19

STREET	MAP	GRID
Ludlam St	2	H 20
Luther Pl	2	H 19
Luyster St	3	H 18
Lyn Ct	2	J 23
Lynbrook Ct	2	J 22
Lynch St	2	H 20
Lyndon Pl	3	H 15
Lynhaven Pl	9	Q 19
Lynmar Ct	2	H 23
Lynn Av	8	O 22
Lynridge La	2	J 22
Lyons St	3	H 17
Lyric Pl	3	M 18
Mac Niece Pl	9	N 16
MacArthur Av	3	E 19
Madison St (NP)	7	O 25
Madison St	2	G 23
Madsen La	8	O 23
Magel La	8	R 20
Magenta La	8	Q 21
Mager Ct	8	R 19
Magerus St	3	H 18
Magnolia La	3	D 19
Magnolia La	3	M 18
Main St	7	L 23
Main St (NP)	7	N 25
Main St	2	D 22
Maize Ct	3	J 15
Majestic Ct	9	N 19
Majestic Dr	3	M 19
Major Trescot La	7	Q 26
Makamah Beach Rd	7	P 27
Makamah Rd	7	P 25
Makanna Dr	2	J 23
Makin Pl	2	K 23
Malcolm's Landing	7	M 25
Mallard Cove	7	L 24
Mallard Dr	1	A 26
Manchester Rd	2	L 20
Mander La	8	O 21
Mangin Rd	8	R 20
Manhattan Pl	2	H 22
Mannetto Ct	3	E 17
Mannetto Hill Rd	3	E 17
Manning Dr	8	Q 21
Manor Pl	2	F 20
Manor Rd	8	M 20
Manor Rd N	2	M 21
Mansfield La	8	P 21
Mansfield La S	8	O 21
Maple Av	7	O 25
Maple Cir	7	N 25
Maple Hill Rd	2	G 23
Maple Mall	8	R 20
Maple Pl	2	F 21
Maple Pl	2	L 22
Maple Pl	3	H 17
Maple Ridge Ct	9	P 17
Maple Rd	3	H 19
Maple Road Ext	2	L 23
Mapleshade Ct	2	J 22
Mapletree La	3	G 18
Maplewood Dr	7	N 23
Maplewood Rd	3	J 19
Mara Rd	2	J 21
Marcelle Ct	7	Q 25
Marcher Av	2	J 20
Marcia Ct	1	L 25
Marcus Dr	4	G 13
Marcy Av	3	G 19
Margaret La	2	L 20
Margo La	2	F 24
Margo Pl	2	F 24
Maria Ct	2	K 20
Maridon La	8	Q 21
Marie Dr	2	F 23
Marine St	1	F 24
Mariners Ct	1	K 26
Mariners La	7	M 25
Marion La	2	F 23
Marion Pl	3	K 18
Marirod Ct	7	Q 24
Mark Ct	3	E 18
Mar-Kan Dr	7	N 25
Markham Pl	8	P 22
Markwood La	8	O 21
Marlboro Dr	2	E 20
Marlin St	9	P 15
Marlowe Pl	2	M 21
Marsh La	1	B 27
Marshall La	8	Q 22
Martha Ct	2	L 23
Martha Dr	3	E 15
Martin Pl	7	O 26
Marvin La	8	R 20
Mary Ct	3	E 16
Mary La	3	E 16
Maryanne Ct	2	J 23
Maryland St	9	N 15
Mary's La	2	L 24
Masefield Dr	8	M 21
Mason Ct	9	P 19
Maspeth Dr	3	H 17
Massey Ct	3	H 15
Mather Ct	3	H 16
Mathews St	3	J 17
Matilda La	2	G 20
Maurice La	2	G 21
Maxess Rd	4	G 14
Maxess Rd	3	G 15
Maxwell Ct	1	H 24
May Hill La	3	E 16
May St	2	H 21
Mayapple La	8	R 22
Mayfair Dr	2	E 23
Mayflower Ct	2	K 23
Mayo Av	3	F 19
Maywood Ct	3	G 17
McCormick St	9	O 15
McCrodden St	4	L 14
McCulloch Dr	9	Q 17
McFadden Dr	8	R 23
McGovern Pl	9	R 15
Mckay Rd	2	F 21
McKenzie St	2	F 24
McKinley Ter	1	K 25
McKinney Av	7	N 25
McLane Ct	9	Q 18
McLane Dr	9	Q 18
McNulty St	9	Q 16
Meade Dr	2	L 23
Meadow Ct	2	J 21
Meadow Farm La	2	E 22
Meadow Haven La	9	P 19
Meadow La	1	D 26
Meadow Lawn St	2	G 23

STREET	MAP	GRID
Meadow Pl	7	O 26
Meadow Pond Ct	2	K 22
Meadowbrook Dr	2	H 20
Meadowdale Dr	3	H 16
Meadowlark Dr	8	P 22
Meadowlark La	3	E 18
Meadowood Ct	2	H 22
Meadowrue La	8	R 22
Meahon Pl	2	K 23
Meath Av	3	F 19
Mechanic Ct	2	F 23
Mechanic St	2	F 22
Medford La	8	Q 21
Medical Cir	7	Q 24
Mehan La	9	Q 16
Melia Wy	3	K 20
Melissa Ct	3	L 16
Melody La	2	H 23
Melrose Av	8	P 23
Melrose Ct	3	L 17
Melrose Pl	8	O 23
Melrose Rd	3	K 17
Melview Ct	3	H 17
Melville Park Rd	4	G 15
Melville Rd	3	H 18
Memas Ct	9	N 17
Mercer Av	9	P 15
Mercer Ct	3	H 19
Meredith Dr	2	G 21
Meredith Dr	2	M 21
Meriden Pl	3	G 18
Merle Ct	2	L 20
Meroke Ct	2	J 21
Merrill Pl	2	H 23
Merriwind Dr	2	H 22
Merriwood Ct	2	K 23
Merrymeeting La	2	D 24
Metcale La	8	Q 22
Miandra Ct	2	H 21
Michael La	2	K 20
Mickey Ct	2	K 20
Micole Ct	3	M 17
Middle Dr	2	L 20
Middle Hollow Rd	2	D 23
Middlesex Pl	1	J 28
Middleville Rd	7	P 24
Midland St	2	D 22
Midvale Ct	9	R 18
Midwood Dr	2	L 24
Milburn La	2	G 22
Mile End La	4	J 14
Milford La	3	J 17
Mill Dam Ct	2	K 24
Mill Dam Rd	2	G 23
Mill Dam Rd	2	K 24
Mill La	2	G 23
Mill Rd	1	D 24
Milland Dr	2	M 24
Millbrook Ct	9	R 17
Miller Pl	2	H 20
Millet St	9	O 15
Millet St N	9	P 16
Milligan St	9	R 17
Millmohr Ct	2	M 23
Millpond La	2	L 24
Millwood Pl	2	J 23
Milton Pl	2	L 20
Milward La	1	E 24
Mimosa La	3	D 19
Minetta Ct	2	F 22
Mitchell Av	8	Q 22
Modell Ct	8	P 20
Mohawk St	2	K 23
Mohegan Pl	2	J 21
Mona La	3	M 16
Monaton Dr	2	H 21
Monett Pl	2	K 21
Monfort Dr	3	E 18
Monmouth Dr	7	O 23
Monmouth Pl	3	G 17
Monroe Dr	1	K 24
Monroe St	7	O 25
Mont Av	9	N 15
Mont Ct	9	N 15
Montana Pl	2	J 20
Montana St	8	N 21
Montauk St	7	O 24
Montrose La	8	O 23
Montrose Pl	3	K 15
Montvale Ct	8	P 22
Moonedge Rd	7	P 25
Moore Pl	3	H 17
Morahapa Rd	2	L 24
Morris Av	2	J 20
Moscato St	8	N 21
Mott Pl	3	M 15
Mt Misery Rd	3	F 16
Mountain View Ct	7	Q 25
Mountain View Dr	7	Q 25
Mowbray Lane N	2	D 23
Mulberry Dr	2	H 24
Mulford Av	2	H 20
Munson Ct	3	J 17
Murdock St	3	H 18
Murfield Pl	3	H 17
Murray Ct	2	G 22
Mux La	1	D 26
Myrtle Av	2	G 22
Mystic La	7	Q 27
Nancy Ct	2	F 23
Naples La	2	M 22
Narcissus La	7	Q 25
Nash Pl	9	M 19
Nason Pl	3	M 15
Nassau Rd	2	G 22
Nathan Hale Dr	2	F 22
Nathan Pl	3	H 19
Nautilus Av	7	N 25
Neptune Av	3	G 18
Netcong Pl	8	P 21
Nevada Pl	2	J 20
Neville St	3	H 16
Nevinwood Pl	2	K 20
New Dorp Pl	3	H 17
New Harbor Rd	1	J 27
New Jersey Ct	9	N 15
New Jersey St	9	N 15
New St	2	F 22
New York Av	2	F 22
Newark St	8	P 21
Newbrook La	8	R 21
Newbury Pl	8	P 22
Newfoundland Av	8	N 21
Newtown La	8	N 21
Niagara La	8	R 19
Nichols Pl	3	J 19

STREET	MAP	GRID
Nicolette Ct	2	J 19
Nielson St	9	P 15
Nimitz St	3	F 19
Nipawaton Rd	1	G 24
Nita St	8	Q 21
Noah Pl	3	J 18
Noel Av	8	P 23
Noel Ct	1	F 24
Norden La	2	F 20
Norfolk Dr	1	H 27
Norma La	3	L 17
Norma St	8	P 21
Norman Ct	3	L 16
Norman Pl	2	J 22
Normandy Dr	7	P 24
North Creek Rd	1	H 28
North Dr	2	K 23
North Gate	9	R 18
North Haven La	9	P 19
North Hill Dr	8	P 23
North Hill Dr E	8	Q 23
North Honey La	8	Q 23
North La	1	F 25
North La	2	K 21
North Rd	2	M 24
North Run	2	D 20
North Service Rd	3	E 15
North St	2	F 20
North Woodhull Rd	2	G 22
Northcote Dr	4	J 14
Northern State Pkwy	3	F 17
Northern State Pkwy	3	J 17
Northern State Pkwy	9	O 19
Northern State Pkwy (Town Pk)	15	T 18
Northfield Dr	2	K 24
Northgate Cir	4	F 14
Northgate Ct	4	F 14
Northgate Crest	4	F 15
Northgate Dr	8	M 22
Northridge Cir	3	L 19
Northridge St	2	H 21
Northwest Dr	7	N 25
Northwood Cir	2	H 24
Northwood Ct	9	N 18
Norton Dr	7	P 23
Norview Ct	2	G 20
Norway Ct	8	L 20
Norwood Rd	7	O 25
Notch Ct	3	M 17
Noyes La	2	G 23
Nursery Rd	3	G 18
Nutwood Rd	3	H 16
Nyack Dr	8	P 23
Oak Av	2	J 20
Oak Crest Ct	8	P 23
Oak Haven Pl	9	P 19
Oak Hill La	1	E 25
Oak Hill Rd	1	E 25
Oak La	1	E 27
Oak Ridge Dr	3	E 19
Oak Rd	2	F 24
Oak St	7	O 25
Oakcrest Dr	3	J 19
Oakdale Rd	2	K 24
Oakfield Av	9	O 16
Oakhill La	8	N 20
Oakhurst St	3	H 18
Oakland Av	3	J 17
Oakland St	8	P 23
Oakland St	2	G 22
Oakleaf Ct (NP)	7	P 25
Oakleaf Ct	3	E 18
Oakledge Dr	8	Q 22
Oakleigh Pl	7	N 25
Oakley Dr	3	G 19
Oaktree La	3	G 18
Oakwood Dr	1	E 27
Oakwood Dr W	1	D 26
Oakwood Pl	1	J 25
Oakwood Rd	3	F 19
Oakwood St	2	M 22
Oasis Pl	8	Q 22
Oberlon Dr	2	K 21
Obermueller Dr	4	L 14
Ocean Av	7	N 25
Oceanside Ct	7	O 26
Oelsner Dr	7	O 26
Ogden Ct	3	H 19
O'Hara Pl	2	G 24
Old Baylis Rd	4	H 14
Old Bridge Rd	7	Q 24
Old Bk Rd	9	P 16
Old Country Rd	3	E 16
Old Country Rd	9	P 15
Old Crane Ct	2	J 21
Old East Neck Rd	3	H 16
Old Field Rd	2	K 22
Old Hickory La	2	F 23
Old Hills Ct	2	L 22
Old Northport Rd	2	J 23
Old Oak Ct	2	F 21
Old Orchard Pl	1	J 28
Old Pine La	2	M 23
Old South Pa	3	J 16
Old Town La	1	D 26
Old Walt Whitman Rd	3	G 18
Old Winkle Point Rd	1	J 27
Oldwood Ct	3	H 17
Oleander Dr	2	M 22
Olga La	8	Q 19
Olive St	2	G 21
Olmstead La	8	Q 22
Olney Pl	9	Q 17
Olympia Ct	8	O 21
Olympia Pl	8	O 21
Ona Av	3	K 17
Oneida Pl	7	O 24
Oneonta Ct	2	K 23
O'Niel Ct	3	K 16
Ontario St	2	L 20
Opp Ct	3	M 15
Orchard Ct	8	N 23
Orchard Pl	2	G 22
Oregon Dr	2	J 20
Orient Av	8	R 24
Oriole Pl	2	K 20
Oriole Wy	3	M 18
Orleans Ct	9	R 19
Ormond St	9	O 16
Orton Dr	8	P 22
Osage Dr	2	J 21
Oswego Dr	8	N 22
Otego Pl	2	L 21
Otsego Av	9	O 16

STREET	MAP	GRID
Ottawa Av	2	K 23
Overbrook Dr	2	L 23
Overdale Ct	2	H 22
Overhill Rd	3	G 17
Overland Pl	2	F 22
Overland Pl	3	G 17
Overlook Dr	2	H 23
Owen Pl	8	O 22
Oxbow Ct	8	R 22
Oxford Av	3	G 16
Oxford St	7	O 25
Pamela La	8	Q 22
Pan Ct	3	H 18
Pan La	2	F 24
Panorama Dr	2	G 21
Park Av	2	G 23
Park Dr	4	F 14
Park Hill Ct	8	N 20
Park St	7	N 24
Parkridge Ct	2	G 22
Parkside Dr	9	O 18
Parkview Ter	2	G 23
Parkwood La	9	O 18
Parmalee Ct	2	F 22
Parsons Dr	3	M 17
Partridge La	2	J 21
Pashen Pl	9	Q 17
Pasture Ct	8	Q 20
Pasture La	1	J 28
Patri Ct	9	P 17
Patricia Dr	8	Q 20
Patrician Ct	8	N 22
Patrician Dr	8	N 22
Patrick Dr	3	E 16
Patriot Ct	2	F 23
Patton Pl	3	E 19
Paul Revere La	2	M 23
Paula St	8	Q 21
Paulding St	1	F 24
Pauline La	7	O 24
Paumanauk Dr	2	M 22
Paumonok Dr	3	F 19
Payne St	2	H 21
Peabody Rd	2	E 21
Peachtree La	3	G 19
Pearl Pl	8	L 21
Pearltree La	3	G 18
Pearsall Pl	2	G 22
Pearwood Dr	2	F 20
Pebble Hill Ct	7	Q 25
Pebble Hill Dr	7	Q 26
Pebble La	3	J 18
Peg's Ct	2	F 21
Peg's La	2	F 21
Pembroke Av	3	G 15
Pembury Ct	4	J 14
Penataquit Pl	2	F 23
Penelope La	8	N 19
Penfield Dr	8	P 20
Penn Ct	3	J 16
Penn Dr	3	J 16
Pennington Dr	2	F 21
Penny Dr	2	J 19
Penrose Pa	9	P 19
Pentagon Ct	3	J 18
Peppermill La	9	N 17
Perri Pl	9	Q 16
Perth Pl	8	Q 22
Peter Ct	3	K 19
Peterborough Dr	1	J 27
Pettit Ct	3	L 16
Pettit Dr	3	L 16
Pewter Pl	9	P 18
Phaetons Dr	3	E 16
Phaetons Gate	3	E 16
Pheasant Cir	2	D 24
Pheasant La	1	E 27
Pheasant La	1	K 28
Pheasant Run La	9	O 15
Phillip Ct	2	H 21
Phyllis Dr	9	P 19
Pickering Pl	9	Q 18
Pickwick Hill Dr	2	G 21
Pidgeon Hill Rd	3	J 19
Pierce St	1	K 24
Piermont Ct	3	G 17
Pierre Dr	9	R 19
Pierson Pl	3	H 18
Pike Ct	7	O 24
Pilgrim Pa	2	E 22
Pine Acres Blvd	10	O 14
Pine Acres Ct	9	O 15
Pine Av	2	J 20
Pine Dr	7	P 24
Pine Dr	2	D 22
Pine Edge Pl	9	O 15
Pine Hill Ct	8	N 23
Pine Hill Dr	3	M 18
Pine Hill La	9	Q 16
Pine Hollow Ct	2	L 21
Pine Hollow La	2	L 21
Pine Pl	2	F 21
Pine Pl	2	L 22
Pine Point	1	E 25
Pine Ridge St	4	F 15
Pine Tree Rd	3	G 19
Pinebrook Ct	3	K 16
Pineland Ct	9	O 15
Pinelawn Rd	3	G 15
Pinewood Dr	2	K 20
Pinoak Ct	2	K 20
Pinta Ct	2	M 22
Pioneer Blvd	3	H 18
Pioneer Ct	3	K 16
Piper St	7	Q 23
Pippin La	1	E 24
Pitt Pl	9	Q 17
Plains Ct	3	J 19
Plainwood Rd	3	H 17
Plane Tree La	9	M 17
Platt Pl	2	G 22
Playa Pravda	2	J 22
Pleasant St	2	K 20
Pleasant View Ct	2	J 22
Plover La	1	C 25
Plumb Ct	2	H 21
Plumtree La	3	G 19
Plymouth Rd	3	L 18
Plymouth St	9	P 15
Pocket Ct	7	N 23
Poe Pl	8	P 23
Poet La	2	M 21
Polk Av	7	O 24
Polly Dr	2	F 22
Polly Pl	2	H 22

STREET	MAP	GRID
Polo St	9	R 16
Pomper Ct	9	P 19
Pomper Dr	9	P 19
Pond Dr	1	J 28
Pond Field Ct	2	D 23
Pond Rd	2	D 24
Pond View Ct	2	J 23
Ponderosa Dr	3	F 16
Ponderosa La	3	F 16
Ponds Edge Ct	2	J 20
Poplar Av	3	H 19
Poplar Pl	2	D 22
Porpoise Ct	7	M 25
Porterfield Ct	3	J 17
Portland St	2	D 22
Post Dr	2	M 22
Poster Pl	3	J 18
Potter La	2	G 23
Prairie Rd	2	K 20
Preakness Ct	2	L 21
Prescott Av	9	N 15
President St	2	G 20
Preston St	2	F 23
Prime Av	2	G 23
Primrose La	2	H 24
Princess Ct	2	L 21
Princeton Dr	9	O 19
Printer Ct	2	K 20
Priory Ct	4	J 14
Priscilla Av	9	P 15
Private Rd	7	Q 24
Private Rd (HB)	1	J 25
Pvt Rd	1	K 25
Promenade Dr	3	E 18
Prospect Av	7	N 25
Prospect Dr N	2	H 20
Prospect Dr S	3	H 19
Prospect Rd	1	L 25
Prospect St	2	F 22
Pudding La	3	M 16
Pueblo St	2	K 24
Pulaski Rd	2	K 21
Pumpkin St	8	P 22
Purdy Av	8	R 22
Puritan Pl	2	E 23
Putnam Pl	2	H 20
Quail Hill Rd	1	E 25
Quaker Pa	2	E 22
Quay Ct	2	L 24
Quayle Ct	2	J 20
Quebec Dr	3	H 19
Queens St	2	H 22
Quill Pl	8	P 22
Quintree La	3	J 17
R.R. Av	8	O 23
Rachel Av	8	R 20
Radcliff Dr	2	F 23
Railroad Pl	2	G 20
Railroad St	2	G 20
Railroad St	2	L 22
Rainer St	3	H 17
Raines St	3	H 17
Raintree Rd	4	L 14
Rambling Rd	7	Q 25
Ramita La	8	Q 20
Rancher Pl	2	F 21
Randi Ct	3	J 15
Randolph Dr	9	P 17
Randou Dr	2	H 23
Raphael St	2	J 21
Raspberry Ct	4	G 13
Rassmussen Pl	3	H 17
Raven Pl	3	F 18
Rawlings Dr	3	K 15
Ray Ct	4	L 14
Ray Pl	7	O 24
Raybor Rd	9	Q 19
Recreation La	2	F 24
Rector Ct	2	L 21
Red Cedar Ct	3	M 16
Red Deer La	2	J 22
Red Maple La	9	N 18
Red Oak Ct	9	P 18
Redbrook Ct	3	F 15
Reddington Ct	3	M 16
Redwood Dr	3	M 18
Regal Dr	2	G 21
Regency La	9	N 19
Regent Pl	2	J 22
Regina Av	9	P 17
Regina Ct	2	J 19
Rego Ct	3	J 19
Reinhart Ct	3	H 16
Remly La	3	J 17
Remsen St	8	P 21
Renee Pl	8	Q 20
Rensselaer Dr	9	R 19
Renwick Av	2	K 22
Republic Rd	4	G 13
Reservoir Av	7	N 24
Reservoir Pl	7	N 24
Reservoir Rd	3	G 18
Revere Dr	2	F 22
Revere Pl	7	Q 26
Revona La	2	F 21
Reybold Ct	1	B 28
Reynolds St	3	H 19
Richard La	2	H 23
Richbourne La	4	J 14
Richlee Dr	8	Q 22
Richmond Pl	2	F 21
Richwood Pl	3	H 19
Ridge Dr	3	G 18
Ridge Rd	2	D 22
Ridge View La	2	K 23
Ridgecrest St	2	G 21
Ridgefield Rd	2	K 24
Ridgewood St	7	P 23
Ridings Gate	7	P 25
Ridings Rd	7	P 25
Ridley Ct	2	L 23
Riga La	3	K 15
Rigger Ct	2	K 20
ROW (LH)	1	B 26
ROW (LH)	1	D 25
ROW (LH)	1	E 26
ROW	2	C 23
ROW	2	H 24
Rimlet Dr	8	R 20
Rinaldo Rd	7	P 25
Ring Neck Ridge	1	D 26
Ringler Dr	8	Q 22
Ripley Dr	7	N 24
Robert Dr	2	J 20
Robert Lennox Dr	1	H 27
Roberta La	8	Q 19
Roberts Pl	3	H 17
Robertson Pl	3	G 15

STREET	MAP	GRID
Robin Dr	2	L 20
Robin La	3	F 18
Robin Pl	3	G 17
Robin Rd	3	M 18
Rocco Dr	8	O 22
Rochester Ct	2	F 23
Rocklyn Ct	2	J 22
Rockne St	2	L 21
Rockrose La	8	O 21
Roderick Ct	8	Q 21
Rodsfield Ct	8	N 20
Roe St	3	J 17
Roebling Pl	8	P 22
Rofay Dr	8	O 19
Rogers Av	2	L 20
Rogers Dr	2	E 21
Rogues Ct	2	K 20
Rolling Hills Dr	2	F 21
Roma La	3	E 18
Romack Rd	8	N 20
Romany Wy	8	Q 21
Romeo La	9	Q 19
Ronald La	9	R 19
Rondel La	9	Q 19
Ronny St	8	Q 21
Roosevelt Av	7	O 24
Roosevelt Av S	2	L 21
Rope Ct	3	G 18
Rosalie Pl	8	Q 20
Rose Ct	7	Q 25
Rose Pl	2	L 20
Rose Pl	9	L 20
Rosemont Ct	2	J 21
Rose's Ct	9	O 19
Rosewood Pl	3	H 17
Roslyn St	8	N 21
Ross Av	3	G 16
Rotterdam St	2	L 20
Rough Riders Ct	2	E 22
Round Swamp Rd	3	E 17
Roundtree Dr	3	K 15
Roundwood Ct	3	L 15
Rover La	2	L 20
Rowena La	8	Q 23
Rowland Pl	7	M 25
Rowley Dr	7	P 24
Roxanne Ct	2	H 21
Roxbury St	3	J 19
Royal La	8	R 23
Royal La	9	N 19
Royal Oak Dr	2	G 21
Royce Rd	9	O 17
Rubin's Ct	9	O 19
Ruby La	3	K 19
Rugby Ct	1	J 27
Ruland Pl	4	G 14
Ruland Rd	4	G 13
Rupert Pl	3	H 16
Rural Pl	8	Q 20
Rusco St	2	E 22
Rushmore St	3	H 18
Russell Ct	7	P 25
Russet La	2	H 24
Rustic Gate La	3	L 15
Rutgers La	2	K 21
Ruth St	3	L 19
Rutland La	3	H 16
Rutledge Av	7	N 25
Ruwaner Ct	2	M 21
Ryder Av	3	L 15
Ryder Ct	9	N 15
Rye St	9	O 15
Sabath Day Pa	2	G 22
Sabrina Ct	3	M 19
Saddle Bk Ct	9	N 15
Saddle La	3	J 18
Saddler Ct	3	H 18
Sage Ct	2	G 21
Sage Hollow Ct	3	L 17
Sailfish Pl	7	N 25
St Andrews Dr	2	E 23
St Ann Ct	3	H 19
St George Ct	3	K 15
Salem Ct	2	K 23
Salem Ridge Dr	2	K 22
Salisbury Dr N	8	O 23
Salisbury Dr S	8	N 23
Salt Aire Pl	7	N 25
Sammis St	2	G 22
Sampson Pl	3	F 19
Sandgate Pl	3	H 16
Sandpiper La	7	Q 23
Sandra Ct	2	H 19
Sandra Dr	9	N 17
Sandy Hollow Rd	2	M 23
Sandy St	8	P 21
Sanford St	2	K 19
Sapphire Pl	3	K 19
Sarah Dr	9	O 16
Saratoga Av	8	N 22
Sarina Dr	8	P 20
Savings Ct	8	N 22
Saw Mill La	2	D 21
Saw Mill Rd	2	D 21
Saxon St	3	J 17
Saylor Pl	2	H 23
Schaefer St	3	H 19
Schiller Av	3	H 19
Schley Pl	3	F 19
Schoenfield La	3	H 17
Scholar Ct	8	P 22
School House Wy	9	P 16
School La	1	C 24
School La	2	K 20
School St	8	M 24
Schooner Rd	7	N 26
Schubert Ct	3	K 18
Schwab Rd	3	H 18
Scott Dr	3	H 17
Scott St	3	M 15
Scudder Av	7	M 24
Scudder Pl (NP)	7	N 24
Scudder Pl	2	F 22
Sea Cove Rd	7	N 25
Sea Ridge Ct	2	F 24
Sea Spray Dr	2	L 24
Seacrest Dr	1	F 27
Seaforth La	1	A 26
Seaman Neck Rd	9	O 15
Seaside Ct	7	O 26
Seaview Av	7	O 24
Seaview Ter	7	N 24
Seaward Ct	2	D 21
Sedgwick St	2	F 20
Seeley Pl	2	F 24
Segrove Pl	2	G 20

Suffolk Co.

Town of Huntington / Town of Islip

Suffolk Co.

Suffolk Co.

Suffolk Co.

STREET	MAP	GRID	
Nebraska Av	10	U	14
Neel Ct	23	J1	12
Neil Pl	21	E1	18
Nelson St	15	C1	19
Nemeth St	22	F1	15
Neptune Ct	11	U	9
Neptune Wk	18	C1	4
Neptune Wk (SA)	18	Z	4
Nevada Av	16	V	12
New Hampshire Av	10	U	13
New Jersey Av	16	V	13
New St	17	C1	10
New York Av	16	U	13
Newberry St	16	W	14
Newbrook La	16	V	12
Newham Av	16	W	14
Newman St	16	W	14
Newport St	23	M1	11
Newton Av	11	S	8
Newton Pl	15	W	17
Newton St	23	J1	12
Niagara St	16	W	11
Nichol's Rd	15	B1	16
Nichol's Rd	15	C1	18
Nicole Ct	22	H1	14
Nicoll Av	16	A1	15
Nicolls Rd	22	L1	17
Nicon Ct	15	X	18
Nikia Dr	16	X	11
Nikon Dr	16	X	12
Nimbus Rd	22	L1	15
Nimitz Av	9	T	15
Nina St	22	J1	15
Noble St	16	W	14
Nolin St	16	W	14
Norgate Dr	23	J1	10
Norma Av	10	R	11
Norman Dr	22	D1	15
Norman La	15	Y	17
Normandy Dr	22	J1	14
North 1st St	23	H1	12
North 1st St	21	E1	19
North 2nd St	21	E1	19
North 3rd St	22	H1	13
North 3rd St	21	D1	19
North 4th St	21	D1	19
North 5th St	21	D1	19
North 6th St	21	D1	19
North 7th St	21	D1	17
North Atlantic St	15	X	17
North Bay Wk	18	Z	5
North Briarwood Av	11	R	9
North Cedar Av	21	F1	18
North Champlin Dr	16	Y	14
North Chicot Av	11	R	9
North Cliff Av	23	H1	12
North Clinton Av	10	T	12
North Connecting Rd	15	C1	17
North Dr	21	E1	18
North Dyre Av	11	R	9
North Express Dr	21	D1	17
North Fehr Wy	10	R	14
North Fire Rd	10	U	13
North Gardiner Dr	10	S	14
North Greenlawn Av	16	A1	14
North Huron St	21	D1	19
North McConnell Av	23	L1	12
North Monroe Av	10	Q	10
North Ocean Av	16	X	11
North Ocean Av	21	E1	18
North Ontario St	21	D1	18
North Peters Blvd	15	Y	16
North Research Dr	16	Y	14
North St	11	Q	9
North Thompson Dr	10	S	14
North Washington Av	21	E1	18
North Windsor Av	10	T	11
North Windsor Blvd	10	T	12
Northfield La	11	S	9
Northfield Rd	15	W	18
Northwood Blvd	15	Y	15
Northwood Ct	23	M1	12
Norwood St	16	A1	13
Nostrand Av	15	W	16
Nugent Av	10	S	13
Oak Av	22	G1	13
Oak Av	10	R	11
Oak Ct	16	Y	11
Oak Dr	21	F1	18
Oak Grove Ct	23	L1	12
Oak Neck La	10	S	10
Oak Neck Rd	11	S	10
Oak Rd	23	K1	11
Oak St	15	U	15
Oak St	16	U	10
Oak St	18	Y	3
Oak St	23	J1	12
Oak St	23	M1	12
Oak St	9	U	15
Oak Wk	18	A1	4
Oakdale Av	15	Y	16
Oakdale Av	21	E1	18
Oakdale Bohemia Rd	22	E1	12
Oakforest Dr	15	B1	17
Oakland Av	15	X	17
Oakland Av	16	W	11
Oakland St	9	V	17
Oakley Pl	11	P	8
Oakmont La	16	W	10
Oakridge Dr	10	U	12
Oaks Av	15	X	15
Oaks Ct	10	U	10
Oakton Av	16	D1	11
Oaktree Dr	16	W	11
Oakwood	22	F1	12
Oakwood Av	11	Q	9
Oakwood Av	15	A1	17
Oakwood Av	22	K1	13
Oakwood Av	23	L1	12
Oakwood Av	10	U	14
Oakwood Blvd	16	V	12
Oakwood Hills Dr	16	A1	10
Oakwood La	16	Z	10
Oakwood Rd	23	F1	12
Ocean Av	15	W	16
Ocean Av	16	V	10
Ocean Av	16	X	10
Ocean Av	22	F1	14
Ocean Av	22	F1	13
Ocean Av	23	M1	11
Ocean Av	10	R	13
Ocean Av	21	E1	17
Ocean Av Ext	17	X	10
Ocean Breeze Wk	18	C1	4
Ocean Crest Wk	18	B1	4
Ocean Pathway	18	B1	4
Ocean Rd	18	C1	4
Ocean View Av	16	C1	11
Oceanside St	16	A1	14
Oceanview Wk	18	C1	4
Ockers Dr	23	F1	12
Oconee Wk	11	U	9
O'Connell Ct	16	C1	11
O'Connell Rd	23	C1	11
Officials Av	22	J1	17
Ogden Rd	11	Q	9
Ohio Av	16	V	12
Ohio Av	16	V	13
O'Kane St	15	Y	15
Oklahoma Av	10	U	13
Olander Ct	11	S	9
Old Broadway Av	22	K1	12
Old Nichol's Rd	15	B1	16
Old Pond Ct	11	S	8
Old Post Dr	15	B1	18
Olean St	16	Z	13
Oliva Ct	10	R	10
Olive St	15	Y	15
Olive St	23	H1	11
Oliver St	22	J1	16
Olm St	16	X	14
Omni La	22	M1	15
Onehtah Dr	15	V	15
Oneida St	15	D1	19
Oniel Av	10	V	11
Ontario Dr	10	S	12
Ontario St	15	D1	18
Opal St	22	K1	15
Orange St	16	Y	13
Orange St	16	Z	14
Oray St	16	W	14
Orbit La	15	Y	18
Orchard Dr	17	T	10
Orchard St	15	C1	18
Oregon Av	10	V	12
Orgas St	22	J1	16
Orgill Av	10	R	14
Orient Av	9	V	17
Orinoco Dr	11	R	9
Orinoco Dr (BR)	10	T	10
Oriole Pl	16	W	14
Orleans St	16	W	11
Ormond Av	16	C1	11
O'Rourke St	16	W	14
Orowoc Av	16	X	10
Orowoc St	16	X	12
Ort Ct	22	J1	14
Orville Dr	22	G1	15
Osage Pl	10	S	12
Oscar St	10	U	11
Oswego Dr	10	T	12
Otis La	11	T	9
Otis Pl	16	B1	13
Otis Rd	16	B1	13
Oval Dr	15	Z	17
Overlea Ct	16	W	10
Overlook Dr	16	B1	11
Oversouth St	23	J1	11
Overton Av	23	J1	12
Overton St	23	J1	12
Ovid Pl	10	S	10
Oxford Rd	9	V	16
Oxford St	16	W	13
Pace Ct	11	S	9
Pace Dr S	11	S	8
Pacific St (IS)	15	B1	17
Pacific St	15	X	17
Pacific St	16	B1	12
Pacific St	10	U	11
Pacific Wk	18	Z	4
Paddock St	22	K1	16
Palermo St	16	A1	15
Palfrey Av	10	T	12
Palm Rd	10	V	11
Palm St	16	X	14
Palmer Cir	23	H1	10
Palmer Dr	23	H1	10
Palmer St	16	W	14
Palmetto St	16	X	15
Pam Ct	22	G1	14
Pamela La	10	V	14
Pamlico Av	22	E1	17
Pamoqua La	11	Q	8
Pamoqua La W	11	Q	8
Pandora Dr	9	T	16
Pansmith La	11	Q	8
Papoose La	22	K1	13
Paprocki Av	11	Q	9
Par La	9	T	16
Par La N	9	T	16
Par La S	9	T	16
Paradise La	10	T	14
Pardee Av	16	X	11
Paris Ct	11	P	9
Park Av	15	Z	18
Park Av	10	U	11
Park Av	10	U	12
Park Av	9	U	15
Park La	11	Q	9
Park Pl	16	Z	12
Park Row Blvd	15	Z	15
Park View La	15	Z	15
Parkside St	22	J1	15
Parkview Wy	22	F1	15
Parkway Blvd	21	D1	18
Parkway Gardens Blvd	15	C1	18
Parkway Pl	15	D1	18
Parkwood Rd	11	P	8
Parkwood St	15	C1	17
Parr Dr	21	E1	19
Parsons Landing	16	Y	10
Partington St	22	J1	13
Pat Ct	22	F1	13
Pat Dr	22	F1	13
Patchogue-Holbrook Rd	22	L1	17
Patco Ct	15	A1	16
Patricia Av	11	R	9
Patricia Ct	23	F1	12
Patrician St	22	L1	15
Patton St	9	T	15
Pauchogue Av	16	A1	11
Paul Dr	22	J1	17
Paul Pl	21	F1	18
Paulanna Av	23	L1	11
Pauline St	22	J1	16
Pauls Ct	15	A1	18
Paulsen St	22	J1	16
Paumanake Av	11	Q	9
Pawnee St	15	D1	18
Peach Pl	10	S	13
Peach St	16	X	14
Peachtree Ct	22	J1	15
Peacock Pl	16	W	14
Pear St	16	X	14
Pearl Ct	11	Q	10
Pearl Ct	22	H1	13
Pearl St	15	C1	17
Pearl St	22	G1	14
Pearl St	22	J1	15
Pearson Ct	11	T	9
Pease La	11	R	8
Pecan St	15	C1	18
Peck Av	16	T	14
Peckham Av	16	X	12
Peconic St	15	D1	16
Peconic St	22	E1	17
Peconic St W	15	C1	16
Peggy Dr	23	G1	12
Pelham Dr	9	V	17
Pembroke Ct	10	U	12
Penataquit Av	16	V	11
Penataquit Av	16	V	12
Penataquit Dr	10	S	11
Pennant Wk	18	Z	4
Penney St	10	Q	11
Pennsylvania Av	10	V	13
Pennsylvania Av	9	V	15
Pennsylvania Dr	9	V	15
Pepperidge Rd	23	E1	11
Pequot La	16	A1	11
Percy Williams Dr	16	Y	10
Perimeter St	22	J1	15
Periwinkle Dr	22	H1	14
Perkal St	10	U	11
Perry St	9	U	16
Pesce Ct	22	F1	15
Peter Farber St	22	K1	16
Peter La	22	G1	14
Peter Paul Dr	11	R	8
Peters Blvd	15	Y	15
Peters Blvd	16	C1	10
Peters Blvd	10	S	12
Peterson St	16	W	14
Petrel Wk	18	Y	5
Pheasant Pl	16	W	14
Phelps Dr	17	U	10
Philip St	22	J1	16
Philips St	22	F1	14
Phyllis Ct	22	K1	13
Phyllis Pl	10	Q	10
Pia Ct	15	C1	18
Pic Ct	16	W	14
Pilar La	23	G1	12
Pilgrim Rd	9	S	15
Pilot Wk	18	Z	3
Pine Acres Blvd	10	S	14
Pine Acres Blvd (BR)	10	T	12
Pine Aire Dr	10	R	14
Pine Av	11	Q	10
Pine Av	22	E1	17
Pine Av	22	F1	15
Pine Av	21	E1	18
Pine Av	10	R	10
Pine Blvd	15	B1	16
Pine Ct	15	U	15
Pine Dr	10	S	12
Pine Dr	10	T	11
Pine Edge Av	15	B1	16
Pine Grove Blvd	10	T	14
Pine La	23	K1	13
Pine Oak La	10	T	14
Pine St	15	Y	15
Pine St	18	Y	3
Pine St	23	J1	11
Pine St	23	M1	12
Pine St	9	U	15
Pine Wk	18	A1	4
Pinebrook Pl	10	V	12
Pinecone La	15	C1	17
Pinedale Rd	15	Z	18
Pineland Pl	16	W	13
Pinetop Dr	15	X	16
Pinetree La	16	B1	11
Pineview Blvd	15	Y	15
Pineville Rd	15	Z	16
Pinewild Rd	15	V	15
Pinewood Av	15	A1	16
Piney St	16	B1	12
Pioneer St	15	W	15
Piper Ct	11	S	7
Piper La	22	G1	14
Pirates Wk	18	B1	4
Placid Ct	22	J1	14
Plad Blvd	27	M1	17
Pleasant Dr	10	S	13
Pleasant La	16	W	10
Pleasant St	15	C1	17
Pleasantview Dr	15	Z	15
Plum Pl	16	Y	11
Plum St	16	Y	13
Plume Ct	10	T	13
Plunket St	16	W	14
Plymouth Av	10	T	10
Plymouth Ct	11	U	10
Plymouth Rd	15	W	18
Poe La	16	W	14
Poet Pl	22	J1	16
Polly Dr	15	T	16
Pond Rd	16	D1	12
Pond Rd	22	F1	14
Pond Rd	22	F1	16
Poplar La	23	K1	11
Poplar Pl	10	S	12
Poplar St	15	Z	12
Poplar St	16	X	13
Poplar St	23	J1	11
Port Av	21	D1	18
Portside Dr	22	J1	14
Post Office Rd	16	A1	10
Potomac La	22	K1	14
Potter Av	15	Y	15
Potter Blvd	16	T	10
Potter Blvd	10	S	13
Powell Av	15	Z	16
Prescott Ct	23	J1	11
President Dr	22	F1	12
President St	23	F1	12
Preston St	16	W	14
Prime Pl	15	X	17
Princess Av	10	T	14
Princess Ct	16	C1	11
Princeton St	16	X	12
Princeton St	10	U	12
Pringle St	22	J1	15
Privet Pl	10	S	12
Prospect Av	11	Q	9
Prospect Av	11	V	10
Prospect Av	15	Z	16
Prospect Dr	9	V	15
Prospect Pl	15	X	18
Prospect Pl	10	S	14
Prospect St	15	A1	16
Provost St	16	C1	10
Public Rd	15	C1	18
Pueblo Ct	22	K1	13
Purdy Av	23	L1	11
Purick St	22	M1	13
Puritan Rd	23	J1	11
Quail Dr	9	T	16
Quail Run	16	Z	10
Quality St	16	C1	11
Quarles St	16	X	14
Quay Ct	11	S	8
Queen Anne Pl	15	Y	17
Queen St	10	Q	13
Quinn Pl	9	U	15
Quintuck La	16	A1	10
Rabro Dr	15	W	17
Race Pl	23	F1	12
Rachels Wy	22	J1	17
Radburn Dr	15	Z	18
Radcliff Dr	16	X	14
Raft Av	22	K1	14
Railroad Av	15	A1	16
Railroad Av	15	Y	16
Railroad Av	23	H1	12
Railroad Av	21	G1	17
Railroad Av	21	H1	17
Railroad Pl	10	V	11
Railroad Plaza	16	U	10
Railroad St	23	L1	12
Railroad St	10	V	11
Rajon Rd	28	M1	14
Raleigh La	11	Q	9
Ralph Av	15	W	16
Ramm Ct	9	T	17
Ranick Rd	15	W	17
Rasons Ct	15	W	17
Raven Wk	18	A1	4
Ray Ct	16	W	13
Raymond St	15	B1	17
Raymond St	16	X	11
Raynor St	22	F1	17
Recreation Pl	16	W	10
Redington St	10	V	11
Redmen St	16	A1	12
Redmond Av	10	V	11
Redwood Dr	16	B1	11
Reese Av	9	V	15
Regina Ct	16	W	13
Regina Dr	22	J1	12
Reil Pl	10	U	11
Reilly St	10	Q	11
Remington Blvd	22	D1	16
Renee Dr	22	L1	12
Renee Dr	23	G1	12
Resiak Ct	22	J1	16
Revelyn Ct	22	J1	13
Revere Dr	22	J1	13
Rex Ct	16	W	13
Reynolds Rd	11	R	9
Rhode Island Av	10	V	13
Rhodes Av	10	U	11
Rianna Ct	16	V	14
Richard Av	16	Z	12
Richards Wk	18	Z	4
Richardson La	16	Y	11
Richland Blvd	10	T	12
Richmar Dr	22	J1	13
Richmond Blvd	15	D1	18
Richmond St	16	W	13
Richwood La	15	C1	19
Ricky Rd	21	E1	18
Riddle St	16	W	14
Ridge Av	15	A1	16
Ridge Ct	15	X	17
Ridgefield Rd	15	W	18
Ridgeway Blvd	10	S	11
Ridgewood Av	15	V	16
Ridgewood Ct	22	M1	13
Ridgewood St	10	R	12
Rigney St	16	W	14
Rime La	28	M1	15
Rita Dr	15	V	16
Ritchie St	10	V	10
River Rd	16	C1	11
River St	23	J1	11
Rivera La	23	G1	11
Riverdale Rd	23	F1	12
Riverview Av	16	C1	11
Riverview Ct	16	C1	11
Riviera Ct	16	B1	11
Robbins Av	16	Y	12
Robert Moses Causeway	10	R	10
Robert Moses Twin Causeway	11	S	7
Robert Moses Twin Causeway	12	T	5
Robert Pl	16	Y	12
Roberts St	22	J1	16
Robin Hill Pl	16	W	15
Robin La	15	W	15
Robin La	10	U	11
Robin Wk	18	A1	4
Robinhood Dr	16	A1	13
Rock Rd	16	B1	13
Rockaway St	16	A1	14
Rockaway St	10	R	11
Rocket Dr	16	A1	13
Rodeo Dr	9	R	15
Roderick Rd	10	Q	10
Rodney Av	16	Z	13
Roe Ct	16	Y	11
Roebling Ct	22	H1	16
Rogers Rd	22	F1	14
Rolan Ct	16	A1	13
Roland Pl	16	W	13
Rollin La	9	U	16
Rollstone Av	23	H1	12
Roma Av	15	A1	15
Romaine Av	16	X	12
Roman La	11	Q	9
Roman St	16	X	12
Ronald Av	22	K1	13
Roosevelt Av	16	X	12
Roosevelt Av	22	E1	15
Roosevelt Av	23	H1	12
Roosevelt Blvd	15	Y	17
Roosevelt Pl	10	R	11
Roosevelt St	16	Y	12
Roosevelt St	9	V	15
Roosevelt St	10	U	11
Roosevelt St	15	X	15
Root Av	16	A1	11
Rose Ct	16	A1	11
Rose Dr	23	G1	12
Rose Dr	21	E1	18
Rose La	10	U	12
Rose St	15	C1	18
Rose St	15	Y	16
Rose St	16	Y	11
Rose St	22	J1	12
Rosemary Pl	16	A1	10
Rosemore Av	15	Y	16
Rosevale Av	21	E1	19
Rosewood Pl	10	S	13
Rosewood St	15	Z	15
Roslyn Rd	9	V	16
Roslyn St	16	A1	12
Roslyn St	16	Z	12
Ross Av	10	U	11
Rotledge St	9	U	16
Rowe Pl	10	S	10
Roxbury Av	16	C1	11
Roxbury Ct	16	C1	11
Roy Av	10	Q	11
Royal Oak Ct	22	L1	16
Rudder Dr	22	M1	16
Rugby St	9	V	17
Runyon St	10	S	10
Russell Av	22	J1	17
Russell Rd	23	D1	11
Ruth St	10	Q	10
Ruzicka Pl	22	G1	14
Ryan St	11	R	9
Rye Ct	16	W	13
Sachem Rd	16	D1	11
Sage St	15	X	15
Sagebrush La	15	B1	17
Sagtikos State Pkwy	9	S	15
Sail, The	17	Z	10
Sailor St	10	V	10
St Andrews Dr	9	S	15
St Charles Rd	22	J1	16
St James St	22	J1	15
St Johns St	15	Y	15
St Johns St	22	G1	12
St Louis	16	W	13
St Marks Cir	15	B1	17
St Mark's La	16	Y	10
St Peters Dr	9	S	15
Sal Ct	22	H1	14
Salem Ct	15	W	18
Salem Pa	15	W	18
Salem St	16	Z	13
Salt Meadow La	23	M1	11
Saltmeadow Ct	23	L1	11
Saltmeadow La	23	L1	11
Sampson Av	15	B1	16
Sampson St	22	H1	13
Sampson St	10	U	11
San Juan Dr	15	C1	18
San Rafael Av	22	L1	16
Sand La	15	B1	17
Sand Wk	18	A1	4
Sandpiper La	16	A1	10
Sandpiper Wk	18	A1	4
Sandra Av	10	R	10
Santa Anita Ct	22	L1	15
Santam Ct	16	T	12
Sarah St	10	U	11
Sassafras St	15	X	15
Satelite Dr	16	A1	13
Satinwood St	15	Z	15
Sauters St	22	M1	13
Savoy Av	10	T	14
Saxon Av	16	W	13
Saxton Av	23	H1	11
Sayville Av	22	G1	14
Sayville Blvd	22	K1	13
Scaup Ct	16	W	13
Schaefer Av	22	G1	16
Schember Rd	10	R	12
Schley St	15	B1	17
Schmidt Av	22	H1	16
Schneider La	15	X	17
School House La	15	X	18
School House Rd	16	A1	10
School St	11	Q	9
Scopelitis Ct	21	K1	17
Scotch Pine Dr	15	B1	17
Scott Av	10	P	10
Sea Breeze Wk	18	B1	4
Sea Cliff St	16	Z	14
Sea Wk	18	Z	4
Seabay Wk	18	Y	4
Seafield La	10	U	10
Seal St	16	A1	13
Seaman Av	23	K1	11
Sears Rd	11	Q	9
Seaspray La	11	P	8
Secatogue Av	16	A1	11
Secatogue Rd	11	R	8
Secaucus La	16	A1	11
Sejon Dr	23	K1	12
Seley Cross	16	B1	13
Seminole Dr	10	T	11
Seminole St	15	D1	18
Seneca Dr	10	S	11
Seneca St	15	D1	18
Sequams La	11	P	8
Sequams La E	11	Q	8
Sequams La N	11	P	8
Sequams La W	11	P	8
Sequoia Wy	22	L1	15
Serene Pl	15	C1	19
Serpentine La	15	B1	17
Service Rd	22	J1	13
Service Rd	10	U	10
Seusing Blvd	21	D1	18
Seville Blvd	23	K1	13
Sexton Dr	11	S	8
Seymour Av	16	A1	12
Shadow Grove La	22	L1	15
Shady Brook La	11	Q	8
Shady Ct	11	T	9
Shady La	15	A1	15
Shafter St	15	B1	17
Shamokin La	16	A1	11
Shandon Ct	15	Z	18
Shaw Av	16	X	11
Shebar Dr	16	Y	10
Sheets Av	22	J1	17
Sheffield Av	10	U	12
Sheila Ct	22	M1	16
Shelby Av	22	J1	16
Sheldon St	15	A1	15
Shell Wk	18	A1	4
Shelter Rd	15	D1	18
Sheppard Ct	10	V	14
Sheridan St	16	W	14
Sherman Av	11	Q	9
Sherman St	9	T	16
Sherry St	16	A1	11
Sherwood Dr	16	A1	12
Sherwood La	22	L1	15
Shinnecock La	16	Z	10
Shirley St	22	F1	15
Shoal Dr	11	S	7
Shore Ct	16	X	12
Shore Dr	16	C1	12
Shore La	10	V	10
Shore Rd	11	U	9
Shore Rd (BR)	23	H1	10
Shore Wk	18	B1	4
Short St	16	Z	16
Sid Ct	15	Z	18
Silva St	22	J1	16
Silverleaf La	15	A1	17
Simeon Woods Rd	15	X	17
Simmons Dr	16	B1	11
Singingwood Dr	22	L1	17
Sioux Dr	10	T	12
Sioux St	15	D1	19
Skidmore Pl	11	R	8
Skip La	10	R	14
Skipper Dr	11	S	7
Skookwams Ct	11	Q	8
Skylark Dr	22	L1	16
Slade Pl	10	S	11
Slate La	15	B1	17
Slone Ct	23	L1	12
Slope La	15	Z	18
Smith Av	16	X	10
Smith Av	10	U	10
Smith Ct	10	V	11
Smith St	15	Y	15
Smith St	23	J1	12
Smith St	10	T	11
Smithtown Av	22	G1	16
Snedecor Av	11	R	8
Snedecor Av	23	L1	11
Snowberry La	15	A1	17
Soka Gill Av	21	E1	17
Somerset Av	16	Z	11
Somerset Dr	22	K1	17
Somerville St	9	T	15
Sonia Rd	10	S	13
Sorowoc La	16	W	13
Sotzen Av	22	J1	17
South 1st St	22	F1	15
South 1st St	10	S	14
South 2nd St	22	F1	16
South 2nd St	10	R	14
South 3rd St	22	F1	16
South 3rd St	10	R	14
South 4th St	22	F1	15
South 4th St	10	R	14
South 5th Av	10	U	14
South Atlantic Av	11	V	10
South Bay Av (BR)	11	U	9
South Bay Av	11	V	9
South Bay Av	17	X	9
South Bay Wk	18	Z	5
South Briarwood Av	11	R	8
South Chicot Av	11	R	8
South Clinton Av	10	U	10
South Connecting Rd	21	C1	17
South Country Rd	11	T	9
South Country Rd	16	Z	11
South Country Rd	23	C1	12
South Dr	21	E1	18
South Dr	21	F1	18
South Dyre Av	11	R	8
South Express Dr	15	D1	17
South Fehr Wy	10	R	14
South Friedner La	22	F1	13
South Harrison Av	16	Z	11
South Lawn Av	15	A1	16
South Pk Av	10	V	10
South Research Dr	16	Y	14
South Rd	15	Y	15
South Roberts St	22	J1	15
South Shore Ct	16	X	12
South Side Av	10	R	11
South St	11	Q	9
South St	16	C1	10
South St	16	V	10
South St	23	K1	12
South Technology Dr	16	Y	14
South Union Av	16	U	10
South Wk	18	A1	4
South Windsor Av	11	U	10
Southern Blvd	21	C1	21
Southern State Pkwy	10	T	12
Southfield Rd	11	T	9
Southport St	15	C1	16
Space Ct	15	Z	17
Spacecraft La	15	Y	18
Spad La	22	M1	15
Sparrow Pl	16	W	14
Sparton La	15	Z	18
Speed St	16	X	15
Spence Av	21	M1	17
Spence St	10	T	14
Sperry Ct	16	X	13
Spiral Rd	28	M1	16
Split Cedar Dr	15	B1	17
Sportsman Pl	16	X	15
Sportsmen St	15	A1	15
Spray Ct	23	L1	12
Springdale Dr	15	D1	17
Springfield Cir	15	A1	15
Springmeadow Dr	22	K1	16
Spruce Av	11	Q	10
Spruce Av	22	G1	13
Spruce Av	10	R	10
Spruce Dr	22	M1	15
Spruce Dr	21	F1	18
Spruce La	15	A1	15
Spruce La	23	L1	11
Spruce St	15	A1	16
Spruce St	10	U	11
Spruce St	9	U	15
Spruce Wk	18	A1	4
Sprucewood Blvd	15	Z	15
Spur Dr	10	V	13
Spur Dr N	16	A1	13
Spur Dr N	16	V	13
Spur Dr N	10	T	13
Spur Dr S	16	A1	13
Spur Dr S	16	V	12
Spur Dr S	10	T	12
Spur La	10	V	13
Squaw La	22	K1	13
St Johns St	23	G1	12
St Lawrence St	22	J1	13
Stacom St	16	X	13
Stahley St	16	W	13
Standish Rd	9	V	16
Stanley St	10	R	10
Starlight Dr	16	Z	11
State Hwy 27	16	U	11
State Hwy 27A	11	Q	8
State Hwy 111	15	X	15
State Hwy 454	15	X	18
Station Av	23	D1	12
Station St	16	D1	12
Stein Dr	10	U	13
Stellenwerf Av	16	Z	11
Stephen Ct	22	L1	13
Stephen Rd	22	L1	15
Stephens Ct	15	X	17
Stephens Dr	15	X	17
Stepney La	16	W	14
Sterling Pl	22	H1	12
Steuben St	15	W	15
Stewart St	16	Z	11
Stewart St	10	R	12
Stillman Ct	22	M1	12
Stockton St	9	U	17
Storey Av	15	Y	16
Storey Blvd	10	S	11
Storm Dr	22	M1	17
Straw La	15	B1	17
Strong St	16	X	15
Strum St	16	X	14
Stub St	9	U	16
Studley St	16	W	13
Stumrel St	16	X	13
Stuyvesant Rd	23	E1	12
Stuyvesant St	9	V	17
Suellen Ct	16	Y	11
Suellen Rd	16	Y	11
Suffolk Av	15	X	15
Suffolk Av	9	T	15
Suffolk Av	9	U	15
Suffolk La	17	Z	11
Sugarwood La	15	A1	16
Sullivan St	10	R	12
Summerfield Cir	15	A1	15
Summerwood Rd	22	L1	15
Sun Ct	16	W	13
Sunburst Blvd	15	Z	15
Sunburst Ter	15	A1	15
Sunflower Dr	22	H1	14
Sunflower La	15	B1	17
Sunny Glenn Wy	22	L1	17
Sunny La	11	S	9
Sunrise Av	22	J1	13
Sunrise Dr	22	J1	13
Sunrise Hwy	16	U	11
Sunrise Hwy	22	D1	12
Sunrise Hwy	28	N1	15
Sunrise Hwy (BR)	10	S	11
Sunrise Rd	22	E1	15
Sunset Dr	23	H1	11
Sunset Pl	11	Q	9
Sunset Rd	10	T	10
Sunwood Cir	15	A1	15
Surf Av	16	X	10
Surf Rd	18	C1	4
Surf View Wk	18	C1	4
Surf Wk	18	Y	4
Surfside Cove	11	S	8
Sutton Ct	11	Q	9
Sutton Pl	15	B1	16
Sutton Pl	16	Y	11
Suydam La	23	K1	11
Swallow La	9	T	17
Swan Ct	16	W	10
Swan Pl	16	W	13
Swayze St	23	J1	12
Sweeneydale Av	10	T	13
Swindon Row	22	J1	13
Sycamore Av	22	E1	17
Sycamore Av	22	F1	15
Sycamore La	15	A1	17
Sycamore St	16	X	14
Sycora La	15	B1	17
Sylvan Av	22	M1	12
Sylvan Ct	11	Q	8
Sylvan St	10	U	12
Sylvia Cir	21	J1	17
Sylvia Dr	11	Q	10
Tabor St	16	W	13
Taft Av	16	X	12
Taft St	9	V	15
Tahlulah La	11	Q	8
Tamarack St	16	Y	12
Tamarack St	16	Z	15
Tanglewood Rd	11	R	8
Tanner St	22	J1	17
Tappen Av	16	Y	11
Tariff St	23	H1	12
Tate St	22	J1	15
Taylor Av	16	Z	12
Taylor Av	10	S	14
Teal Cres	16	C1	10
Technology Dr	16	Y	14
Teddy Ct	15	C1	18
Tee Pl	21	E1	18
Teleky Pl	22	E1	16
Tellar Dr	16	A1	13
Telstar La	15	Y	18
Tennessee Av	10	V	13
Teresa La	23	G1	12
Tern Ct	11	S	9
Tern Ct	16	A1	10
Terrace Ct	15	D1	19
Terrace Dr	21	F1	18
Terrace Rd	22	M1	13
Terry Blvd	22	J1	16
Terry Rd	15	B1	20
Terry Rd	15	C1	18
Terry Rd	22	D1	17
Terry St	23	J1	11
Tex Ct	16	X	12
Texas Av	10	V	12
Thaddeus La	11	Q	8
Thayer Pl	11	S	8
Thomas St	9	T	17
Thomas St	10	U	12
Thompson Av	18	D1	4

Suffolk Co.

STREET	MAP	GRID
Thompson Dr	10	S 11
Thompson Dr	10	S 12
Thorn La	23	E1 11
Thorpe La	16	A1 11
Thrift St	15	C1 16
Thrush Dr	9	T 17
Thunder Rd	22	M1 16
Ticondiroga Dr	22	H1 14
Tide Ct	23	E1 12
Tillie St	17	V 11
Timber Point Rd or Old Place Pa	16	A1 11
Timber Ridge Ct	22	J1 12
Timber Ridge Dr	15	Z 18
Timber Ridge Dr	22	L1 16
Timberline Dr	15	W 15
Tojan Dr	16	A1 12
Toni Pl	15	Y 16
Toomey Rd	10	Q 11
Toppy La	10	R 13
Tory Ct	22	K1 15
Tower Mews	16	C1 11
Tower St	23	H1 12
Town House Village	15	A1 17
Town Line Ct	15	B1 19
Town Line Rd	15	W 18
Town Line Rd	21	C1 19
Tracy La	17	B1 11
Trade Zone Ct	22	H1 15
Trade Zone Dr	22	H1 15
Trader La	16	W 13
Tranquil Ct	23	L1 11
Tree Av	15	X 15
Tremont Av	15	V 17
Tremper St	22	K1 15
Trim St	10	U 11
Trout St	23	F1 12
Troy St	16	Z 13
Trues Dr	11	S 8
Trumpet La	22	J1 16
Tucker Dr	22	L1 13
Tudor La	10	U 12
Tulip Av	23	G1 11
Tulip St W	10	U 12
Tulip West St	16	U 12
Tupelo La	16	Z 11
Turul Pl	22	E1 16
Tuttle St	22	J1 16
Twig Av	15	X 15
Twin Bark Av	22	J1 16
Twin Lawns Av	15	X 15
Twin River Dr	16	D1 12
Tyler Av	23	H1 11
Udalia Ct	11	Q 9
Udalia Rd	11	Q 9
Udall Rd	10	Q 10
Uncas St	15	D1 19
Union Av	16	X 11
Union Blvd	11	P 9
Union Blvd	10	S 10
Union Pkwy	22	F1 16
Union Pl	16	X 10
Union St	22	F1 15
Union St	23	H1 11
Urn Ct	16	X 13
Ursula Ct	15	C1 18
Utica St	16	V 12
Vail St	16	Y 11
Val Ct	22	K1 15
Vale Dr, The	21	F1 18
Valencia St	15	C1 18
Valerie Ct	22	J1 13
Valerie Pl	16	A1 10
Valley Forge Dr	22	J1 14
Valley Rd	21	F1 18
Valley Stream St	16	A1 13
Val-Ray Blvd	15	Y 17
Van Bomel Blvd	16	D1 11
Van Buren Av	10	Q 11
Van Buren St	9	U 17
Van Cedar Av	9	U 15
Van Horn Av	22	J1 17
Van Schack Pl	15	C1 17
Van St	16	X 13
Vanderbilt Av	15	D1 18
Vanderbilt Av	15	V 16
Vanderbilt Blvd	16	D1 11
Vanderbilt Motor Pkwy	9	S 17
Ventura La	11	S 10
Vera Ct	11	P 8
Verka Ct	23	K1 12
Vermont Av	10	V 13
Vern Ct	16	X 14
Veronica St	22	J1 15
Versa Pl	22	J1 13
Veterans Memorial Hwy	15	Y 18
Veterans Memorial Hwy	22	D1 16
Vicksburg Dr	22	J1 14
Victor St	22	J1 15
Victory Dr	15	D1 19
Victory St	15	C1 18
View Ct	16	Y 12
Viking Ct	22	F1 13
Viking Dr	11	S 7
Village Dr	15	A1 18
Village La	15	Z 18
Village La	22	F1 14
Vincent Pl	23	F1 12
Vincent St	22	F1 14
Viola Pl	16	A1 11
Violet St	15	A1 16
Virgil Dr	16	X 13
Virginia Ct	22	H1 13
Vita Dr	15	X 16
Voorhis Dr	9	T 16
Waco La	22	L1 15
Wagon Wy	21	D1 19
Wagstaff La	11	Q 8
Wainwright St	15	C1 18
Walbridge Av	10	U 13
Wald St	22	J1 16
Wall Pl	21	E1 17
Wall St	16	Z 11
Wall St	22	F1 14
Wallace St	16	X 12
Walnut Av	22	F1 15
Walnut Av	22	F1 17
Walnut Av	22	G1 13
Walnut St	15	Y 15
Walnut St	16	Y 12
Walnut Wk	18	A1 4
Walter Av	15	C1 18
Walter St	9	T 15
Walton St	9	U 16
Wampum La	11	Q 8
Wantagh Av S	16	Z 12
Ward St	10	R 11
Warren St	9	V 17
Warwick La	11	S 9
Washington Av	16	V 12
Washington Av	16	Z 12
Washington Av	22	E1 15
Washington Av	23	G1 11
Washington Av	10	Q 11
Washington Av	10	R 14
Washington Av	9	V 17
Washington St	16	Z 12
Washington St	22	J1 12
Washington St	10	R 11
Wateredge Ct	23	E1 11
Waterford Rd	22	E1 12
Waterview Av	21	E1 19
Watson Pl	16	X 11
Watson St	16	Z 11
Watts Pl	10	R 11
Wavecrest Av	11	Q 9
Wavecrest Dr	16	Y 11
Waverly Av	22	M1 17
Wayne Av	9	V 17
Wayne St	15	C1 19
Weaver Rd	23	G1 12
Webster Av	10	Q 11
Webster Rd	16	X 12
Wedgewood Dr	15	C1 18
Weeks Av	15	Z 16
Weichers Av	21	E1 18
Weichers Pl	21	F1 18
Weldon St	16	W 13
Wells Dr	10	T 14
Wendover Rd	23	J1 11
Wendy La	9	T 16
Wenman Av	16	W 11
Wensley La	16	B1 10
Wensley La	17	B1 10
Wenwood Rd	15	X 18
West 1st St	21	E1 19
West 1st St	10	Q 10
West 2nd St	21	E1 19
West 2nd St	10	Q 10
West 3rd St	21	E1 19
West 3rd St	10	Q 10
West 4th St	21	D1 19
West 4th St	10	Q 10
West 5th St	21	D1 19
West 5th St	10	R 10
West 6th St	21	D1 19
West 6th St	10	R 11
West 7th St	21	D1 19
West 8th St	21	D1 19
West 9th St	21	F1 18
West 10th St	21	F1 18
West 11th St	21	F1 18
West Admiral's Dr	17	T 9
West Av	23	H1 11
West Bay Dr	11	R 8
West Bayberry Rd	17	X 9
West Belmont St	10	Q 12
West Ct	10	R 10
West Dr	21	F1 18
West Dr	10	U 11
West End Av	15	V 17
West Golf St	22	F1 13
West Islip Blvd	11	Q 9
West Islip Rd	11	P 8
West Lakeland St	10	Q 12
West La	11	U 10
West La	23	H1 11
West Lighthouse Wk	18	Y 3
West Oakdale St	10	Q 12
West Orange St	16	X 13
West Plum St	16	X 13
West Rd	23	L1 12
West Secatogue La	11	R 8
West Shore Dr	23	E1 12
West Shore Rd	23	D1 11
West Side Av	10	V 11
West Spruce St	16	Y 12
West St	11	Q 9
West Wk	18	A1 3
West Wk	18	B1 4
West Wk (SA)	18	Y 3
West White St	9	T 16
West William St	10	U 11
West Willow St	16	X 13
West Wind Dr	22	F1 13
Westbridge Dr	22	K1 15
Westbury St	16	B1 12
Westgate Dr	22	G1 14
Westgate Dr	23	J1 10
Westminster Dr	22	G1 14
Westminster La	10	Q 10
Westway Av	22	H1 13
Westwood Blvd	10	S 14
Westwood Dr	15	W 15
Wexford Ct	22	E1 12
Wexford Dr	23	E1 12
Whalen Ct	16	X 13
Wharf Wy	11	S 8
Wheeler Av	9	U 15
Wheeler Rd	15	X 17
Wheeler Rd	15	X 18
Whig Ct	22	K1 15
Whipple St	9	U 16
White Oak La	16	Z 10
White Spruce La	15	W 18
White St	9	U 17
Whitehall Ct	22	L1 16
Whitetail La	15	A1 16
Wichard Dr	22	F1 13
Wicks Rd	9	T 17
Widgeon Ct	16	C1 10
Wilbur Pl	22	G1 15
Wilbur St	17	U 11
Wilcox La	16	W 13
Wildwood Ct	16	Z 10
Wildwood Rd	15	D1 18
Wiley St	16	X 13
Wilherm La	11	Q 8
Wilken La	16	W 13
Willett Av	23	H1 12
Willetts La	11	Q 8
William Av	15	Y 16
William Av	16	Y 11
William St	15	Z 16
William St	16	Z 11
William St	22	H1 14
William St	23	L1 11
William St	9	T 15
William St	10	U 12
Williamsburgh La	15	D1 19
Willoughby Pl	11	P 8
Willoughby St	15	W 16
Willow Av	16	Y 11
Willow Brook Av	16	W 11
Willow St	15	Z 15
Willow St	16	Y 13
Willow St	23	J1 11
Willow St	23	K1 11
Willow Wood Dr	23	F1 12
Willowview Ct	22	F1 15
Wilmot Rd	18	C1 4
Wilshire La	23	E1 12
Wilson Blvd	15	Y 15
Wilson Blvd	16	Y 14
Wilson Blvd	17	Y 12
Wilson St	22	F1 14
Wilson St	10	R 11
Wilson St	9	U 16
Wilton Ct	16	C1 10
Windermere Dr	22	L1 15
Winding La	15	B1 17
Windmill Gate Dr	23	F1 12
Windmill Rd	23	G1 12
Windsor Ct	22	K1 17
Windsor Pl	11	U 9
Windsor Pl	15	A1 16
Windsor St	16	W 12
Windwatch Dr	15	A1 18
Windwood Rd	22	F1 13
Winfield Av	9	V 17
Winganhauppauge Av	16	Y 12
Winganhauppauge Rd	16	Y 13
Wingham Dr	16	Y 11
Winne La	16	W 13
Winnetica La	16	A1 11
Winnifred St	10	U 11
Winona La	16	A1 11
Winston Dr	16	W 13
Winthrop Rd	9	V 16
Winthrop St	16	W 13
Winwood Ct	16	Y 11
Winwood La	22	L1 15
Wisconsin Av	10	U 13
Wisconsin Ct	10	T 14
Witmer Ct	15	B1 17
Wittberg St	16	X 13
Wittman La	9	T 16
Wohseepee Dr	10	S 10
Wood La	15	C1 19
Wood St	9	U 15
Woodbine Av	10	U 12
Woodbury Rd	15	X 17
Woodcliff Rd	16	B1 13
Woodcrest Dr	15	X 18
Woodhollow Rd	16	B1 11
Woodhull La	23	J1 12
Woodland Av	15	A1 16
Woodland Dr	17	T 9
Woodland Dr	17	Z 11
Woodland Dr	23	K1 11
Woodland Dr (BR)	10	T 10
Woodland St	16	A1 11
Woodlawn Av	15	Y 16
Woodlawn Av	16	D1 12
Woodlawn Pine Av	21	E1 18
Woodlea Av	10	U 12
Woodleigh Ct	22	L1 16
Woodmere St	16	A1 13
Woodmont Ct	22	M1 16
Woods Edge Ct	15	A1 18
Woods Pl	16	B1 13
Woods Rd	16	B1 13
Woodside Av	16	Y 11
Woodside Av	22	N1 16
Woodside St	15	X 18
Woody La	23	F1 12
Wurz St	16	X 13
Wyandanch Av	16	Z 11
Wyandanch Rd	22	K1 13
Wyandotte La	16	A1 11
Wyndham La	22	K1 17
Wyndham Rd	9	V 16
Wyoming Av	10	V 12
Yale Ave	22	F1 12
Yale St	16	X 12
Yalta Dr	15	X 17
Yankee St	16	X 13
Yarnell St	9	T 15
Yen Ct	16	X 13
Yerk St	15	C1 18
Yew Ct	16	X 13
Yockel Av	16	A1 11
Yonda Dr	22	H1 12
Yukon Ct	16	X 13
Yuma La	16	A1 11
Zane Ct	16	X 13
Zavra St	22	F1 14
Zena Ct	16	W 13
Zeus Ct	16	X 13
Zoe Ct	10	V 12
1st Av	15	Y 16
1st Av	16	Z 11
1st Av	22	L1 12
1st Av	10	V 11
1st Av	9	V 15
1st Ct	16	V 10
1st Ct	21	E1 19
1st Pl	15	A1 16
1st St	11	S 8
1st St	16	X 10
1st St	22	E1 17
1st St	22	F1 17
1st St	22	J1 16
1st St	22	J1 17
1st St	22	L1 12
1st St	23	H1 12
1st St	10	U 14
1st St	9	U 15
2nd Av	15	Y 16
2nd Av	16	Z 11
2nd Av	22	L1 12
2nd Av	10	U 11
2nd Av	9	U 15
2nd Ct	16	W 10
2nd Ct	21	E1 19
2nd Pl	17	U 11
2nd Pl	10	U 11
2nd St	11	S 9
2nd St	16	X 10
2nd St	22	J1 16
2nd St	22	J1 17
2nd St	22	L1 13
2nd St	23	H1 12
2nd St	10	U 14
2nd St	9	U 15
3rd Av	15	Y 15
3rd Av	16	Z 11
3rd Av	17	U 11
3rd Av	22	K1 13
3rd Av	22	L1 12
3rd Av	10	U 11
3rd Av	10	U 15
3rd Ct	21	E1 19
3rd St	11	S 9
3rd St	22	E1 16
3rd St	23	H1 12
3rd St	9	U 15
4th Av	10	U 11
4th Av	10	U 15
4th Dr	22	E1 16
4th St	11	S 9
4th St	23	H1 12
4th St	9	V 15
5th Av	15	D1 17
5th Av	18	A1 4
5th Av	15	U 15
5th Av	10	T 11
5th Industrial Ct	10	T 13
5th St	11	S 9
5th St	22	E1 16
5th St	22	J1 16
5th St	23	H1 11
6th Av	10	U 14
6th St	16	Z 13
6th St	22	E1 16
6th St	9	V 15
7th Av	10	U 14
7th St	11	S 9
7th St	16	A1 13
7th St	22	E1 15
7th St	9	V 15
8th Av	10	U 14
8th St	15	D1 15
8th St	9	V 15
9th Av	15	D1 16
9th Av	10	U 14
9th St	16	A1 13
9th St	10	S 10
10th Av	10	U 14
10th St	16	A1 13
11th St	22	G1 13
13th Av	15	D1 16
13th St	22	G1 13
13th St	22	J1 16
14th St	22	G1 14
17th Av	15	C1 17
18th Av	15	C1 16
18th Av	10	U 13
19th Av	15	C1 16
19th Av	10	U 13
20th Av	10	U 13
21st Av	10	U 13
22nd Av	10	U 13
23rd Av	10	U 13
38th St S	16	W 13
39th St	16	W 13
40th St	16	X 13
41st St	16	X 13
42nd St	16	X 13
43rd St	16	X 12
44th St	16	X 12
45th St	16	X 12
46th St	16	X 12
47th St	16	X 12

RIVERHEAD

STREET	MAP	GRID
Ackerly St	41	Q2 27
Adele Ct	36	Q2 28
Adelia Pa	40	W2 31
Aldersgate Dr	41	R2 28
Alexander Hamilton Rd	31	F2 27
Aliperti Rd	40	Y2 29
Amen Cor	41	R2 29
Andrea Ct	41	S2 28
Anna Ct	31	B2 29
Apple La	31	D2 30
Arrowhead Av	41	R2 28
Atwater St	36	N2 30
Audra La	41	X2 27
Augusta Al	41	R2 28
Bailey's Ct	31	C2 28
Baiting Hollow La	36	M2 29
Baiting La	36	M2 29
Ballmann Ct	41	R2 27
Baltusrol Blvd	41	R2 28
Barbara Ct	31	C2 27
Barnes Rd	31	C2 27
Bay Av	41	W2 27
Bay Ct	41	R2 28
Bay Harbor	41	W2 27
Bay Run La	40	X2 31
Bayberry La	40	V2 31
Bayberry Pa	36	Q2 30
Bayberry Rd	31	D2 29
Bayside Av	41	X2 27
Baywood Ct	36	M2 30
Baywood Dr	36	M2 30
Beach Av	41	V2 27
Beach Club La	31	C2 30
Beach Rd	41	A3 29
Beach Rd	31	D2 30
Beach Rd	41	Z2 28
Beach Wk	40	U2 31
Beach Wy	36	J2 30
Beech St	31	C2 29
Bell Av	41	U2 27
Benjamin Pl	41	S2 26
Benjamin St	31	C2 28
Berry La	31	D2 30
Birch La	31	E2 30
Birchwood	36	P2 26
Birdie Ct	31	E2 29
Black Pine St	36	N2 28
Bluebird Pl	41	S2 27
Bluegrass Ct	41	U2 28
Bluff Dr	36	K2 30
Booker Dr	41	S2 28
Breezy Point Rd	31	E2 29
Broad Av	41	T2 28
Broadview Cir	31	C2 29
Brook St	41	S2 26
Brookside Av	41	X2 27
Brown St	41	T2 26
Brown St	41	X2 27
Buckskin La	41	R2 28
Calico Ct	41	R2 28
Calverton Ct	32	D2 26
Calverton Dr	31	E2 27
Cambridge Ct	31	C2 29
Camping Grounds La	41	Y2 28
Carls Pl	41	S2 27
Carnoustie Ct	41	R2 29
Carol Ct	36	K2 28
Caroline Ct	41	V2 28
Carrie Ct	31	D2 29
Castle Ct	32	C2 26
Cavlga Wy	31	F2 27
Cedar Av	41	R2 26
Cedar Ct	41	A3 29
Cedar Dr	36	O2 30
Cedar Pa	36	Q2 31
Cedar Rd	36	H2 29
Cedar Rd	31	E2 30
Cedar St	31	D2 30
Cedar St	41	V2 27
Center Dr	36	O2 30
Center St	41	X2 27
Center St	41	Y2 28
Central Av	31	B2 30
Charles St	31	C2 28
Charles St	41	S2 27
Cherokee Wy	31	E2 27
Cherry La	31	D2 30
Chestnut Ct	41	R2 28
Chris Ct	40	T2 30
Church La	40	V2 29
Church La	41	V2 28
Circle Dr	41	Y2 28
Claus Av	41	Q2 26
Cliff Rd	31	E2 30
Cliff Rd N	31	D2 30
Cliff Rd W	31	D2 30
Cliff Wy	36	J2 30
Clover Pl	40	U2 30
Colonial Dr	41	W2 28
Columbus Av	37	Q2 26
Commerce Dr	36	P2 27
Constable Dr	36	O2 27
Corwell Av	41	T2 26
Corwin St	41	S2 26
Cottage La	37	Q2 26
Cottage La	41	Q2 26
Cotton Tail Ct	31	C2 27
Country Rd	36	H2 27
County Route 22	41	Y2 29
County Route 23	40	V2 30
County Route 25	32	D2 26
County Route 43	41	S2 27
County Route 48	40	S2 30
County Route 54	31	F2 28
County Route 58	36	O2 26
County Route 63	41	R2 26
County Route 73	41	R2 26
County Route 94	41	R2 26
County Route 94A	41	R2 26
County Route 105	41	U2 27
Court St	41	R2 26
Cove St	41	U2 27
Cranberry St	41	R2 27
Creek Rd	31	B2 30
Cricket Ct	32	C2 26
Cross	36	P2 26
Cross Rd	31	C2 30
Cross-River Dr	41	T2 29
Cross-River Dr (Union Av)	40	S2 30
Crows Nest Dr	36	N2 30
Cruise St	36	N2 30
Crystal Dr	41	V2 28
Cutlas St	36	N2 30
Daisy Ct	31	D2 29
Daly Ct	41	T2 27
Daly Dr	41	T2 27
Daniel Ct	32	C2 26
Deane St	31	E2 29
Debbie La	31	D2 28
Deep Hole Rd	36	M2 27
Deer Field Cres	32	D2 26
Deer Run	31	D2 28
Dennis Ct	41	Q2 28
Derby Ct	41	U2 28
Diana Ct	31	C2 27
Doctor's Pa	41	R2 29
Dogwood Dr	31	C2 28
Dogwood La	31	D2 29
Dogwood La S	31	D2 29
Dogwood Rd	31	E2 30
Dolores Av	36	Q2 27
Dolphin Way La	36	O2 31
Doris Av	41	S2 27
Doug La	41	Y2 28
Dover Ct	31	C2 29
Downs Blvd	41	Z2 28
Duane St	41	Q2 26
Dunlookin La	41	Z2 27
Duryea St	41	R2 27
East 2nd Av	36	H2 28
East 3rd Av	36	H2 29
East 4th Av	36	H2 29
East 5th Av	36	H2 29
East Av	41	R2 26
East Av	41	S2 26
East Ct	31	D2 29
East Dr	36	O2 28
East Fairview Av	40	U2 31
East Main St	41	S2 26
East Meadow Rd	36	M2 28
East Rd	31	C2 30
East St	41	X2 27
East Woodland Dr	31	C2 29
Eckel Ct	41	Q2 28
Edgar Av	41	U2 28
Edwards Av	36	J2 30
Edwards Av	36	L2 27
Edwards La	41	U2 28
Eight Bells Rd	36	N2 30
Eileen Cir	40	Y2 30
Elbert St	31	C2 28
Elizabeth Dr	31	E2 29
Ellen St	41	R2 29
Elton Pl	41	R2 26
Elton St	41	R2 26
Emerald La	31	C2 29
Emmetts La	31	B2 29
Fairway Av	41	T2 27
Fairway Dr	31	E2 29
Fanning Blvd	41	S2 28
Fanning St	36	P2 26
Farm Rd E	31	D2 28
Farm Rd N	31	D2 29
Farm Rd S	31	D2 28
Farm Rd W	31	D2 29
Farwood	36	O2 26
Fawn Crossing	32	D2 27
Faye St	31	E2 30
Fern Rd	36	H2 29
Fire La	31	F2 29
Fishel Av	41	S2 27
Flagg Hill Dr	36	K2 30
Flanders Rd	41	S2 26
Flora La	41	T2 27
Florence Ct	36	L2 27
Forest Dr	41	T2 28
Forest Hollow La	31	E2 28
Forest La	31	C2 30
Founders Pa	36	J2 30
Fox Chaser Pl	41	W2 27
Fox Hill Dr	36	K2 30
Fox La	41	Y2 29
Fox Run La	41	T2 27
Fox Trail Ct	40	V2 30
Francis St	31	C2 28
Franklin St	41	R2 26
Freds La	41	Z2 28
Fresh Pond Av	36	H2 28
Front St	31	C2 28
Front St	41	Y2 27
Further La	41	T2 27
Garfield Langhorne Rd	31	E2 27
Gatewood	36	P2 26
George Benson Wy	36	J2 29
Gerald St	32	D2 26
Gerald St	31	E2 29
Gina La	41	R2 29
Gladys Rd	31	C2 30
Glen Rd	36	H2 29
Glynwood	37	P2 26
Golden Spruce Dr	36	O2 27
Goodale Ct	41	R2 27
Goose La	36	L2 27
Gordon Ct	36	L2 28
Grant Dr	41	U2 28
Great Rock Dr	31	D2 29
Green Ash St	36	N2 28
Green St	41	Y2 28
Green Tree Dr	36	P2 28
Greenbrier Rd	31	B2 29
Gregory Pl	41	Q2 27
Gregory Wy	31	F2 29
Griffing Av	41	R2 26
Grove St	41	S2 28
Grumman Blvd	32	E2 25
Gully Rd	31	C2 29
Hallock St	41	R2 27
Halsey Rd	40	W2 31
Hamilton Av	41	R2 26
Harbor Rd	41	V2 27
Harper Rd	36	H2 29
Harrison Av	41	Q2 27
Hearthstone La	36	O2 30
Heights Pl	41	R2 27
Hemlock Wy	36	N2 28
Henry Lewis La	40	W2 31
Heritage La	41	W2 28
Herod Point Rd	31	D2 30
Herricks La	40	X2 31
Hickory La	36	H2 29
Hidden Acres Pa	32	D2 27
Hidden Pheasant Ct	32	C2 26
Hidden Pond Pa	31	C2 27
High Hill Rd	31	C2 29
High Meadow La	41	Z2 28
High View Dr	31	C2 29
Hill Dr	36	O2 30
Hill St	31	B2 29
Hill St	31	E2 30
Hilton Ct	41	V2 28
Hinda Blvd	36	P2 26
Hobson Dr	41	U2 27
Hollow Ct	36	M2 29
Holly Berry Ct	32	C2 26
Holly Tree La	41	Z2 28
Hornpipe Dr	36	N2 30
Horton Av	36	N2 29
Horton Ct	32	G2 24
Howard St	31	E2 29
Howell Av	41	S2 27
Howell Ct	41	S2 27
Howell La	41	S2 26
Hubbard Av	41	T2 27
Hubbard Tr	41	V2 27
Huckleberry Hill	41	U2 29
Hulse Av	31	E2 30
Hulse Av	31	C2 28
Hulse Landing Rd	31	F2 29
Ida La	40	V2 29
Imperial Wy	31	C2 27
Industrial Blvd	36	P2 26
Inwood	36	O2 26
Iroquois Wy	31	E2 27
Ivy Cir	31	C2 29
J.T Blvd	37	P2 26
Jackson Rd	41	T2 27
Jacobs La	31	C2 29
Jacobs La	41	V2 27
Jakes La	36	L2 27
James Dr	40	T2 31
James St	41	T2 26
Jean Ct	36	O2 30
Jeanie La	40	V2 29
Jerome Cir	41	T2 27
Jills Wy	36	L2 29
Joan Ct	31	C2 27
John Jay Rd	31	F2 27
Josephine Dr	31	C2 27
Josica Dr	41	U2 28
Joyce Dr	41	Q2 28
June Ct	40	Y2 30
Karen Ct	31	F2 29
Karlin Dr	36	L2 27
Kathy La	41	R2 28
Katie Dr	31	C2 28
Kay Rd	32	D2 26
Kimberly Ct	36	L2 28
Kimmel La	41	Y2 28
Kindling Wood	37	P2 26
Kingfish Ct	36	P2 30
Kings Dr	41	R2 27
Kings Hwy	36	H2 29
Kirby La	41	Z2 28
Kirk Av	41	T2 26
Kratoville Av	36	Q2 26
Kristen Pl	31	F2 29
Kroemer Av	36	O2 26
Lagoon Ct	41	X2 27
Lagoon Ct W	41	X2 27
Lagoon St	41	X2 27
Lakeview Ct	41	R2 28
Landing La	36	J2 30
Laurel Bay Av	40	Z2 30
Laurel Bay La	46	A3 29
Laurel Ct	31	C2 29
Laurel Hollow	31	D2 28
Laurel Hollow Ct	31	E2 30
Laurel La	36	H2 29
Laurel La	31	C2 30
Laurin Rd	32	D2 26
Leafwood	36	P2 26
Leafy Wy	41	W2 27
Legend La	41	Y2 28
Leonard St	31	C2 28
Lewin Dr	31	E2 30
Lewis St	41	S2 27
Lincoln St	41	R2 26
Linda Av	41	T2 28
Linda La E	36	O2 30
Linda La W	36	O2 30
Line Rd	32	E2 25
Little Bay Rd	31	C2 30
Lockitt Dr	41	X2 27
Locust Rd	31	E2 30
Locust St	31	C2 28
Locust St	41	X2 27
Lois Ct	41	R2 28
Long Island Expwy	36	M2 26
Long View Dr	36	O2 30
Long View Rd	31	D2 30
Lorraine	41	Z2 28
Lorraine Ct	40	Y2 30
Louise Ct	36	O2 30
Lovers La	41	W2 27
Lowe Dr	40	T2 31
Lyn La	36	K2 30
Madison St	41	T2 26
Main Rd	41	T2 28
Malcolm Wy	36	O2 27
Mallard Ct	36	P2 30
Manor La	41	X2 29
Manor Rd	36	M2 27
Manor Rd	32	F2 23
Maple Av	41	S2 26
Maple La	41	A3 29
Maple Rd	36	H2 29
Maple Rd	31	D2 30
Maplewood La	41	T2 27
Marcy Av	41	Q2 27
Marge La	36	K2 29
Marine St	36	N2 30
Mary Ct	36	O2 30
May Dr	36	M2 27
McDermott Av	41	S2 26
McDonald Pl	41	R2 27
McVeigh La	41	A3 29
Meadow Ct	31	C2 28
Meadow Dr	36	J2 29
Meadow La	41	T2 27
Meadow Pa	31	C2 28
Meetinghouse Creek Rd	41	V2 28
Megan's Wy	32	D2 26
Melene Av	41	S2 27
Melissa Ct	41	Z2 28
Melissa La	40	X2 30
Meroke Tr	32	C2 26
Merritt's Pond Rd	41	R2 27
Michaels La	31	C2 27
Michigan Wy	31	F2 27
Middle Country Rd	32	D2 26
Middle Rd	36	N2 27
Midfield Pl	36	O2 27
Midland St	36	N2 30
Midway Dr	41	S2 28
Mill Rd	37	P2 27
Millbrook La	41	S2 26
Moet Dr	41	R2 29
Morningside Av	41	X2 27
Mystic Ct	36	P2 30
Nadel Ct	41	Q2 28
Nadel Dr	41	Q2 28
Nancy Ct	36	O2 30
Nate's Wy	40	T2 30
Nautical Dr	36	N2 30
Newton Av	41	S2 27
North Appolo Dr	40	V2 29
North Corwell Av	41	S2 26
North Country Rd	31	C2 29
North Howell Av	41	S2 27
North Howell Ct	41	S2 27
North Railroad Av	41	Y2 28
North Side Rd	31	C2 30
North Wading River Rd	31	C2 29
North Wk	40	U2 31
North Woods Dr	31	C2 30
Northern Pkwy	41	R2 27
Northgate Cir	36	M2 29
Northview Ct	41	U2 29
Northville Tpke	41	S2 27
Northwoods Rd	36	N2 27
Nugent Dr	41	Q2 26
Oak Dr	36	H2 29
Oak Dr	41	R2 29
Oak Dr	41	Z2 28
Oak La (Pvt)	31	C2 30
Oak Rd	31	E2 30
Oak St	31	B2 30
Oak St	31	E2 30
Oak St	41	X2 27
Oak Tr	31	C2 30
Oakland Dr N	41	R2 28
Oakland Dr S	41	S2 28
Oakland Dr W	41	R2 28
Oakleigh Av	36	K2 30
Oakwood Dr	32	E2 23
Oakwood Dr	31	E2 30
Old Country Rd	36	O2 26
Old Farm Rd	41	R2 28
Old Field Ct	31	D2 29
Old Orchard Rd	31	D2 30
Old River Rd	32	F2 24
Old Stone Rd	36	H2 27
Oliver St	31	B2 29
Oliver St	41	R2 27
Oneida Wy	31	F2 27
Osborn Av	36	P2 27
Osprey Av	41	S2 27
Ostrander Av	41	R2 27
Overbrook St	36	N2 30
Overhill Rd	31	C2 28
Overlook Dr	40	T2 31
Overlook Dr	31	C2 29
Overlook Dr	41	V2 27
Palane E	36	L2 30
Palane N	36	L2 30
Palane S	36	L2 30
Pansy Ct	31	D2 29
Par Ct	31	E2 28
Park Dr	36	O2 30
Park Pl	36	H2 30
Park Pl	41	S2 27

Index

Suffolk Co.

Town of Riverhead / Town of Shelter Island / Town of Smithtown

STREET	MAP	GRID
Park Rd	36	N2 30
Park St	31	E2 29
Parkway St	36	Q2 26
Patti La	36	P2 28
Peach St	31	D2 30
Peacock Ct	40	V2 30
Peacock Pa	40	V2 30
Pebble Beach Pa	41	R2 28
Peconic Av	41	R2 26
Peconic Bay Blvd	41	V2 27
Peninsula Pa	41	R2 27
Penny Dr	36	H2 27
Pennys Rd	40	S2 31
Pheasant Ct	36	P2 30
Pheasant La	36	L2 27
Philip St	41	S2 27
Philips La	40	U2 30
Phil's Rd	41	V2 28
Phyllis La	41	Z2 28
Pier Av	40	V2 31
Pine Av	41	V2 27
Pine Cone Ct	32	C2 26
Pine St	31	D2 30
Pintail Ct	36	P2 30
Pirate St	36	N2 30
Plainview Dr	31	C2 29
Plover Ct	36	P2 30
Pleasant Ct	36	M2 28
Point St	41	Y2 28
Pond View Blvd	31	B2 29
Pond View Rd	41	R2 27
Pondwood	36	P2 26
Preserve, The	36	M2 28
Primrose La	41	W2 27
Princeton Blvd	31	E2 26
Promenade Dr	40	V2 29
Prospect Pl	41	S2 26
Pulaski St	36	P2 26
Purple Beech St	36	N2 28
Pye La	41	Z2 28
Rabbit Run	41	R2 28
Railroad St	41	R2 26
Ralph Dr	40	T2 31
Ravine Rd	31	E2 30
Raynor Av	36	Q2 27
Red Fox Pa	31	C2 28
Redbird Pl	41	S2 27
Redleaf Ct	36	O2 27
Red Oak Ct	36	M2 28
Reeves Av	36	N2 28
Remsen Rd	31	C2 29
Riley Av	36	L2 27
Rita Ct	31	C2 29
Rita's Ct	41	Z2 29
River Av	41	T2 26
River Rd	36	N2 26
River Rd	32	F2 23
Riverside Dr	41	S2 26
Roan La	41	R2 28
Roanoke Av	36	O2 30
Roanoke Av	36	P2 30
Roanoke Av	41	Q2 27
Robert St	41	T2 27
Robert's Pa	31	C2 27
Robinson Pkwy	41	R2 26
Rocklein Rd	31	C2 29
Rose Ct	36	L2 27
Roundwood Blvd	36	P2 26
Ruby Dr	41	V2 29
Ruth Ct	41	T2 27
Saddle Lake Dr	41	R2 28
St Andrews Av	41	R2 29
St Johns Pl	41	R2 26
St Mary's Dr	41	Z2 28
Sandalwood La	41	T2 27
Sandpiper Dr	36	P2 30
Sandy Ct	36	O2 30
Sandy Hollow Ct	37	Q2 26
Scallop La	41	Y2 27
School St	41	Q2 27
Schultz Rd	32	D2 24
Schyler Ct	41	T2 28
Sea Breeze Dr	36	N2 31
Seacove Ct	41	Y2 27
Seacove La	41	Y2 28
Seaman Rd	41	Z2 28
Sebastian Dr	36	O2 30
Seril Ct	41	V2 28
Service Rd	31	F2 27
Service Rd A	36	M2 27
Shade Tree La	41	U2 28
Shady La	31	F2 30
Shady La	41	V2 27
Shirley St	31	E2 30
Shore Rd	41	Y2 27
Short Rd	31	C2 30
Short St	36	O2 28
Sigal Av	41	S2 27
Silver Beech La	36	J2 29
Simeon Rd	40	W2 31
Smith La	41	Z2 28
Smugglers Pa	40	V2 31
Sound Av	31	F2 28
Sound Dr	40	T2 31
Sound Rd	31	B2 29
Sound Shore Rd	40	T2 31
Soundbreeze Tr	31	D2 30
South Apollo Dr	41	W2 29
South Dr	36	O2 30
South Jamesport Av	41	Y2 28
South Pa	36	H2 27
South Railroad Av	41	Y2 28
South Rd	31	C2 30
Southern Pkwy	41	R2 27
Southfield Rd	36	M2 28
Southfields Rd	41	U2 29
Southview Ct	31	C2 29
Splish Splash Dr	36	L2 26
State Hwy 25	32	G2 27
State Hwy 25A	31	G2 27
Stephen Dr	31	C2 27
Stoll Dr	40	Y2 30
Sue La	41	R2 28
Suffolk Av	31	E2 30
Summit Dr	36	J2 30
Sun Ct	41	W2 28
Sun Up Tr	41	W2 28
Sunny Line Dr	36	H2 27
Sunrise Av	41	T2 27
Sunrise Av	41	X2 27
Sunset Blvd	31	B2 30
Sunwood Dr	31	F2 28
Susan Dr	31	C2 27
Susan Pl	36	M2 28
Sweezy Av	41	Q2 26
Sylan Pl	31	E2 29

STREET	MAP	GRID
Sylvan Dr	31	E2 30
Tanger Dr	36	N2 26
Tanglewood	36	O2 26
Tara La	41	T2 28
Telephone St	41	R2 27
Terry Pl	41	T2 27
Terry Rd	31	D2 30
Theodore Roosevelt Rd	31	E2 28
Tide Ct	31	C2 29
Timber Dr	36	H2 27
Timothy La	41	Z2 29
Town Beach Rd	41	Z2 28
Treasure Dr	36	N2 30
Triangle La	36	L2 27
Trout Bk La	41	U2 27
Tuthills La	40	V2 29
Tuts La	41	Y2 28
Twomey Av	36	L2 29
Tyte Dr	41	T2 27
Union Av	41	S2 26
Union Av	41	T2 29
Veronica La	40	U2 29
Veterans Cir	31	E2 26
Victor St	41	U2 27
Village Green N	36	K2 28
Village Green S	36	K2 28
Vinmar La	41	A3 29
Vista Ct	41	Y2 28
Wading River-Manorville Rd	31	C2 28
Warner Ct	36	L2 30
Warner Dr	36	L2 30
Washington Av	41	R2 26
Washington Av	41	X2 28
Waterview Ct	36	O2 31
Wema La	31	E2 30
Wesley Av	41	Y2 28
Wesley Pl	41	T2 27
West Apollo Dr	40	V2 29
West Dr	36	N2 28
West Fairview Av	40	U2 31
West La	41	U2 29
West Main St	41	Q2 26
West St	41	Q2 26
West St	41	Y2 27
West Woodland Dr	31	C2 29
Westwoods Blvd	41	U2 28
White Birch Ct	41	Y2 28
White Spruce Dr	31	C2 27
White's Rd	41	V2 27
Widgen Ct	36	P2 30
Wildwood Av	31	E2 30
Wildwood Dr	36	H2 27
Wildwood Rd	31	E2 30
Wildwood Rd	31	F2 29
Williams Wy N	36	L2 29
Williams Way S	36	K2 28
Williamson La	41	A3 28
Willow Pond Dr	36	P2 31
Willow St	41	X2 27
Willow St	41	Y2 28
Wilowski Wy	41	X2 27
Wilson Av	41	S2 27
Winds Wy	41	Y2 27
Windwood	37	P2 26
Windy Acres La	40	X2 31
Winged Foot Wy	41	R2 28
Winters La	41	Q2 26
Witt La	41	U2 28
Woodchuck Hollow La	31	C2 29
Woodchuck Pa	31	C2 28
Woodcliff Tr	36	K2 30
Woodcrest Av	36	Q2 27
Woodland Ct	32	D2 27
Woodlawn Dr	36	O2 30
Wyl La	36	K2 30
Yellowbird Pl	41	S2 27
Youngs Av	36	M2 28
Zdunko La	36	O2 30
Ziemacki La	41	Y2 29
Zion St	41	U2 27
Zophar Mill's Rd	31	B2 29
1st Av	36	H2 29
1st St	36	G2 29
1st St	36	K2 30
1st St	36	O2 27
1st St	36	O2 28
1st St	36	Q2 27
1st St	31	D2 30
1st St	31	E2 30
1st St	41	T2 27
2nd Av	36	H2 28
2nd St	36	H2 29
2nd St	36	K2 30
2nd St	36	N2 28
2nd St	36	O2 27
2nd St	36	Q2 27
2nd St	31	D2 30
2nd St	31	E2 30
2nd St	41	R2 26
2nd St	41	T2 27
2nd St	41	Y2 27
2 1/2 St	31	E2 30
3rd Av	36	H2 28
3rd St	36	H2 29
3rd St	36	K2 30
3rd St	36	N2 28
3rd St	36	O2 27
3rd St	36	Q2 27
3rd St	31	D2 30
3rd St	31	E2 30
3rd St	41	R2 26
3rd St	41	T2 27
3rd St	41	Y2 28
4th Av	36	G2 29
4th St	36	G2 28
4th St	36	K2 30
4th St	36	N2 28
4th St	36	Q2 27
4th St	31	D2 30
4th St	31	E2 30
4th St	41	Y2 28
5th Av	36	G2 29
5th St	36	G2 28
5th St	36	K2 30
5th St	36	N2 28
5th St	31	D2 30
5th St	31	E2 30
5th St	41	R2 26
6th Av	36	G2 29
6th St	36	G2 28
6th St	36	K2 30
6th St	36	N2 28
6th St	31	D2 30
6th St	31	E2 29

STREET	MAP	GRID
6th St	41	Y2 28
7th Av	36	G2 29
7th St	36	G2 28
7th St	36	K2 30
7th St	31	D2 30
7th St	31	E2 29
7th St	41	Y2 28
8th St	36	G2 28
8th St	36	K2 30
8th St	31	E2 29
8th St	41	Y2 28
9th St	36	H2 28
9th St	36	K2 30
9th St	31	E2 29
10th St	36	K2 30
10th St	31	E2 29
11th St	36	K2 30
11th St	31	E2 29
12th St	36	K2 30
12th St	31	E2 29
14th St	31	E2 29
15th St	31	E2 29
16th St	31	E2 29
17th St	31	E2 29
18th St	31	E2 29
19th St	31	F2 29
20th St	31	F2 29
21st St	31	F2 29
22nd St	31	F2 29

SHELTER ISLAND

STREET	MAP	GRID
Apple Orchard La	51	T3 36
Auburn Pl	51	R3 39
Baldwin Rd	51	T3 38
Bartman Rd	51	T3 39
Bateman Rd	51	S3 38
Bay Av	51	R3 39
Bay Av	51	S3 37
Bay Rd	51	S3 39
Bay Shore Dr	51	R3 37
Bayview Av	51	Q3 39
Bayview Rd	51	R3 38
Behringer La	51	Q3 38
Belvedere Rd	51	P3 38
Bevan Pl	51	R3 39
Blueberry La	51	R3 37
Bluff Av	51	R3 39
Bonnie La	51	T3 39
Bootleggers Al	51	Q3 37
Bowditch Rd	51	R3 38
Brander Parkway	51	Q3 37
Bridge St	50	R3 39
Burns Rd	51	T3 38
Burro Hall La	51	R3 38
Carousel La	50	S3 40
Cartwright Rd	51	T3 39
Cedar Av	51	R3 39
Charlie's La	51	S3 37
Chase Av	51	R3 39
Chequit Av	51	R3 39
Cherry La	51	U3 38
Clark Pl	51	U3 37
Clinton Av	50	R3 39
Clinton Av Ext	51	R3 40
Club Dr	51	X3 39
Cobbets La	51	S3 39
Coecles Pl	51	T3 39
Community Dr	51	Q3 38
Congdon Rd	51	T3 38
Conrad Rd	51	S3 37
Country Club Dr	50	T3 40
County Route 42	51	P3 38
County Route 69	51	U3 38
County Route 114	51	U3 36
County Route 115	51	R3 38
County Route 116	51	S3 37
County Route 117	51	T3 38
Cove Wy Joy Dr	51	S3 37
Cozy La	51	R3 37
Crab Cr Rd	51	Q3 37
Crescent Wy	50	T3 40
Daniel Lord Rd	51	R3 38
Dawn La	50	T3 41
Deer Park La	51	T3 37
Dering La	50	S3 40
Dering Woods La	50	S3 40
Dering Woods Rd	50	S3 40
Dickerson Dr	51	S3 37
Dina Rock Rd	50	T3 40
Dogwood La	51	T3 37
Duvall Av	51	T3 38
East Brander Pkwy	51	R3 36
East Thomas St	51	S3 38
East View Rd	50	T3 41
Easy St	51	S3 38
Emerson La	51	T3 38
Evans Rd	51	S3 37
Fox Hollow Run	51	T3 37
Fred's La	51	R3 37
Fresh Pond Rd	51	T3 37
Gardiner Wy	50	S3 40
Gardiners Bay Dr	50	T3 40
Gazon Rd (Pvt)	51	R3 37
George Fox La (Pvt)	51	T3 39
Gibbs Rd	51	S3 37
Ginny Dr	51	T3 38
Glynn Dr	51	Q3 38
Grace's La	51	S3 37
Grand Av	51	R3 39
Great Circle Dr	50	T3 40
Hager Rd	51	S3 37
Harbor Head Rd	50	U3 40
Havens Rd	50	S3 40
Hay Beach Rd	50	T3 41
Hedges Rd	51	S3 39
Heritage Dr	51	T3 37
Heron La	51	T3 36
Hiberry La	50	T3 41
Hidden Pa (Pvt)	51	Q3 37
Hill Crest Dr	51	Q3 37
Hill Rd	51	S3 37
Hillside Dr	51	R3 38
Hilo Dr	51	Q3 38
Hudson Av	51	U3 39
Ian's La	51	S3 37
Irene La	51	U3 37
Island Wy	51	T3 40
Ivy Pl	50	T3 40
James St	51	R3 39
Jaspa Rd	51	S3 38
Johnston	51	T3 39
Jupiter's La	51	U3 38
Lake Dr	51	T3 37
Lakeview Dr	51	T3 37
Landing La	51	R3 38
Lari La	51	T3 39

STREET	MAP	GRID
Lesser Rd	51	S3 37
Lilliput La	51	Q3 37
Linda Ct	51	T3 38
Linda Rd	51	U3 37
Little Ram Island Dr	51	V3 39
Locust Av	51	R3 39
Locust La	51	U3 38
Locust Point Rd	50	S3 40
Locust Woods Dr	51	T3 39
Manhanset Rd	51	T3 40
Manwaring Rd	51	S3 39
Marc St	51	T3 38
Margaret's Dr	51	R3 37
Meadow La	51	U3 38
Meadow Pl	51	R3 39
Meadow St	51	R3 39
Menantic Rd	51	R3 38
Menhadden La	50	U3 40
Merkel La	51	U3 37
Middle Har-Bay Rd	51	W3 39
Mimosa Pl	51	Q3 38
Montclair Av	51	R3 36
Neck Rd	51	R3 39
New York Av	51	R3 39
Nicoll Rd	50	S3 40
North Brander Pkwy	51	R3 36
North Cartwright Rd	51	U3 38
North Ferry Rd	51	S3 39
North Midway Rd	51	S3 39
North Ram Island Dr	51	W3 39
North Silver Beach Rd	51	R3 36
Nostrand Pkwy	51	P3 38
Oak Rd	51	X3 38
Oak Tree La	51	R3 36
Oakwood Av	51	R3 39
Ole Buck Run	51	Q3 37
Orchard La	51	Q3 37
Orchard Rd	51	S3 39
Orient La	50	T3 41
Osprey La	51	T3 36
Osprey Rd	51	T3 36
Overlook Pl	51	T3 40
Oxford Av	51	R3 39
Peconic Av	51	Q3 36
Penny's Pa	51	Q3 37
Peppermill La	51	T3 37
Petticoat La	51	Q3 36
Pheasant Cir	51	U3 36
Pheasant La	51	U3 36
Point La	50	T3 41
Point La	50	U3 40
Poplar Av	51	P3 38
Price La	51	U3 38
Primrose Pl	51	T3 40
Private Rd	51	U3 37
Private Rd	55	W3 36
Proposed Rd	51	T3 36
Prospect Av	51	P3 38
Prospect Rd	51	Q3 38
Prospect Av	51	R3 39
Prospect Pl	51	R3 39
Quail Hedge La	51	S3 39
Quail Run	51	T3 37
Quaker Pa	51	T3 39
Rainbow Cir	51	R3 39
Ram Island Dr	51	U3 40
Ram Island Rd	51	T3 39
Ravine Av	51	R3 39
Rebel Rd	51	Q3 37
Robin La	51	U3 37
Rocky Point Av	51	P3 38
Rocky Point Rd	51	Q3 37
Rocky Point Ter (Pvt)	51	P3 38
St John St	51	R3 39
St Mary's Rd	51	T3 38
Sandpiper Rd	51	T3 37
School St	51	S3 38
Sea Gate Rd	51	T3 37
Sea Gull Rd	51	U3 36
Sean's Cir	51	Q3 38
Serpentine Dr	51	Q3 39
Sheep Pasture La	51	T3 40
Shelterlands Pa	51	T3 37
Shore Rd (DH)	50	S3 40
Shore Rd	51	Q3 38
Shorewood Rd	51	T3 36
Short Rd	51	R3 38
Simpson	51	R3 37
Sleepy Hollow Rd	51	R3 38
Smith St	51	S3 38
South Cartwright Rd	51	T3 38
South Ferry Rd	51	T3 37
South Midway Rd	51	S3 37
South Ram Island Dr	51	W3 39
South Silver Beach	51	R3 36
South St	50	S3 40
Southwick La	51	T3 39
Spring Garden Av	51	R3 39
State Hwy 114	55	U3 36
Stearns Point Rd	51	Q3 38
Strawberry La	51	T3 37
Strobel Rd	51	R3 38
Sudee Gln	51	Q3 37
Summerfield La	51	R3 39
Sunny Side Av	51	R3 38
Sunset La	51	U3 36
Sunshine Rd	51	S3 38
Sylvan Pl	51	R3 39
Sylvan Rd	51	R3 39
Sylvester Rd	50	S3 40
Tarkettle Rd	51	S3 37
Terry Dr	51	Q3 38
Thomas Av	51	T3 38
Thompson Rd	51	U3 37
Tims Tr	51	Q3 37
Tower Hill Av	51	R3 39
Town Foxen Cr Rd	51	U3 38
Tuthill Dr	51	W3 39
Valley Rd	51	R3 38
Valley Rd	51	U3 37
Wade Rd	51	T3 39
Ward St	51	S3 37
Washington St	51	R3 39
Waverly Pl	51	R3 39
Weck Av	51	R3 39
Wesley Av	51	R3 39
West Har-Bay Rd	50	U3 39
West Neck Rd	51	Q3 38
West Thomas St	51	S3 38
Westmoreland Dr	51	Q3 37
Westview Dr	50	T3 41
Wheeler Dr	51	R3 36
White Birch	51	R3 36

STREET	MAP	GRID
Williette Av	51	T3 39
Willow La	51	U3 39
Willow Pond Rd	51	T3 37
Winthrop Rd	51	S3 39
Woodbine Wy	50	T3 40
Worthy Wy	51	Q3 37
Yoco Rd	50	S3 40

SMITHTOWN

STREET	MAP	GRID
Abbey Dr	9	S 18
Abbot Rd	14	V 21
Aberdeen Rd	15	X 19
Acacia Rd	13	X 24
Acorn La	9	S 17
Acorn Rd	13	C1 24
Adams Av	15	U 17
Adams Ct	21	D1 20
Addie La	14	C1 20
Adrienne Ct	15	A1 19
Adrienne La	15	Z 19
Aesop La	14	D1 22
Agren La	21	E1 20
Albatross La	14	Y 21
Alberta Ct	14	Z 20
Alden Ct	20	E1 22
Alden Ct E	20	E1 23
Alden Ct N	20	D1 22
Alder Dr	13	X 24
Alexander Av	21	E1 22
Alfred La	14	V 22
Algonquin La	9	T 19
Alice La	15	V 19
Allegany Pl	9	R 19
Allenby Dr	7	R 26
Allison Ct	15	A1 19
Alma Av	21	F1 20
Alma Lind La	21	E1 20
Alo Ct	14	C1 21
Alpine Ct	15	V 19
Alpine Pl	21	G1 20
Amapola La	14	W 23
Amboy La	21	E1 21
Amherst La	14	U 21
Amsterdam Rd	14	V 20
Andam Wy	20	D1 23
Andover Ct	8	T 21
Andrea La	15	V 19
Angela Ct	14	C1 22
Angela La	21	E1 22
Angelica Ct	15	A1 19
Ann Ct	13	W 24
Ann Marie Dr	14	C1 22
Annandale Rd	8	U 22
Annette Av	14	B1 20
Antrim Ct	8	T 21
Apple La	9	T 19
Apple Tree Dr	15	Z 19
Applewood Rd	14	C1 23
Arbor La (HH)	13	B1 23
Arbor La	15	Z 19
Arbutus Dr	14	W 24
Arbutus Rd	8	U 20
Archer La	14	W 24
Arden La	8	T 22
Ardito Av	8	U 23
Ardmore Pl	14	W 23
Ardra Ct	15	V 19
Argyle Pl	14	V 20
Arjay La	9	S 17
Arkay Dr	15	U 18
Arlene Pl	8	T 22
Arlington Av	14	B1 22
Arlington Ter	21	F1 22
Arlyne La	8	U 21
Armand Ct	13	C1 25
Armon St	21	E1 20
Armor Ct	14	W 24
Aron St	14	A1 22
Arrowood Dr	20	D1 24
Artesian Wy	13	X 25
Arthur Dr	14	B1 22
Arthur Pl	15	B1 19
Arthurs Ct	21	D1 22
Asbury Dr	14	V 20
Ash Ct	14	A1 21
Ashford Dr	21	G1 20
Ashland Dr	14	W 23
Ashleigh Dr	20	D1 25
Ashley Loop	7	S 25
Ashlon Dr	8	T 21
Ashly Cir	9	T 19
Aspatuck Ct	8	T 22
Aspen Ct	14	C1 23
Aspen Rd	14	X 23
Astor Av	14	D1 22
Astor Ct	8	T 20
Atlas Pl	14	C1 20
Atterbury Dr	14	Z 21
Attridge Dr	14	W 22
Audubon St	21	E1 20
August Cres	9	S 18
Austin Blvd	9	S 17
Autumn Ct	15	V 19
Autumn Dr	15	U 18
Avalon Cir	14	B1 21
Avenue A	7	T 24
Avenue B	8	T 23
Avenue K	8	T 23
Averly Pl	14	V 20
Avery Ct	21	E1 21
Azaelia Ct	8	S 20
Bacon Rd	13	C1 25
Balboa Dr	14	U 23
Balis Dr	14	W 23
Balsam La	8	T 21
Bambi La	9	S 18
Bank Av	14	Z 21
Barbera Rd	14	U 22
Bareback Ct	13	Z 25
Barkley La	21	E1 21
Barley Pl	8	R 21
Barn La	14	C1 24
Barnes St	14	A1 22
Barrett Ct	21	D1 21
Barry La	14	U 21
Barton La	15	Z 19
Bass Ct	14	Z 20
Basswood La	14	Z 20
Bauss Rd	21	D1 19
Bayard St	21	F1 20
Bayberry La	14	U 19
Baylor Dr	14	B1 21
Bea St	21	F1 21
Beach Hill Dr	7	S 26
Beach Plum La	13	C1 26

STREET	MAP	GRID
Beau Jol Ct	14	C1 20
Beauregard Dr	21	F1 21
Beaver Dr	14	X 24
Bee Dr	15	W 18
Beech St	21	F1 20
Beechwood La	8	T 20
Belford La	14	V 21
Belinda Ct	14	B1 20
Bella Ct	14	C1 20
Bellemeade Av	14	Z 21
Belmar La	8	S 21
Belmont Dr	15	V 19
Bennett St	8	T 23
Benson Pl	21	G1 20
Bentley Ct	20	E1 23
Bentley Ct E	20	E1 23
Bentley Ct S	20	D1 22
Bentley Ct W	20	D1 22
Berg Av	8	T 24
Berkley Pl	14	A1 20
Bernard St	7	S 24
Berryhill Dr	7	S 24
Bethal La	8	R 22
Bethany Dr	8	T 21
Bette La	8	S 20
Beverly Ct	7	S 26
Beverly Rd	8	U 21
Beverly Rd	14	B1 20
Beverly Rd	21	F1 20
Bezel La	15	B1 19
Bianco Ct	14	Z 20
Birch Ct	21	G1 21
Birch Dr	14	X 24
Birch La (HH)	20	D1 25
Birch Rd	13	W 24
Birchbrook Dr	14	Z 21
Bishops Rd	14	W 22
Black Gum Tree La	14	U 24
Blackman St	14	B1 21
Blackwell Rd	15	C1 19
Blanchard St	14	A1 22
Blue Spruce La	8	T 20
Bluegrass La	8	R 21
Bluff Rd	13	Z 26
Blydenburgh Av	14	Z 21
Bobann Dr	21	D1 21
Bonarck La	21	D1 21
Bond La	21	E1 21
Boney La	13	Y 25
Bonnie Dr	7	R 26
Bonnie Gate	14	W 23
Bonny Ct	15	B1 19
Borrell Dr	14	A1 22
Boulder Wy	15	U 19
Bow Dr	15	A1 19
Bow Dr E	15	B1 19
Bowers Ct	21	E1 20
Bowers Ct	14	Z 21
Bowman La	13	W 24
Box Pl	15	A1 19
Boxwood Dr	14	V 24
Brackenwood Rd	13	C1 25
Bradford St	21	E1 19
Bradley Ct	14	X 22
Bradshaw La	7	R 25
Brae Mar St	14	B1 20
Bragg Dr	21	F1 21
Bralo Ct	13	U 24
Branch Brook Dr	14	Z 20
Branch Dr	14	A1 20
Brand St	13	U 24
Brandy Ct	21	F1 21
Brandy La	21	F1 21
Branglebrink Rd	13	A1 23
Brasswood Rd	20	D1 23
Bread And Cheese Hollow Rd	7	R 25
Breeze Hill Rd	7	R 26
Breezy Hill Dr	7	S 24
Breezy Hollow	14	A1 23
Brewster Av	7	R 24
Bri Ct	21	D1 19
Brian St	9	S 18
Briaroot Dr	15	Y 19
Briarwood Ct	13	C1 24
Brich St	21	G1 21
Bridge Branch Rd	14	W 20
Bridle Ct	8	S 23
Bridle Pa	13	Z 24
Bridlepath Rd	14	Z 21
Brilner Dr	14	A1 20
Bristol La	14	W 23
British Colony Rd	7	R 26
Broadley Av	14	C1 21
Broadview Av	13	U 25
Broadview Dr	8	T 20
Broadway	14	Z 20
Brocton La	14	X 23
Bronwyn Ct	21	D1 20
Brook Ct	14	Z 20
Brook La	14	Y 20
Brookfield Rd	7	R 26
Brooks Av	21	D1 19
Brookstan Rd	21	E1 21
Brookvale La	21	F1 21
Browning St	14	B1 21
Brown's Rd	14	C1 21
Brown-Wood La	20	D1 24
Bruce La	14	U 23
Bruce La N	14	U 23
Bruce La S	14	U 23
Bryan Meadow Dr	8	R 24
Buckingham Ct	14	A1 23
Burgundy La	14	C1 20
Burham Ct	14	Y 23
Burham Dr	14	X 23
Burlington Blvd	14	Y 20
Burr Av	8	U 23
Burr La	21	E1 22
Bury Ct	8	T 22
Butterfly Dr	9	U 19
Buttonwood Pa	14	Y 20
Buxton Wy	15	B1 19
Byrd Ct	8	U 23
Byron Rd	8	T 21
Cabot Ctr	20	E1 23
Cabot Ct	9	U 17
Cabot Ct Common	20	D1 22
Cabot Ct N	20	E1 23
Cabot Ct S	20	D1 22
Cabot Ct W	20	D1 22
Cabot Pa	20	D1 22
Cactus La	14	W 23
Cake Walk Ter	14	Y 22
Caldwell Av	14	B1 22

STREET	MAP	GRID
Caleb's Pa	15	W 17
Calico Tree Rd	15	Z 19
Callahan's Beach Rd	7	S 25
Callahan's Rd	7	S 25
Cambon Av	20	D1 23
Cambon Pl	21	D1 21
Cambridge Dr	14	A1 20
Camelia Pl	15	U 19
Camelot La	14	D1 22
Cameo Rd	8	R 21
Cameron Ct	8	T 22
Candlelight Ct	14	A1 21
Candy La	8	R 22
Canna Dr	9	U 19
Canterbury La	21	D1 20
Capitol Ct	9	U 18
Captain Richard's La	7	R 25
Caramel Ct	8	S 22
Caramel Rd	8	S 22
Cardinal La	13	Z 24
Cardinal La	15	V 18
Carl Ct	21	E1 20
Carldon Rd	8	T 21
Carlson Av	8	U 23
Carlson Ct	14	U 24
Carlton Pl	21	F1 20
Carman La (HH)	14	A1 24
Carman La	14	C1 21
Carmella La	21	E1 22
Carnegie Dr	14	B1 22
Carol La	20	D1 22
Caroline Av	14	B1 20
Carow Pl	14	B1 23
Carr Ct	21	E1 21
Carriage Dr	14	V 23
Carriage House Rd	14	A1 21
Carrie Ct	14	Y 21
Caryl Pl	14	W 23
Cassata St	8	U 23
Castle Ct	21	D1 20
Catherine Av	14	B1 20
Cathy Ct	21	D1 19
Cayuga Pl	9	R 19
Cedar Av	21	E1 20
Cedar Grove Av	21	F1 19
Cedar Pl	13	U 25
Cedar Ridge Av	15	A1 19
Cedar Rd	14	X 23
Cedar St	7	T 23
Cedar St	14	C1 23
Cedar St	9	U 19
Cedar St	14	Z 21
Cedar St N	7	T 24
Cedarfield Ter	20	D1 25
Cedarwood La	9	S 17
Central Rd	14	V 21
Chapel Hill Ct	21	F1 21
Chapel Hill Rd	21	F1 21
Chapman Rd	21	D1 20
Chardonnay Rd	8	U 22
Charlemange Dr	14	C1 21
Charles Ct	21	F1 19
Charter La	8	U 21
Chase, The	14	A1 23
Chassyl Rd	9	T 19
Chatham Rd	8	T 21
Cherokee La	9	T 19
Cherry La	14	Y 21
Chester St	15	B1 19
Chester St	21	F1 20
Chestnut Ct	9	T 19
Chestnut St	21	D1 19
Chestnut Stump Rd	7	S 24
Chivalry La	21	D1 20
Chris Ct	7	S 24
Christa Ct	21	F1 21
Christina Ct	14	C1 22
Christopher Ct	14	C1 22
Church St	8	U 23
Churchill La	8	U 20
Churchill Rd	7	R 25
Cinderella La	20	D1 22
Cindy Dr	14	A1 22
Cindy St	14	W 20
Claremont Ct	14	A1 21
Clarissa La	8	S 20
Clark St	14	Y 22
Clearbrook Dr	14	A1 20
Cleremont Av	14	B1 23
Cleveland Pl	15	B1 19
Cleveland St	15	D1 19
Cleveland St	14	B1 22
Cliff Dr	14	V 22
Clifford Blvd	15	Z 19
Cliftwood Pl	14	W 23
Clime Ct	14	B1 22
Clinton Av	14	B1 23
Cloister St	15	V 19
Clover Dr	15	U 19
Clover La	13	D1 23
Clover La	13	W 23
Clubhouse La	15	C1 19
Clyde Pl	14	W 23
Coach La	14	W 23
Cobb La	8	S 20
Cobblers La	20	D1 23
Cobblestone Ct	21	D1 20
Cobblestone La	21	F1 21
Coconut Dr	8	S 22
Cody Pl	21	E1 21
Coe Ct	14	B1 21
Colby Dr	14	W 23
Coles Dr	21	G1 21
Colgate Dr	14	B1 22
Collins Av	7	U 24
Colonial Dr	15	U 19
Colonial Rd	14	Y 21
Colony Ct	14	W 21
Columbia Ct	14	Y 20
Columbine La	14	V 23
Columbus Av	14	V 22
Columbus Av	14	Z 20
Comanche La	9	S 19
Commack Rd	7	T 23
Commack Rd	9	R 17
Commack Rd (Bread & Cheese Hollow Rd)	9	R 18
Commander La	21	D1 20
Commerce Dr	9	T 17
Concord Dr	7	S 25
Concord Dr S	7	S 25
Concord La	14	V 21
Connoly Dr	21	F1 20

Suffolk Co.

Town of Smithtown

Index

Suffolk Co.

Town of Smithtown / Town of Southampton

STREET	MAP	GRID
Ott Pl	8	R 21
Overhill Dr	14	X 22
Overlook Ct	14	Z 23
Overton Ct	21	F1 19
Overton Pass	13	C1 24
Owl La	15	V 18
Oxford La	14	A1 20
Ozone Rd	14	C1 21
Paddington Cir	14	B1 21
Paddock Dr	8	S 23
Palin Pl	14	W 23
Palmer La	8	T 20
Pam Dr	9	S 18
Pantzer St	14	A1 22
Park Av	8	U 24
Park Av	14	C1 21
Park Av	14	C1 22
Park Cir	21	E1 19
Park Ct	14	A1 21
Park Dr	8	U 23
Park St	8	T 23
Park St	21	F1 22
Park Woods La	8	T 23
Parkside Av	20	D1 24
Parkside Dr	14	W 23
Parkview Dr	8	T 20
Parkway Dr N	9	S 18
Parkway Dr S	9	S 18
Parla Ct	7	S 24
Parnell Dr	14	V 21
Parsnip Pond Rd	21	E1 21
Parson's La	13	Y 24
Partridge Dr	9	T 19
Partridge La	13	Z 24
Pasture Rd	14	V 22
Patiky St	8	U 23
Patricia Ct	14	X 22
Patricia La	21	G1 20
Patrick's Wy	14	C1 22
Patton Rd	14	C1 22
Paul La	8	U 21
Pauline Pl	15	A1 19
Pawnee Dr	9	S 19
Peacock La	9	T 19
Pear Ct	20	D1 23
Peary La	8	U 23
Pebble Pl	8	S 21
Peconic Ct	8	T 22
Pelican Rd	15	A1 19
Penguin La	9	T 19
Penn Dr	14	B1 22
Penn St	14	B1 21
Penny La	13	B1 23
Penny La	21	G1 21
Peony La	8	U 20
Peppermill Ct	8	U 21
Peppermint Rd	8	R 22
Pequa La	9	S 19
Percy St	14	Z 21
Periwinkle Ct	14	B1 21
Persimmon Ct	21	E1 21
Peter Ct	20	D1 24
Peyton Pl	15	A1 19
Pheasant Dr	9	T 19
Pheasant Run	13	X 25
Phillips La	21	F1 20
Philson Ct	8	U 21
Phyllis Ct	13	X 24
Pia Blvd	14	A1 22
Pickwick Ct	8	T 20
Pickwick Dr	8	S 20
Pierrepont St	14	B1 23
Pierson St	15	C1 19
Pimlico Ct	8	S 22
Pimlico Dr	8	S 22
Pine Acre Dr	14	W 22
Pine Dr	15	C1 19
Pine Dr E	21	E1 19
Pine Hollow Rd	9	U 18
Pine Point	13	X 25
Pine Ridge Dr	14	V 20
Pine Rd	14	X 23
Pine St	14	C1 22
Pine St	21	F1 20
Pine St	21	G1 21
Pine St	9	U 19
Pinecone La	9	T 19
Pineland St	21	E1 20
Pinetree Ct	8	S 22
Pinewood Ct	21	D1 19
Pinewood Dr	9	S 17
Pinoak La (HH)	13	C1 24
Pinoak La	9	U 19
Piper Ct	13	C1 24
Piper La	13	B1 23
Pittoni Dr	9	S 18
Plaisted Av	15	Z 20
Plane Tree La	20	D1 24
Plant Av	15	V 17
Plantation Dr	15	A1 19
Platt Av	14	Y 20
Plaza Ct	14	A1 21
Plaza Dr	14	A1 21
Pleasant Dr	21	E1 19
Plowboy Pa	8	R 21
Plum Tree La	8	R 20
Plymouth Blvd	14	V 21
Pond Pa	14	Z 22
Pond View Cir	14	A1 20
Ponderosa La	21	D1 20
Poplar Dr	14	W 22
Poplar La	8	T 21
Poppy La	8	T 20
Potter Ct	13	X 23
Power Dr	15	W 17
Premier Ct	21	D1 21
Prescott La	14	Y 21
Primrose La	14	V 23
Prince Charming Rd	21	D1 21
Prince Valiant Ct	21	D1 20
Princeton Av	14	Z 20
Priscilla Rd	14	V 21
Private Rd	13	A1 23
Private Rd	13	X 24
Prospect Av	14	B1 21
Prospect St	14	Y 21
Pulaski Rd	8	R 23
Pumpkin Rd	21	D1 22
Pups Pa	7	S 24
Purdue La	14	A1 22
Putnam Ct	9	R 19
QT Pa	9	S 18
Quail Hollow Ct	13	Z 24
Quail Pa	13	Z 24
Quail Pl	9	T 19
Quaker La	14	V 21
Quantuck Ct	8	T 22
Quay Rd	15	W 19
Queens Av	14	V 23
Quensel Ct	21	F1 20
Quenzer St	14	D1 20
Quincy La	15	B1 19
Quist La	14	C1 21
Radburn Dr	8	T 21
Radcliffe Rd	8	T 20
Radford Rd	21	F1 20
Railroad Av	20	C1 23
Rainbow Dr	15	A1 19
Raleigh La	8	U 23
Ralph Av	21	F1 20
Ramondo La	14	V 21
Ramsey Rd	8	T 21
Ranson St	14	B1 22
Raphael Blvd	15	C1 19
Rapone La	15	X 19
Rassapeague Rd	13	A1 23
Raven Dr	9	T 19
Ravenwood Dr	14	W 23
Ray La	15	Z 19
Raynier Pl	21	D1 20
Reagan Ct	20	D1 22
Red Oak Rd	13	C1 24
Redleaf La	9	S 18
Redwood La	14	Z 21
Reed St	15	A1 19
Reeves St	14	A1 22
Regal Ct	14	A1 22
Regency Ct	14	C1 20
Regina Dr	9	S 18
Reinhart Ct	13	B1 23
Remsen St	14	B1 23
Renown St	21	F1 22
Rensselaer Dr	9	R 19
Renwick Av	8	U 23
Retta La	9	R 19
Reydon Wy	8	T 22
Rhett Ct	9	S 19
Rhoda Av	14	B1 20
Rhododendron Rd	13	D1 25
Rhonda La	9	S 18
Rice La	14	A1 21
Ricefield La	9	T 18
Richard Pa	13	Z 26
Richie Ct N	20	D1 23
Richie Ct S	20	D1 23
Richmond Blvd	21	G1 21
Richmond Pl	15	B1 19
Richmond Pl	9	R 19
Ridge Rd	7	R 25
Ridge Rd	14	V 21
Ridgely Rd	15	B1 19
Ridgewood La	7	R 25
Riesling Ct	8	U 21
Rita Cres	9	S 18
River Heights Ct	14	Y 22
River Heights Dr	14	X 22
River Hollow La	13	Y 25
River Rd	13	Z 24
River Rd (Nissequogue Riv Rd)	14	Z 24
Riverview Ter	14	Z 22
Riviera Dock Rd	13	X 24
Riviera Dr	14	X 22
Roanoke Ct	8	T 22
Robin Dr	9	V 18
Robin Hill La	13	B1 23
Robin Hood Ct	21	D1 20
Robin La	7	U 24
Rochelle La	7	R 24
Rockland Ct	8	R 20
Rockland Pl	21	G1 20
Rodney St	14	B1 23
Rogers La	14	V 21
Rolling Hills Dr	21	D1 19
Roman Ct	21	F1 21
Romeo Dr	14	V 21
Ron Ct	15	U 19
Ronald Ct	21	E1 20
Ronde Dr	9	T 19
Roosevelt Av	21	D1 19
Roosevelt Av	14	U 21
Roosevelt Dr	14	V 21
Rosalia Ct	14	A1 21
Rosanne Ct	21	E1 20
Rose Ct	8	U 20
Rose La	15	Y 19
Rose St	14	X 23
Rosevale Av	21	E1 19
Roseville Av	14	B1 22
Rosewood Rd	13	X 24
Rotondi Ct	14	A1 21
Roundabout Rd	14	X 21
Roundtree Dr	14	W 23
Roundtree Rd	14	V 24
Rowan St	14	X 23
Roxbury Dr	8	T 21
Roy Dr	21	D1 20
Royal Ct	21	D1 20
Rumford Rd	14	V 23
Russet Ct	7	T 24
Russet La	21	F1 22
Rutgers St	14	A1 22
Ruth Blvd	8	R 20
Ruth St	14	X 23
Rutherford St	14	B1 22
Rutland Gate	15	W 18
Rye Pl	8	S 21
Saber Dr	14	V 23
Saber La	14	W 23
Sachem Hill Pl	14	Z 23
Saddle La	13	Z 25
Saddle Rd	20	D1 25
Sagebrush La	14	W 23
Saggese Cir	14	C1 21
Saggese La	14	C1 20
Sailer St	14	D1 22
St James Av N	14	B1 23
St James Pkwy	21	E1 20
St James Rd	21	F1 20
St Johnland St	13	W 24
St Nicholas Av	21	F1 22
Salem Pa	15	W 18
Sally's Pa	7	S 24
Salonga Woods Rd	7	S 24
Salt Box Ct	14	A1 21
Salt Hay Wy	14	Z 22
Salvatore Ct	21	D1 20
Sammis St	14	B1 22
Samuel St	14	C1 20
San Juan Dr	21	C1 18
Sandalwood Dr	15	Z 20
Sandalwood Dr	14	A1 20
Sanders Pl	21	E1 20
Sandpiper Ct	14	X 21
Sandra Dr	15	A1 19
Sandy Ct	21	F1 22
Sandy Dr	14	W 22
Sandy Hill Dr	8	T 20
Sandy Hollow Dr	8	U 20
Saneck Rd	13	C1 25
Sankey's Pa	21	F1 21
Sansun La	21	D1 22
Sara Ct	14	D1 21
Sarah Dr	15	Z 19
Sarah Dr	21	F1 21
Saratoga St	9	R 19
Saturn Blvd	15	Z 19
Saw Mill Rd	9	S 19
Saxon Ct	15	W 19
Scarborough Dr	14	B1 21
Scarlet Dr	9	S 19
Scholar La	8	R 21
School House Rd	21	F1 19
School St	8	U 22
School St	14	B1 22
Schubert Dr	15	V 19
Schuyler Dr	8	R 20
Scott Ct	7	S 25
Scott La	14	W 22
Scott La	14	Z 21
Seatuck Ct	8	T 22
Seaver Ct	15	Z 19
Seaver La	15	Y 19
Seawanhaka Av	21	E1 20
Selmar Ct	7	U 24
Seminole Dr	9	S 19
Seneca Dr	9	S 19
Senne Rd	7	R 26
Sequoia Dr	15	Z 19
Serene Pl	21	C1 19
Sergent Ct	14	C1 22
Sesame St	14	V 23
Seusing Blvd	21	D1 18
Shady La	14	Y 20
Shady Pl	14	C1 21
Shaker Ridge La	8	S 21
Shandon Rd	8	T 21
Sharon Ct	14	X 23
Shawnee La	9	T 19
Shay Dr	8	U 23
Sheffield St	21	D1 20
Sheila Dr	15	Z 19
Shelley Ct	8	U 20
Shelton Ct	8	T 21
Shenandoah Blvd	21	E1 21
Shep Jones La	13	C1 25
Sheppard La	14	B1 20
Sherbrook Dr	15	Z 19
Sherry La	15	A1 19
Sherwood Dr	14	C1 22
Sheryl Cres	14	W 22
Shetland La	14	B1 22
Shinbone La	9	S 18
Shinnecock Ct	8	T 22
Shirley Ct	8	T 20
Shirley Pl	8	T 23
Shore Dr	14	Z 23
Shore Rd	13	W 25
Shore View Ct	14	C1 21
Short Beach Rd	13	X 25
Short Ct	14	C1 21
Short Pa	13	Z 25
Short St	8	T 23
Sigal St	14	Z 20
Silo Rd	8	S 21
Silver Pond Cres	8	T 22
Singer La	14	Z 21
Sioux Dr	9	S 19
Siracusa Blvd	8	U 20
Skunk Hollow Rd	13	C1 24
Sleepy Hollow	21	F1 20
Sleepy Hollow Ct	7	S 24
Smith La	13	Z 24
Smith St	21	E1 20
Smith's La	8	S 20
Smithtown Blvd	15	C1 20
Smithtown Blvd	14	B1 20
Smithtown Cres	14	V 21
Smithtown Port Jefferson Rd (North Country Rd)	13	C1 24
Smithtown to St Johnland Rd	13	X 24
Somers La	8	S 21
Somerset Dr	8	T 21
Somerset Pl	13	Y 25
Sorrel Hill La	9	U 18
Sound Rd	7	R 26
Sound View	14	Z 23
Soundview Ct	13	W 25
Soundview Dr	7	S 26
South Av	14	A1 20
South Ct	14	C1 20
South Gate	15	Y 19
South Hillside Av	21	D1 21
South Lakebridge Dr	14	V 23
South Lot Rd	14	Z 22
South Pa	13	Z 25
South Plaisted Av	15	Z 19
South Pond La	15	A1 19
Southern Blvd	14	C1 21
Space Wy	15	Z 19
Sparrow La	15	V 18
Sparton La	8	T 21
Speaker St	8	R 20
Spectacle Lake Dr	21	E1 19
Spencer Wy	14	W 23
Spinnaker Ct	7	S 25
Spitrail Pl	8	S 21
Spout La, The	14	Z 22
Spring Hollow Rd	13	A1 23
Springbriar La	14	V 22
Springmeadow Ct	8	T 23
Springmedow Dr	8	T 23
Spruce Ct	14	A1 22
Spruce Dr	21	E1 19
Spruce St	14	X 23
Squire La	13	W 24
Squire Pa	14	A1 23
Stacey La	8	U 21
Standish Pl	14	B1 20
Standish Pl	21	C1 20
Stanley Pl	15	Z 19
Stanwich Rd	8	U 21
Stardom Ct	14	C1 23
Starlight Dr	8	S 20
State Hwy 25	21	G1 21
State Hwy 25	14	V 20
State Hwy 25A	13	C1 24
State Hwy 25A	7	T 24
State Hwy 25A	14	A1 21
State Hwy 25A	14	W 23
State Hwy 25A	14	X 21
State Hwy 111	14	Z 20
State Hwy 347	14	C1 21
State Hwy 454	8	R 20
State St	21	F1 22
Stattel Dr	8	U 23
Steep Bank Rd	14	Z 23
Stengel Pl	14	X 22
Sterling Dr	21	F1 21
Sterling La	15	Z 19
Steuben Blvd	21	E1 19
Steven Pl	15	B1 19
Steven Pl W	15	A1 19
Stillwater La	13	A1 23
Stillwater Rd	13	Z 25
Stirrup La	8	S 23
Stone Edge La	21	D1 20
Stone Gate Ct	14	X 22
Stonegate	14	Z 23
Stony Brook Rd	21	F1 22
Stony Hill Pa Dr	14	Y 22
Stonywood Rd	9	S 18
Storybook La	21	D1 22
Storyland Rd	20	D1 22
Strawberry Knoll Ct	7	R 24
Strongs Ct	14	Z 21
Stuyvesant La	14	V 21
Suburban La	14	C1 20
Suffolk Ct	9	U 18
Summerset Dr	14	X 21
Summit Dr	14	B1 20
Summit Tr	13	Y 24
Sundale Ct	14	Z 21
Sunflower Dr	9	U 18
Sunhill Rd	15	B1 19
Sunken Meadow Rd	7	R 24
Sunken Meadow State Pkwy	8	S 19
Sunken Meadow State Pkwy	7	T 24
Sunken Meadow State Pkwy	9	R 18
Sunny Rd	14	C1 22
Sunrise La	14	Y 20
Sunset La	15	Y 19
Supreme Ct	15	W 19
Susan Ct	8	T 20
Susan Dr	7	S 24
Sussex La	21	E1 20
Sutton Pl	13	A1 23
Suttonwood Dr	9	S 18
Swallow La	15	W 18
Swan La	15	W 18
Swan Pl	13	A1 23
Sweet Hollow Ct	13	A1 23
Sweetbriar Dr	7	Y 21
Sy Ct	21	F1 21
Sybil Pl	14	X 22
Sycamore Av	21	F1 20
Sycamore Dr	14	W 23
Sycamore La	8	S 21
Sycamore Rd	13	X 24
Sylvan Rd	15	Z 19
Taffy Ct	8	T 23
Taft Dr	14	W 20
Takats La	14	C1 22
Talbot La	14	V 21
Tall Pines La	21	D1 20
Tall Tree La	14	Y 20
Tallmadge Rd	7	R 25
Tammi Ct	14	V 22
Tanglewood Dr	15	Y 19
Tanyard Pl	7	T 24
Tap Ct	21	D1 21
Tara Ct	21	F1 20
Tara La	8	S 21
Tarleton Ct	7	T 25
Tarleton La	7	T 25
Teal La	14	X 23
Teal Wy	13	Z 24
Teapot La	14	Z 22
Tern Pl	9	T 19
Terrace Dr	9	U 19
Terrace La	14	A1 21
Terri Dr	14	V 22
Terrill La	7	U 24
Terry Ct	21	G1 20
Terry La	8	R 20
Terry Rd	14	B1 19
Thatch Pond Rd	14	Z 22
Theodore St	14	Z 20
Thistle Ct	14	X 22
Thistle La	8	T 23
Thomas Dr	15	Z 19
Thomas Pl	14	Y 21
Thompson Av	14	B1 24
Thompson Hill Rd	13	C1 24
Thompson St	7	U 24
Three Pond Rd	14	Z 22
Three Sisters Rd	20	C1 24
Thrush Dr	14	X 20
Tide Mill La	14	Z 23
Tide Mill Rd	14	Z 23
Tiffany Ct	21	F1 21
Tiffany La	15	Z 19
Tillotson Av	14	B1 23
Timber Croft Wy	15	V 19
Timber La	7	R 25
Timber Ridge Dr	8	U 22
Timberbrook Rd	7	R 26
Timothy Ct	8	R 21
Timothy Ct	8	U 20
Timothy La	14	B1 23
Tishner La	14	A1 20
Tomkins Ct	9	R 19
Tony Dr	14	V 22
Torlen Ct	15	Z 19
Tower Pl	14	B1 22
Tower St	21	F1 22
Town Commons Dr	14	B1 20
Town Line Rd	8	R 20
Town Line Rd	15	Y 19
Tracklot Rd	13	Z 24
Traister Ct	14	A1 21
Tredwell Av	14	B1 23
Tree Top Ter	14	Y 23
Treetop Pa	21	C1 19
Treetop Path Rd	15	C1 19
Trent Ct	14	Y 23
Trent La	14	Y 23
Trescott Pa	7	T 25
Triple Oak La	13	Y 25
Troon Rd	20	D1 23
Truesdale Ct	7	T 25
Truval La	21	D1 21
Truxton La	8	T 22
Tuck, The	14	A1 23
Tuckahoe La	9	S 19
Tulane Ct	7	T 25
Tulip La	14	T 20
Tulip Rd	14	X 24
Tulip St	21	E1 20
Tulipwood Dr	9	S 18
Turtle Crossing	13	Z 25
Tusa Ct	14	A1 22
Tusculum Rd	8	T 20
Tween Ct	14	A1 22
Twilight La	15	Y 19
Twin Oaks Dr	7	U 24
Twixt Hills Rd	14	Z 22
Tyler Rd	14	Y 22
Tyram St	8	T 21
Unity Ct	21	D1 21
Upper Old Dock Rd	13	W 25
Ursular Ct	14	Y 22
Val Ct	9	S 18
Valant Ct	14	V 20
Valiant Ct	15	B1 19
Valley Av	14	Y 22
Valley Pa	13	Z 26
Valley Rd	7	U 25
Valley Wood Rd	9	T 19
Valley Wood Rd (Broadview Dr)	14	U 19
Valleywood Ct E	13	C1 25
Valleywood Ct W	13	C1 25
Valmont La	9	S 18
Valtop La	21	D1 21
Van Buren Ct	14	C1 20
Vanburen St	14	B1 23
Vance St	8	R 20
Vanderbilt Av	14	B1 23
Vanderbilt Motor Pkwy	15	T 17
Vanderbilt Motor Pkwy	9	S 17
Vanderbilt Pkwy	9	P 18
Vassar Pl	14	Y 20
Verbena Dr	8	T 20
Verdi St	14	X 23
Vernon Pl	14	Y 20
Veronica Ct	14	X 22
Veterans La	8	U 23
Veterans Memorial Hwy	8	S 20
Veterans Memorial Hwy	15	U 19
Vicar Ct	14	C1 20
Victoria Ct	13	C1 25
Vie Pl	21	F1 21
Viking Ct	21	E1 20
Villa La	8	U 21
Village Wy	14	A1 21
Vine Rd	14	W 23
Vineyard Ct	14	D1 23
Violet La	8	S 20
Violet Rd	13	X 24
Virginia Av	21	G1 20
Virginia Rd	21	F1 20
Vista Pl	21	D1 21
Vivian La	21	F1 22
Wade Dr	21	F1 21
Wadsworth Pl	14	Z 20
Wagner La	21	F1 21
Wagon Wy	21	D1 19
Wallis La	13	Y 25
Walnut Ct	21	F1 20
Walnut Rd	13	X 24
Walnut St	21	F1 20
Walnut St	14	X 23
Walter Ct	8	T 20
Walter Dr	21	E1 20
Wanda La	15	Z 19
Wandering Wy	14	Z 23
Waner St	8	S 20
Warbler La	9	T 19
Ward Dr	14	X 23
Ware Pl	14	X 23
Wartburg Ct	8	T 23
Wartburg Dr	8	T 23
Washburn Av	21	F1 21
Washington Av	15	B1 19
Washington Av	14	C1 23
Washington Blvd	8	T 21
Washington Ct	14	V 21
Washington Dr	14	W 23
Watercrest Ct	13	B1 23
Waverly Av	14	Y 21
Wayfarer La	14	Z 23
Wayne Pl	9	R 19
Wayside La	14	V 21
Weatherstone Wy	14	A1 21
Webster Pl	15	B1 19
Weldon La	8	T 21
Wellington Dr	20	D1 25
Wellwood Rd	20	D1 24
Welsley La	15	Z 19
Wenmore Ct	8	T 21
Wenmore Rd	8	T 21
Wesleyan Ct	8	U 21
Wesleyan Rd	8	T 21
West Av	14	A1 20
West Ct	14	X 23
West Dr	8	U 23
West Pond Ct	15	A1 19
Westbrook La	15	Z 19
Westcliff La	21	F1 21
Westminster Ct	14	C1 20
Weston La	14	V 21
Westwood La	14	W 23
Wetherill La	13	B1 23
Wexford Ct	14	B1 22
Wheatly Pl	8	R 21
Wheelright Wy	14	A1 21
Whisper Hill	13	Y 25
Whisper La	14	Z 20
Whispering Woods Dr	14	V 22
White Av	14	D1 22
White Birch Ct	14	A1 21
White Birch La	8	S 20
White Cliff La	21	E1 21
White Oak Dr	9	U 19
White Pine Ct	14	Y 23
White Spruce Cir	9	T 19
Whitney Ct	14	Y 21
Whitney Gate	14	Y 21
Whittier Dr	13	X 24
Wichard Blvd	8	T 21
Wicks La	14	B1 23
Wicks Pa	9	T 18
Wicks Rd	9	T 19
Wiigs Rd	15	B1 19
Wild Flower Dr	15	W 22
Wild Run	15	V 19
Wilderness Rd	13	Z 25
Wildwood Ct	20	D1 23
Wildwood La	14	Y 20
Wildwood St	21	G1 22
William St	14	B1 20
Williams Blvd	21	F1 21
Williams Ct	14	C1 22
Williamsburg Dr	7	S 25
Williamsburgh La	15	D1 19
Willow La	7	U 24
Willow Ridge Dr	14	X 22
Willow St	14	Z 21
Wilson Av	14	C1 20
Win Pl	21	F1 20
Windham Cres	14	X 23
Windmill Ct	14	A1 21
Windsor Hill	13	Y 25
Windwood Dr	21	E1 21
Windy La	7	R 26
Wing St	21	F1 22
Wink Pl	14	W 23
Winnecomac Cir	8	S 23
Winners Cir	21	D1 21
Winona St	14	W 21
Winslow La	14	W 23
Winston Dr	8	U 20
Wireless Blvd	9	T 18
Wisteria Ct	14	B1 21
Wood Duck Ct	14	Z 21
Wood La	15	Z 19
Wood View Dr	21	D1 20
Woodcrest Ct	13	A1 23
Woodcrest Dr	13	Z 24
Woodcutters Pa	13	Z 24
Woodfield Av	7	R 26
Woodhill Pa	13	Z 25
Woodhollow Ct	7	T 24
Woodhollow La	7	T 24
Woodhollow Rd	14	Z 20
Woodland Dr	14	W 23
Woodland Dr	14	Z 21
Woodland La	14	V 20
Woodland Pa	7	U 24
Woodlawn Av	20	C1 23
Woodlawn Av	14	B1 22
Woodlot Rd	13	B1 23
Woodmere Dr	7	R 26
Woodrow La	14	V 20
Woodstock Pl	21	G1 20
Woodvale Av	7	U 25
Woodvale La	7	U 25
Woodvale Pl	7	U 24
Wren Ct	8	U 20
Wren Dr	15	V 18
Wyandanch Blvd	15	U 19
Wyoming St	9	R 19
Wysocki Ct	14	C1 20
Yale La	13	W 24
Yardley La	21	E1 21
Yarmouth La	21	E1 21
Yates Av	9	R 19
Yellow Brick Ct	7	S 24
Yellow Brick Rd	7	S 24
Yens Wy	13	Z 26
Yorktown Pl	7	S 25
Zinnia Ct	8	S 20
1st Av	8	U 23
1st Av	14	C1 23
1st St	8	T 23
1st St	14	C1 23
1st St	21	E1 20
1st St	21	G1 20
1st St E	14	V 24
2nd Av	14	C1 23
2nd St	8	T 23
2nd St	14	C1 23
2nd St	21	E1 20
2nd St E	14	V 24
2nd St W	14	V 24
3rd Av	14	C1 23
3rd St	14	C1 23
3rd St	21	E1 20
3rd St	21	G1 20
3rd St E	14	V 24
4th Av	8	T 23
4th St	20	C1 23
4th St	14	C1 23
4th St	21	E1 20
4th St	21	G1 20
5th Av	8	T 23
5th Av	14	C1 23
5th Av	14	Z 20
5th St	14	C1 23
5th St	21	E1 20
6th Av	8	T 23
6th Av	14	C1 23
6th Av	14	Z 20
6th St	14	C1 23
6th St	21	E1 21
7th Av	20	D1 23
7th Av	8	T 23
7th Av	14	Z 20
7th St	14	C1 23
8th Av	8	T 23
8th St	21	D1 21
9th Av	8	T 23

SOUTHAMPTON

STREET	MAP	GRID
Aberdeen Dr	47	C3 24
Aberdeen La	52	U3 32
Aberdeen La	47	L3 23
Acorn Pa	42	A3 21
Actors Colony Rd	52	V3 35
Adam La (WB)	43	T2 19
Adams La (SY)	54	N3 23
Adams La	42	Z2 21
Adelphi Cir	48	E3 22
Aider Av	54	N3 26
Ajay Ct	48	E3 22
Alanson La	48	E3 21
Albany Av	41	U2 25
Alden La	43	U2 18
Aldrich La	54	O3 24
Alexis La	38	P2 18
Alfies Wy	57	W3 28
Alissa La	42	V2 23
Allamoro Rd	42	A3 22
Ambelside La	57	V3 25
Amber La	43	Q2 17
Amherst Rd	55	U3 32
Amity St	56	W3 32
Amy's Pa	42	Z2 21
Anchor Rd	55	U3 32
Anchor St	41	T2 25
Anderson Rd	48	D3 23
Andrews La	43	Y2 19
Andrews Rd	54	L3 24
Andy's La	38	O2 18
Ann Av	41	R2 24
Anns La	54	N3 23
Anthony La	43	W2 18
Apaucuck Cove La	43	R2 17
Apaucuck Rd	43	R2 17
Aqua Dr	47	G3 23
Arbor Ct	47	D3 23
Arbor La	52	T3 31
Arbor La	47	D3 23
Arbutus La	47	C3 24
Arbutus Rd	47	J3 24
Archibald Wy	56	W3 32
Ardmore La	47	D3 23
Argonne Rd	48	C3 22
Argyle Rd	43	Y2 19
Arlen Ct	41	T2 26
Armande St	54	N3 24
Arnold Bess Dr	48	B3 21
Arnold St	43	R2 20
Art Village Cir	54	L3 24
Arthur Av	56	W3 29
Arthur St	43	S2 18
Arthur St	42	U2 24
Artist Colony La	54	M3 23
Ash La	53	Q3 29
Ash St	42	Z2 21
Ash St	41	S2 25
Ashwood Ct	53	N3 28
Aspatuck Rd	43	T2 18
Atlantic Av	57	V3 25
Atlantic Av	48	C3 22
Atterbury Rd	47	H3 23
Auburn Cir	48	E3 22
B Rd	48	L3 21
Bailey Rd	54	L3 23
Baldwin Dr	52	U3 34
Bam La	56	V3 29
Barclay Dr	52	U3 35
Barker La	43	V2 18
Barkers Island Rd	54	K3 25
Barnhart St	54	M3 23
Baron's La (Pvt)	54	Q3 23
Barracuda Rd	42	A3 20
Barrett Dr	41	Z2 25
Barrett Dr N	41	Z2 26
Barrow Pl	47	J3 23
Bath House Rd	47	H3 24
Bathing Beach Rd	47	G3 24
Bay Av	52	S3 32
Bay Av	53	M3 27
Bay Av	53	S3 26
Bay Av	48	B3 22
Bay Av	42	Y2 20
Bay Crest	42	Z2 21
Bay Dr	48	E3 22
Bay La	54	T3 25
Bay Meadow La	43	Q2 17
Bay Rd	47	H3 23
Bay Rd (WG)	43	R2 16
Bay Rd (QG)	43	X2 19
Bay St	53	L3 28
Bay St (SH)	55	W3 33
Bay View Av	56	V3 32
Bay View Ct	52	T3 34
Bay View Dr	52	T3 32
Bay View Dr	52	U3 33
Bay View Dr (NH)	55	V3 35
Bay View Dr	53	O3 29
Bay View Dr (QG)	43	W2 17
Bay View La	41	U2 25
Bay View Rd N	53	P3 30
Bay View Rd W	53	P3 30
Bay Woods Dr	47	C3 24
Bayberry Landing	47	J3 25
Bayberry La (NH)	52	U3 34
Bayberry La	39	O2 16
Bayberry La (QG)	43	W2 19
Bayberry La	42	Z2 20
Bayberry Rd	47	F3 24
Baybury La	48	E3 21
Baycrest Av	43	R2 17
Bayfield Ct	43	S2 17
Bayfield La	43	S2 16
Bayfield La	43	T2 17
Bayside Av	43	Z2 19
Bayview Av	47	E3 24
Bayview Dr	47	E3 23
Bayview Dr	43	Q2 17
Bayview Ter	53	O3 29
Bayview Ter	47	B3 24
Baywood Rd	53	O3 29
Beach La	43	W2 18
Beach Plum Rd	52	R3 32
Beach Rd	54	L3 21
Beach Rd	43	T2 18
Beach Rd	43	A3 18
Beach St	42	Z2 21
Beachcomber La	54	R3 23
Beachdale Rd	47	F3 24
Beachland Av	42	A3 20
Beachwood Dr	53	L3 26
Beatrice Dr	48	D3 21
Beaver La W	43	R2 19
Beaverdam Rd	43	R2 17
Beck's Pa	56	V3 29
Beechnut Ct	42	A3 21
Bell Av	41	T2 25
Bellows Ct	54	P3 23
Bellows La	54	P3 24
Bellows Pond Rd	42	A3 23
Bellows Ter	54	P3 23
Bergen Av	47	B3 25
Bernadine St	54	M3 24
Bernard Pl	52	S3 32
Beth La	48	C3 22
Bettina Ct	47	B3 25
Beverly Dr	42	Z2 21
Big Fresh Pond Rd	53	M3 26
Birch Av	41	S2 25
Birch Av	41	W2 25
Birch Ct	37	Q2 24
Birch Creek Rd	41	X2 25
Birch St	52	S3 32
Birch St	41	S2 25
Birchwood La	42	Z2 21
Bishop Av	43	R2 18
Bishop Ct	54	M3 23
Bishop La	43	S2 18
Bishop Pl	47	E3 24
Bishops La	54	M3 24
Bishops La	54	N3 24
Bittersweet Av	47	D3 24
Bitter Sweet La	52	P3 31
Bittersweet	47	D3 23
Bittersweet S	47	D3 23
Black Watch Ct	47	J3 23
Blank La	53	R3 28
Blue Heron Wy	52	U3 34

Suffolk Co.

Index

Suffolk Co.

Town of Southampton

STREET	MAP	GRID
Meadowmere Pl	54	N3 22
Meadows East	56	V3 30
Meadows W	56	V3 29
Mecox Fields La	57	V3 25
Mecox La	54	R3 25
Mecox Rd	53	T3 26
Meeting House La	54	O3 23
Meeting House La Ext	54	P3 23
Melissa Ct	47	D3 23
Merchant's Pa (Simpson Rd)	56	X3 29
Mermaid La	48	C3 19
Middle La	53	M3 26
Middle Line Hwy	53	P3 29
Middle Line Hwy (SH)	56	W3 31
Middle Pond La	47	K3 23
Middle Pond Rd	47	J3 23
Middle Rd	48	A3 21
Midgie La	47	F3 24
Midhampton Av	43	X2 20
Midhampton Ct	43	X2 20
Midland St	43	W2 18
Midocean Dr	57	V3 25
Mildred Pl	47	E3 23
Mill Creek Cl	54	Q3 25
Mill Pond La	54	R3 25
Mill Pond Rd	38	P2 18
Mill Race	48	D3 21
Mill Rd	53	S3 28
Mill Rd	52	R3 32
Mill Rd	38	P2 17
Mill Rd (WB)	43	S2 18
Miller Rd	54	N3 24
Millfarm La	54	P3 25
Millicent Dr	53	O3 28
Millpond Rd	48	D3 21
Mills Pl	41	U2 25
Millstone Brook Rd	53	M3 26
Millstone Brook Rd	47	K3 25
Millstone Dr	53	M3 27
Millstone La	47	L3 26
Millstone Rd	52	R3 31
Milton Rd	54	N3 25
Mineola Ct	48	C3 21
Missapogue Ct	53	M3 26
Mitchell La	53	T3 28
Mitchell Pl	42	Y2 20
Mitchell Rd	43	T2 17
Mohawk Av	54	S3 25
Moneybogue La	43	T2 17
Montauk Hwy	53	S3 26
Montauk Hwy	54	K3 23
Montauk Hwy	54	Q3 25
Montauk Hwy	48	A3 22
Montauk Hwy	47	D3 23
Montauk Hwy	47	G3 23
Montauk Hwy	38	P2 18
Montauk Hwy	43	Q2 18
Montauk Hwy	43	U2 18
Montauk Hwy (QG)	43	X2 19
Montauk Hwy	42	Y2 20
Montauk Hwy	56	Y3 28
Montauk Hwy	42	Z2 21
Montrose La	53	T3 26
Moon Av	41	W2 25
Morris Cove La	56	V3 32
Morrison La	54	T3 25
Mortimer St	43	T2 18
Moses La	54	M3 24
Mostyn Pl	43	T2 17
Mt Misery Dr	56	X3 31
Mountain Laurel Rd	54	M3 25
Mulberry Dr	52	U3 32
Mullen Hill La	53	P3 30
Munchogue Dr	52	S3 32
Murphy Dr	48	C3 21
Murray Av	57	V3 28
Murray La	54	Q3 23
Murray Pl	54	Q3 23
Nadine Dr	43	R2 18
Narod Blvd	53	T3 26
Narrow La	57	V3 28
Narrow La	57	X3 28
Narrow La	53	S3 27
Narrow La (SV)	54	P3 24
Narrow La S	53	R3 27
Nash Av	41	W2 25
Nassau Rd	48	C3 22
Nassau St (SH)	55	W3 33
Nassau St	41	U2 25
Nautilus Ct	48	D3 21
Nautilus Dr	48	D3 21
Nautilus La	48	D3 21
Neptune Av	48	B3 22
Netz Pl	41	V2 25
New North Highway	54	K3 25
New North Hwy Rd	47	J3 25
New St	39	P2 16
New Town Ct	47	E3 24
Newberry La	54	O3 25
Newlight La	53	T3 27
Newman Av	57	V3 27
Newtown Rd	47	C3 24
Newtown Rd	47	E3 24
Niamogue La	43	X2 17
Nicholas Ct	54	L3 24
Nickerson La	38	N2 17
Nidzyn Av	38	O2 17
Norbury Rd	48	E3 21
Norris La	57	W3 28
North Bay Av	38	N2 19
North Captain's Neck La	54	M3 23
North Dr	52	U3 35
North Harbor Dr	52	V3 34
North Haven Wy	52	U3 35
North Hwy	47	F3 24
North Jessup Av	43	W2 19
North Magee St	54	L3 26
North Main St	54	O3 24
North Oak Dr	47	D3 23
North Phillips Av	38	O2 18
North Quarter Rd	38	Q2 18
North Rd	42	Z2 21
North Rd	47	G3 24
North Rolling Woods La	47	C3 23
North Sea Mecox Rd	54	N3 25
North Sea Dr	53	N3 27
North Sea Rd	53	L3 28
North Sea Rd	53	M3 27
North Sea Rd	54	N3 26
North Sea Rd (SV)	54	O3 24
North Shore Rd	47	E3 23
North Valley Rd	52	T3 32
North View Hills Ct	52	S3 32
North View Hills Dr	52	S3 32
North Westbury Rd	48	E3 22
North Wooley St	54	P3 24
Northside Dr	53	Q3 30
Northway La	38	N2 20
Northwest Rd	56	X3 29
Northwoods Rd	41	R2 25
Norton Pl	53	N3 28
Norwood Rd	42	A3 21
Notamiset Rd	43	U2 18
Notre Dame Rd	52	U3 32
Nowedonah Av	54	R3 26
Noyac Av	52	S3 32
Noyac Bay Av	52	R3 32
Noyac Harbor Rd	52	R3 32
Noyac Long Beach Rd	52	T3 32
Noyac Pa	53	S3 28
Noyac Rd	52	P3 31
Noyac Rd	52	U3 32
Noyac Rd	53	N3 27
Nugent Dr	41	Q2 26
Nugent St	54	O3 23
Oak Av	52	Q3 32
Oak Av	53	M3 27
Oak Av	41	U2 25
Oak Ct	41	R2 25
Oak Ct	43	D3 22
Oak Dr	52	R3 32
Oak Dr	52	S3 32
Oak Dr (NH)	52	U3 34
Oak Dr	48	D3 23
Oak Grove Rd	53	O3 30
Oak La	52	Q3 32
Oak La (NH)	52	V3 34
Oak La	48	B3 22
Oak La	48	D3 21
Oak Pl	53	N3 28
Oak Rd	52	S3 32
Oak St	41	S2 25
Oak St	57	W3 27
Oak St (SV)	54	O3 23
Oak St	48	B3 22
Oak St	48	C3 22
Oak St	42	Y2 21
Oak St (WB)	43	T2 18
Oak View Rd	53	O3 29
Oakhurst Rd	47	F3 24
Oakland Av	56	W3 32
Oakland La	42	A3 20
Oaks Av	41	W2 26
Oaktree La	48	A3 21
Oakville Av	42	V2 22
Oakwood Rd	42	A3 21
Ocame Av	43	U2 18
Ocean Av	48	C3 22
Ocean Av (QG)	43	X2 18
Ocean Av	42	Z2 21
Ocean Rd	57	V3 26
Ocean View Pkwy	53	P3 29
Ocean View Rd	47	F3 23
Oceanview Av	47	H3 23
Oceanview Dr	47	H3 23
Ogden La	43	W2 18
Ogden La	43	X2 17
Old Barn La	57	Z3 27
Old Country Rd	54	R3 25
Old Country Rd	38	M2 19
Old Country Rd (QG)	43	W2 19
Old Country Rd	42	Y2 20
Old Depot Rd	43	W2 19
Old Farm Rd	57	W3 29
Old Field La	54	N3 23
Old Field Rd	53	M3 27
Old Fish Cove Rd	53	M3 27
Old Fort La	47	K3 23
Old Main Rd	43	V2 19
Old Meadow Bend	43	T2 17
Old Meeting House Rd	43	U2 18
Old Mill La	38	P2 17
Old Mill Rd	54	R3 25
Old Montauk Hwy	38	P2 18
Old North Hwy	47	F3 24
Old Oaks La	43	X2 19
Old Orchard Rd	53	N3 28
Old Point Rd	43	X2 19
Old Pond La	39	O2 17
Old Quogue Riverhead Rd	43	V2 20
Old Quogue Rd	41	S2 26
Old Riverhead Rd	42	T2 20
Old Riverhead Rd E	47	D3 23
Old Riverhead Rd W	47	B3 23
Old Sag Harbor Rd	53	O3 28
Old Sag Harbor Rd	53	S3 29
Old Sag Harbor Rd	53	T3 30
Old Squires Rd	47	B3 24
Old Squiretown Rd	47	C3 24
Old Town Crossing	54	P3 23
Old Town Rd	54	P3 24
Old Trail Rd	53	P3 29
Old West Hampton Rd	43	R2 20
Oliver's Cove La	53	T3 26
On the Bluff	52	T3 35
Oneck La	43	S2 18
Oneck Pl	43	S2 17
Oneck Rd	43	S2 17
Oneck Ter	43	S2 17
Orchard Av	52	Q3 32
Osborn Ct	57	Y3 27
Osborne Av	54	P3 24
Osceola La	47	K3 23
Osprey Av	42	A3 20
Osprey Wy	53	T3 27
Overlook Dr	47	K3 24
Overlook La	52	T3 32
Ox Pasture Rd	54	M3 23
Oxford Ct	54	M3 24
Palmer Ter	56	W3 32
Palm Dr	42	Z2 21
Palo Alto Dr	48	E3 22
Park Av	52	Q3 32
Park Cir	43	V2 19
Park La	48	E3 22
Park Pl	43	Q2 18
Park Pl	41	R2 25
Parkside Av	53	O3 28
Parkview Ct	47	A3 24
Parkway Rd	52	U3 32
Pkwy, The	53	M3 26
Parlato Dr	43	T2 17
Parlato Pl	43	T2 17
Parrish Pond Ct E	54	L3 24
Parrish Pond La	54	L3 24
Parrish Pond Ct W	54	L3 24
Parrish Rd	53	M3 26
Parsonage La	57	X3 27
Parsonage Pond Rd	57	Y3 27
Partridge Dr	52	U3 31
Paths End Ct	53	P3 28
Patrick St	43	R2 19
Paul's La	57	U3 26
Paumanok Rd	53	T3 30
Pawnee St	47	F3 23
Payne Av	55	V3 34
Paynes La	42	Y2 20
Peacock Pa	42	V2 20
Pebble Wy	41	S2 25
Peconic Av	52	P3 31
Peconic Av	53	M3 27
Peconic Av	41	R2 26
Peconic Bay Av	53	O3 29
Peconic Cres	47	G3 24
Peconic Hills Ct	53	O3 29
Peconic Hills Dr	53	O3 29
Peconic Overlook	47	F3 24
Peconic Rd	47	G3 24
Peconic Tr	41	U2 25
Peg's La	41	R2 25
Pelham St	54	N3 24
Pelletreau St	54	O3 24
Peninsula Dr	52	U3 32
Pennant La	42	V2 22
Penniman Point Rd	43	X2 18
Penny La	48	E3 21
Pepi Ct	47	D3 23
Pepperidge La	48	E3 21
Percy Av	43	R2 18
Percy Pl	47	F3 24
Percy St	43	R2 18
Periwinkle La	48	D3 21
Peters La	57	Y3 26
Peters La	43	U2 19
Petrel La	47	C3 25
Petrel Rd	47	J3 23
Pharoh's Wy	42	Y2 20
Pheasant Ct E	54	Q3 24
Pheasant Ct N	54	Q3 24
Pheasant Ct S	54	Q3 24
Pheasant Ct W	54	Q3 24
Pheasant Cove Ct	54	Q3 25
Pheasant Dr	57	U3 28
Pheasant La (SV)	54	Q3 23
Pheasant La	38	O2 17
Pheasant La E	38	O2 17
Pheasant Rd	52	U3 31
Pheasant Run	43	W2 19
Pheasant Wk	57	V3 25
Pheasants Crossing	54	R3 25
Phillips Av	41	S2 25
Phillips Av	38	O2 18
Phillips La	47	J3 23
Piconic View	47	H3 23
Pierce Av	53	P3 29
Pierpont St	54	P3 23
Pierson Ct	54	R3 24
Pierson Rd	41	W2 25
Pin Oak La	43	T2 18
Pine Av	41	W2 26
Pine Ct	37	Q2 24
Pine Ct	48	C3 22
Pine Crest La	52	T3 32
Pine Dr	48	F3 22
Pinegrove Ct	41	S2 25
Pine Grove Ct	38	P2 18
Pine La	48	B3 22
Pine La (QG)	43	W2 18
Pine Neck Av	52	S3 32
Pine Neck Rd	48	A3 21
Pine Pa	42	Q2 24
Pine Path Ct	37	Q2 24
Pine Rd	52	S3 32
Pine Rd	47	G3 23
Pine St	57	W3 27
Pine St (SV)	54	P3 23
Pine St	47	B3 22
Pine St	48	D3 21
Pine St	41	R2 25
Pine St (WB)	41	S2 25
Pine St	43	T2 18
Pine St	42	Z2 21
Pine Tree Ct	42	A3 21
Pine Tree La	48	A3 21
Pine Tree La	39	P2 17
Pine Tree La	42	Z2 21
Pine Tree Pl	47	E3 24
Pine Tree Rd	53	O3 30
Pine View La	48	C3 22
Pinewood La	48	C3 22
Pioneer La	54	L3 26
Plant St	54	P3 24
Platt Ter	54	M3 23
Pleasant Av	43	R2 17
Pleasant La (SV)	54	M3 23
Pleasant La	42	X2 21
Pleasure Dr	42	V2 23
Plume Grass Wy	43	R2 18
Point Rd	41	U2 26
Point Rd (QG)	43	V2 18
Pointe Mecox La	57	U3 25
Polk St	41	U2 25
Polo Grounds La	42	W2 21
Pond Dr	41	R2 25
Pond La (SV)	54	O3 23
Pond La	41	R2 25
Pond Rd	43	R2 16
Ponquoque Av	47	D3 23
Poplar St	48	C3 22
Port Elizabeth	48	C3 21
Port St	41	T2 25
Porter Dr	47	H3 24
Post Av	53	P3 29
Post Crossing	54	O3 24
Post La (SV)	54	P3 23
Post La (QG)	43	X2 18
Post Pl	53	N3 26
Potato Rd	57	Z3 26
Potato Barn Rd	54	R3 25
Potato Field Ct	54	P3 24
Potato Field La	54	P3 24
Potunk La	43	T2 17
Powell Av	54	O3 24
Powers Dr	47	K3 23
Poxabogue La	57	X3 28
Princeton Rd	52	U3 32
Priscilla Av	41	U2 25
Private	56	V3 29
Private (QG)	43	X2 19
Private Rd (NH)	55	V3 33
Private Rd	54	L3 24
Private Rd	54	O3 25
Private Rd	47	B3 25
Private Rd	48	F3 22
Proprietors La	54	R3 25
Prospect Av	48	D3 21
Public Rd	43	R2 16
Pulaski Av	54	O3 24
Pulaski St	54	O3 24
Quahog La	43	W2 18
Quail Run	47	D3 24
Quantuck Bay La	43	V2 18
Quantuck Bay Rd	43	V2 18
Quantuck La	43	W2 17
Quaquanantuck La	43	W2 17
Quarter Ct	38	Q2 18
Quimby La	57	V3 25
Quogo Neck La	43	W2 17
Quogue Av	41	U2 25
Quogue Plz Tr	43	W2 19
Quogue St	42	Z2 21
Quogue St (Main St)	43	V2 18
Quogue-Riverhead Rd	42	W2 21
Ragnar La	54	M3 26
Railroad Av	57	V3 28
Railroad Plaza	54	O3 24
Rampasture Rd	48	C3 20
Ranch Ct	56	X3 29
Randall Rd	53	M3 26
Randall St	41	S2 25
Randall St	42	Z2 20
Rawson Rd	53	P3 31
Raymonds La	54	N3 23
Raynor Dr	43	R2 17
Raynor Rd	54	N3 25
Re Ct	48	E3 22
Realnautic Ct	47	B3 25
Rebadam La	47	K3 23
Red Cedar Point Rd	41	A3 25
Red Cedar Rd	53	O3 30
Red Creek Cir	47	B3 25
Red Creek Rd	42	Z2 24
Red Rd	54	N3 26
Redcoats La	52	U3 34
Redfield La	43	T2 18
Redwood Rd	56	V3 32
Reeves Bay Tr	41	U2 25
Regents Park Rd	43	X2 19
Registry, The	42	V2 22
Remsen La	39	N2 17
Reynolds Dr	43	S2 17
Ridge Dr	52	U3 33
Ridge La	47	F3 23
Ridge Rd	52	T3 32
Ridge Rd	47	H3 23
Ridgeway Rd	47	C3 25
Ridgewood La	48	C3 22
R O W	52	S3 32
Ring Neck Rd	39	P2 17
Risa Ct	42	V2 23
Riverdale Dr	48	E3 22
Riverhead-B186 Hampton Bays Rd	42	X2 24
Riverhead-Hampton Bays Rd	47	A3 24
Riverhead-Hampton Bays Rd	41	W2 25
Riverhead-Moriches Rd (Lake Av)	41	Q2 24
Riverhead-Quogue Rd	41	S2 25
Riverside Av	41	U2 25
Riverview Dr	39	P2 17
Road B	54	L3 21
Road L La	48	D3 19
Roberta Ct	48	F3 22
Robertson Dr	52	U3 34
Robertson La	48	D3 21
Robin Dr	57	V3 28
Robin Hood La	53	L3 26
Robins La	53	N3 28
Robins Nest Rd	41	Z2 25
Robinson Rd	54	N3 26
Roger St	56	W3 32
Rogers Av	43	T2 19
Rogers Av Ext	43	T2 19
Rogers Ct	52	S3 32
Rogers La	39	O2 17
Rogers St	54	P3 23
Rogusa La	43	W2 17
Rolling Hill Ct	53	P3 30
Rolling Hill Ct E	52	U3 31
Rolling Hill Rd	48	A3 21
Rolling Woods La	47	C3 23
Roman Rd	54	N3 25
Romana Dr	48	B3 21
Roosevelt Av	53	M3 27
Rose Av	53	M3 27
Rose Hill Rd	53	O3 29
Rose Hill Rd	54	S3 26
Rose St	55	W3 33
Rose Wy	57	V3 25
Rosebud La	43	W2 20
Roseeriar La	42	Z2 21
Rosemary La	56	X3 31
Roses Grove Rd	53	O3 29
Rosewood Ct	54	S3 26
Rosewood Dr	52	U3 31
Rosewood La	54	S3 26
Rosko Dr	54	N3 23
Round Pond Rd	56	W3 31
Rowland Ct	48	E3 21
Royal Av	41	W2 25
Royal Av N	41	W2 26
Rugby Rd	43	Y2 19
Ruggs Pa	52	S3 32
Russell Rd	48	C3 22
Ruth Pl	47	F3 24
Rutyne Cir	47	D3 23
Sachem La	42	W2 21
Sag Harbor Tpke	56	V3 31
Sagamore Rd	47	F3 23
Sagaponack Main St	57	X3 26
Sage St	56	W3 32
Sagg Rd	57	W3 27
Sagg Rd	56	X3 30
St Andrews Rd	47	J3 24
St Andrews Rd	47	L3 24
St Jhones Rd	47	D3 22
St Jhons Rd	48	D3 22
Saltmeadow La	52	U3 35
Sams Creek Rd	57	V3 25
Sandalwood Ct	48	C3 22
Sanderling La	42	Z2 20
Sandgate La	47	H3 24
Sandpiper Ct	43	Q2 17
Sandpiper La	57	V3 25
Sandringham La	47	J3 23
Sandune Ct	57	X3 26
Sandy Ct	48	D3 21
Sandy Hollow Rd	54	N3 25
Sandy's La	38	O2 18
Sanford Pl	54	O3 24
Sawasett Av	57	V3 28
Sayres Pa	56	Z3 28
Scallop Pond Rd	53	L3 27
Schaefer La	43	X2 17
School La	43	T2 17
School St	57	V3 27
School St	48	D3 22
School St (WP)	43	T2 18
Schooner La	48	F3 22
Schwenks Rd	54	P3 25
Scotch Mist La	47	J3 23
Scotline Dr	57	Y3 28
Scott Rd	53	L3 26
Scotts Landing Rd	53	N3 29
Scrimshaw Dr	53	P3 30
Scrub Oak Rd	43	W2 19
Scuttle Hole Rd	53	S3 26
Scuttle Hole Rd	56	U3 29
Sea Crest Dr	47	F3 24
Sea Farm La	56	V3 29
Sea Field Point	43	U2 17
Sea Gull Hill Rd	52	U3 34
Seabreeze Av	43	R2 18
Seafield La	43	U2 17
Seagate Av	43	R2 18
Seaponack Dr	52	T3 35
Seascape La	57	W3 26
Seascape La (QG)	43	V2 18
Seashell La	47	D3 23
Seashore Av	42	Z2 21
Seaside Av	48	B3 22
Seatuck	39	N2 17
Seaweed Rd	53	N3 28
Sebonac Inlet Rd	54	K3 26
Sebonac Inlet Rd	54	L3 25
Sebonac Rd	54	L3 25
Second Neck La	43	X2 18
Seely La	52	U3 34
Seletine Wy	57	V3 28
Selfridge St	43	R2 19
Seneca Dr	47	F3 23
Settlers La	54	P3 24
Seven Ponds Rd	54	P3 25
Seven Ponds-Town Rd	53	P3 27
Shady Cove La	52	T3 31
Shadyrest Dr	52	P3 31
Shagbark La	38	P2 18
Shell Rd	48	C3 22
Shelter Island Av	52	V3 35
Sheppard St	43	U2 17
Sheridan Rd	47	B3 25
Sherman Av	48	D3 21
Sherwood Rd	53	N3 26
Sherwood Rd	48	B3 21
Shinnecock Av	42	Z2 21
Shinnecock Hills Rd	47	J3 24
Shinnecock La	48	C3 22
Shinnecock Pl	47	E3 24
Shinnecock Rd (SV)	54	M3 21
Shinnecock Rd	42	A3 20
Shinnecock Rd (QG)	43	X2 18
Shinnecock Rd	48	E3 21
Shore Av	41	U2 26
Shore Dr	53	M3 26
Shore Dr	53	O3 29
Shore La	43	Q2 17
Shore Rd	53	M3 27
Shore Rd	48	C3 22
Shore Rd (WB)	43	S2 17
Shore Rd	41	Z2 25
Short Beach Av	52	U3 34
Short Beach Rd	52	U3 33
Short Pa	43	S2 17
Shrubland Rd	47	J3 24
Silver Bk Dr	41	U2 25
Silver La	57	V3 26
Sims Av	52	U3 32
Skinner St	54	O3 24
Skyes Neck Ct	42	Z2 21
Smith St	41	U2 26
Snake Hollow Rd	57	U3 28
Snog Harbor La	43	S2 17
Somerset Av	54	M3 23
Southampton Hills Ct	53	P3 29
South Bay Av	38	N2 18
South Beach Rd	47	H3 23
South Country Rd	38	N2 18
South Country Rd	38	P2 17
South Country Rd	43	U2 18
South Crestview Dr	38	P2 17
South Dr	52	U3 35
South Ferry Rd	55	U3 36
South Harbor Dr	52	V3 34
South Hill St	54	M3 23
South Main St	54	O3 23
South Oak Dr	47	D3 23
South Old Country Rd	38	P2 19
South Old Country Rd	43	Q2 17
South Peninsula Dr	47	C3 24
South Redwood Rd	52	U3 32
South Rd	43	R2 18
South St	53	L3 28
South St (SV)	54	O3 24
South Valley Rd	52	T3 32
South Valley Rd	47	F3 23
Southway Dr	47	H3 23
Southwind	39	N2 17
Southwood La	43	V2 19
Speonk Shore Rd	39	P2 16
Speonk-Riverhead Rd	38	P2 19
Spinnaker Wy	53	N3 27
Spinny Rd	42	X2 21
Spinny Rd N	42	X2 23
Spring La	52	T3 32
Spring Pond La	47	J3 25
Spring St	56	W3 32
Springville Rd	48	C3 22
Spruce La	48	B3 22
Spruce St	42	Z2 21
Spruce St	48	B3 22
Squabble La	54	Q3 23
Squires Av	42	Z2 21
Squires Blvd	47	C3 24
Squires East Landing Rd	47	D3 25
Squire's La	48	E3 21
Squires Pond Rd	47	C3 25
Squires West Landing Rd	47	C3 25
Squiretown Rd	47	C3 24
Stacy Dr	43	S2 16
Stafford Ct	52	U3 31
Staller Blvd	48	D3 22
Staller Dr	42	V2 22
Stanley's Wy	54	N3 25
Starfish La	48	D3 21
State Hwy 24	47	B3 23
State Hwy 24	41	Q2 25
State Hwy 24	41	W2 25
State Hwy 27	54	Q3 24
State Hwy 27	47	B3 23
State Hwy 27	47	F3 24
State Hwy 27	38	Q2 21
State Hwy 27	57	U3 27
State Hwy 27	42	W2 22
State Hwy 114	52	V3 34
State St	48	D3 21
Station Rd	54	R3 25
Station Rd	43	S2 18
Station Rd	43	W2 19
Stephen Halsey Pa	54	R3 24
Stern Av	41	T2 25
Stevens La	43	T2 17
Stewart Av	43	S2 20
Stillwater La	43	S2 17
Stock Farm La	52	U3 35
Stokes La	38	O2 16
Stone La	43	X2 19
Stonewood La	47	D3 23
Stony Ct	48	C3 22
Stony Hill Rd	52	T3 32
Stony Well Ct	48	D3 22
Stoveboat Rd	53	P3 30
Straight Pa	53	M3 27
Strathmore Ct	38	P2 18
Strongs La	53	S3 27
Stuart Ct	47	D3 23
Studio La	54	L3 23
Suffolk Av	41	U2 25
Suffolk Av	43	X2 19
Suffolk Rd	48	C3 22
Suffolk St	56	W3 32
Sugar Loaf Rd	47	H3 23
Summerfield La	57	U3 25
Summit Blvd	43	R2 18
Sun Valley Rd	48	E3 22
Sunninghill Rd	53	P3 28
Sunrise Av	57	V3 28
Sunrise Hwy	48	A3 23
Sunrise Hwy	38	K2 19
Sunrise Hwy	42	R2 21
Sunrise Hwy	42	X2 22
Sunrise Hwy Ext	47	C3 23
Sunrise Hwy Ext	47	F3 24
Sunset Av (WB)	43	T2 18
Sunset Av	43	Y2 19
Sunset Av	47	E3 24
Sunset Beach Av	55	U3 34
Sunset Dr	52	U3 33
Sunset La	43	T2 18
Sunset Ridge	47	F3 24
Sunset Rd	52	U3 34
Sunswick La	43	U2 17
Surf St	48	C3 22
Surfside Dr	57	V3 25
Susan St	56	W3 32
Swamp Rd	54	L3 22
Swans Neck La	53	T3 26
Sweet Briar Rd	47	J3 23
Sweetgrass Rd	43	Q2 17
Sylvan Av	41	W2 25
Sylvan Av N	41	W2 26
Sylvan La	52	T3 31
Sylvan Pl	42	W2 20
Tall Oak La	38	P2 18
Tall Oak La	43	W2 18
Tamarack Ct	42	Z2 21
Tamarack La	42	Z2 21
Tanager La	53	Q3 28
Tanners Neck Rd	43	Q2 17
Tansey La	56	W3 29
Tarpon Rd	42	A3 20
Temple Av	41	W2 25
Temple Av N	41	W2 25
Tepee St	47	F3 23
Terrace Dr	54	L3 24
Terrace La	48	C3 22
Terrace Rd	48	B3 22
Terry Ct	54	O3 23
Thistle Patch La	52	U3 34
Tiana Cir	48	C3 21
Tiffany Wy	53	T3 28
Tony Tiska's Pa	53	S3 29
Topping Dr	41	R2 25
Toppings Field Ct	57	V3 27
Toppings Pa	56	W3 30
Towd Point Rd	53	M3 28
Town Line Rd	56	X3 31
Townsend Av	41	V2 25
Toylsome La	54	O3 23
Toylsome Pl	54	P3 23
Tracy Dr	52	U3 34
Trail Ct	53	P3 28
Trail Rd	48	E3 22
Trail, The	47	D3 24
Tramposch La	48	E3 22
Treadwell Rd	52	R3 32
Tree Haven La	41	V2 25
Trees La	57	X3 26
Trelawney La	57	V3 27
Triton La	48	B3 18
Trout La	54	N3 26
Trout Pond Rd	52	S3 32
Truman La	42	Z2 20
Trynz La	48	E3 21
Tuckahoe La	54	L3 24
Tuckahoe Rd	47	K3 23
Tulip Av	48	E3 22
Tunnell Ter	47	B3 25
Turtle Cove Dr	53	N3 28
Turtle La	43	X2 18
Turtle Pond Rd	53	O3 29
Tuthill La	39	O2 17
Tuttle Av	38	N2 19
Tuttle Pl	43	T2 17
Twin View Dr	53	N3 29
Tyler St	41	U2 25
Tyndall Rd	52	U3 34
Uncle Leo's Pa	53	S3 27
Underhill Dr	47	K3 24
Union St	48	D3 22
Union St (SH)	56	W3 32
Upland Dr	47	J3 23
Upper Red Creek Rd	41	Z2 25
Upper Seven Ponds Rd	54	Q3 25
Vail Av	41	S2 26
Vail Av	42	Y2 20
Vail Ct	43	S2 20
Valley Rd	52	T3 32
Valorie Rd	54	N3 25
Van Brunt St	54	O3 24
Van Houten St	41	S2 25
Victoria Rd	47	F3 23
Viking La	42	V2 22
Village La	54	P3 24
Village La	43	W2 18
Vine St	48	B3 22
Vitali Cilli Av	56	V3 32
Wainscott Harbor Rd	56	Y3 29
Wakefield Rd	47	C3 24
Wakeman Ct	48	E3 22
Wakeman Rd	48	E3 21
Walker Av	43	Y2 20
Walker Ct	43	Y2 20
Wall St	54	O3 23
Walnut Av	43	Y2 20
Walnut St	52	S3 32
Walnut St (SV)	54	O3 23
Ward's Pa	47	D3 24
Warfield Wy	53	O3 28
Warner Rd	47	D3 23
Warren St	54	O3 24
Wash Dr	48	C3 22
Wash St	55	W3 33
Washington Av	48	D3 21
Washington Dr	42	A3 21
Washington Heights Av	47	D3 24
Washington Heights Sq	47	D3 23
Washington Rd	47	F3 24
Water Mill-Towd Rd	53	O3 28
Wateredge Rd	53	N3 28
Watermill Heights	53	P3 27
Watersedge Ct	43	T2 17
Watersedge Dr	43	W2 17
Wauhope Rd	48	E3 22
Wayne Ct	43	S2 18
Wedgewood Rd	42	Y2 20
Weesuck Av	42	Y2 20
Weidner La	53	P3 29
Wells La	48	D3 21
Werewolf Pa	53	Q3 29
West Beach Dr	53	N3 29
West Dr	52	U3 35
West End Av	43	Y2 20
West Gate Rd	54	L3 23
West Harbor Dr	55	V3 34
West Henry St	56	V3 32
West La	43	U2 19
West La	41	V2 25
West Main St	54	O3 23
West Neck Cir	47	K3 26
West Neck La	47	K3 25
West Neck Point Rd	47	K3 26
West Neck Rd	54	L3 26
West Prospect St	54	N3 24
West Side Av	43	X2 20
West St	53	L3 28
West Tiana Rd	48	A3 21
West Trail Rd	53	P3 29
West Water St	56	V3 33
Westbridge Rd	43	T2 16
Westbury Rd	48	E3 21
Westerly Ct	48	E3 22
Westerly Rd	47	C3 24
Westminster Rd	54	T3 26
Westway Dr	47	H3 23
Westwood La	52	T3 32
Wetzel Ct	39	O2 17
Whalebone Landing Rd	53	P3 30
Whalers Dr	56	W3 31
Whalers Wk	52	U3 33
Wharf St	55	W3 33
Wheaton Wy	54	T3 25
Whippoorwill Ct	42	V2 20
Whippoorwill La	42	V2 21
Whispering Fields	53	R3 27
White Birch La	38	P2 17
White Birch Tr	42	A3 21
White Bk Dr	41	T2 25
White La	48	E3 21
White Oak La	54	L3 25
White Oak La	43	S2 17
White St (SV)	54	N3 24
White St (SH)	56	W3 32
Whites La	54	L3 25
Whitewood Ct	42	A3 21
Whitfield Rd	54	O3 25
Whiting Rd	42	A3 20
Whitney Rd	52	U3 32
Wickapogue Rd	54	P3 23
Wickatuck Dr	52	T3 32
Wickatuck La	52	T3 31
Widgeon La	56	X3 31
Widgeon La	42	Z2 20
Widgeon Wy	39	Q2 15
Widgeon Wy	39	M2 14
Widow Coopers Pa	52	U3 35
Widow Gavitts Rd	56	W3 30
Wild Cherry La	42	A3 21
Wild Duck La	41	Z2 25
Wild Goose La	53	U3 26
Wildcherry La	52	U3 34
Wildwood La	47	F3 23
Wildwood La (QG)	43	V2 18
Wildwood Pa	42	Q2 24
Wildwood Path Tr	37	Q2 24
Wildwood Rd	52	Q3 31
Wildwood Tr	37	Q2 24
Wilkes La	57	Y3 27
William Pl	54	P3 24
William St	47	E3 23
William St	56	W3 32
Williams Wy	57	W3 27
Williams Wy	54	N3 24
Willis St	54	O3 24
Williz Valley Rd	53	P3 28
Willow Dr	42	Z2 21
Willow La	43	W2 18
Willowood Ct	O2	38 18
Willow Rd	54	S3 26
Willow Shade La	48	A3 21
Willow St	54	O3 24
Wilson Av	48	C3 21
Wilson Rd	53	P3 30
Wiltshire St	54	O3 24
Wind Mill La	47	F3 24
Windemere Cl	48	D3 21
Windermere Dr	52	U3 33
Winding Wy	54	Q3 25
Windmill La	53	T3 27

Index

Suffolk Co.

Town of Southampton / Town of Southold / Places

STREET MAP GRID

Windmill La 54 O3 23
Windward Wy 54 N3 24
Windwood Ct 38 Q2 18
Winnebogue La 43 V2 18
Wintergreen La 38 Q2 18
Wintergreen Wy La 43 W2 18
Wipperwill La 48 A3 21
Wireless Wy 53 O3 26
Wisteria Dr 38 O2 18
Wolf Swamp La 53 L3 26
Wood Edge Ct 53 P3 26
Wood Rd Tr 41 U2 25
Wood Thrush La 53 Q3 28
Wood View La 47 B3 25
Woodbine Pl 53 N3 26
Woodbridge Av 43 U2 18
Woodcock La 39 P2 17
Wooded La 47 B3 24
Woodedge Tr 43 W2 19
Woodfield Av 42 A3 20
Woodhollow Dr 38 O2 18
Woodhull Av 41 R2 25
Woodland Av 43 T2 18
Woodland Ct 53 O3 29
Woodland Dr 57 V3 28
Woodland Dr 53 P3 29
Woodland Dr 41 R2 25
Woodland La 43 X2 19
Woodland Rd 55 V3 35
Woodland Wy 43 W2 19
Woodleigh Pl 42 W2 20
Woodridge Rd 48 E3 22
Woodruff La 56 W3 29
Woods La 53 N3 27
Woodvale St 52 U3 31
Woodview Rd 42 Z2 20
Woody Ct 53 P3 28
Wooley St 54 P3 24
Wooleys Dr 53 O3 28
Worchester Ct 56 W3 29
Wyandanch La 54 P3 23
Yale Dr 48 E3 22
Yale Rd 56 V3 32
1st St 52 U3 33
2nd St 52 U3 33
3rd St (NH) 52 U3 33
3rd St 53 N3 28
5th Av 38 P2 19

SOUTHOLD

Aborn La 45 K3 32
Ackerly Pond La 44 K3 37
Adams St 50 R3 41
Airway Dr 46 D3 32
Albacore Dr 44 O3 39
Albertson La 50 N3 40
Albo Dr 46 B3 31
Aldrich La 40 Y2 31
Aldrich La Ext 40 Y2 32
Alois La 46 C3 31
Anchor La 44 N3 36
Anderson Dr 44 K3 39
Angler's La 50 R3 41
Ann Wy 44 L3 38
Ann's Wy 44 L3 38
Apartment La 50 Q3 42
Apple Ct 44 L3 37
Aquaview Dr 50 R3 44
Arrow La 44 E3 35
Arshamomaque Av 44 N3 38
Atlantic Av 50 Q3 42
August La 51 P3 39
Back La 49 V3 44
Bailey Av 50 Q3 42
Barley La 44 L3 38
Bartley Ct 46 C3 31
Basin Rd 44 O3 36
Bay Av 50 R3 41
Bay Av 50 S3 43
Bay Av 46 C3 31
Bay Haven La 44 M3 35
Bay Home Rd 44 N3 38
Bay Rd 50 R3 41
Bay Shore Rd 51 P3 39
Bayberry La 50 N3 40
Bayberry Rd 44 L3 36
Bayberry Rd 45 K3 32
Bayview Av 44 N3 39
Bayview Av 40 A3 33
Bayview Dr 50 S3 42
Bayview Rd 44 M3 36
Baywater Av 44 K3 36
Beach Ct 50 S3 42
Beachwood La 44 M3 36
Beachwood Rd 46 E3 32
Beckwith Av 44 L3 38
Beech La 49 X3 45
Bennet Rd 50 Q3 41
Bennet Rd Ext 50 Q3 41
Bennett La 44 L3 37
Bergen Av 40 Z2 32
Big Pond La 40 W2 31
Bight Rd 49 Y3 45
Birch Av 44 M3 36
Birch Dr 46 B3 30
Birch Dr S 46 B3 30
Birch Rd 44 J3 38
Birdseye Rd 49 U3 44
Blossom La 44 L3 37
Blue Marlin Dr 44 O3 39
Boisseau Av 44 L3 39
Booth Pl 50 Q3 41
Booth Rd 44 K3 39
Bow Rd 44 L3 35
Bray Av 46 B3 31
Breaknock Rd 44 K3 36
Break Water Rd 40 A3 33
Breistadt Ct 44 L3 37
Briar Pl 44 O3 36
Bridge La 44 F3 36
Bridge La 45 K3 32
Bridge St 50 Q3 41
Brigantine Dr 44 N3 36
Broad St 50 Q3 42
Brown St 50 Q3 40
Browns Hill Rd 49 W3 45
Budd Pond Rd 44 N3 38
Bungalow La 46 D3 32
Burgundy Ct 44 L3 39
Burtis Pl 44 H3 37
Byrnes La 50 R3 41
Caleb Wy 50 P3 41
Calves Neck Rd 44 M3 37
Camp Mineola E Ext 46 D3 31
Camp Mineola Rd 46 C3 32
Captain Kidd Dr 40 Z2 33
Cardinal La 50 Q3 42
Carole Rd 50 M3 40
Carpenter Rd 45 K3 33
Carpenter St 50 R3 41
Carroll Av 44 J3 36
Case St 50 R3 41
Cedar Beach 44 O3 35
Cedar Birch La 49 A4 44
Cedar Dr 44 Q3 36
Cedar Dr 50 S3 43
Cedar La 50 S3 42
Cedar Point Dr E 44 O3 35
Cedar Point Dr W 44 N3 35
Cedar Point Rd 44 O3 35
Cedarfields Dr 50 P3 41
Cemetery Rd 50 S3 43
Center St 46 D3 31
Center St (GR) 50 Q3 41
Central Av 50 R3 41
Central Dr 40 Z2 33
Chablis Pa 44 L3 39
Champlain Pl 50 Q3 42
Chapel La 50 O3 40
Chardonnay Dr 44 L3 39
Chestnut Rd 44 J3 38
Christopher St 44 M3 37
Circle Dr 50 R3 44
Clark Rd 44 M3 39
Clark St 50 Q3 40
Clear View Rd 44 O3 35
Clearview Av 44 L3 37
Clearview Av W 44 L3 36
Clearwater La 45 K3 32
Cleaves Point Rd 50 S3 42
Clipper Dr 44 N3 36
Colonial Rd 44 M3 36
Colony Rd 44 N3 39
Columbia Rd 52 M3 36
Condor Ct 40 A3 29
Corey Creek La 45 L3 36
Corey Creek Rd 52 M3 36
Corwin La 44 L3 37
Corwin St 50 Q3 40
Cottage Pl 44 M3 38
County Route 48 44 F3 35
County Route 48 44 K3 38
County Route 48 46 B3 32
County Route 48 50 N3 40
County Route 48 50 P3 41
County Route 48 40 Y2 31
County Route 84 40 A3 32
Cox La 44 E3 35
Cox Neck Rd 46 A3 32
Cres Wy 46 A3 31
Cres, The 50 R3 43
Crescent Wy 40 A3 31
Crittens La 44 M3 37
Cross Wy, The 50 R3 43
Custer Av 44 L3 37
Daisy Rd 40 Z2 33
Daly La 44 M3 38
Dawn Dr 50 R3 42
Dayton Rd 44 N3 37
Dean Dr 46 F3 32
Deep Hole Dr 46 E3 32
Delmar Dr 46 A3 30
Delmar Dr W 46 A3 30
Demarest Rd 49 X3 45
Depot La 44 E3 35
Diachun Rd 46 A3 29
Diamond La 44 H3 37
Dickerson St 44 G3 37
Diederichs Rd 49 W3 44
Digman's Rd 44 E3 35
Dogwood La 44 J3 38
Dogwood La 50 S3 42
Dogwood La 40 Z2 33
Dolphin Dr 44 O3 39
Donna Dr 46 E3 32
Douglas Rd 49 W3 43
Dune Dr 40 W2 32
Dylan's Ter 44 E3 35
Eagle Nest Ct 40 A3 29
East De Bexeidon Rd 44 N3 38
East Gillette Dr 50 S3 42
East La 50 T3 42
East Legion Av 46 C3 31
East Rd 40 A3 33
Ed's Rd 44 M3 36
Edwards La 49 W3 45
Egret La 50 Q3 42
Elizabeth La 44 L3 36
Emerson Rd 45 K3 35
Emma Dr 40 A3 30
Esplanade, The 55 V3 35
Factory Av 46 B3 32
Farmveu Rd 40 Z2 31
Fassbender Av 44 H3 36
Fiddler La 50 R3 42
Fire Rd 3 50 R3 44
Fletcher St 50 V3 43
Flint St 50 Q3 40
Fords Rd 44 L3 36
Founders La 44 L3 38
Founders Pa 44 M3 38
Four Winds Ct 44 N3 25
Franklin Av 50 P3 40
Front St 50 Q3 41
Frost Rd 44 N3 38
Gagen's Landing Rd 44 M3 37
Garden Ct 44 L3 37
Gardiners La 44 L3 37
Gilbert St 44 L3 37
Gillette Dr 50 S3 42
Gin La 44 M3 35
Gina St 46 A3 30
Glenn Rd 44 L3 36
Glover St 44 K3 37
Goldin Av 44 M3 39
Goose Creek La 44 M3 36
Grandview Dr 49 X3 45
Grange Rd 44 K3 36
Great Peconic Bay Blvd 46 A3 29
Greenfield La 44 K3 38
Greenhill La 50 P3 42
Greenway Rd E 49 Z3 45
Greenway Rd W 49 Z3 45
Greenway, The 50 R3 43
Grigonis Pa 44 L3 37
Grissom La 44 L3 36
Griswold St 44 L3 37
Grove Dr 44 O3 36
Grove Rd 44 M3 39
Gull Pond La 50 R3 42
Hallock La 40 Y2 32
Halls Creek Dr 46 E3 32
Halyoke Av 49 W3 44
Harbor Lights Dr 44 N3 37
Harbor River Rd 49 V3 44
Harbor Rd 49 W3 43
Harper Rd 44 M3 37
Harper Rd W 44 L3 37
Harvest La 40 Z2 31
Heather Pl 46 A3 29
Henry's La 44 H3 36
Herwin Blvd 44 O3 39
Hiawatha's Pa 44 L3 36
Hickory Av 44 M3 36
Hickory Rd 44 J3 38
Highwood Rd 44 M3 36
Hillcrest Dr 49 X3 45
Hillcrest Dr N 49 X3 45
Hill Rd W 44 L3 37
Hilltop Pa 44 J3 39
Hippodrome Dr 44 N3 38
Hobart Rd 44 M3 38
Hobson Dr 46 B3 31
Hoey La 44 M3 38
Homestead Wy 50 P3 41
Hope La 44 J3 37
Horton Av 46 B3 32
Horton La 44 K3 39
Howard Av 40 A3 32
Huckleberry Hill Rd 49 T3 42
Hummel Av 44 L3 38
Huntington Blvd 44 G3 37
Hyatt Rd E 44 K3 39
Hyatt Rd N 44 K3 39
Hyatt Rd W 44 K3 39
Illinois Av 40 A3 32
Indian Neck La 44 J3 35
Indian Neck Rd 44 J3 35
Inlet Dr 40 Z2 33
Inlet La 50 R3 41
Inlet Pond Rd 50 P3 42
Inlet Wy 52 O3 35
Island View La 51 P3 39
Jackson Landing Rd 40 A3 32
Jackson St 46 G3 32
Jacobs La 44 N3 36
Jasmine La 44 K3 37
Jennings Rd 44 K3 39
Jernick La 44 L3 37
Jockey Creek Dr 44 L3 37
Johns Rd 46 C3 31
Johnson Ct 50 Q3 41
Johnson Pl 50 Q3 40
Joseph St 46 A3 30
Kaplan Av 50 Q3 41
Kayleigh's Ct 50 S3 43
Kenney's Rd 44 J3 38
Kerwin Blvd 50 O3 39
Kimberly La 44 M3 37
Kimogener Point Rd 46 G3 32
Kingfisher La 50 Q3 42
King St 49 V3 43
Kirkup La 40 Z2 31
Knapp Pl 50 Q3 42
Knoll Cir 50 S3 42
Korn Rd 44 M3 38
Kraus Rd 46 C3 31
Lake Ct 44 J3 38
Lake Dr 44 J3 38
Lake Dr 44 O3 36
Lake Wy 46 A3 31
Lakeside Dr N 44 O3 35
Lakeside Dr S 44 O3 35
Lakeview Av 44 G3 36
Lakeview Ter 50 T3 43
Landing La 50 R3 41
Landing Pa 44 L3 36
Landon La 44 M3 37
Lands End Rd 49 A4 45
Larson La 44 H3 37
Latham La 49 A4 45
Laurel Av 44 M3 39
Laurel Bay La 46 A3 29
Laurel Lake Dr 46 A3 31
Laurel Wy 46 A3 31
Laurelwood Dr 46 A3 29
Leeton Dr 44 J3 38
Leeward Dr 44 N3 36
Legion Av 46 B3 32
Leon Rd 44 M3 39
Leslie's Rd 44 J3 35
L'Homme Dieu 44 M3 38
Liberty La 44 M3 36
Lighthouse La 44 M3 37
Lighthouse Rd 44 K3 39
Linda Rd 40 Z2 33
Linnet St 50 Q3 40
Lipco Rd 46 B3 32
Lisa Dr 44 M3 38
Little Peconic Bay La 44 N3 35
Little Peconic Bay Rd 45 K3 33
Locust Av 44 M3 38
Locust Ct 50 S3 42
Long Boat La 49 Y3 45
Long Creek Dr 44 M3 39
Long Wy, The 50 R3 43
Longview La 44 N3 35
Lower Rd 44 K3 37
Ludlum Pl 50 R3 41
Lupton Point Rd 46 D3 32
Luthers (Breakwater) Rd 40 A3 34
Madison Av 50 Q3 41
Madison St 50 Q3 41
Maidstone La 40 W2 31
Maier Pl 44 M3 38
Mailler Ct 44 L3 37
Main Bayview Rd 44 L3 36
Main Rd 46 B3 31
Main Rd 49 S3 42
Main Rd 49 U3 43
Main Rd 49 X3 45
Main Rd (gw) 50 P3 40
Main Rd 50 R3 42
Main St 44 M3 37
Major Pond Rd 49 W3 43
Majors Pa 44 K3 39
Mallard La 50 Q3 42
Manhasset Av 50 R3 42
Manor Pl (GR) 50 Q3 41
Manor Pl 50 S3 42
Maple Av 44 K3 36
Maple La 44 M3 38
Maple La 49 U3 44
Maple La 50 R3 42
Maple Pl 50 S3 43
Maple Rd 44 K3 38
Maple St 50 Q3 41
Marine Pl 50 R3 42
Marion La 50 S3 43
Marion Pl 50 S3 43
Mark La 46 B3 32
Marlene La 46 B3 31
Marratooka Rd 46 D3 32
Masters Rd 46 B3 30
Mathews La 44 E3 35
McCann La 50 P3 42
McDonald Crossing 46 B3 29
McDonald Rd 46 B3 29
Meadow Beach La 46 E3 32
Meadow La 44 M3 39
Meadow La 50 R3 41
Mechanic St 44 L3 38
Mechanic St E 44 L3 38
Meday Av 40 A3 32
Mesrobian Dr 46 A3 29
Miami Av 44 H3 36
Middle Rd 44 G3 35
Middle Rd 44 J3 37
Middle Rd 44 L3 38
Middle Rd 46 B3 32
Middletown Rd 50 Q3 41
Midfarm Rd 44 M3 37
Midland Pkwy 44 M3 38
Midland Pl 50 S3 42
Midway Ct 44 M3 35
Midway Rd 52 N3 35
Mill Creek Dr 44 M3 39
Mill Rd 44 H3 36
Miller Rd 40 A3 32
Minnehaha Blvd 44 L3 36
Miriam Rd 40 A3 33
Mockingbird La 44 M3 38
Monsell Pl 50 Q3 41
Moores La N 50 P3 41
Mt Beulah Av 44 L3 39
Mulford Ct 49 X3 45
Munn La 49 U3 44
Nakomis Rd 44 L3 36
Nassau Point Rd 46 L3 32
Nassau Point Rd 45 K3 34
Naugles Rd 40 A3 33
Navy St 49 V3 43
Nelson Dr 49 V3 43
New Suffolk Av 46 C3 32
New Suffolk Rd 46 G3 32
Nickles La 44 M3 38
North Bayview Rd 44 M3 37
North La 50 S3 42
North Oakwood Dr 46 A3 29
North Parish Dr 46 B3 31
North Riley Av 46 C3 31
North Rd 44 L3 39
North Rd 44 K3 37
North Rd 44 M3 39
North Rd to Bayview 44 M3 37
North Sea Dr 44 J3 38
North Sea Dr 49 Z3 45
North St 50 Q3 41
North View Dr 49 W3 45
Northfield Rd 44 N3 36
Oak Av 44 M3 36
Oak Ct 50 S3 43
Oak Dr 44 N3 36
Oak Pl 46 B3 31
Oak St 46 B3 32
Oak St (GR) 50 Q3 41
Oaklawn Av 44 L3 37
Oakwood Dr 44 M3 37
Oakwood Dr 44 O3 35
Oakwood Rd 44 J3 38
Old Cove Rd 50 M3 40
Old Farm Rd 49 W3 43
Old Jule La 46 C3 32
Old Main Rd 44 N3 39
Old Main Rd 46 B3 31
Old Main Rd 49 X3 45
Old Main Rd 49 Y3 45
Old Main Rd (gw) 50 P3 40
Old Main Rd 40 Z2 30
Old Menhaden Rd 45 K3 33
Old Orchard La 49 S3 42
Old Salt Rd 46 C3 31
Old Shipyard La 44 M3 38
Oldfield Ct 40 Z2 31
Opechee Av 44 L3 35
Orchard La 52 O3 35
Orchard Rd 44 M3 38
Orchard St 49 W3 44
Oregon Rd 44 E3 35
Orient State Pkwy 49 Y3 43
Oriole Dr 44 M3 38
Oriole La 50 Q3 42
Osprey Nest Rd 50 S3 42
Osprey La 50 Q3 42
Osprey Rd 50 R3 42
Osseo Av 44 L3 35
Owaissa Av 44 L3 35
Oyster Pond La 49 V3 44
Pacific St 46 C3 32
Paradise Point Rd 44 O3 35
Paradise Shore Rd 44 N3 36
Park Av 44 N3 39
Park Av 46 D3 31
Park St 50 R3 41
Park View La 49 Z3 45
Park Wy 44 M3 37
Parkers Landing Rd 45 K3 35
Parkview Dr 49 Z3 45
Parsons Blvd 50 S3 42
Pasture La 46 E3 32
Pauls La 44 H3 36
Peck Pl 44 L3 37
Peconic La 44 J3 36
Penn Av 40 A3 32
Pete Hill Rd 49 V3 44
Peters Neck Rd 49 W3 43
Petty Rd 44 L3 37
Petty's Dr 49 Y3 45
Pheasant Pl 51 P3 39
Pine Av 44 M3 36
Pine Neck Rd 44 L3 37
Pine Pl 50 S3 42
Pine Rd 44 J3 38
Pine St 46 B3 32
Pine Ter 50 S3 43
Pipes Neck Rd 50 O3 40
Platt Rd 49 W3 44
Pleasant Pl 44 M3 35
Plum Island La 49 Z3 45
Point Rd 49 A4 45
Point Rd 51 P3 36
Pond Av 44 M3 38
Private Rd #1 49 S3 44
Private Rd #2 50 S3 43
Queen St 50 P3 41
Rabbit La 50 T3 42
Racketts Ct 49 V3 44
RR Dr 40 A3 30
Rambler Rd 44 N3 35
Reeve Av 46 C3 31
Reydon Dr 44 N3 36
Rhoda Rd 40 Z2 33
Richard St 46 E3 32
Richmond Rd 44 M3 39
Richmond Rd E 44 M3 39
Riley Av 46 C3 31
Robin Rd 49 X3 44
Robinson La 45 K3 35
Robinson Rd 44 O3 36
Robinson Rd 50 R3 42
Rochelle Pl 46 C3 31
Rocky Point Rd 50 R3 43
Rogers Rd 44 M3 38
Rose La 40 A3 33
Rosewood Dr 40 A3 32
Rowe Dr 49 W3 43
Roxanne Rd 44 M3 37
Ruth Rd 40 Z2 33
Ryder Farm La 49 Z3 45
Sage Rd 44 O3 39
Sage Spur 51 P3 39
Sailor La 45 K3 32
Sailor Needle 46 C3 31
Salt Marsh La 44 G3 37
Sandpiper La 50 Q3 42
Sandy Beach Point Rd 50 R3 41
Sandy Beach Rd 50 R3 41
Schooner Dr 44 N3 36
Seawood Dr 44 N3 36
Selah La 40 A3 33
Shepard Dr 44 L3 36
Ship's Dr 44 N3 36
Shipyard La 50 S3 42
Shirley Rd 46 B3 32
Shore Dr 50 P3 40
Short La, The 50 R3 43
Sigsbee Rd 46 B3 31
Silvermere Rd 50 P3 40
Skippers La 49 V3 44
Sleepy Hollow La 44 L3 36
Smith Dr N 44 L3 36
Smith Dr S 44 L3 36
Snug Harbor Rd 49 R3 42
Sound Av 44 G3 37
Sound Av 46 B3 31
Sound Beach Dr 40 Z2 33
Sound Dr 50 P3 42
Sound Rd 54 Q3 42
Sound View Av 44 H3 37
Sound View Av 44 K3 39
Sound View Av 50 M3 39
Sound View Av Ext 44 K3 39
Sound View Rd 49 Y3 45
Sound View Rd 49 Z3 45
South Harbor Dr 44 K3 36
South La 49 T3 42
South Oakwood Dr 46 A3 29
South St 44 L3 37
South St (GR) 50 Q3 41
South View Dr 49 W3 45
Southern Blvd 50 R3 43
Spring La 44 J3 35
Square Rigger La 44 N3 36
Squndview Av W 44 H3 36
Stanley Rd 40 Z2 32
Stars Rd 49 S3 44
Stars Rd W 49 S3 44
State Hwy 25 44 K3 38
State Hwy 25 49 R3 42
State Hwy 25 49 Z3 45
State Hwy 25 (gw) 50 O3 40
State Hwy 25 (GR) 50 R3 41
State Hwy 25 50 T3 43
State Hwy 25 40 A3 30
State Hwy TRK 25 40 Z2 31
State Hwy 25 45 J3 35
State Hwy TRK 25 44 M3 40
State Hwy TRK 25 44 F3 35
State Hwy TRK 25 46 A3 32
State Hwy TRK 25 (gw) 50 P3 41
Sterling Av 50 R3 41
Sterling Forest Rd 44 J3 37
Sterling Pl 50 Q3 42
Sterling St 50 Q3 41
Stevenson Rd 49 U3 44
Stony Shore Dr 50 N3 40
Strand, The 50 R3 43
Stratmors Rd 44 N3 36
Summer La 44 M3 36
Summit Dr 40 Z2 33
Summit Rd 44 M3 36
Sun La 44 L3 36
Sung Harbor Rd 50 R3 42
Sunny La 44 J3 35
Sunnyside Rd 44 L3 38
Sunrise Wy 44 O3 35
Sunset Dr 40 Z2 33
Sunset La 44 N3 35
Sunset La 50 Q3 42
Sunset Pa 44 J3 39
Sunset Wy 52 O3 35
Sutton Pl 50 Q3 42
Sylvan Dr 50 S3 42
Tabor Rd 49 V3 44
Takaposa Rd 44 M3 35
Tall Tree Cir 40 W2 31
Tanager La 50 Q3 42
Tarpon Dr 44 O3 39
Tasker La 50 Q3 42
Teepee Tr 44 L3 35
Terry Ct 44 K3 37
Terry La 44 M3 37
Terry Pl 44 L3 36
Theresa Dr 46 E3 32
Thomas St 44 M3 38
Thomson Blvd 50 Q3 42
Three Waters La 49 A4 45
Topsail La 44 N3 36
Town Creek La 44 L3 38
Town Harbor La 44 M3 38
Town Rd 49 S3 44
Traveler St 44 L3 38
Truman's Pa 50 T3 43
Tuckers La 44 K3 38
Tuthill Rd 44 M3 39
Uhl La 49 Z3 45
Vail Av 44 G3 36
Victoria Dr 44 M3 36
Village La 49 V3 44
Vincent St 49 V3 44
Wabasso St 44 L3 36
Wabun St 44 L3 35
Walnut Av 46 B3 32
Walter Av 50 P3 40
Wampum Wy 44 L3 35
Washington Av 50 Q3 41
Washington Av Ext 50 Q3 41
Water Ter 44 N3 35
Water Wy 40 W2 31
Watersedge Wy 44 M3 35
Waterview Dr 44 L3 36
Webb St 50 Q3 41
Wells Av 44 L3 37
Wells La 51 P3 39
Wells Rd 44 J3 36
Wendy Dr 46 B3 29
West Creek Rd 44 L3 36
West Dr 44 J3 38
West Lake Dr 52 N3 35
West La 44 N3 35
West La 50 S3 42
West Mill Creek Dr 44 M3 39
West Mill Rd 40 A3 32
West Shore Dr 44 N3 36
West St 50 Q3 41
West Wood La 50 P3 42
Westland Rd 44 J3 38
Westphalia Av 40 A3 32
Whalers Rd 49 Y3 44
White Eagle Dr 40 A3 29
Wiggins La 50 R3 42
Wiggins St 50 Q3 40
Wigwam Wy 44 L3 35
Wilburs Pa 40 W2 31
Wild Cherry Wy 50 N3 40
Williams Rd 44 L3 36
Williamsburgh Dr 44 L3 36
Willow Dr 50 S3 43
Willow Point Rd 44 N3 38
Willow Pond La 44 L3 36
Willow St 49 V3 43
Willow Terrace La 49 V3 43
Wills Creek Dr 46 E3 32
Wilmarth Av 50 Q3 41
Windjammer Dr 44 N3 36
Windward Rd 49 Y3 45
Wood End Wy 44 M3 37
Wood La 50 R3 41
Wood La 45 K3 35
Woodside La Ext 40 A3 29
Yennecott Dr 44 M3 38
Youngs Av 44 L3 39
Youngs St 49 V3 44
Zacks La 44 E3 35
Zena Rd 40 Z2 33
1st St 46 B3 30
1st St (nk) 46 H3 32
1st St (GR) 50 Q3 41
2nd Av 44 H3 37
2nd St 46 B3 30
2nd St (nk) 46 H3 32
2nd St (GR) 50 Q3 41
3rd St 46 B3 30
3rd St (nk) 46 H3 32
3rd St (GR) 50 Q3 41
4th Av 50 Q3 41
4th St 46 B3 30
4th St (nk) 46 H3 32
4th St (GR) 50 Q3 41
5th Av 50 Q3 41
5th St 46 B3 30
5th St (nk) 46 G3 32
5th St (GR) 50 Q3 40
6th Av 50 Q3 41
6th St 46 B3 30
6th St (GR) 50 Q3 40
7th St 46 B3 31
7th St (GR) 50 Q3 40
8th St 46 B3 31
8th St (gw) 50 Q3 40
9th St 50 Q3 40
10th St 50 Q3 40

PLACES

Amagansett 60 J4 31
Amity Harbor 5 J 5
Apaquogue 57 D4 28
Aquebogue 41 U2 27
Art Village 54 L3 24
Atlantique 18 B1 4
Babylon 11 O 8
Baiting Hollow 36 L2 29
Barcelona Neck 55 Y3 33
Barnes Hole 60 J4 33
Bay Shore 16 V 10
Bayberry Dunes 30 Q1 8
Bayport 23 L1 12
Bayside Park 5 G 5
Bayview 44 N3 36
Baywood 10 R 12
Beach Hampton 60 M4 30
Belle Terre 19 K1 29
Bellport 29 U1 13
Bixedon 44 N3 38
Big Ram Island 51 W3 39
Blue Point 23 M1 12
Bohemia 22 H1 14
Brentwood 9 V 15
Bridgehampton 57 U3 28
Bright Waters 10 T 11
Calverton 37 K2 25
Canoe Place 47 D3 24
Captain Kidd Estates 40 Z2 33
Cedar Beach 44 N3 35
Center Moriches 34 F2 16
Centereach 21 H1 21
Centerport 2 L 23
Centerville 36 P2 30
Central Islip 15 X 16
Cherry Grove 24 H1 5
Cobb 54 R3 25
Cold Spring Harbor 2 C 22
Commack 8 R 20
Copiague 5 H 7
Coram 26 Q1 22
Coram Hill 27 R1 21
Corneille Estates 18 B1 4
Cow Neck 46 K3 38
Crane Neck 19 D1 29
Davis Park 30 P1 7
Deer Park 10 O 13
Deerfield 53 Q3 28
Dering Harbor 50 S3 40
Devon 60 L4 32
Ditch Plains 62 A5 35
Dix Hills 9 N 18
Dunewood 18 Z 4
East Commack 8 T 20
East Farmingdale 4 G 11
East Half Hollow Hills 9 P 16
East Hampton 60 E4 29
East Hampton Beach 61 Q4 32
East Hampton North 60 E4 30
East Holbrook 22 L1 15
East Islip 16 A1 11
East Marion 50 S3 43
East Moriches 39 J2 17
East Northport 8 P 23
East Patchogue 28 R1 14
East Quogue 42 X2 21
East Setauket 19 H1 28
East Shoreham 31 Z1 29
East Yaphank 33 Z1 20
Eastport 38 M2 19
Eatons Neck 1 J 27
Edgewood 10 S 14
Elwood 8 O 20
Fair Harbor 18 A1 3
Farmingville 21 M1 20
Fire Island Pines 24 K1 6
Fireplace 59 H4 36
Fireplace Neck 34 X1 14
Fishers Island 63 W4 54
Five Corners 21 G1 19
Flanders 42 V2 25
Flowerfield 20 D1 24
Flying Point 54 R3 24
Fort Salonga 7 R 26
Freetown 56 E4 31
Gardiners Island 58 N4 38
Georgica 56 B4 28
Georgica Neck 57 B4 28
Gerard Park 59 J4 36
Gordon Heights 27 R1 22
Grace Estate 55 A4 35
Grassy Hollow 55 B4 34
Great Hog Neck 44 M3 36
Great River 16 C1 10
Greenlawn 2 M 22
Greenport 50 Q3 41
Greenport West 50 O3 40
Hagerman 28 S1 15
Halesite 2 H 23
Half Hollow Hills 10 L 14
Hampton Bays 47 D3 23
Hampton Park 54 O3 26
Hardscrabble 56 B4 30
Hauppauge 15 Y 18
Hayground 53 T3 26
Holbrook 22 K1 17
Holtsville 21 M1 18
Huntington 2 H 22
Huntington Manor 2 G 20
Huntington Sta 2 H 21
Islip Terrace 16 Z 13
Jamesport 41 Y2 27
Jericho 56 C4 29
Jessup Neck 52 P3 34
Kings Park 14 V 23
Kingstown 59 H4 33
Kismet 18 Y 3
Lake Grove 21 E1 21
Lakeland 15 D1 18
Laurel 40 Z2 30
Lindenhurst 11 L 8
Little Neck 1 K 25
Little Ram Island 51 V3 39
Lloyd Neck 1 C 26
Lower Melville 4 H 14
Maidstone Park 59 G4 36
Manetto Hills 3 E 16
Manorville 32 E2 23
Mastic 34 B2 16
Mastic Beach 34 C2 14
Mattituck 40 A3 32
Mecox 57 U3 26
Medford 27 Q1 18
Melville 3 F 15
Middle Island 26 U1 23
Middleville 7 R 24
Mill Hills Estates 55 A4 33
Montauk 61 X4 35
Montauk Beach 61 V4 34
Moriches 33 E2 17
Mt Sinai 25 N1 28
Napeague 61 P4 33
Nassau Point 45 K3 33
Nesconset 21 D1 20
New Suffolk 46 G3 32
Nissequogue 19 C1 27
North Amityville 5 G 8
North Babylon 10 O 11
North Bay Shore 10 V 12
North Bellport 28 T1 15
North Centereach 21 K1 22
North Great River 16 A1 14
North Harbor 52 V3 34
North Haven 52 V3 34
North Lindenhurst 5 K 9
North Patchogue 28 N1 17
North Sea 53 N3 27
North Selden 20 M1 22
North Side Hills 53 Q3 31
North Smithtown 14 Y 23
Northampton 42 R2 23
Northville 40 U2 30
Noyac 52 R3 31
Noyac Side Hills 52 Q3 31
Oakdale 22 E1 12
Oakville 42 W2 22
Ocean Bay Park 24 D1 5
Ocean Beach 24 C1 4
Old Field 19 D1 29
Old Lonelyville 18 A1 4
Old Mastic 34 D2 15
Old Stony Brook 19 D1 27
Orient 49 V3 44
Orient Point 49 Y3 44
Pantigo 60 H4 30
Patchogue 22 M1 14
Peconic 44 H3 36
Pine Neck 52 S3 33